Love, Justice, and Autonomy

Philosophers have long been interested in love and its general role in morality. This volume focuses on and explores the complex relation between love and justice as it appears within loving relationships, between lovers and their wider social context, and the broader political realm. Special attention is paid to the ensuing challenge of understanding and respecting the lovers' personal autonomy in all three contexts.

Accordingly, the essays in this volume are divided into three thematic sections. Section I aims at shedding further light on conceptual and practical issues concerning the compatibility or incompatibility of love and justice within relationships of love. For example, are loving relations inherently unjust? Might love require justice? Or do love and justice belong to distinct moral domains? The essays in Section II consider the relation between the lovers on the one hand and their broader societal environment on the other. Specifically, how exactly are love and impartiality related? Are they compatible or not? Is it unjust to favor one's beloved? Finally, Section III looks at the political dimensions of love and justice. How, for instance, do various accounts of love inform how we are to relate to our fellow citizens? If love is taken to play an important role in fostering or hindering the development of personal autonomy, what are the political implications that need to be addressed, and how?

In addressing these questions, this book engenders a better understanding both of conceptual and practical issues regarding the relation between love, justice, and autonomy as well as their broader societal and political implications. It will be of interest to advanced students and scholars working on the philosophy of love from ethical, political, and psychological angles.

Rachel Fedock is a Senior Lecturer and Honors Faculty Fellow at Barrett, the Honors College at Arizona State University, USA. Her research focuses on ethics, feminist ethics, moral psychology, the philosophy of love, and care.

Michael Kühler is "Privatdozent" (roughly equaling Associate Professor) at the University of Münster, Germany. He is the co-editor of *The Limits of Moral Obligation* (Routledge, 2016) and *Autonomy and the Self* (2013).

Raja Rosenhagen is an Assistant Professor of Philosophy at Ashoka University, India. His research interests include philosophy of mind, epistemology, philosophy of science, logic, love, Indian philosophy, and cross-cultural philosophy.

Routledge Studies in Ethics and Moral Theory

Cultivating Our Passionate Attachments
Matthew J. Dennis

Reason and Ethics
The Case Against Objective Value
Joel Marks

Offense and Offensiveness
A Philosophical Account
Andrew Sneddon

Virtue, Narrative, and Self
Explorations of Character in the Philosophy of Mind and Action
Edited by Joseph Ulatowksi and Liezl van Zyl

The Authority of Virtue
Institutions and Character in The Good Society
Tristan J. Rogers

Getting Our Act Together
A Theory of Collective Moral Obligations
Anne Schwenkenbecher

Love, Justice, and Autonomy
Philosophical Perspectives
Edited by Rachel Fedock, Michael Kühler, and Raja Rosenhagen

For more information about this series, please visit: https://www.routledge.com/Routledge-Studies-in-Ethics-and-Moral-Theory/book-series/SE0423

Love, Justice, and Autonomy
Philosophical Perspectives

Edited by Rachel Fedock, Michael
Kühler, and Raja Rosenhagen

NEW YORK AND LONDON

First published 2021
by Routledge
52 Vanderbilt Avenue, New York, NY 10017

and by Routledge
2 Park Square, Milton Park, Abingdon, Oxon, OX14 4RN

Routledge is an imprint of the Taylor & Francis Group, an informa business

© 2021 Taylor & Francis

The right of Rachel Fedock, Michael Kühler, and Raja Rosenhagen to be identified as the authors of the editorial material, and of the authors for their individual chapters, has been asserted in accordance with sections 77 and 78 of the Copyright, Designs and Patents Act 1988.

All rights reserved. No part of this book may be reprinted or reproduced or utilized in any form or by any electronic, mechanical, or other means, now known or hereafter invented, including photocopying and recording, or in any information storage or retrieval system, without permission in writing from the publishers.

Trademark notice: Product or corporate names may be trademarks or registered trademarks and are used only for identification and explanation without intent to infringe.

Library of Congress Cataloging-in-Publication Data
Names: Fedock, Rachel, editor. | Kühler, Michael, editor. | Rosenhagen, T. Raja, editor.
Title: Love, justice, and autonomy : philosophical perspectives / edited by Rachel Fedock, Michael Kuhler, and Raja Rosenhagen.
Description: New York, NY : Routledge, 2021. | Series: Routledge studies in ethics and moral theory | Includes bibliographical references and index.
Subjects: LCSH: Interpersonal relations. | Love–Social aspects. | Justice--Social aspects. | Autonomy–Social aspects.
Classification: LCC HM1106 .L597 2021 (print) | LCC HM1106 (ebook) | DDC 302–dc23
LC record available at https://lccn.loc.gov/2020037274
LC ebook record available at https://lccn.loc.gov/2020037275

ISBN: 978-0-367-33264-8 (hbk)
ISBN: 978-0-429-32399-7 (ebk)

Typeset in Sabon LT Std
by KnowledgeWorks Global Ltd.

Contents

Preface   vii

1 Introduction   1
RACHEL FEDOCK, MICHAEL KÜHLER, AND RAJA ROSENHAGEN

SECTION I
Justice Within Relationships of Love   21

2 The Amorality of Romantic Love   23
ARINA PISMENNY

3 Autonomy, Love, and Receptivity   43
CARTER LANE JOHNSON

4 A Minimalist Account of Love   61
GETTY L. LUSTILA

5 "Someone I Would Have Hated to Be:" The Threat of Love in *Rear Window* and *Vertigo*   79
TROY JOLLIMORE

6 Murdochian Presentationalism, Autonomy, and the Ideal Lovers' Pledge   102
RAJA ROSENHAGEN

7 Dialogical Love and Its Internal Normative Fabric   131
ANGELIKA KREBS

8 Tolerance, Love, and Justice   150
CHRISTIAN MAURER

vi *Contents*

9 Abandonment and the Egalitarianism of Love 167
   TONY MILLIGAN

SECTION II
Loving Partiality and Moral Impartiality 183

10 Dissolving the Illusion of the Love and Justice Dichotomy 185
    RACHEL FEDOCK

11 Love and Our Moral Relations with Others 201
    NORA KREFT

12 Acting Out: How Personal Relationships Provide
    Basic Moral Practical Reasons 216
    SHANE GRONHOLZ

13 Love for One's Own or Justice for All? 240
    MARILYN FRIEDMAN

SECTION III
The Political Dimension of Love and Justice 257

14 Love's Extension: Confucian Familial Love
    and the Challenge of Impartiality 259
    ANDREW LAMBERT

15 Love as Union and Political Liberalism 289
    MICHAEL KÜHLER

16 The Freedom that Comes with Love 307
    NIKLAS FORSBERG

17 Love, Activism, and Social Justice 327
    BARRETT EMERICK

List of Contributors 345
Index 349

Preface

We first thought about putting together a volume on the controversial relations between love, justice, and autonomy when the three of us presented a panel entitled *Love and Justice: Can Union Views Do Justice to Just Love?* during the SEP-FEP Joint Annual Philosophy Conference that was held in August 2016 at the Regent's University, London. It soon became clear that we wanted to expand on the topic and go beyond a discussion of only union theories of romantic love. The present volume is the result of this idea and we would like to take this opportunity to express our heartfelt gratitude to everyone involved. First and foremost, we would like to thank our contributors who not only took the time and effort to write excellent original contributions for the volume but also showed unwavering patience with its at times slow progress, aggravated by intercontinental moves and, near the end, the onset of a global pandemic. Many thanks are due also to Allie Simmons and Andrew Weckenmann from Taylor & Francis who, besides being models of patience, supported the idea for this volume right from the start. We cannot stress enough how much we appreciate their help and support in putting this volume together.

Rachel Fedock, Michael Kühler, and Raja Rosenhagen
July 2020

1 Introduction

Rachel Fedock, Michael Kühler, and Raja Rosenhagen

Justice, Respect for Autonomy, and Love

Questions concerning love and its role in morality (and *vice versa*) have existed since antiquity. They have given rise to a long and complex debate about the nature of love, the lovers' emotional and attitudinal characteristics, and about how love shapes and is in turn shaped by the lovers' self-understanding and their autonomy. In this context, important questions arise concerning the relation between love and justice, be it

1. within relationships of (romantic) love,
2. about love's alleged incompatibility with morality's demand for general impartiality, or
3. regarding the implications of both of the aforementioned tensions for the political realm.

Arguably, acts of love may come into conflict with considerations of justice when rather than considering the claims of everyone involved equally and impartially, one favors a loved one over others. Moreover, lovers may be prone to interfere with the freedom or autonomy of their beloved out of concern for their well-being, which apparently goes against the moral demand of respecting everyone's autonomy, including the beloved's. Given that both love and morality are undoubtedly of central concern in our lives, how can these apparent tensions between love, justice, and respect for autonomy be addressed or resolved? And which implications would need to be incorporated in a broader, political perspective on the matter? In order to address these questions, the central notions of love, justice, and autonomy obviously need to be clarified. The following introductory sketch is intended to provide some conceptual background on the topic.

First of all, equality, fairness, and impartiality are all essential aspects of justice (for an overview concerning the notion of justice, see Miller 2017). Justice has often been construed in relation to equality and fairness, where the latter includes the claim that persons are to receive their due.

This seminal idea can be found in Plato's *Republic* (Plato 2013a, 2013b) and has been famously enshrined in the formula *suum cuique* (to each his own) by Ulpian in the 3rd century and later by emperor Justinian in the early 6th century (cp. Frier 2016). Aristotle classically conceived of justice in terms of *equitable* distributions of benefits and burdens in society as well as rectifying unjust distributions (cp. Aristotle EN, Book V).[1] The basic underlying and still prevalent idea is that equality functions as the default position against which possible inequalities need to be justified. Equal cases need to be treated equally. The burden of proof, thus, lies with inequality (cp. Tugendhat 1997, 70). Of course, unequal treatment can be shown successfully as just by pointing to morally relevant and differing characteristics, e.g., desert or need. Yet what may count as morally relevant characteristic is, in turn, in need of (moral) justification. Moreover, equality needs to be specified, i.e., whether something is considered an equal basis of moral judgment or which kind of equality is supposed to be the aim of moral action. Unsurprisingly, both aspects are a matter of contention and the question "equality of what?" has spawned an intense debate (see Gosepath 2011, section 3).

Still, one of the undisputed core elements of modern morality is the idea that all persons are moral equals. This idea is most forcefully advocated by Immanuel Kant, when he contends that persons do not have a price, which characterizes weighable and replaceable items, but dignity, which makes persons irreplaceable and of unweighable value (cp. Kant 2011, 97–99). Likewise, the idea of persons as moral equals can be found in John Stuart Mill's appropriation of Jeremy Bentham's dictum of classical utilitarianism: "everybody to count for one, nobody for more than one" (cp. Mill 1861, 257f.), viz., when Mill discusses justice and morality's impartiality (for an overview of the notion of impartiality, see Jollimore 2020). Being impartial, then, means treating all persons as equals and judging a situation irrespective of the particular persons involved, only based on morally relevant characteristics.

More recently, John Rawls famously defined justice as fairness, where persons are regarded as free (autonomous) and equal, rational citizens, who share the burdens in a fair society, grounded in two principles of justice: "First: each person is to have an equal right to the most extensive basic liberty compatible with a similar liberty for others. Second: social and economic inequalities are to be arranged so that they are both (a) reasonably expected to be to everyone's advantage, and (b) attached to positions and offices open to all" (as he first stated them in Rawls 1971, 60). Rawls's lexical ordering of both principles, according to which possible further advantages are prohibited if they come at the cost of infringing on people's equal liberties as stated in the first principle, once again shows the importance of equality and fairness when it comes to how people should be regarded, viz., as having equal value, no matter their position in society. While Rawls recognizes that persons are born into unequal societal positions, these undeserved inequalities should be compensated for in order to ensure that all enjoy fair opportunities (cp. Rawls 1971, 100). Accordingly, the principles of justice form the bedrock of society and are the essential element of Rawls's social contract theory. This theory also exemplifies the role of impartiality, since the so-called original position, which includes the *veil of ignorance*, is defined in a way that avoids any possible partiality (cp. Rawls 1971, 118–22, 130–42). The original position is the hypothetic starting point where citizens determine the just principles of their society. In this position, they need to decide under a veil of ignorance, stripping them of any knowledge about their personal values, preferences, and place in society. Hence, it is ensured that their point of view is impartial. Ultimately, the equal respect for persons thus grows out of this conception of fairness and an impartial perspective, which are both in turn grounded in a fundamental assumption of equality.

Furthermore, Rawls at first followed Kant's conception of persons, who are considered to be morally autonomous, equal, and rational (Rawls 1980).[2] Persons possess equal worth and deserve equal respect, specifically because of and for their autonomous rational will. These notions are captured in Kant's three formulations of the categorical imperative (see Kant 2011). The first states to act only on that maxim which at the same time can be willed as universal law. This formulation exemplifies impartiality, since principles are applied to all persons equally and no one can receive special treatment. In other words, one ought to view the application of justice from an objective perspective. The second formulation requires that we respect all persons, including ourselves, equally and never treat persons merely as a means, which specifically consists in respecting a person's autonomous, rational will. Persons are, in turn, autonomous because they can set laws for themselves, more specifically the moral law as expressed in the categorical imperative. The third formulation states that as autonomous, rational agents, we ought to act such that we could legislate universal law in an imagined kingdom of ends. This formulation reveals the source of our dignity, i.e., our value as human beings, in our autonomous rational will that can legislate universal law and not merely act in accordance with it. So for Kant, our equality is grounded in our autonomous rational will, where autonomy consists of our ability to set the moral law for ourselves from an impartial perspective. And as we are all equal, everyone's autonomous will ought to be respected.

Respect for a person's autonomy is thus not only an important part of considerations of justice in particular but a fundamental part of modern morality in general (for an overview, see Christman 2015). It is the centerpiece of Kantian ethics, and while utilitarianism does not put autonomy front and center as Kantianism does, it is traditionally considered to contribute crucially to people's well-being, which is why strong moral reasons are needed for overriding it by other aspects of the situation in question (cp. Mill 1859, 1861). In sum, equality, fairness, impartiality, and respect for autonomy are mutually supporting notions.

In contrast, partiality, i.e., treating someone differently just because the person has a special connection to oneself, is considered unjust or unfair in modern morality (see Jollimore 2020). At the very least, partiality is in need of moral justification. The question is therefore whether there are some special circumstances that set aside moral impartiality or that can, in fact, morally justify treating certain persons more favorably than others because of some personal connection. Arguably, family bonds, relationships of love, or friendships might qualify as morally relevant characteristics, thereby making a corresponding partiality morally justified. If so, it could also be concluded that everyone is being treated fairly.

However, even if this were granted, it only holds for differentiating between loved ones and other persons. Yet, what about questions of how to treat one's beloveds and the temptation to interfere with their freedom or autonomy, even if only out of concern for their well-being or flourishing? When following Kant or Rawls, such interfering would apparently mean *dis*respecting their autonomy and *not* treating them as equals. Granted, in the case of family relations, parents are certainly morally justified when they engage in paternalistic behavior toward their, especially smaller, children—which neither Kant, Mill, nor Rawls deny. However, relationships of romantic love present a different challenge, and it is far from clear that lovers are justified in interfering with their beloved's freedom or autonomy, even if it might be for their own sake. No wonder, therefore, that references to autonomy play such an important part also in the discussion on love's relation to morality. However, it is important to note that these references typically do not have the narrow Kantian definition of autonomy (as the ability to set the moral law for oneself) in mind. So, what is autonomy?

In partially explicit opposition to Kant's narrow definition, recent debate on autonomy has taken a broader approach and understands *personal autonomy* as a general capacity of self-governance (for an overview, see Buss and Westlund 2018). Accordingly, personal autonomy is meant to describe a person's capacity of deciding and acting, i.e., in general leading her life, based on her own convictions, consisting especially of her desires, preferences, values, or principles. Being autonomous, thus, also means to be (sufficiently) independent of undue influences, be these external influences by other people, like coercion or manipulation, or internal influences, like addictions or other mental influences experienced as alien to oneself.

The debate on personal autonomy has been largely shaped by individualist accounts and corresponding criticisms (see, e.g., Christman 1989; Taylor 2005). Individualist accounts analyze personal autonomy solely in relation to a person's internal traits and capabilities. Most notably,

Harry G. Frankfurt has argued that autonomy consists in a specific hierarchical structure of a person's will, which basically consists in our capacity of (metaphorically) stepping back from our desires and considering whether we identify ourselves with them (cp. Frankfurt 1971, 1988). The details of Frankfurt's approach and the corresponding criticism are not important for the purpose at hand. What matters, rather, is this: on individualist approaches, love may be considered either as an influence that endangers the lover's autonomy—e.g., when we speak of being "madly" in love or being no longer able to see things clearly because of being in love—or, on the contrary, as an authentic source of the lover's autonomy. The latter position is notably defended by, again, Frankfurt, when he identifies love, or what we care about, as the source of our identity or self (cp. Frankfurt 1994, 1999, 2004). Assuming that we decide and act based on what (or whom) we love and, thus, based on who we essentially are, Frankfurt claims that this may be regarded as an authentic and, therefore, autonomous expression of our self.

However, while both of these individualist considerations discuss love in relation to the *source* of authenticity and autonomy, either endangering autonomy or being constitutive of it, love may very well also be analyzed in terms of being the *result* of personal autonomy. These kinds of individualist approaches reject an essentialist idea of the self as something to be merely discovered, including what or whom one loves, and instead opt for a—likely even existentialist—perspective, according to which we are able to—or even unavoidably must radically—choose who we want to be, including what and whom we want to love (cp. Fromm 1956; Lehrer 1997; Kühler 2014). Admittedly, this would imply giving up the influential understanding of love as something over which we have no control, especially when love is considered to be, at least primarily, a specific emotion.

In any case, these all too brief remarks already show the variety of options of how love's relation to personal autonomy may be discussed against individualist accounts of the latter. However, things get even more complicated once one also adds relational accounts of personal autonomy to the mix (see Mackenzie and Stoljar 2000; Oshana 2006). In recent decades, these accounts have gained substantial popularity, not the least due to a number of corresponding criticisms of individualist accounts. For individualist accounts are taken to fall short of addressing precisely enough autonomy endangering as well as autonomy enabling social conditions. While individualist accounts simply take a person's reflective capabilities for granted, relational accounts emphasize that we need to grow up in a suitable social environment in order to be capable of developing into an autonomous person in the first place. If we are not treated with respect and recognized as a person with dignity, so that we can develop corresponding attitudes toward ourselves, notably self-trust, self-respect, and self-esteem (cp. Anderson and Honneth 2005, 130f.), we would arguably not be able to become autonomous persons—although we may be able to remain autonomous even in a hostile social environment once we have developed our capacity for personal autonomy. Stronger relational accounts, on the other hand, go a step further and claim that these social conditions are *constitutive* of personal autonomy, i.e., we cannot be or remain autonomous unless they are met.

Since loving relationships are obviously a tremendously important part of a person's social environment, on relational accounts, love may influence personal autonomy even more. Being loved may be considered as contributing substantially to enabling or promoting one's autonomy. However, this claim only holds if love comprises an attitude toward the beloved that fosters their autonomy enabling or promoting self-attitudes, i.e., that supports the beloved in developing and maintaining attitudes such as self-respect or self-esteem. Accordingly, this idea explains well how love may not only be considered compatible with the lovers' respective individual autonomy but even enabling and promoting it (cp. notably Velleman 1999).

However, relational accounts have also put much emphasis on identifying and criticizing social conditions that endanger personal autonomy, including close personal relationships (see Oshana 2014). For especially loving relationships may also include interpersonal dynamics that diminish a person's flourishing as an autonomous individual—although it might be a matter of contention if such relationships should still be considered relationships of love. Most notably, feminist authors have shown how more or less subtle manipulations up to straightforward "gaslighting" or treating the beloved based on restrictive gender stereotypes diminishes and endangers the beloved's—i.e., for the most part women's—autonomy.

In sum, while personal autonomy broadens the view in comparison to Kant's narrow notion and is of central importance to modern ethics, it is far from clear how it should be analyzed exactly. Moreover, the variety of theoretical approaches creates a multitude of possibilities how personal autonomy may relate to love, i.e., in what sense love may be supportive of or even required for our capacity of being autonomous and, on the contrary, in which sense it may endanger autonomy.

What complicates the matter even further is the fact that the notion of love is, of course, far from clear as well. Traditionally, three different notions of love have been distinguished: love as *eros*, love as *philia*, and love as *agape* (for an extensive historical and critical discussion, see Singer 2009a, 2009b, 2009c). As per the account epitomized in Plato's *Symposion* (Sheffield and Howatson 2008), *eros* is associated with passionate and romantic love. Though typically (but not necessarily) carnal in its initial stages, *erotic* love can be purified, as it were, into love of beauty itself, perhaps even further. *Philia*, on the other hand, is meant to characterize the relation of mutual well-wishing and support in the dimension of the good. According to Aristotle, *philia* refers to the loving relationship that relates true friends and, in its lesser forms, people who share certain goals or pleasures (cp. Aristotle EN, books VIII & IX). *Agape*, finally, is said to refer to a kind of selfless and unconditional love. In the Christian tradition, the term is associated with love's highest form, charity, and is said to be properly attributed to the bond between man and the divine but is also used as a label for the love the religious person is to feel for her neighbor (see Soble 1989).

In highlighting the lover's desire, *eros* is arguably a more self-centered love, including a specific partiality toward the beloved. Accordingly, it seems rather natural to assume that such loving partiality is in tension with morality's required impartiality. *Philia* and *agape*, on the other hand, do not seem to present quite the same pressing challenge. Following Aristotle's seminal discussion, *philia* usually requires the lovers or friends to be virtuous persons, which also includes the virtue of justice. *Agape* in the sense of neighborly love is even the explicit manifestation of equality and impartiality in love.

In addition to this traditional distinction between *eros*, *philia*, and *agape*, another possible grouping of theoretical approaches to analyze love may be helpful for the topic at hand (cp. Kühler 2020, where the following overview is mostly borrowed from; cp. also Klonschinski and Kühler 2021):

1. individualist accounts, according to which love is analyzed in terms of a purely individual stance that takes the beloved as its object,
2. interpersonal accounts, according to which love is conceived as a dialogical relation between the lovers who are thus both considered subjects of their loving relationship, and
3. union accounts, according to which the lovers "merge" into a *we*, i.e., abandon their individual identities and together form a new *we*-identity.

Individualist accounts of love come in different flavors. They might analyze love in terms of a specific emotion, volition, or a more general stance. They might argue that love is rational in that there are reasons *for* love. Alternatively, they might argue that, on the contrary, love is arational and is, conversely, the source of reasons, viz., reasons *of* love (for an overview, see Helm 2017). What all of these individualist accounts have in common is that they take love to be something attributable exclusively to the lover, with the beloved merely being the *object* of this love. What it means to love someone then often includes the idea of *caring about* the beloved, i.e., wanting the beloved to flourish and being actively engaged in promoting the beloved's well-being and flourishing, as it has traditionally been attributed to *philia*. As Frankfurt puts it in his influential account of love as caring, "[l]ove is, most centrally, a disinterested concern for the existence of what is loved, and for what is good for it" (Frankfurt 2004, 42; see also Frankfurt 1999). Moreover, as mentioned above, what a person loves or cares about is, in turn, a source of the lover's own identity and autonomy (Frankfurt 1994, 138; 1999; 2004). Yet the point of individualist accounts is to locate this source in the loving person herself. The beloved person, therefore, does not necessarily have any impact on the lover's identity. Loving another person does not imply any changes to the lover's identity because of this love—and if such changes occurred, these would be conceived as accidental. Accordingly, individualist accounts of love allow for each lover's identity to remain basically unchanged. Mutual love can, thus, only be explained in terms of each lover's individual and independent stance of love that just so happens to have the respective other person as its object.

In contrast, interpersonal accounts of love take mutual love as their starting point and claim that love should be analyzed in terms of a *shared* relationship. Notably, Angelika Krebs defends such an account (cp. Krebs 2014, 2015, cp. also her chapter in this volume). She argues that love's nature is *dialogical*. Mutual lovers are not only both subjects of their shared love, but each lover also has an intrinsic interest in the sharing of their lives. "Partners share what is important in their emotional and practical lives. [...] [L]ove is the intertwining of two lives" (Krebs 2014, 22). Moreover, the sharing of lives includes that the lovers are open to changes in their individual identities because of their love (cp. Rorty 1987). Hence, interpersonal accounts of love include the claim that each lover's individual identity will unavoidably—and willingly—be affected by their dialogical love. "In sharing emotions and actions, the partners engage in a mutual building of selves. How they view and respond to each other shapes their characters" (Krebs 2014, 22).

The *locus classicus* for union accounts, finally, is Plato's *Symposium*. According to the myth conveyed by Aristophanes (cp. Sheffield and Howatson 2008, 189c–93), humans were once "double-creatures" with four legs, four arms, and two heads. Because of their strength and hubris, they even posed a threat to the gods themselves, so Zeus split them in halves, yielding our current appearance. Ever since each of these halves desperately looks for its other half and yearns for being reunited with it. Love is, therefore, nothing but the desire for unity and, if fulfilled, the union itself. Now, obviously, the idea of lovers being (re-)united or merging must not be taken literally. Recent union accounts usually do not rest on ontological claims about the creation of a new entity. Instead, union accounts' central claim is that lovers merge in the sense of sharing a *we*-identity and *we*-autonomy (cp. Fisher 1990, 26–35; Nozick 1990; for a discussion of how to understand the lovers' union, see Merino 2004). The main idea is that lovers no longer see themselves as independent individuals but as fundamentally belonging together. Union accounts, thus, go one step further than interpersonal accounts. While interpersonal accounts claim that the lovers keep their individual identities and autonomy—although their identities are affected by their dialogical love—union accounts often readily admit that love as union is incompatible especially with individual autonomy (cp. Fisher 1990, 28; Nozick 1990, 71; for intricate discussions of the matter, see Soble 1997; Friedman 1998, see also Kühler's chapter in this volume). However, it should be noted that union accounts may include a stronger or weaker claim when it comes to the lovers' we-identity. Stronger versions of union accounts comprise the claim that the new we-identity completely redefines or replaces the lovers' prior individual identities. Weaker versions, on the other hand, leave some room for each lover to retain their respective individual identity and consider the new we-identity merely as a supplement to or a partial modification of the lovers' individual identities.

The intriguing point of this threefold distinction of theories of love for the topic at hand is that each of these approaches implies a specific framing of possible conflicts between love and justice as well as autonomy on all three levels mentioned at the beginning, i.e., within loving relationships, concerning the conflict between love's partiality and morality's impartiality, and regarding the political dimension. First, following individualist accounts, all of these possible conflicts allow for a traditional individualist analysis and discussion, according to which individual interests, preferences, and autonomy can be pitted and weighed against each other. Accordingly, justice within loving relationships would amount to a discussion about whether benefits and burdens are distributed fairly among the individual lovers in their relationship. Love's partiality would manifest itself in a lover's preference for the beloved in comparison to everyone else. Finally, at least the liberal, likewise individualist, political tradition would not face fundamental problems when it comes to incorporating love as an individual personal stance—although this obviously does not mean that all ensuing problems of loving partiality vs. now political impartiality may easily be fixed; it merely means that they may easily enough be analyzed and discussed against a shared individualist background.

Interpersonal accounts of love, on the other hand, yield a different framework and are arguably more challenging for an otherwise individualist moral and political point of view. Although interpersonal accounts stress that lovers remain individually autonomous, their identities get affected and may undergo significant changes. Consequently, if a person's identity is considered to be the source of authenticity for making autonomous choices, a lover's individual autonomy is affected, after all. Yet, this is usually not considered as negatively interfering or even impeding the lover's autonomy, for the underlying changes in identity because of love are taken to be welcomed, even pursued intrinsically.

Moreover, interpersonal accounts of love stress that loving someone includes valuing and promoting the beloved's individual autonomy. If so, it would seem that interpersonal accounts are well equipped to address and even ensure justice within loving relationships. However, given that the lovers value their relationship intrinsically, it appears to be quite possible that this may result once again in a tension between love's partiality and morality's impartiality, now understood in terms of the lovers being partial toward their relationship in comparison to other people. The latter would, in turn, present a challenge for acknowledging loving relationships as special from a political point of view, although it might be argued that the traditional concept of marriage precisely serves as the corresponding instrument in political thought and practice.

Finally, love as union likely yields the most challenging framework when it comes to taking justice and the political realm into account. Especially with stronger versions of union accounts, the idea of the lovers sharing a we-identity and abandoning their respective individual identity and autonomy seems to make it impossible even to address the question of justice within love, at least in the usual sense. However, it is perfectly conceivable to raise the question of how exactly the shared we-identity came about and to what degree the (previously) individual lovers are represented in it. Hence, questions about justice within loving relationships can still be raised but require a substantial reformulation in terms of their content, including questions about how autonomous the individual lovers' initial or continued identification with their shared we-identity actually is. While weaker versions of union accounts readily allow for such questions to make sense, stronger versions of union accounts arguably exclude any individual stance toward the shared we-identity to begin with. If so, the question would be to what degree the lovers' shared we-identity may be considered an acceptable source of authenticity for the lovers' autonomy, be it in terms of their individual autonomy or their shared we-autonomy—assuming that the redefinition of each lover's identity in terms of the shared we-identity may still be considered as individually autonomous to begin with. Furthermore, union accounts of love in any version seem to present an even more pressing tension between love's partiality and morality's impartiality. For how could the lovers not favor their *we* in comparison to everyone else? Yet in principle, it seems to be perfectly conceivable that the lovers actually value morality's impartiality, especially if they consider themselves as no longer being separate individuals. Just like individuals are capable of valuing impartiality, so is the lovers' *we*, or so it could be argued. Although love as union certainly allows for an *égotisme à deux*, it does not imply it. In any case, love as union certainly presents an even greater challenge for modern political thought than interpersonal accounts due to the apparent abandonment of the lovers' respective individual identity and autonomy.

Overview of Contributions

Following the above sketch of possible tensions between love, justice, and autonomy, the contributions to this volume engage in the critical discussion of these tensions from three perspectives, which mark the volume's three sections:

1. Justice Within Relationships of Love
2. Loving Partiality and Moral Impartiality
3. The Political Dimension of Love and Justice

Section 1: Justice Within Relationships of Love

Contributions in this first section aim at shedding light on conceptual and practical issues concerning the (in-)compatibility of love and justice *within* relationships of love, with the notion of justice construed primarily in terms of respect for autonomy between the lovers. In this respect, *Arina Pismenny* takes the tension head-on and argues in her contribution "The Amorality of Romantic Love" that romantic love does not include a moral dimension. She starts from the opposing view that romantic love is, according to a number of authors, an intrinsically moral phenomenon. The alleged connection between love and morality is elucidated in terms of reasons *for* and reasons *of* love. Romantic love, on such views, is a response to moral reasons—the moral qualities of the beloved. Similarly, the reasons love produces are also taken to be moral in nature. Since romantic love is a response to moral qualities and a source of moral motivation, it is itself moral. Pismenny's contribution aims to cast doubt on both these claims. By employing the model of emotional rationality, she contends that a moralistic fallacy is committed when reasons for love are construed as moral. Reasons of love are also not essentially moral, as she goes on to argue, but rather of both moral and nonmoral kinds, and they are in part determined by cultural narratives and norms pertaining to love. Romantic love, she concludes, is not moral in nature; morality is extrinsic to love.

In his contribution "Autonomy, Love, and Receptivity," *Carter Johnson* focuses on respect for autonomy within loving relationships. Being in a loving relationship apparently includes the risk either to give up one's own autonomy or to abridge the autonomy of the beloved. Moreover, since loving relationships can produce dispositions, one risks developing a long-term disposition to do so. In order to protect against this risk, Johnson argues, a person can develop a contrary disposition, one that will nurture autonomy, and claims that receptivity is such a disposition. He defines receptivity as the ability to be with someone without having to impose careless or compulsive expectations. This definition is bolstered by using research from psychology and neuroscience about biases, defense mechanisms, and other cognitive and motivational features common to most people. Since receptivity involves sufficient control of or independence from these cognitive and motivational features, and since such features are often what causes breaches in autonomy, Johnson concludes that receptivity enables one to have loving relationships without damaging the autonomy of oneself or the other.

In his contribution "A Minimalist Account of Love," *Getty Lustila*, too, addresses the prima facie conflict between the values of love and autonomy. How can we bind ourselves to a person and still enjoy the fruits of self-determination? He argues that the solution to this conflict lies in recognizing that love is the basis of autonomy: one must love a person in order to truly appreciate their autonomy. To make this case, Lustila defends a *minimalist account of love*, according to which love is an agreeable sensation that is experienced when considering the existence of another person. On this view, the lover does not desire anything from the beloved but works to attend to their presence. Love, then, puts us in a position to appreciate the beloved in their particular way of being. By accepting the presence of the beloved, we gain a sense of their autonomy. The roots of this account of love are found in the writings of Damaris Cudworth Masham, but Lustila also draws on the work of Kieran Setyia, David Velleman, and Kyla Ebels-Duggan to elaborate on and defend Masham's views.

Troy Jollimore takes on a more skeptical view again. In his contribution "'Someone I Would Have Hated to Be.' The Threat of Love in *Rear Window* and *Vertigo*," he looks at two films by Alfred Hitchcock, *Rear Window* (1954) and *Vertigo* (1958). Both films showcase our anxieties about romantic love, connecting them with the view that such love is transformative, i.e., tends to open lovers to radical changes, including alterations of their very identities. Moreover, these changes are to a large degree unpredictable and uncontrollable. This suggests, Jollimore argues, that love, at least in some cases, can pose a deep threat both to our continued well-being and, perhaps more profoundly still, to our autonomy. If this is right, then some of the most powerful reasons for avoiding love might arise from love itself: both love of ourselves, and the love we direct toward others. In light of these considerations, the anxiety felt about love by the protagonists of these films is, as Jollimore concludes, entirely understandable.

Like Lustila and Johnson, Raja Rosenhagen, in his contribution "Murdochian Presentationalism, Autonomy, and the Ideal Lovers' Pledge," examines the relation between love and autonomy aiming to make it intelligible why and how just love fosters autonomy. He draws on two sources: presentationalism, a position in the debate on experience's rational role, and Iris Murdoch's account of love as just attention. Presentationalism and Murdoch's view, he argues, are natural bedfellows and yield *Murdochian presentationalism*. On it, just love requires just attention and the continuous acknowledgment that the beloved, their concepts, and their ends are different from us and that both lovers' concepts, views, and experiences may be muddled, selfish, and murky. Since different responses to identical circumstances can be equally rational, just lovers are both humbly willing to learn from their beloved and ever-ready to compassionately respond to them. Rosenhagen thus couches ideal loving relationships in terms of the joint project of cleansing the lovers' respective outlooks by removing selfish fantasies and excising—through action and explication—heteronomous factors, so as to ultimately increase the lovers' ability to treat each other justly, do well by each other, to increase their freedom and autonomy, and to orient them, gradually, toward what is real and good.

In her contribution "Dialogical Love and Its Internal Normative Fabric," *Angelika Krebs* engages in a further clarification and defense of her recently developed dialogical conception of romantic love (Krebs 2015). According to this view, romantic lovers share what is important in their lives and are internally, that is, by virtue of their love, committed to contribute to and respect the other's autonomy. In order to understand romantic love, she argues that we need to understand how two people can truly share feelings and actions and what kind of obligations go along with this. Max Scheler and Edith Stein offer some valuable insights on this issue. First, Krebs introduces three major models of romantic love: the fusion model, the care model, and the dialogue model. She then argues in support of the third model, which views romantic love essentially as a form of sharing, and reconstructs the thoughts of Max Scheler and Edith Stein about sharing. Krebs goes on to argue that Edith Stein's perceptions, which in turn are extensions of Max Scheler's work, constitute a convincing account of collective feeling and acting and thus of what lies at the heart of romantic love. In closing, she updates this account on the basis of current philosophical understanding.

In his contribution "Tolerance, Love and Justice," *Christian Maurer* discusses the relation between love and tolerance and its implications for justice within loving relationships, which has been surprisingly underrepresented in recent debate. He proposes a conception of love as a robust-yet-fragile phenomenon experienced by weak human agents and goes on to discuss some differences between tolerance and forbearance. The latter is conceived as a form of patient endurance of deeply objectionable difference in values, which is often associated with love and hope. On the other hand, tolerance—a more distant reaction—is often thought to be incompatible with love. However, Maurer argues that not only forbearance but also tolerance is psychologically and morally compatible with love. To some extent, he follows John Bowlin's discussion of forbearance and tolerance but bases his own discussion on the specific conception of love as a robust-yet-fragile phenomenon. Within such love, and within certain limits, Maurer argues, at least some deeply objectionable differences may be tolerated, yet this may render difficult the wholehearted acceptance of the other because it involves some degree of alienation. The motive for tolerance in such love may be a concern for justice combined with a concern for the loving relationship.

In the final contribution to the first section, "Abandonment and the Egalitarianism of Love," *Tony Milligan* broadens the view further. While focusing on love as an emotion, he assumes that it is central to various forms of religious commitment, particularly so in the case of the Christian tradition which appeals to an egalitarian worthiness of love's recipients. However, Milligan suggests, and to some extent argues, that appeals to love's unconditionality and to constancy which are prevalent in Christian discourse work better in some domains than in others. More specifically, an unconditional constancy in the context of intimate sexualized love can be problematic by reinforcing submissive gender roles, conflicting with a concern for equality, and clashing with a reasonable concern for agent well-being. There are loves, Milligan contends, which we ought to end insofar as we are able to do so.

Section 2: Loving Partiality and Moral Impartiality

Contributions in this section shift the focus from the internal fabric of loving relationships to relations between lovers and others. This raises questions about a possible tension between love's apparent partiality and the impartiality demanded by morality. *Rachel Fedock* explicitly addresses this shift in perspective in her contribution "Dissolving the Illusion of the Love and Justice Dichotomy," while arguing that justice and love are, in fact, interconnected, where one makes little sense in isolation from the other. Love and justice have often been conceived as not only sharply distinct, but divergent in their aims and sometimes, conflicting in their demands. Justice has been perceived as having no place in loving relations, while some have argued that the particularistic and partial nature of loving is inconsistent with impartial, universal morality. Fedock refers to this perceived contrast as the "love and justice dichotomy (LJD)." After briefly examining a few theories of love and care to illustrate the history of the LJD and exploring those theorists whose work challenges the LJD, particularly Velleman's, she lays out the beginnings of a feminist-focused theory of love, which focuses on empowering and promoting the autonomy of the beloved. This results in a further breaking down of the LJD. Drawing upon these challenging works and her own conception of love, she concludes that the LJD is an illusion.

Nora Kreft shares the idea that love and justice are not only compatible but even more closely related. In her contribution "Love and Our Moral Relations with Others," she defends this claim against the background of Philip Pettit's account of love as robust care. Pettit argues that if A loves B, then A provides care for B not only in all actual scenarios, given certain prompts or triggers, but also over a certain range of hypothetical scenarios. Further, according to Pettit, being so disposed is more than being motivated to provide care, it is also a matter of having reason to do so. There is a sense in which, as a lover, one *ought* to provide care for one's beloved, given the right prompts. However, Pettit goes on to say that the reasons of love—the reasons to provide care for the beloved—can be outweighed by other reasons, notably moral reasons, e.g., to help a stranger in dire need instead of consoling one's beloved on a minor matter. While Kreft agrees with Pettit that the lover should help the stranger and that this does not undermine her status as a genuine lover, she disagrees that the situation is correctly analyzed in terms of reasons of love being outweighed by reasons to help the stranger. Instead, Kreft argues that love itself gives us a reason to help the stranger. In helping the stranger, the lover is in fact (also) acting out of love for her beloved, not in spite of it. More generally, Kreft defends the position that love gives us reasons to respect and care not only for the beloved but also for *other* human beings, at least to some, further specifiable extent and in certain, further specifiable situations. She thereby invokes a long tradition in philosophy to view love as a morally virtuous attitude—an attitude that has the potential to change our moral relations not just with our beloved, but to a certain degree with everyone.

While the previous two contributions attempt to show how love includes a moral perspective, thus allowing for morality's impartiality, *Shane Gronholz* puts the matter on its head. In his contribution "Acting Out: How Personal Relationships Provide Basic Moral Practical Reasons," he asks whether love's partiality might not be even called for on moral grounds. He starts from the everyday observation that people at least at times behave partially toward their friends or loved ones. To behave partially is to show favoritism toward certain groups or individuals, to put their interests ahead of the interests of others, to treat them *better* than one treats everyone else. He then raises the question of whether those kinds of actions are wrong, permissible, or rather morally required. Gronholz argues that we are, in fact, morally permitted, and sometimes morally required, to give preferential treatment to those with whom we have certain kinds of personal relationships. This is because he believes that such relationships provide *basic* moral practical reasons that apply to our treatment of our friends, but not to others. He explicates the concept of these reasons in terms of *relational reasons* and defends the accompanying normative moral claim that we *ought* to love our friends.

However, such a partial loyalty to one's beloved or friends might provoke more serious moral challenges. In her contribution "Love for One's Own or Justice for All?," *Marilyn Friedman* discusses how love's loyalty may present a lover with a painful dilemma in case the beloved engages in serious moral wrongdoing. Many people identify themselves and are identified by others in terms of a social group (race, religion, nationality, gender, etc.) to which they belong and to which they may feel a strong attachment. Although often beneficial for their members, a person's social identity group may engage in serious moral wrongdoing or injustice toward other groups or their members. In such cases, Friedman contends, a member of the wrongdoing group may face a painful dilemma. A strong attachment, or love, for her own group inclines a member toward continuing to support her identity group under varying circumstances. However, when the group commits injustice, it seems appropriate for members to condemn and oppose their own group in the name of justice. These conflicting options are possibly irreconcilable. Friedman surveys this dilemma, explores five ways of responding to it, and considers whether content-neutral autonomy helps to resolve it.

Section 3: The Political Dimension of Love and Justice

Unsurprisingly, the contributions thus far have shown a great variety and partially opposing positions on the possible tensions between love, justice, and autonomy. Whatever stance one takes on any of the issues previously discussed will arguably have broader political implications. Since loving relationships play an important role in society, it is an open question of how to incorporate any position on the relation or tension between love and justice in a more encompassing political framework. The contributions in this final section address such implications for the political realm.

Andrew Lambert's contribution "Love's Extension: Confucian Familial Love and the Challenge of Impartiality" ventures beyond the confinements of a debate rooted only in Western tradition and explores the political implications of love in the Confucian tradition. The most prominent form of love in the Confucian tradition is familial love, which is also central to ethical conduct and good character. Lambert discusses potential Confucian responses to the demands of impartiality. This is timely, he contends, because the Confucian family-centric approach to society, and its relevance in contemporary China and beyond, has been questioned by scholars who have identified a conflict between a thoroughgoing commitment to family and ethical impartiality. Various defenses of Confucian thought have been offered, including impartiality is, in fact, an important value in the classical texts; public institutions from outside the tradition could be introduced to formalize and strengthen impartiality and are compatible with traditional social values; and the defense of alternative regulative ideals internal to the tradition, which are accorded priority over impartiality. Lambert assesses the merits of these responses before exploring an alternative line of argument: that Confucian familial attachments can sometimes achieve that at which impartiality aims, but without appealing to impartiality as a foundational moral ideal. Such an approach to ethics has its limits, Lambert admits, but shows promise in the regulation of everyday social life in localized communities. More importantly, he argues that the Confucian tradition of familial ethics can engage in a critical dialogue with ethics in the tradition of liberal individualism.

In his contribution "Love as Union and Political Liberalism," *Michael Kühler* follows up on liberalism's individualism and discusses its compatibility with union accounts of romantic love. According to liberal thought, each person is treated as an individual, i.e., as a separate subject independent of any group affiliations. Moreover, everyone is treated as an equal whose individual autonomy and freedom needs to be respected. Union accounts of romantic love, on the other hand, claim that lovers (at least partially) abandon their individual identities and form a shared *we*-identity. The crucial idea is that lovers no longer regard themselves as separate (autonomous) individuals but as fundamentally belonging together, even including a "pooling" of their autonomy. Taken together, this raises the question of whether or to what degree liberalism is compatible with union accounts of love. Does liberalism leave (sufficient) room for this highly influential and still prevalent understanding of romantic love? In order to answer this question, Kühler discusses core assumptions of liberalism's individualism, distinguishes between a variety of union accounts of love, and argues that liberalism's compatibility with love as union is substantially limited. In fact, he concludes that only one rather weak version of love as union, which is distinctly akin to liberalism's individualism, proves to be compatible.

Aside from its emphasis on individualism, liberalism, of course, focuses on people's freedom. This topic is taken up by *Niklas Forsberg* in his contribution "The Freedom that Comes with Love." Forsberg engages in a detailed discussion of love's implications for the political realm in Iris Murdoch's philosophy, which is well known for love taking center stage. However, the general tendency has been to think that the relevance of Murdoch's conception of love concerns romantic relations between two persons. Thus, little attention has been paid to how this conception of love relates to the communal and to more political notions like justice and freedom. Forsberg's discussion is intended to remedy that by means of elucidating the relations that hold between Murdoch's conception of love and her concept of freedom. What emerges, he argues, is a call for a recognition of the many layers in which freedom is developed. Beyond a restricted notion of freedom as "freedom to choose," there is a notion of freedom that comes in degrees.

In the final contribution to the volume, "Love, Activism, and Social Justice," *Barrett Emerick* analyzes the relationship between love and social justice activism, focusing in particular on ways in which activists rely on either the union account of love (to argue that when one person is oppressed, everyone is oppressed), the sentimentalist account of love (to argue that overcoming injustice is fundamentally about how we feel about one another), or love as fate (to argue that it is in love's nature to triumph over hatred and injustice). Emerick argues that all three accounts, while intelligible and attractive, are seriously problematic, as they tend either to obscure important differences in the ways that various groups are socially situated or to enable inaction by trusting that justice is inevitable. Therefore, Emerick explores alternative, deeper interpretations of each account and their respective relationships to activism.

Notes

1. However, it should be noted that according to Aristotle, justice is not for everyone, only equals. As citizens and slaves are not equals, they ought not be treated as such. While citizens should be treated equally among each other, and slaves as well, Aristotle rejects impartiality between these groups.
2. Later, Rawls revised his position and claimed to have abandoned Kantian metaphysics. Yet, his new *political* conception of the person still includes *regarding* everyone as free and equal, i.e., treating everyone *as if* they were free and equal (cp. Rawls 2001, 18–24; 2005, 29–35).

References

Anderson, Joel, and Axel Honneth. 2005. "Autonomy, Vulnerability, Recognition, and Justice." In *Autonomy and the Challenges to Liberalism*, edited by John Christman and Joel Anderson, 127–49. Cambridge: Cambridge University Press.

Aristotle, E. N. *Nicomachean Ethics*. Translated by W. D. Ross. The Internet Classics Archive. http://classics.mit.edu/Aristotle/nicomachaen.html.

Buss, Sarah, and Andrea Westlund. 2018. "Personal Autonomy." In *The Stanford Encyclopedia of Philosophy*, edited by Edward N. Zalta, Spring 2018. Metaphysics Research Lab, Stanford University. https://plato.stanford.edu/archives/spr2018/entries/personal-autonomy/.

Christman, John, ed. 1989. *The Inner Citadel: Essays on Individual Autonomy*. New York: Oxford University Press.

Christman, John, ed. 2015. "Autonomy in Moral and Political Philosophy." In *The Stanford Encyclopedia of Philosophy*, edited by Edward N. Zalta, Spring 2015. Metaphysics Research Lab, Stanford University. http://plato.stanford.edu/archives/spr2015/entries/autonomy-moral/.

Fisher, Mark. 1990. *Personal Love*. London: Duckworth.

Frankfurt, Harry G. 1971. "Freedom of the Will and the Concept of a Person." In *The Importance of What We Care About*, by Harry G. Frankfurt, 11–25. Cambridge: Cambridge University Press, 1988.

Frankfurt, Harry G. 1988. *The Importance of What We Care About*. Cambridge: Cambridge University Press.

Frankfurt, Harry G. 1994. "Autonomy, Necessity, and Love." In *Necessity, Volition, and Love*, by Harry G. Frankfurt, 129–41. Cambridge: Cambridge University Press, 1999.

Frankfurt, Harry G. 1999. "On Caring." In *Necessity, Volition, and Love*, by Harry G. Frankfurt, 155–80. Cambridge: Cambridge University Press.

Frankfurt, Harry G. 2004. *The Reasons of Love*. Princeton: Princeton University Press.

Friedman, Marilyn. 1998. "Romantic Love and Personal Autonomy." *Midwest Studies in Philosophy* 22: 162–81. https://doi.org/10.1111/j.1475-4975.1998.tb00336.x.

Frier, Bruce W. 2016. *The Codex of Justinian. 3 Volume Hardback Set: A New Annotated Translation, with Parallel Latin and Greek Text*, translated by Fred H. Blume. Annotated, New Translation, Multilingual. Cambridge: Cambridge University Press.

Fromm, Erich. 1956. *The Art of Loving*. New York: Harper Perennial, 2006.

Gosepath, Stefan. 2011. "Equality." In *The Stanford Encyclopedia of Philosophy*, edited by Edward N. Zalta, Spring 2011. Metaphysics Research Lab, Stanford University. https://plato.stanford.edu/archives/spr2011/entries/equality/.

Helm, Bennett W. 2017. "Love." In *The Stanford Encyclopedia of Philosophy*, edited by Edward N. Zalta, Fall 2017. Metaphysics Research Lab, Stanford University. https://plato.stanford.edu/archives/fall2017/entries/love/.

Jollimore, Troy. 2020. "Impartiality." In *The Stanford Encyclopedia of Philosophy*, edited by Edward N. Zalta, Summer 2020. Metaphysics Research Lab, Stanford University. https://plato.stanford.edu/archives/sum2020/entries/impartiality/.

Kant, Immanuel. 2011. *Immanuel Kant: Groundwork of the Metaphysics of Morals: A German–English Edition*. Translated by Mary Gregor and Jens Timmermann. Bilingual. Cambridge: Cambridge University Press.

Klonschinski, Andrea, and Michael Kühler. 2021. "Romantic Love Between Humans and AIs: A Feminist Ethical Critique." In *New Philosophical Essays on Love and Loving*, edited by Simon Cushing. Houndmills: Palgrave Macmillan.

Krebs, Angelika. 2014. "Between I and Thou—On the Dialogical Nature of Love." In *Love and Its Objects. What Can We Care For?*, edited by Christian Maurer, Tony Milligan, and Kamila Pacovská, 7–24. Basingstoke: Palgrave Macmillan.

Krebs, Angelika. 2015. *Zwischen Ich und Du: Eine dialogische Philosophie der Liebe*. Berlin: Suhrkamp.

Kühler, Michael. 2014. "Loving Persons. Activity and Passivity in Romantic Love." In *Love and Its Objects. What Can We Care For?*, edited by Christian Maurer, Tony Milligan, and Kamila Pacovská, 41–55. Basingstoke: Palgrave Macmillan.

Kühler, Michael. 2020. "Love and Conflicts Between Identity-Forming Values." In *International Handbook of Love: Transcultural and Transdisciplinary Perspectives*, edited by Claude-Hélène Mayer and Elisabeth Vanderheiden. Dordrecht: Springer. https://doi.org/10.1007/978-3-030-45996-3.

Lehrer, Keith. 1997. "Love and Autonomy." In *Love Analyzed*, edited by Roger E. Lamb, 107–21. Boulder, CO: Westview Press.

Mackenzie, Catriona, and Natalie Stoljar, eds. 2000. *Relational Autonomy: Feminist Perspectives on Automony, Agency, and the Social Self*. Oxford: Oxford University Press.

Merino, Noël. 2004. "The Problem with 'We': Rethinking Joint Identity in Romantic Love." *Journal of Social Philosophy* 35: 123–32.

Mill, John Stuart. 1859. "On Liberty." In *The Collected Works of John Stuart Mill, Volume XVIII – Essays on Politics and Society Part I*, edited by John M. Robsen, 213–310. Toronto: University of Toronto Press, 1977.

Mill, John Stuart. 1861. "Utilitarianism." In *The Collected Works of John Stuart Mill, Volume X—Essays on Ethics, Religion, and Society*, edited by John M. Robsen, 203–59. Toronto: University of Toronto Press, 1969.
Miller, David. 2017. "Justice." In *The Stanford Encyclopedia of Philosophy*, edited by Edward N. Zalta, Fall 2017. Metaphysics Research Lab, Stanford University. https://plato.stanford.edu/archives/fall2017/entries/justice/.
Nozick, Robert. 1990. "Love's Bond." In *The Examined Life. Philosophical Meditations*, by Robert Nozick, 68–86. New York: Simon & Schuster.
Oshana, Marina. 2006. *Personal Autonomy in Society*. Aldershot: Ashgate.
Oshana, Marina, ed. 2014. *Personal Autonomy and Social Oppression*. New York: Routledge.
Plato. 2013a. *Republic, Volume I*, edited by Christopher Emlyn-Jones and William Preddy. Bilingual. Cambridge: Harvard University Press.
Plato. 2013b. *Republic, Volume II*, edited by Christopher Emlyn-Jones and William Preddy. Bilingual. Cambridge: Harvard University Press.
Rawls, John. 1971. *A Theory of Justice*. Cambridge: Belknap Press.
Rawls, John. 1980. "Kantian Constructivism in Moral Theory." *Journal of Philosophy* 77 (9): 515–72.
Rawls, John. 2001. *Justice as Fairness. A Restatement*. Cambridge: Belknap Press.
Rawls, John. 2005. *Political Liberalism. Expanded Edition*. New York: Columbia University Press.
Rorty, Amelie Oksenberg. 1987. "The Historicity of Psychological Attitudes: Love Is Not Love Which Alters Not When It Alteration Finds." *Midwest Studies in Philosophy* 10 (1): 399–412.
Sheffield, Frisbee C. C., and M. C. Howatson, eds. 2008. *Plato: The Symposium*. Cambridge: Cambridge University Press.
Singer, Irving. 2009a. *The Nature of Love 1. Plato to Luther*. Cambridge: MIT Press.
Singer, Irving. 2009b. *The Nature of Love 2. Courtly and Romantic*. Cambridge: MIT Press.
Singer, Irving. 2009c. *The Nature of Love 3. The Modern World*. Cambridge: MIT Press.
Soble, Alan, ed. 1989. *Eros, Agape, and Philia: Readings in the Philosophy of Love*. New York: Paragon House.
Soble, Alan, ed. 1997. "Union, Autonomy, and Concern." In *Love Analyzed*, edited by Roger E. Lamb, 65–92. Boulder: Westview Press.
Taylor, James Stacey, ed. 2005. *Personal Autonomy. New Essays on Personal Autonomy and Its Role in Contemporary Moral Philosophy*. Cambridge: Cambridge University Press.
Tugendhat, Ernst. 1997. *Dialog in Leticia*. Frankfurt am Main: Suhrkamp.
Velleman, J. David. 1999. "Love as a Moral Emotion." *Ethics* 109: 338–74.

Section I
Justice Within Relationships of Love

2 The Amorality of Romantic Love

Arina Pismenny

Introduction

Philosophical discussions of romantic love[1] are often concerned with its moral dimensions. Indeed, some leading accounts characterize it as an intrinsically moral phenomenon. This means either or both of two things: (1) when in love, we respond to the moral qualities of our beloveds; and (2) love is the primary motivation for treating our beloveds morally. I dispute both of these claims. Using key concepts of the rationality of emotions, I argue that attempts to categorize romantic love as an intrinsically moral phenomenon relying on claim (1) commit a moralistic fallacy. They construct idealized accounts of love rather than providing a realistic picture of it. As regards (2), reasons of love are not reducible to moral reasons. Although they can be moral, they are not so exclusively. Ultimately, they belong in their own category, which isn't determined by the kind of valuing love involves. Rather, reasons of love are grounded in the lover's internal love model, informed by the lover's attachment style and experience, and by social norms pertaining to romantic love. Since both are highly variable, they are unlikely to coincide with morality. Moral norms, therefore, are extrinsic to love. Romantic love is not an intrinsically moral phenomenon.

I begin by sketching a psychological profile of romantic love in the "Romantic love: definitions" section, differentiating between passionate and companionate love. Philosophers often complain that either one or the other should not be considered romantic love. For the purposes of this chapter, either one or both of them together are what the discussion of the morality of love is about. In the "Emotions and rationality" section, I prepare the ground for the discussion of reasons for love by distinguishing between prudent, moral, and aptness norms used to assess the rationality of emotions. The conflation of these norms can result in a moralistic fallacy. This happens when we infer from the claim that an emotional occurrence is immoral that it must also be irrational. The "Love and morality: preliminary distinctions" section lays out preliminary distinctions required to clarify the possible connections between romantic love and morality. It demonstrates that when assessing an emotional state in moral terms, avoiding the moralistic fallacy requires that emotion's aptness or fittingness conditions be the same as the conditions for that emotion's moral assessment. The "Are reasons for love moral reasons" section examines two accounts that attempt to show that reasons for love are moral reasons by appealing to the moral features of the beloved. Both are found to commit a moralistic fallacy. The "Are reasons of love moral reasons" section scrutinizes three attempts to reduce reasons of love to moral reasons. They are the Care View, the Duties of Trust View, and the Moral Deliberation View. Each view gets something right about morality and romantic love. Each one, however, ultimately fails to show that reasons of love are reducible to moral reasons. Reasons of love can be of both moral and nonmoral kinds. This is in part explained by the influence of the cultural narratives of love, a lover's history and attachment style, and other factors. I conclude that because neither reasons for nor reasons of love are intrinsically moral, morality is external to love. Romantic love is not a moral phenomenon.

Romantic Love: Definitions

Although there is no consensus on how to best define romantic love, there are two common contenders. First, romantic love can be characterized as a passionate, obsessive state. It is illustrated by phrases such as being "in love," falling "head over heels," or feeling "madly in love." One finds this sort of love in the stories of Romeo and Juliet, Abelard and Heloise, Tristan and Isolde. Its psychological profile is described by Dorothy Tennov as having intrusive thoughts about the beloveds, violent feelings and desires directed at them, and motivation to seek their company and intimacy (Tennov 1999/1979; Fisher 1992, 2004). It is also characterized by the idealization of the beloveds, to whom the lovers attribute special and unique value, not found in anyone else (Stendhal 1822/1967; Grau 2004; Singer 2009a; Grau and Pury 2014).

Some dismiss this definition of romantic love as referring to nothing more than infatuation or crush, not serious or "real" love (cf. Velleman 1999; Frankfurt 2004). Spontaneous and whimsical, it is bound to end quickly. At best, it will pave the way for a deeper kind of love, the love that lasts: companionate love. Companionate love is characterized by a much calmer emotional state, an acquired intimacy, understanding, and trust between the lovers (Wang and Nguyen 1995; Hatfield and Rapson 1996; Kim and Hatfield 2004). Though less intense, companionate love "is a warm feeling of affection and tenderness that people feel for those with whom their lives are deeply connected" (Kim and Hatfield 2004, 175). It is closely associated with friendship and involves shared values, strong and deep attachment, feelings of comfort, and a long-term commitment. It develops over a long period of time and can last for years, even a lifetime (Contreras, Hendrick, and Hendrick 1986; Hendrick, Hendrick, and Adler 1988; Hatfield and Rapson 1996; Kim and Hatfield 2004).

The dismissal of passionate love as not serious or real seems to rest on the presumed tradeoff between intense passion and deeper connection. One might wonder whether companionate love can justifiably bear the title "romantic." It can, no doubt, retain some or obtain new romantic elements; but it need not arise from passionate love in the first place. Passionate love, on the other hand, should not be dismissed as foolish and pointless. As is illustrated in many works of fiction and films, it can be very powerful and fulfilling and also involve a deep mode of connection.

The distinction between passionate and companionate love can be useful, but for the purposes of this chapter, it makes no difference. I take romantic love to be passionate love that can transform into companionate love, while maintaining some of the elements of passionate love. This conception is sufficient to discuss the morality of both reasons for and reasons of love.

Emotions and Rationality

I argue elsewhere that romantic love is not an emotion but rather a syndrome, comprising a variety of affective, cognitive, and behavioral dispositions (Pismenny and Prinz 2017; Pismenny 2018). Nevertheless, romantic love essentially involves vast if not unlimited emotional dispositions. I will, therefore, use the various rational norms applicable to emotions as a framework for thinking about the rationality of love. This will be useful for two reasons: first, it will help elucidate the relationship between love and reasons; and second, it will help zoom in on the different relationships between love and morality.

Emotions are intentional states (Deonna and Teroni 2012; Tappolet 2016). They represent certain features of the world and ourselves to us. While the question of intentionality of emotions is a complex one, there are at least two kinds of "object" of emotions: the target, which is the primary object of the emotion, and the formal object (Kenny 1963). The target of an emotion is that at which the emotion is directed. The formal object represents the value that supervenes on the focal properties of the target (de Sousa 1987). For example, fear of a dog is directed at a dog, its target, while its formal object is dangerousness. To fear the dog is to attribute to it the property of being dangerous. Emotions, therefore, are evaluations of objects and situations relevant to those who are experiencing them, and each emotion type is individuated by the specific formal object that it attributes to its target.

Insofar as each emotion represents the value it is about, each emotion has its own standard of correctness. An emotion is assessed for correctly or incorrectly representing its target as having a particular value. This standard of correctness is the aptness or fittingness of emotions (de Sousa

1987). An emotion fails to be apt when the value it attributes to its target cannot be shown to be grounded in it. For instance, my anger at my friend for being late is inapt when in fact she is on time, and I have simply misremembered the hour we have agreed upon. Since showing up on time does not ground offensiveness, my anger is unfitting. Perhaps my anger is also inapt if she has left on time but was late because her subway train broke down, and she had no way of alerting me as she had no reception underground. On the other hand, if she simply managed her time poorly, or did not think it was important to meet me on time, my anger at her is fitting and justified, as her attitude and behavior are really insulting.

Even though aptness is the intrinsic norm of rational assessment for any emotion (as it stems directly from the emotion's meaning), it is not the only norm of rationality applicable to them. We often assess emotions from prudential and moral points of view. One might say that I ought not to be angry with my friend for being late, as my anger is just a waste of energy. My anger will not undo her lateness. My anger is unproductive and thus irrational. Or one might insist that patience is a virtue, and therefore, my anger reveals a character flaw. That amounts to regarding my anger as inappropriate in the sense of constituting a moral failure on my part. Furthermore, emotions are also subject to meta-attitudes such as those stemming from cultural norms of feeling and display. For instance, in the United States, a woman's anger is more likely to be deemed inappropriate than a man's (Salerno and Peter-Hagene 2015). These meta-attitudes affect how women experience and express anger. They often feel unjustified in feeling it and are afraid of revealing it lest they be labeled hysterical, etc.

Although it is common to assess emotions from prudential and moral standpoints, it is important to keep these assessments separate from that of aptness. Indeed, to run together aptness and prudential or moral assessments is to commit a prudential or a moralistic fallacy, respectively. As Justin D'Arms and Daniel Jacobson put it, "[T]o commit the moralistic fallacy is to infer, from the claim that it would be wrong or vicious to feel an emotion, that it is therefore unfitting" (D'Arms and Jacobson 2000). Aptness or fittingness is a distinct mode of correctness of emotions.

Romantic love too can be assessed in terms of these norms. From a meta-attitude perspective, in the West, romantic love is considered extremely important for a happy and meaningful life, as well as the most important reason to get married. In some Eastern cultures, by contrast, it is considered unstable and ephemeral, and a poor basis for matrimony (Branden 1980; Beach and Tesser 1988; Triandis 1990; Levine et al. 1995; Dion and Dion 1996; Rothbaum and Tsang 1998; Neto et al. 2000; Nelson and Yon 2019). A given case of love may be prudentially sound when it helps further one's goals such as marriage and childrearing, or impractical as in the cases of unrequited love, or love not directed at one's partner in a monogamous relationship.

The fittingness conditions of love (if there are any) correlate with the formal object of love—lovability—the evaluative property in virtue of which the beloved is lovable. To elucidate this evaluative property, we would need to identify a set of properties that ground it as we have done in the cases of fear and anger. We can assess love from a moral standpoint by examining whether reasons for love are moral reasons, and whether reasons of love motivate us to act morally. In the following sections, I discuss each question in turn.

Love and Morality: Preliminary Distinctions

Evaluating reasons for love from a moral standpoint can take different forms. First, it might be thought that morality dictates that we love certain people—though it seems very unlikely that we *owe* romantic love to anyone.[2]

Second, we might evaluate reasons for love[3] as morally appropriate or inappropriate. Perhaps loving someone for their money is morally condemnable, while loving someone for their character is morally praiseworthy. On a view of this kind, the lovability of one's beloved is grounded in their character traits, which may or may not be moral. If so, love may be apt when the beloved is loved for their humor, wit, attentiveness, and happy disposition (see Keller 2000). Here the aptness and moral assessments are clearly distinct. While an instance of such love may be fitting, it may at the same time be morally problematic if it takes the form of an adulterous affair, or manifests itself through abuse, or becomes a fetishism focusing exclusively on some of the beloved's physical qualities. Similarly, love may be inapt but morally unproblematic, as in the case of the lover's misattribution of qualities—if any such exist—that would ground lovability of the beloved. One may be deluded or tricked into thinking that the beloved is witty, funny, and charming but over time discover that it was all a fantasy or an act. While the beloved might have acted immorally, the lover's love was not morally devious but simply grounded in false assumptions.

Third, it might be that reasons for love are moral reasons in so far as they pick out only moral qualities of the beloved. On such a view, the beloved is loved for their moral character (Abramson and Leite 2011). Construed this way, romantic love is an intrinsically moral phenomenon since its fittingness conditions are defined by the moral virtues of the beloved. It is apt only when someone is loved for their moral character and inapt when the moral character in the beloved is lacking, or the beloved is loved for some nonmoral features.

A worry arises with respect to this last consideration: aren't we committing a moralistic fallacy by conflating the fittingness norms of love with moral norms? It might seem so since the same moral qualities of the beloved are used to assess love for both of these norms. However, when the fittingness norm of love is defined by moral qualities, no fallacy need be committed. It might be that romantic love just is (or is like) a moral emotion, in requiring only moral features to ground the target's possession of the properties that define its formal object (Gibbard 1990; D'Arms and Jacobson 2000). Emotions like guilt, shame, contempt, indignation, and anger are often cited as examples of moral emotions because they deal with notions like personal moral failures, moral failures of others, justice, fairness, desert, and harm. When these emotions are directed at moral features of the situation, they are moral emotions.

It is likely, however, that not all cases of these emotions are purely moral cases (Prinz 2007). For I may be feeling angry that the car broke down, ashamed of my body, guilty of wasting time on Twitter, contemptuous of my friend's poor taste in music. Arguably, these are not examples of moral failures. Thus, if there are purely moral emotions (such as indignation), there are very few of them (Gibbard 1990; Prinz and Nichols 2010).

If love's fittingness conditions are determined by moral properties, then love is an intrinsically moral attitude. Nothing but the lovability of the beloved is relevant to love's fittingness. But we could still make a further moral assessment of a given instance of love. While an instance of love is grounded in the moral qualities of the beloved, it might still be morally problematic because it is adulterous or abusive. Fittingness and moral assessments can still be kept apart, so as to avoid the moralistic fallacy.

This last type of case does not preclude a very intimate connection between love and morality. Moral features, it could be held, are defining features of love. Without them love is unfitting: it gets things wrong either about the beloved or about what is worth loving. Lovability, in such cases, would be a moral property, and the function of love is to correctly identify those who are lovable.

Are Reasons for Love Moral Reasons?

While it is conceivable that reasons for love are moral in nature, is it plausible that they are? What arguments can be offered in support of lovability being a moral property? Two accounts have attempted to show this. The first is that of David Velleman, who argues that lovability is grounded in the beloved's personhood—their rational will and capacity to value (Velleman 1999). The second, due to Kate Abramson and Adam Leite, argues that lovability is grounded in the beloved's moral qualities (Abramson and Leite 2011). I examine each in turn.

David Velleman models his view of love on the Kantian account of respect. He states that from the phenomenological perspective, love feels like an arresting awareness of the person's value that is grounded in their personhood (Velleman 1999, 360). Persons have unconditional moral worth because they are rational and possess the capacity to value. Love is a response to and an appreciation of this worth (Velleman 1999, 365).[4]

For Velleman, love is an intrinsically moral emotion since it is the moral value of persons that love is responding to. Love is apt when the beloved is loved for their personhood. Love is inapt when the beloved is loved for some other qualities such as their good looks and delicious cooking, or if the beloved is not a person. Velleman holds that one advantage of his view is that the beloved is valued the way anyone would want to be valued—for who they truly are, and also as irreplaceable: for "[w]hat makes something truly irreplaceable is a value that commands appreciation for it as it is in itself, without comparison to anything else, and hence without substitutions" (Velleman 1999, 369).

In his attempt to ground lovability in personhood, Velleman's account shows too much and too little.[5] It shows too much since most cases of romantic love involve persons, and so love will rarely be inapt. Every person is equally lovable since all persons possess the same immeasurable value of dignity grounded in personhood. It shows too little, since few would recognize a universal abstract property of personhood or rational will as their reason for loving their beloveds. Rather it is the particularity of the beloved that love highlights and not a universal bare core that persons might have. Velleman acknowledges that we come to love our beloveds on the basis of the singular expression of their personhood, which seems designed to capture the particularity of the beloved (Velleman 1999, 371–372). However, since he insists that it is not the particular qualities that constitute the beloved's lovability, this point only explains rather than justifies a given instance of love.

In effect, Velleman's account commits a moralistic fallacy since his reasons for picking personhood as the quality that grounds lovability are moral ones. He wants to resolve the conflict between love and morality that arises, according to Kant, due to love's partiality;[6] he also thinks that if we love for some other qualities, our loves are superficial and are not loves that take our beloveds as ends in themselves. But while we might value our beloveds as moral beings, valuing them finally need not be reduced to the Kantian notion of ends in themselves.[7]

Kate Abramson and Adam Leite attempt to show that love is an intrinsically moral emotion by arguing that love is fitting when it is a response to moral qualities of the beloved (Abramson and Leite 2011). They point out that when asked why one loves their beloved, it is typical to list the beloved's moral character traits (Abramson and Leite 2011, 678). This kind of response feels more legitimate than appeals to convenience or the beloved's good looks. This may be so in part because we feel that moral traits best capture a person's essence: only thus can a person be loved for who they are. On this view, love is apt when the beloved is loved for their moral character traits. It is inapt if the beloved does not possess good moral character for which the lover takes themselves to be loving them, or if the beloved is loved for qualities other than moral.

Though it seems plausible to identify love's fittingness conditions by attending to answers commonly given to the question of why one loves, there are three main problems with this strategy. First, it is important to determine whether those answers are correct. If love's function is to track moral qualities, then we should expect these qualities to serve as grounds for falling in love. Generally, there is a correlation between what makes emotions apt and their eliciting conditions. Whether the correlation exists is an empirical question. Abramson and Leite rely on characters from *Sense and Sensibility* to illustrate their view. But one need not look far for counter examples: Mr. Darcy, Rhett Butler, Eugene Onegin, Don Juan, Heathcliff, Dorian Gray, Carmen, Salome, Nana, Lulu, and Hedda Gabler are some examples of romantic heroes and heroines with questionable or devious characters. A romantic hero is often a bad boy or an inconsiderate girl, someone with charisma and character rather than moral virtue. Indeed, exhibiting rudeness and standoffishness as a romantic strategy is more likely to catch attention, while being nice is likely to land one in the "friend zone"[8] (for discussion, see McDaniel 2005; Ahmetoglu and Swami 2012). If it is objected that such cases do not exemplify "real love" because they fail to be grounded in moral qualities, that would be manifestly begging the question against the examples just provided.

Second, whether moral properties are the grounding properties of lovability is difficult to determine through self-report, since asking why one loves often arises when the lover's family or friends disapprove of their choice of love object. This puts the lover on the defensive, and they may try to appease the questioner by trying to rectify the beloved's flaws in the eyes of the accusers. Pointing to these qualities does not justify one's romantic love from the aptness point of view. Instead, attempting to show that the beloved is a good person evokes either prudential norms to reassure those concerned that the lover's well-being not be negatively affected by the beloved or moral norms as an *ex-post-facto* rationalization to appease a critic.

Third, when faced with the demand to justify one's love, one is already in love. Indeed, love makes us idealize our beloveds, attaching positive values to their trivial traits, and underplaying or rationalizing their shortcomings. We inflate the goodness of our partners and of our relationships in comparison to others (Rusbult and Buunk 1993; Martz et al. 1998; Murray, Holmes, and Griffin 1996a, 1996b; Showers and Kevlyn 1999). For this reason, referencing the practice of referring to the positive character traits of the beloved in justifying one's love is unhelpful, since this practice does not reveal the grounds for one's love but rather provides rationalizations for its existence. Or it might simply display the qualities that the lover lingers on when thinking about the beloved.

Abramson and Leite commit a moralistic fallacy in taking lovability to be grounded in moral character. Their project is not to identify lovability as an evaluative property to which we respond with love. Instead, they construct a moral ideal of love according to which the lover should love the beloved for their moral virtues.[9] However, since there is no actual correlation between love's eliciting conditions and the moral character of the beloveds, picking moral virtues as grounding features of lovability is arbitrary.

Of course Abramson and Leite could insist that love is essentially morally good by definition. Anything else simply cannot count as "real love" even if it fits the psychological profile described in the "Romantic love: definitions" section. I have been trying to show that such a move begs the question. Romantic love is not an intrinsically moral emotion because lovability cannot be confined to moral qualities. It need not be grounded in either personhood or moral character traits. Moralizing reasons for love results in conflating aptness and moral norms, and in over-intellectualizing love.

Nonetheless, some might claim that love is intrinsically moral because the reasons that love *produces* are moral reasons. I explore this possibility in the next section.

Are Reasons of Love Moral Reasons?

If lovability were a moral property, and love were a fitting response to it, it might have been reasonable to expect love to generate moral reasons for actions: for if love were essentially a recognition and appreciation of the beloved as a moral agent, it would give one a reason to treat them as such. But since lovability is not necessarily a moral property, valuing the beloved does not obviously generate moral reasons. Nevertheless, reasons of love might still be moral reasons. Indeed, quite independently of claims about reasons for love, some have argued that reasons of love are reducible to moral reasons. Others argue that reasons of love are *sui generis*. In this section, I hope to show that a hybrid account of the reasons of love is most plausible: reasons of love can be of either kind.

To do so I consider three views according to which reasons of love are moral reasons. First, on what I call the Care View, reasons of love are moral reasons because they are concerned with promoting the beloved's well-being for its own sake. And this is what morality is inherently about—caring for people. Second, on what I call the Duties of Trust View, reasons of love are moral reasons because a romantic relationship is based on trust, and trust creates moral obligations. Third, on what I call the Moral Deliberation View, reasons of love are moral reasons because moral reasoning is indispensable in practical deliberation generally, not excluding situations involving romantic love.

Before considering these three views, it is worth emphasizing that romantic love has a motivational component. As discussed in the

"Romantic love: definitions" and "Emotions and rationality" sections, love is an affective state (like an emotion) or better, a syndrome that includes dispositions to experience affective states. Emotions such as anger and fear move us to aggress against the wrongdoer, or to freeze or flee. If love is like emotions in this regard, we should expect it to provide a set of motivations of its own. Indeed, recall that romantic love is characterized by the motivation to seek the beloved's company and intimacy. This motivation is enabled both in passionate and companionate types of love. Typically when in love, the lover seeks proximity to the beloved, longs for their company, desires reciprocity, etc. Over time the lover develops an attachment to the beloved, which motivates the lover to sustain the ongoing relationship, and when apart, to long for union (Fisher 1998). Romantic love moves the lover to achieve certain ends.

Several authors have argued that the motivational force of love can be harnessed by the will. Robert Solomon (1973) went as far as to claim that love and other emotions could be chosen. Without going quite so far, Harry Frankfurt is among those who characterize love as volitional. He says it is a "configuration of the will that consists in a practical concern for what is good for the beloved" (Frankfurt 2004, 43). He defines love as "a disinterested concern for the existence of what is loved, and for what is good for it" (Frankfurt 2004, 42). Thus, to love is to care for the beloved's well-being, and to promote it for its own sake (see also Taylor 1976; Newton-Smith 1989; LaFollette 1996; Soble 1997; White 2001; Helm 2010; Abramson and Leite 2011; Wallace 2012, Smuts 2014).[10]

Frankfurt rejects the idea that reasons of love are moral reasons on several grounds. First, the kind of care and valuing that love generates is partial—it is directed toward a particular individual—the beloved—who acquires a special non-fungible value in virtue of being loved (Frankfurt 2004, 39–41). Whereas one might care for the sick or the poor as a generic object: any sick or poor will do, any one of them qualifies as a proper object of care (Frankfurt 2004, 44). Second, for Frankfurt love has its own reasons and duties that stem directly from the love attitude and the value love has for the lover as opposed to moral principles (Frankfurt 1998). He says, "I believe that it is possible to give a better explanation of the unquestionable truth that loving someone or something entails that there are certain things we must do — a more authentic and more illuminating explanation than one that resorts to the notion of moral obligation" (Frankfurt 1998, 6). He continues, "The imperatives of love are not grounded in the strictures of moral obligation but in the compelling facts that loving is of decisive importance to us and that it is rather hard to come by" (Frankfurt 1998, 7). Thus, reasons of love are not reducible to moral reasons because love as a species of caring generates reasons of its own. This brings us to the first of three views to be assessed.

According to what I call the Care View, reasons of love are moral reasons because love has a central role to play in morality. Care, as

The amorality of romantic love 33

disinterested concern for the other, could take the form of treating the other as an end. In that regard, care is like love, if not identical to love, and a capacity for love might need to be cultivated in order to value the well-being of others as much as one's own.[11] As Brook Sadler points out, "a commitment to being morally attentive to another, to treating her as an end-in-herself, is constitutive of a caring relationship with the other, thus blurring the line between an ethics that emphasizes duty and obligation and an ethics of care" (Sadler 2006, 252).[12]

Proponents of the Care View argue that acting from care is a paradigmatic example of moral action. For instance, Katrien Schaubroeck in her "Reasons of Love" points out that Susan Wolf's famous account of moral saints mischaracterizes morality as moralizing. Wolf's moral saint is concerned with the right, and one's duty to uphold it to the exclusion of all else. However, Schaubroeck argues, a truly good moral agent is likely to be concerned with the morally good actions themselves rather than mere commitment to moral principles (Schaubroeck 2019, 295–296). One wants to help those in need because they are in need, not because one has a duty to help. We want to help because we care about the well-being of others. Frankfurt is right that love singles out a particular individual while moral considerations may concern generic classes of people. However, since our moral actions are often directed at particular individuals even if we are not in love relationships with them, caring is arguably at the core of our moral concern for them.

Caring is central to some moral theories as well as many theories of love. Love is a paradigm of caring, an ideal toward which we might strive in our moral treatment of others: "[L]ove [is] an enabling condition of morality in the sense that it provides a firm experience with recognizing the individuality of another being" (Schaubroeck 2019, 297). But does it follow that reasons of love are moral reasons?

For four reasons, we should resist the inference. Reasons of love are not moral reasons, nor are moral reasons reasons of love.

First, although care may be essential both to moral concerns and to love, neither is reducible to care. Nor are love and morality reducible to one another. While loving involves caring, not all caring involves loving. I might care for the well-being of my neighbors, without at the same time having the kind of emotional, cognitive, volitional engagement that loving consists in. Even if moral concerns stem from caring, it doesn't mean that they stem from love. Moreover, care is not a sufficient condition for morality, since we can care about anything, regardless of its moral status.

Second, moral reasons generalize: if they apply in one given case, they apply across all similar cases. This is not so in love. As Frankfurt points out, love is partial. It latches onto a particular individual, bestowing on them a unique non-fungible status. Reasons of love do not generalize because the kind of partial concern one has for the beloved does not extend to all. Additionally, the kind of commitment that love sometimes warrants flies in the face of moral considerations. A lover may be moved to commit immoral acts on behalf of the beloved. If one were to insist that "real love" would never motivate one to do anything immoral, one would again beg the question.

Third, while both love and morality involve disinterested concern for the other, the mode and the grounds of concern are different. The way we care for a stranger is not the way we care for our beloved. We might care for a stranger because we see them in need or in pain. We might be moved to help judging that the person needs help, not because it's our duty to help, or an obligation to help, or because helping is the right thing to do. However, even if the content of our moral motivation does not contain notions of "duty," "right," or "ought," but rather only the specific factors of our situation, such as "this person needs my help!", the mode of concern does not represent the individual as non-fungible or special and is not grounded in romantic love.

Fourth, the notion of care is simply too generic to adequately capture the kind of concern present in either love or moral considerations. In the current discussion, care is narrowly defined as disinterested concern for the other's well-being. But this is only one species of caring. One can care for something instrumentally. In its most general sense care only means valuing, or perhaps appreciating the value of something.[13] Caring *simpliciter* is too thin a concept to differentiate the many states in which it is involved, and too basic a concept to be explained in terms of any more complex one such as love or morality.

If appealing to care does not help in showing that reasons of love are necessarily moral reasons, another possible approach is the Duties of Trust approach. It is described by R. Jay Wallace in his "Duties of Love" (Wallace 2012). According to Wallace, there are special duties[14] of trust, vulnerability, and reciprocity and gratitude that arise from our standing in close relationships with those we love. The duties of trust arise from the expectations the beloved is led to form, thereby obligating the lover to fulfill those expectations. Duties of vulnerability arise with respect to those who are particularly vulnerable to being harmed by the one they love. Duties of reciprocity and gratitude also arise from having benefited from a lover's altruistic actions (Wallace 2012, 177–178). These duties are not special to romantic relationships. They can arise in many different kinds of human interactions. However, they may be particularly salient in romantic relationships given their intimate nature, and the closeness and emotional interconnectedness they establish.

Given their salience, are these moral duties duties of love? Insofar as they arise in love contexts, yes. In so far as they are not unique to these contexts, no. Indeed, the fact that these duties are not unique to romantic love has been used to deny that there are *sui generis* reasons of love. According to what Wallace calls a reductionist account, whatever moral reasons guide any given interpersonal interaction are the same kinds of reasons that guide romantic interactions (Wallace 2012, 176–183). That is, there doesn't seem to be a special set of moral duties that arises between the lovers.

This seems too strong. We might acknowledge that these kinds of moral duties are present in romantic love relationships as well as other kinds of interpersonal relationships but deny that these are the only kinds of reasons applicable to love. Indeed, since love does have a motivational component, it seems to be able to provide the lovers with reasons of its own. These reasons might either stem from the love attitude itself or from the romantic love relationship. Given the typical "goals" of love, loving might motivate one to seek the company of the beloved, court them in hopes of facilitating reciprocation, and take actions that would enable love to continue. Once the relationship is formed, it too provides reasons for action by serving as a normative framework for interaction.

One might find this picture of reasons of love too generic. To imbue it with specificity it is important to recognize the role that social norms play with respect to love. Like all our experiences, our romantic love experiences are informed by our upbringing and cultural context. The social norms that we inherit and internalize inform our ideas of what kinds of reasons love can provide. For example, social norms elaborate on what sort of beloved is appropriate (not a child, a nonhuman animal, and, in not so distant past, not someone of the same sex), how love feelings should be experienced (deeply, intensely), expressed (romantic words and gestures, intimacy), and acted upon (attending to the beloved's needs, self-sacrifice). The social narratives of romantic love have changed over time and differ across societies (Mesquita and Frijda 1992; Kim and Hatfield 2004; Singer 2009a). To the extent that they determine reasons of love, they are not exclusively moral reasons even though they might have the appearance of being moral because of their rigidity.

The apparent rigidity of the reasons of love as supplied by social norms brings us to the last approach to the question of whether reasons of love are moral reasons—the Moral Deliberation View. It is advanced by Brook Sadler, who argues we should reject the idea that social norms provide reasons of love for two reasons: (1) it commits one to an uncritical view of what a romantic relationship should be, endorsing an objectionable social conservatism; and (2) the social norms are not so clearly defined in a contemporary pluralist society (Sadler 2006, 248–249). Rigidly defined norms often promote injustice and limit personal freedom. Thus, it is necessary to engage in moral reasoning in order to critically assess these norms. Furthermore, since there is disagreement about what the norms of love are, in a modern society romantic norms are more like suggestions with which the individual lovers engage critically. When we do, we construct our roles as lovers (Sadler 2006, 250). This too can be aided by moral deliberation.

Sadler is right on both counts. The emergence of various forms of ethical non-monogamy is a case in point. It is particularly poignant because monogamy was and still often is taken to be a moral ideal, whereas ethical non-monogamy is viewed as morally deficient (for discussion, see Brunning 2016; Brake 2017; Jenkins 2017; de Sousa 2017). Furthermore, moral deliberation is relevant when faced with a conflicting romantic narrative: "you are mine" vs. "I love your freedom;" "all is fair in love and war" vs. "love brings out the best in us." However, Sadler's reasoning fails to show that reasons of love are moral reasons. Instead, it demonstrates how moral reasons can figure in the assessment of the norms pertaining to romantic love, modifying them, and reconstructing the ideal of love. It is clear too that this kind of moral assessment is extrinsic to love. Thus, reasons of love cannot be said to be moral reasons in this way.

Sadler insists, "Moral considerations are formative of how we understand what is expected of us and what we are to do in relationships of love and friendship" (Sadler 2006, 251). However, this is only partially so. On the one hand, reasons of love can be critically assessed from the moral standpoint. On the other hand, some reasons of love can be moral reasons when they are a part of a romantic narrative. That is, it could well be that part of one's romantic love model—a kind of personal conception of love—is that one ought to respect and promote the choices of the beloved, etc.

At the same time the phrase, "I did it because I love you," can be meaningful whatever is substituted for "it." Indeed, love can fail along prudential, moral, and other dimensions but it need not fail as love. First, it is clear that love can motivate us to lie, cheat, steal, and murder on our beloved's behalf.[15] The ultimate sacrifice of one's moral self for the sake of the beloved could be the categorical manifestation of one's romantic commitment. Becoming a culprit, sharing the blame, or simply assisting the beloved's ends are all plausible reasons of love. Second, love can move the lover to do the very same things to the beloved: lie, cheat, steal, and even murder them. These actions can be either construed as deeply mistaken acts of beneficence as when the lover lies to protect the beloved's feelings or murders them to rid them of unhappiness and angst of existence, or as malevolent actions intended to harm: "I wish you were dead because I love you" or "I wish you to suffer because I love you" are perfectly intelligible utterances love might motivate. "If he doesn't hit you, he doesn't love you" has been a common attitude among women across cultures (Ben-Ze'ev and Goussinsky 2008).

It is important to recognize that appealing to love in justifying one's abhorrent actions has little merit.[16] Yet, it is also important to recognize that these can be reasons of love, nonetheless. This is evident from the contradictory narratives of love in our and other societies. Furthermore, an even greater specificity with respect to reasons of love can be achieved by looking at individual lovers, discerning their ideas of what love is, and how they practice them. An individual's history, their attachment style,[17] their conceptions of love informed by family histories, personal experiences, and the cultural narratives they inherit, all contribute to the determination of what reasons of love are for them. Indeed, having different conceptions of love is often a cause of great tension between lovers. Given the multitude of factors that contribute to one's reasons of love, their diversity is not surprising. Some of these reasons can be moral reasons if they are a part of one's love model. Yet, it seems that any reason can be a reason of love. Therefore, reasons of love are not reducible to moral reasons.

After surveying the three views that attempts to show that reasons of love are moral reasons, it seems clear that reasons of love can be both moral and nonmoral. For this reason, I think the right view of the reasons of love is the hybrid view: reasons of love can be of both kinds. Even though morality and love have care in common, that shared element does not establish that reasons of love are exclusively moral. The Duties of Trust View demonstrates that some reasons of love can be moral in so far as they arise from moral duties one acquires when one enters an intimate relationship. However, these duties are not exclusive to love; neither are they exhaustive. Lastly, the Moral Deliberation View accurately shows that moral deliberation is relevant in a romantic love context: a moral assessment of reasons of love is often desirable. But that does not show that reasons of love are intrinsically moral. Furthermore, it remains an open question whether the narratives of love that are dominated by moral reasons provide for a better love experience.

Conclusion

I have tried to show that romantic love is not an intrinsically moral phenomenon by arguing that neither reasons for love nor reasons of love are necessarily moral. Reasons for love are not as such moral because lovability is not necessarily a moral property. It can be grounded neither in the Kantian notion of personhood, nor in a collection of moral virtues. The Kantian notion is a nonstarter because personhood is a property possessed by most beloveds in a romantic context—most beloveds are persons. It is also too generic, which makes it incompatible with the particularity and partiality of love. It is not grounded in moral virtues because if love's function were to track the moral character of the beloved, virtuous people would be loved more than those of devious character. Yet, it seems, all kinds of people are loved, and an antihero is just as stereotypical a romantic protagonist as a virtuous person.

Reasons of love are not intrinsically moral reasons because love can provide both moral and nonmoral reasons. Some reasons of love conflict with morality not only because love might endorse immoral acts on behalf of the beloved but also toward the beloved. This is so because cultural scripts, family history, prior experience, and many other factors contribute to one's model of love, and, therefore, to the range of reasons that love might be credited with providing. It is possible to critically assess a particular set of reasons of love from a moral as well as prudential standpoints.

In the end, it is up to the lovers themselves to determine which reasons are reasons of love, and whether some are better than others.

Notes

1. I will be using "love" to mean "romantic love" unless otherwise specified.
2. Although there may not be a duty to love someone romantically, perhaps other kinds of love such as a parent's love for a child can be said to be obligatory(see Liao 2015, but also Protasi 2019).
3. I argue elsewhere that romantic love is not grounded in reasons of any kind (Pismenny and Prinz 2017; Pismenny 2018). I will not defend this view here but assume for the purposes of this paper that there can be reasons for love.
4. Velleman explicitly denies that his account applies to passionate love. He says, "When I say that love is a moral emotion, what I have in mind is the love between close adult friends and relations—including spouses and other life-partners, insofar as their love has outgrown the effects of overvaluation and transference" (Velleman 1999, 351). Since his account applies to spouses and life-partners, however, he must have in mind companionate though not passionate love.
5. There have been numerous articles criticizing Velleman's view. See, for instance, Millgram (2004) and Callcut (2005).
6. See also the much-discussed piece by Bernard Williams (Williams 1981).
7. I thank Christopher Grau for this point.
8. The scare quotes are intended to mark the numerous ways in which the pejorative connotation of the phrase is problematic.
9. For a comprehensive criticism of the view that love should be directed at moral traits, see Smuts (2014).
10. Frankfurt explicitly rejects passionate love as "real love" because it is rarely disinterested (Frankfurt 1999, 166; 2004, 43). Instead, he argues that paradigms of "real love" include self-love and love for one's children.
11. Frankfurt himself thinks that love is the source of final value: "Love is the originating source of terminal value. If we loved nothing, then nothing would possess for us any definitive and inherent worth. There would be nothing that we found ourselves in any way constrained to accept as a final end. By its very nature, loving entails both that we regard its objects as valuable in themselves and that we have no choice but to adopt those objects as our final ends. Insofar as love is the creator both of inherent or terminal value and of importance, then, it is the ultimate ground of practical rationality" (Frankfurt 2004, 55–56).
12. For a developed account of care ethics and critique of deontology and consequentialism, see Held (2006).
13. Frankfurt himself develops an account of caring which he distinguishes from valuing (Frankfurt 1999). According to it, to care is to be committed to having a desire such that it is not discarded or neglected but continues to occupy an important place among one's preferences (Frankfurt 1999, 162). The person is unwilling to give it up. For example, if one truly cares about being a virtuous person, one would be unwilling to let go of that desire. Care is volitional, and love, a species of care, is also volitional. While to value would be to appreciate the value of a particular person, say, to care is to be committed to continue to desire the good of that person for its own sake.
14. Wallace concentrates on defending the *sui generis* duties of love rather than simply reasons (see also Frankfurt 1997, 2004).
15. See Cocking and Kennett (2000).

16. See, for example, Peter Stearns' analysis of the defense in the so-called crimes of passion (2010). Men (but not women) were often acquitted for killing their adulterous spouses.
17. On attachment see Bowlby (1969), Ainsworth et al. (1978), Hazan and Shaver (1987), van Ijzendoorn and Kroonenberg (1988), and Marazziti et al. (2010).

References

Abramson, Kate, and Adam Leite. 2011. "Love as a Reactive Emotion." *The Philosophical Quarterly* 61 (245): 673–699.

Ahmetoglu, Gorkan, and Viren Swami. 2012. "Do Women Prefer 'Nice Guys'? The Effect of Male Dominance Behavior on Women's Ratings of Sexual Attractiveness." *Social Behavior & Personality: An International Journal* 40 (4): 667–672.

Ainsworth, Mary D. Salter, Mary C. Blehar, Everett Waters, and Sally N. Wall. 1978. *Patterns of Attachment: A Psychological Study of the Strange Situation*. Hillsdale, NJ: Erlbaum.

Beach, Steven R. H., and Abraham Tesser. 1988. "Love and Marriage: A Cognitive Account." In *The Psychology of Love*, edited by Robert Sternberg and Michael Barnes, 330–355. New Haven, CT: Yale University Press.

Ben-Ze'ev, Aaron, and Ruhama Goussinsky. 2008. *In the Name of Love: Romantic Ideology and Its Victims*. New York: Oxford University Press, USA.

Bowlby, John. 1969. Attachment and Loss: *Vol. 1. Attachment*. New York: Basic Books.

Brake, Elizabeth. 2017. "Is 'Loving More' Better?: The Values of Polyamory." In *The Philosophy of Sex: Contemporary Readings*, edited by Raja Halwani, Alan Soble, Sarah Hoffman, and Jacob M. Held, 7th ed., 201–219. New York, NY: Rowman & Littlefield.

Branden, Nathaniel. 1980. *The Psychology of Romantic Love*. New York: Bantam.

Brunning, Luke. 2016. "The Distinctiveness of Polyamory." *Journal of Applied Philosophy* 35 (3): 1–19.

Callcut, Daniel. 2005. "Tough Love." *Florida Philosophical Review* 5 (1): 35–44.

Cocking, Dean, and Jeanette Kennett. 2000. "Friendship and Moral Danger." *The Journal of Philosophy* 97 (5): 278–296.

Contreras, Raquel, Susan S. Hendrick, and Clyde Hendrick. 1996. "Perspectives on Marital Love and Satisfaction in Mexican American and Anglo-American Couples." *Journal of Counseling & Development* 74 (4): 408–415.

D'Arms, Justin, and Daniel Jacobson. 2000. "The Moralistic Fallacy: On the 'Appropriateness' of Emotions." *Philosophy and Phenomenological Research* 61 (1): 65–90.

de Sousa, Ronald. 1987. *The Rationality of Emotion*. Cambridge, MA: MIT Press.

de Sousa, Ronald. 2017. "Love, Jealousy, and Compersion." *In Oxford Handbook of Philosophy of Love*, edited by Christopher Grau and Aaron Smuts. New York, NY: Oxford University Press.

Deonna, Julien, and Fabrice Teroni. 2012. *The Emotions: A Philosophical Introduction*. New York: Routledge.

Dion, Karen, and Kenneth Dion. 1996. "Cultural Perspectives on Romantic Love." *Personal Relationships* 3: 5–17.

Fisher, Helen. 1992. *Anatomy of Love: A Natural History of Mating, Marriage, and Why We Stray*. New York: Ballantine Books.
Fisher, Helen. 1998. "Lust, Attraction, and Attachment in Mammalian Reproduction." *Human Nature* 9 (1): 23–52.
Fisher, Helen. 2004. *Why We Love: The Nature and Chemistry of Romantic Love*. London: Macmillan.
Frankfurt, Harry G. 1998. "Duty and Love." *Philosophical Explorations* 1 (1): 4–9.
Frankfurt, Harry G. 1999. *Necessity, Volition, and Love*. Cambridge: Cambridge University Press.
Frankfurt, Harry G. 2004. *The Reasons of Love*. Princeton: Princeton University Press.
Gibbard, Allan. 1990. *Wise Choices, Apt Feelings: A Theory of Normative Judgment*. Cambridge: Harvard University Press.
Grau, Christopher. 2004. "Irreplaceability and Unique Value." *Philosophical Topics* 32 (1/2): 111–129.
Grau, Christopher, and Cynthia L. S. Pury. 2014. "Attitudes towards Reference and Replaceability." *Review of Philosophy and Psychology* 5 (2): 155–168.
Hatfield, Elaine, and Richard L. Rapson. 1996. "Stress and Passionate Love." In *Stress and Emotion: Anxiety, Anger, and Curiosity*, edited by C. D. Spielberger and I. G. Sarason, Vol 16, 29–50. Washington, DC: Taylor and Francis.
Hazan, Cindy, and Phillip Shaver. 1987. "Romantic Love Conceptualized as an Attachment Process." *Journal of Personality and Social Psychology* 52 (3): 511–524.
Held, Virginia. 2006. *The Ethics of Care: Personal, Political, and Global*. New York: Oxford University Press on Demand.
Helm, Bennett W. 2010. *Love, Friendship, and the Self: Intimacy, Identification, and the Social Nature of Persons*. New York: Oxford University Press.
Hendrick, Susan S., Clyde Hendrick, and Nancy L. Adler. 1988. "Romantic Relationships: Love, Satisfaction, and Staying Together." *Journal of Personality and Social Psychology* 54 (6): 980–988.
Jenkins, Carrie. 2017. *What Love Is: And What It Could Be*. New York: Basic Books.
Keller, Simon. 2000. "How Do I Love Thee? Let Me Count the Properties." *American Philosophical Quarterly* 37 (2): 163–173.
Kenny, Anthony. 1963. *Action, Emotion and Will*. London: Routledge and Kegan Paul.
Kim, Jungsik, and Elaine Hatfield. 2004. "Love Types and Subjective Well-Being: A Cross-Cultural Study." *Social Behavior and Personality: An International Journal* 32 (2): 173–182.
LaFollette, Hugh. 1996. *Personal Relationships: Love, Identity, and Morality*. Malden, MA: Blackwell Press.
Levine, Robert, Suguru Sato, Tsukasa Hashimoto, and Jyoti Verma. 1995. "Love and Marriage in Eleven Cultures." *Journal of Cross Cultural Psychology* 26 (5): 554–571.
Liao, S. Matthew. 2015. *The Right to be Loved*. New York: Oxford University Press.
Marazziti, Donatella, Giorgio Consoli, Francesco Albanese, Emanuela Laquidara, Stefano Baroni, and Mario Catena Dell'Osso. 2010. "Romantic Attachment and Subtypes/Dimensions of Jealousy." *Clinical Practice and Epidemiology in Mental Health: CP & EMH* 6: 53–58.

Martz, John M., Julie Verette, Ximena B. Arriaga, Linda F. Slovik, Chante L. Cox, and Caryl E. Rusbult. 1998. "Positive Illusion in Close Relationships." *Personal Relationships* 5 (2): 159–181.
McDaniel, Anita K. 2005. "Young Women's Dating Behavior: Why/Why Not Date a Nice Guy?" *Sex Roles* 53 (5/6): 347–359.
Mesquita, Batja, and Nico H. Frijda. 1992. "Cultural Variations in Emotions: A Review." *Psychological Bulletin* 112 (2): 179—204.
Millgram, Elijah. 2004. "Kantian Crystallization." *Ethics* 114 (3): 511–513.
Murray, Sandra L., John G. Holmes, and Dale W. Griffin. 1996a. "The Benefits of Positive Illusions: Idealization and the Construction of Satisfaction in Close Relationships." *Journal of Personality and Social Psychology* 70 (1): 79–98.
Murray, Sandra L., John G. Holmes, and Dale W. Griffin. 1996b. "The Self-Fulfilling Nature of Positive Illusions in Romantic Relationships: Love Is Not Blind, but Prescient." *Journal of Personality and Social Psychology* 71 (6): 1155–1180.
Nelson, Alex J., and Kyu Jin Yon. 2019. "Core and Peripheral Features of the Cross-Cultural Model of Romantic Love." *Cross-Cultural Research* 53 (5): 447–482.
Neto, Félix, Etienne Mullet, Jean-Claude Deschamps, José Barros, Rosario Benvindo, Leôncio Camino, Anne Falconi, Victor Kagibanga, and Maria Machado. 2000. "Cross-Cultural Variations in Attitudes Toward Love." *Journal of Cross-Cultural Psychology* 31 (5): 626–635.
Newton-Smith, W. 1989. "A Conceptual Investigation of Love." In *Eros, Agape and Philia: Readings in the Philosophy of Love*, edited by Alan Soble, 199–217. St. Paul, MN: Paragon House.
Pismenny, Arina. 2018. "The Syndrome of Romantic Love." Doctoral Dissertation, New York: City University of New York, The Graduate Center. CUNY Academic Works. https://academicworks-cuny-edu.ezproxy.gc.cuny.edu/gc_etds/2827.
Pismenny, Arina, and Jesse Prinz. 2017. "Is Love an Emotion?" In *The Oxford Handbook of Philosophy of Love*, edited by Christopher Grau and Aaron Smuts. New York: Oxford University Press.
Prinz, Jesse. 2007. *The Emotional Construction of Morals*, 1st ed. Oxford: Oxford University Press.
Prinz, Jesse, and Shaun Nichols. 2010. "Moral Emotions." In *The Moral Psychology Handbook*, edited by John M. Doris, 111–146. New York: Oxford University Press.
Protasi, Sara. 2019. "'Mama, Do You Love Me?': A Defense of Unloving Parents." In *The Routledge Handbook of Love in Philosophy*, edited by Adrienne M. Martin, 35–46. New York: Routledge.
Rothbaum, Fred, and Bill Yuk-Piu Tsang. 1998. "Lovesongs in the United States and China: On the Nature of Romantic Love." *Journal of Cross-Cultural Psychology* 29 (2): 306–319.
Rusbult, Caryl E., and Bram P. Buunk. 1993. "Commitment Processes in Close Relationships: An Interdependence Analysis." *Journal of Social and Personal Relationships* 10 (2): 175–204.
Sadler, Brook J. 2006. "Love, Friendship, Morality." *The Philosophical Forum* 37 (3): 243–263.

Salerno, Jessica M., and Liana C. Peter-Hagene. 2015. "One Angry Woman: Anger Expression Increases Influence for Men, but Decreases Influence for Women, during Group Deliberation." *Law and Human Behavior* 39 (6): 581–592.

Schaubroeck, Katrien. 2019. "Reasons of Love." In *The Routledge Handbook of Love in Philosophy*, edited by Adrienne M. Martin, 288–299. New York: Routledge.

Showers, Carolin J., and Suzanne B. Kevlyn. 1999. "Organization of Knowledge about a Relationship Partner: Implications for Liking and Loving." *Journal of Personality and Social Psychology* 76 (6): 958–971.

Singer, Irving. 2009a. *The Nature of Love: Plato to Luther*, 2nd ed. Vol. I, III vols. The Irving Singer Library. Cambridge, MA: MIT Press.

Singer, Irving. 2009b. *The Nature of Love: Courtly and Romantic*, 2nd ed. Vol. II, III vols. The Irving Singer Library. Cambridge, MA: MIT Press.

Singer, Irving. 2009c. *The Nature of Love: The Modern World*, 2nd ed. Vol. III, III vols. The Irving Singer Library. Cambridge, MA: MIT Press.

Smuts, Aaron. 2014. "Is It Better to Love Better Things?" In *Love and Its Objects: What Can We Care For?*, edited by Christian Maurer, Tony Milligan, and Kamila Pacovská, 91–107. London: Palgrave Macmillan.

Soble, Alan. 1997. "Union, Autonomy, and Concern." In *Love Analyzed*, edited by Roger Lamb, 65–92. Boulder, CO: Westview Press.

Solomon, Robert C. 1973. "Emotions and Choice." *Review of Metaphysics* 27(1): 20–41.

Stearns, Peter. 2010. "Jealousy in Western History: From Past toward Present." In *Handbook of Jealousy: Theory, Research, and Multidisciplinary Approaches*, edited by Sybil Hart and Maria Legerstee, 7–26. Malden, MA: Wiley-Blackwell.

Stendhal. 1822. *On Love*, translated by H. B. Scott-Moncrieff and C. Scott-Moncrieff. New York: Crosset and Dunlap.

Tappolet, Christine. 2016. *Emotions, Values, and Agency*. Oxford: Oxford University Press.

Taylor, Gabriele. 1976. "Love." *Proceedings of the Aristotelian Society, JSTOR* 76: 147–164.

Tennov, Dorothy. 1979. *Love and Limerence: The Experience of Being in Love*. New York: Scarborough House.

Triandis, Harry C. 1990. "Cross-Cultural Studies of Individualism and Collectivism." In *Current Theory and Research in Motivation*, edited by J. J. Berman, 37: 41–133. Nebraska Symposium on Motivation. Lincoln, NE: University of Nebraska Press.

van Ijzendoorn, Marinus H., and Pieter M. Kroonenberg. 1988. "Cross-Cultural Patterns of Attachment: A Meta-Analysis of the Strange Situation." *Child Development* 59 (1): 147–156.

Velleman, J. David. 1999. "Love as a Moral Emotion." *Ethics* 109 (2): 338–374.

Wallace, R. Jay. 2012. "Duties of Love." *Proceedings of the Aristotelian Society Supplementary Volume* 86 (1): 175–198.

Wang, Alvin Y., and Ha T. Nguyen. 1995. "Passionate Love and Anxiety: A Cross-Generational Study." *The Journal of Social Psychology* 135 (4): 459–470.

White, Richard. 2001. *Love's Philosophy*. Lanham, MD: Rowman & Littlefield.

Williams, Bernard. 1981. "Persons, Character and Morality." In *Moral Luck: Philosophical Papers 1973–1981*, 1–19. Cambridge: Cambridge University Press.

3 Autonomy, Love, and Receptivity

Carter Lane Johnson

Introduction

Loving relationships can set people free. They can make one wiser, happier, and stronger. They can open up unpredicted options. In short, they can promote autonomy. Loving parents can nurture their children from infancy so that they become competent self-rulers; romantic or sexual lovers can catapult each other into new maturity. As bell hooks (2000: Ch. 1) says, love can further the growth of the spirit—one's overall personhood and one's capacity to be one's own person.

However, as the arts copiously testify, loving relationships can threaten autonomy. Romantic lovers are compared to prisoners ("You almost had your hooks in me, didn't you dear?/You nearly had me roped and tied") or slaves ("He spoke and said many things, of which I understood only a few; one was *Ego dominus tuus*") or detrimentally irrational ("When my love swears that she is made of truth,/I do believe her, though I know she lies").[1] Parents are notorious for impeding the autonomy of their adult children; later in life, adult children caring for their parents can put up complementary impediments.[2] Whenever people love one another in a way that involves such close living together or working together, and whenever people care so strongly about those to whom they are connected, there is the risk of either control or abjection. Whatever definition of autonomy one adopts, whether grounded in self-legislated rational maxims (Kant 2015 [1788]: 30; Korsgaard 1996: 25), what a person cares about (Frankfurt 1999), rational capacities (Christman 1991), or even a more relational account (Meyers 1987), the threat remains, because there seem to be few limits to one person's ability either to control or be controlled by another.

Unless people abandon either loving relationships or autonomy, they need an option that allows for both genuine love and the protection of autonomy. I argue that receptivity is a disposition that can reliably promote autonomy for both parties to loving relationships.

I first outline two threats to autonomy in loving relationships: giving up one's own autonomy and becoming controlling and neglecting the other's autonomy. The risk is not simply the continued frustration of autonomy in isolated acts, but the further risk of eroding a person's disposition to be autonomous. For this reason, I consider not what kind of act can honor autonomy in loving relationships, but what kind of disposition can do so.

I propose receptivity. Previous philosophical understandings of receptivity have had two shortcomings: receptivity is not always distinguished from other attitudes, such as attentiveness, and it has not yet been defined in terms of such sciences as psychology and neuroscience. I define it as the disposition to be with someone without having to place expectations carelessly or compulsively. This definition is both distinct from definitions of other attitudes and, as shall be shown, uses concepts from the sciences. After explaining receptivity, I show that, because the risks to autonomy come from careless or compulsive expectations, a disposition that frees lovers from such expectations can protect autonomy in their relationship. I conclude by offering suggestions about the cultivation of receptivity.

It might be useful to stipulate at the beginning that I do not consider cases in which lesser autonomy is unavoidable or justified.[3] For instance, Eva Feder Kittay (1999) argues that most people are dependent on others at some phases of life and that many people, such as those with permanent cognitive disabilities, require more guidance than others for their whole lives. Sometimes, lack of independence and a concomitant paternalism are normal rather than exceptional. However, I am concerned with relationships between similarly abled people at comparable stages of life (including independent adult parents and their adult children). When I talk about paternalism, I mean unjustified paternalism.

The Risk of Giving Up One's Autonomy

In loving relationships, there is a risk that one will give up one's autonomy to the beloved. In other words, one risks resigning control over oneself, either over an important area of one's life or over one's life as a whole. One risks being controlled.

In being controlled, one might ignore one's own conflicting needs or preferences. Or one might obliterate them, so that one's own needs or preferences are in accordance with those of the person exercising control, that is one might form adaptive preferences (Elster 1983; Sen 1995; Nussbaum 2001). According to my judgment and those of some feminist theorists (such as Cudd 2006; Taylor 2009), forming such adaptive preferences counts as a surrender of autonomy rather than a legitimate exercise of it (as Friedman 2003; Khader 2009 think; and see Meyers 1987), in the same way that Mill considers it impossible to autonomously sell oneself into slavery (1859, Ch. 5).

Why would someone give up their own autonomy? Perhaps for the sake of maintaining a relationship that they fear, the other party will end unless placated. Perhaps as a gift to the beloved, as a grand romantic gesture. Perhaps as a way of evading responsibility, in what the existentialists would call "bad faith."

Feminist attention to the problem of autonomy within loving relationships suggests further motives (Blum et al. 1973; Card 1990; Hoagland 1990; Houston 1990; and see Soble 1994). Women are encouraged to be self-effacing and sacrificial; the patriarchal "right way" to be a woman is to be heteronomous. Or they can believe that it is a moral duty incumbent upon them in their role as wife or mother or daughter or friend. The risk is greatest when the loving relationship is within a household or family. Because women earn less money, have fewer job opportunities, and face greater vulnerability to violence outside of relationships, sometimes there is no way for them to leave, and the best they can do for the sake of their own survival is to compromise their self-rule (Gordon 1988; Okin 1989; Sen 1989). For these reasons, the risk of giving up one's autonomy in a loving relationship is greater for women.

The Risk of Control

The complementary risk is that a person can become controlling, choosing to exercise an undue measure of control in the relationship.

Definitions of Paternalism: The Same Problem, the Same Solution

Discussions of control and the abridgment of autonomy suggest a discussion of paternalism. There are several definitions of paternalism, primarily coming from political philosophy. Dworkin (1972: 65) defines it as "the interference with a person's liberty of action justified by reasons referring exclusively to the welfare, good, happiness, needs, interests or values of the person being coerced," although in later work he makes his definition less exclusive (Dworkin 2020). Arneson (1980: 471) defines it as "restrictions on a person's liberty which are justified exclusively by consideration for that person's own good or welfare, and which are carried out either against his present will (when his present will is not expressly overridden by his own prior commitment) or against his prior commitment (when his present will is expressly overridden by his own prior commitment)." Archard (1990: 36) defines paternalism toward Q as aiming "to bring it about that with respect to some state(s) of affairs which concern Q's own good Q's choice or opportunity to choose is denied or diminished," when the "belief that this behavior promotes Q's good is the main reason" and "Q's belief that [the paternalistic behavior] does not promote Q's good" is discounted. Shiffrin (2000: 217) argues that paternalism does not have to be for the sake of someone's good. Gert and Culver (1976: 49–50) require that it involve "breaking a moral rule."

For each of these definitions, paternalism involves disregard for the other's autonomy, whether this disregard is the actual obstruction of the person's will (either by going against that will or by impeding the options open to that will) or merely negligence concerning the person's will. Whatever definition of paternalism, if it is unjustified, then the threat to the autonomy of the other remains.

For each of the definitions, paternalism is a threat to the autonomy of the beloved in the same way, namely, through disregard. For some, this disregard is negligence, a failure to think of the other's will when it is relevant. For others, the disregard is an ultimate decision in favor of one's own judgment rather than the other's. Either way, the various definitions of paternalism suggest a common solution: a cultivation of stronger regard for the autonomy of the other. The problem is that it can be difficult to balance this regard with the other motivations common to love, especially benevolence.

Benevolence and Paternalism

Insofar as one desires that a person be harmed or insofar as one is indifferent toward a person's welfare, one does not love the person. An indifferent or malicious person might have attitudes, such as strong emotional dependence, that common usage permits as a referent of the English word "love." But without benevolence and valuation, this attitude will not count as love in the sense of an admirable and desirable attitude toward friends, lovers, and offspring. It will not be the sort of thing that philosophers and conscientious people hope to cultivate. So, benevolence, willing the good of another person, is an essential component of love.

If I will the good of the other person, I might conceive of her good based on what she has told me. But, even if I base my conception of her good on the most explicit testimony she can give, I will probably bring in some interpretation of my own. For instance, if she tells me that she values jazz music, I might interpret this to mean that she values the music of Ella Fitzgerald and Miles Davis. This might be true, or perhaps she values the music of John Coltrane instead; whether I am right or wrong, I have taken an interpretive leap. And few of us confine ourselves to such narrow interpretations of the other's good. Few of us restrict our understanding of their good to what they have explicitly told us. For instance, most people think of the other's good as involving bodily safety and mental adequacy, even if the other has never told us so.

Further, lovers cannot easily avoid acting on their own interpretations of the other's good. If one is at the supermarket and has been given only a partial grocery list, one might have to guess in order to complete it. Or if someone dearly loved is injured or sick or otherwise in no condition to make a choice for themselves in a moment of crisis, when nonaction would be obviously more deleterious, one might have to make it for them. So, it is unavoidable that sometimes one must act on one's interpretation of the other's good.

Since it is so easy to make assumptions about the other's good and since it is sometimes unavoidable to act on these assumptions—and since it is widely acknowledged that this is unavoidable—therefore it is easy to make assumptions and act on them even when doing so is inappropriate. It might be inappropriate either because of insufficient warrant for one's beliefs about the other's good. It might be inappropriate because, even if one has sufficient warrant, it is not one's place to act on another's behalf.

In other words, even for the most well-intentioned and informed lover, there is the risk of unjustified paternalism. This is why Angelika Krebs (2014 and in this volume) argues that a "curative" model of love, based on care for the other, can encourage one to conduct a loving relationship too one-sidedly.

So, every loving relationship, even if perfectly intentioned, risks becoming paternalistic. This is a grave risk because autonomy is an irreplaceable good for a person. If one is paternalistic, one can interfere with the autonomy of the person one loves. Whether romantic partner, parent, sibling, friend, or otherwise, one can go behind their back, can make choices that restrict or direct the options open to them, can discourage them from freely chosen options either subtly or baldly, and more.

On the other hand, as Christopher Bennett (2003) has ably argued, loving relationships can promote autonomy. One can nurture the autonomy of another person, encourage them to consider more options and to pursue options they might be doubtful over, provide the care and assistance necessary for them to pursue difficult options, and more.

Paternalism is a likely risk for relationships between men and women, especially in families. Fathers and daughters, husbands and wives, and even mothers and sons can fall into a pattern of control and abridgement of autonomy. This can happen simply from the man's expectations of being in control, but it is more pernicious because harder to fault (in practice) when it is done out of concern or benevolence. It is also likely with any parent/child relationship well into adulthood and even old age, regardless of the sex or gender of either member.

How to ensure that loving relationships promote autonomy and that they will be free of paternalism?

Attitudes, Not Acts

While great harm can come from isolated acts of control or surrender, the worse damage is often done by patterns of behavior. One person might hazard an act of control, the other person might capitulate, and by repetition this initiation and response becomes a regular duet, sustained antiphonally. A pattern of behavior can become so imprinted in the psyche that it becomes a disposition. In this way, loving relationships can lead one to develop habits of undue paternalism—not merely exceeding one's authority but becoming authoritarian—or of undue compliance—not merely of being controlled but of becoming controllable.

This can happen when the compromises that must accompany any loving relationship are too excessive, often gradually and without the participants realizing that they have become unequal in power. One person asks a little too much, the other gives a little too much, and so on recursively until the imbalance is drastic. Since these patterns of behavior are often the result of interpersonal negotiations ill managed, it can be difficult or impossible to assign willingness or culpability to one party more than the other. It might be that one person didn't intend to take, and that the other didn't intend to give away, autonomy. The long and complex history of the relationship might obviate a distinction between willingly giving up autonomy and unwillingly losing it. Either way, the person who has lost a significant measure of autonomy might be not forcibly enclosed but rather contentedly habituated.

It is not enough, then, to consider isolated cases in which autonomy is threatened. There need to be provisions against patterns of behavior and the imprint of a disposition to paternalism or a disposition to compliance. In order to protect autonomy in loving relationships, then, there must be some means to ensure that one either will not develop a disposition that will undermine autonomy or will be able to counteract such a disposition.

Dispositions, by definition, last longer and are a source of action more often than occurrent desires, feelings, or judgments. An occurrent desire, feeling, or judgment, or even an isolated act, is not an adequate provision against a disposition. Consider someone who should exercise more but is habitually lethargic. An isolated act or occurrent mental state will not change them from a lethargic person into a person who exercises; rather, they need to cultivate a disposition to exercise. So, the best way to prevent or counteract a disposition is to cultivate another, opposed disposition.

What disposition can enable one to respect autonomy—one's own and their beloved's—in loving relationships? What disposition could allow one to detect threats to autonomy and to handle the threats adequately, especially when these threats are promoted by social inequities and by motivations that unavoidably belong to love such as benevolence? One promising candidate is the disposition to receptivity.

What Receptivity Is

Receptivity can be roughly characterized as the ability to have one's cognitive, desiderative, and emotional interior in good enough order to notice (to be "receptive of") what is really the case, either about others or about oneself. There are, then, at least two main components: awareness of external conditions having to do with a person, and sufficient control of or independence from internal conditions to allow this awareness. But such a characterization remains rough. There is already considerable literature on receptivity, although, as will become clear, there is need for clarification and a firmer conceptual foundation.

It has of late come to philosophical attention through Carol Gilligan's (1982) psychological study of care and rose to prominence through the care ethics of Nel Noddings (1984). Noddings highlights receptivity as a trait of a caring person. She uses "receptivity" to mean a style of "affective engrossment," something like prereflectively taking on another person's feelings or concerns as one's own: "I see and feel with the other … I have been invaded by this other" (30–35).[4]

More recently, receptivity has been of interest to political theorists concerned with the emotional and cognitive dispositions most likely to improve the character of citizens under democracy. A pioneer in this overall project is Martha Nussbaum (2013), though she offers no definition. Nikolas Kompridis (2011) discusses "reflective receptivity," the ability to engage with new conditions of intelligibility. That is, a receptive person is willing to reconsider the conceptual framework with which they understand ideas, reasons, or conversations. Jennifer Nedelsky (2011) takes receptivity to be a way of being attentive to particulars without having to sort them into categories, including the categories of good and bad. She thinks this can aid understanding and creativity in politics.

These studies have done the indebting work of giving receptivity its own plinth in the hall of philosophically respectable concepts. However, the accounts of receptivity could further distinguish it from related attitudes and more fully explain not simply what behaviors characterize receptivity but what its psychological and neural bases are.

The feminist work on receptivity does not sufficiently distinguish the concept from a family of related ones, such as attentiveness, reciprocation, or empathy when it ought to be kept distinct from each. For instance, Joan Tronto (1998) says "caring about" includes "attentiveness, that is, of being able to perceive needs in self and others and to perceive them with as little distortion as possible."

Receptivity is distinct from attentiveness, reciprocation, and empathy. Nobody is as attentive as the relentlessly critical. Overbearing parents and venomous frenemies devote great cognitive focus to us, often to our needs as well as our faults, but we would rightly call such impositions the opposite of receptive. Likewise, a person can reciprocate through an attitude of transactional advantage or manipulativeness without being receptive of the other person. And empathy, a notoriously complex and contested concept,[5] is usefully distinguished from receptivity, understood as the ability to know people as they are rather than trying to inhabit their experience.

Further, an account of receptivity would be more complete if it more fully employed the work of psychologists and neuroscientists. It could explain what is going on when a person is being receptive—not simply in the operationalized terms of moral or political outcomes but in terms of what goes on, so to speak, in the person's head. Further, a psychological account can suggest ways that a person might become more receptive. By understanding receptivity on a psychological and even neuropsychological level, a person can more easily think of ways to modify behavior and monitor mental processes in a way that can increase receptivity.

The dual needs to distinguish receptivity from related attitudes and to offer a psychological account of its internal workings have prompted me to define receptivity as being with someone without having to place expectations either carelessly or compulsively. Each of the elements of the definition needs explanation: *being with*, *careless expectations*, and *compulsive expectations*.

Being with

To be with someone, in the sense that is relevant here, is to participate in some activity for a stretch of time in a way that includes the other person. Being with includes working with, hanging out with, marrying, killing time with, talking with, being present to (as in counseling or chaplaincy), and so on. It need not involve a goal-directed activity, nor need it involve an intrinsically collective project such as co-authoring or tango. It can include activities, or perhaps it would be better to say passivities, that are non-deliberate and in which awareness is minimal. Perhaps the only requirement is that one be doing something while another person is connected to one in some way. Being with can be short term, such as building a shed in the backyard, or long term, such as lifelong cohabitation.

There are philosophical traditions surrounding conceptions of being with. For example, Martin Buber (1937) examines something similar in the I-Thou relation, while Emmanuel Levinas (2000) studies what it means to encounter the other face to face. Perhaps the modern investigation of being with began with Hegel (1977 [1807]), who treats encounter with the other as the beginning of self-awareness.

Everyone has to be with other people at least some of the time. But one can be with others in many ways: without noticing that one is with them; while having trouble noticing anything but being with them, as when we undergo limerence in the presence of a crush; for their sake, for one's own, or for both, or for neither. Being with, in itself, does not presuppose compassion or attention or intention.

Careless Expectations

An expectation is careless when it is imposed without duly considering whether it is an appropriate expectation.

The most obvious cases of careless expectations result from bias. Everyone has biases instilled by society. Some of the most well-known and egregious examples of carelessly placing expectations come from biases about sex, gender, race, class, "ability," neurotypicality, and other such troubled categories. When people unreflectively depend on a female coworker for nurturance or support, when people are startled at the justified anger of a black person, when people are indignant at any pushback from someone in the service professions, and so on, these come from carelessly placing expectations on the other. Sometimes these are called implicit biases. But Edouard Machery (2016) persuasively argues that they do not belong in a special category, as if they were ontically different from explicit biases. They are not implicit mental states; they are simply dispositions that often go unnoticed. (See also Gendler 2011.)

There is evidence from psychology that biases are manifestations of cognitive tendencies basic to the human mind. Tversky and Kahneman (1974) and Kahneman and Frederick (2002) argue that, in addition to the cognitive "system" that operates by careful rule-based thinking, there is another "system" that operates by heuristics—unreflective cognitive moves that make it easier to solve problems. One common heuristic, "representativeness," substitutes difficult questions such as degree of probability for the relatively easy task of comparing things to each other. Thus, instead of figuring out the probability that someone will have good intentions by gathering information about their character, the heuristic would work by comparing their outward appearance to a set of stereotypes and finding the closest match. (And see Pohl 2004 for more research on biases.)

This account of bias is not the only psychological theory that can offer exposition of careless expectations. Schank and Abelson (1977) first proposed and Bower, Black, and Turner (1979) provided some empirical evidence for the idea that human beings learn a large number of "social scripts." A script is an arrangement of narrative elements, such as a cast of typical characters, a collection of typical props, and a series of typical actions, that allow one to understand both stories and real-life interactions. The idea is that human beings do well when they can interpret situations by classing them into familiar narratives. When a person recognizes a social situation as an instantiation of a script that is already known, this allows them to know quickly how to behave. They are already familiar enough with the situation that they can fill in a lot of details never made explicit. For instance, one knows, even if one is not told, that if Joe entered a restaurant and ordered soup, then he probably sat down and looked at a menu.

People learn scripts having to do with the family: the Thanksgiving dinner script, the bedtime story script, the sex talk script, the curfew script. Similarly, people learn scripts having to do with sex and romance. These scripts often come from the arts and entertainment, from the other person(s) in the relationship, or from previous relationships. For instance, accustomed to a boyfriend who listens to one, when one has a new boyfriend one might give him cues so that he can listen.

Compulsive Expectations

An expectation is placed compulsively when someone places it on another person because of a strong need or desire. Compulsion need not be the sort the American Psychological Association's (2013) DSM describes. That is, it need not present itself as something that disrupts the person's life or that is recognized as irrational or that seems to be out of control. If a person feels a strong need or desire to do something, that can count as being compelled, as the word is used in ordinary language.

Compulsive expectations, then, are not the special property of people with a diagnosable condition. We all have strong needs or desires. For instance, although it can be healthy to withdraw from social contact if people are asking too much of one, my own impulse to withdraw activates too early and too often; if I regularly gave in to this impulse, my behavior could count as compulsively placing expectations on others. I both assume that they are being too demanding and expect them to give me more space.

People sometimes compulsively place expectations in order to buttress or shield their conception of themselves. Carl Jung suggests that, since people want to be good, they have a tendency to ignore those character traits in themselves which they deem bad. Ignored by the conscious mind, these character traits become the person's "shadow." People frequently "project" these unflattering character traits onto another person or group. If a person's shadow continues to be ignored and projected, it paradoxically gains stronger control over their behavior, both the way they treat others and the way they conduct their private affairs (Jung 1959, Ch. 2). For instance, if one is secretly afraid of being cowardly, then one will refuse to admit the times one has been cowardly and instead will seek out ways to interpret others' behavior as cowardly.

Further, the human capacity for affective response develops far ahead of our capacity for extended rational thought. We all know danger before we can understand it. Psychologists have long theorized that we develop "defense mechanisms"—behaviors by which we attempt to survive whatever it is that threatens us as children, behaviors hastily formed at an impressionable age that can persist unrecognized for the rest of our lives (Freud 1937). For instance, a person might be overly suspicious of everyone who offers help, or deliberately provoke people to see how forbearing they will be, or perpetuate other unnecessary habits for the sake of greater safety.

Neuroscience has begun to show that the human brain develops chemical and electrical patterns to deal with need and danger long before these patterns can be shaped by rational reflection. In a recent volume of the journal *Current Opinion in Behavioral Sciences*, theorists argue that, in order to learn and preserve these patterns, human beings have "survival circuits" that reliably activate the brain and nerves in the required way. In some ways, we learn these patterns from experience, including what we are taught by society (Fanselow 2018; Olsson et al. 2018). Yet, to some degree, we inherit such patterns through natural selection (Mobbs and Le Doux 2018), especially through the evolution of the amygdala (de Voogd et al. 2018) and hypothalamus (Canteras 2018; Yamaguchi and Lin 2018). Although neither learned nor inherited patterns are immutable, even when they are based in the structures of the brain (Fine et al. 2013), it requires deliberate work to shape ourselves rather than to be shaped by them.

These patterns can cause us to place compulsive expectations on others. We have strong desires to meet our needs and avoid danger. Even when we are not in need or danger, situations that appear threatening to us can activate the defense mechanisms or survival circuits whose purpose is to preserve the life of the animal at all costs. Few desires are harder to resist, few behaviors are harder to unlearn. If our response to need or danger is either to control or to submit in the hope of remaining secure, then we might impose expectations bequeathed to us by an ungainly genetic heritage. Hence expectations such as finding someone strong who can take care of one, or someone weak upon whom one can exercise one's strength; hence the unreasonable demands of unhappy lovers; hence the willingness to obey parents who will not let one grow up; hence the inability to let children grow up.

Receptivity and Autonomy

Careless Expectations, Compulsive Expectations, and Loss of Autonomy

Paternalism can enter a relationship through careless expectations, especially if these are based on unquestioned scripts. There are plenty of loving relationships in which paternalism was never appropriate but is part of the script, as with inequitable gender norms. There are other cases in which paternalism becomes outmoded, as when a parent must relate to a child who is now an independent adult.

Paternalism can enter not only through expectations placed carelessly but through those placed compulsively, whenever the compulsive expectation is partly or entirely based on the desire to benefit the other person. Motivation is further complicated by the difficulty of separating the person's needs from one's own. Many people need to be needed. A person might insist on meddling in their wife's business because they cannot believe that they are loved unless they are benefiting the person they want to love them. Many people need not to be needed but to be right. For instance, someone might have a deep-seated need to prove their intelligence, resourcefulness, or competence. For them the most important kind of competence might be taking care of others or knowing what has to be done for them.

Just as careless or compulsive expectations can lead to paternalism, so they can lead to giving up one's autonomy. In psychology, the ability to separate one's own happiness, basic needs, and emotional stability from those of other people is called differentiation. Mostly following the work of Murray Bowen (1974) and using a scale developed by Elizabeth Skowron and Myrna Friedlander (1998), some psychologists suggest that differentiation in intimate relationships is important for a healthy ability to voice one's needs, to regulate one's own emotions, and to manage conflict in the relationship (Olver, Aries, and Batgos 1989; Skowron and Dendy 2004). Empirical research seems to bear this out in a wide variety of settings (Spencer and Brown 2007; Alaedein 2008; Skowron 2011; Lam and Chan-so 2013; Rodríguez-González et al. 2015), although the studies are inconclusive (Miller, Anderson, Keals 2007). People have notorious difficulty practicing differentiation with regard to their families or sexual partnerships. It is plausible to think this is because of the careless and compulsive expectations present in such relationships. Some of the expectations come from the other person with whom one is relating. But some of the expectations are one's own. Consider an adult whose relationship with their parents is controlled by their need for their parents' acceptance, or the wife who has internalized gender norms so that she places expectations of docility and altruism on herself.

Receptivity and Expectations

As shown, both paternalism and giving up one's autonomy often come from careless or compulsive expectations. For example, many people who are paternalistic (as I discussed before) are so because they do not accept the real needs of the beloved. This can be because of careless expectations, if they think that they already know the person's needs because of the script they are following. It can be because of compulsive expectations, if they are compelled to expect the beloved or the relationship to be a certain way and the real needs of the beloved would not allow that. As for giving up autonomy, a person might do so for many reasons. Perhaps, because of her careless expectations, she thinks that each person fills a role in a relationship, one being in charge and the other being submissive. Or perhaps she has a compulsive expectation: to be the one who gives the most to the relationship, to be someone people are grateful to for all she has given up, to be looked after and safe and free of responsibility.

Receptivity toward the other person is to be with them without imposing careless or compulsive expectations. This is to be aware of the scripts one has learned, or at least to be willing to confront, acknowledge, and manage them when they are revealed. It is to labor at the discovery of and familiarity with the patterns one has developed for, as psychologists would say, defense mechanisms, or, as some neuroscientists would say, along one's survival circuits. In addition to this awareness, it is the cultivation of the willingness to make decisions based not on these expectations but on what becomes evident about the person and about what they need once these expectations have been unmasked.

Thus, the person who has learned the script that to love is to control can be made aware of this script and can discern beyond it the respect that the other person needs. Thus, the person who believes that they have carefully considered the other person's independence but decided they know best can ask themselves again whether this is true or whether they have relied on an unacceptable bias or script.

Further, receptivity can draw attention to paternalism or giving up autonomy. A person might not notice when they are being paternalistic. They might have genuine concern and benevolence for the beloved. This might be all that she is aware of in her motivations, and she might therefore think she has license to act in ways that do not honor the beloved's autonomy. It might not even occur to her that she is failing to honor the beloved's autonomy. She might say, "How could that be true since I care about her?" Similarly, in giving up their autonomy, a person might not know that they are doing so. They might think that they are being generous or nurturing or simply a good person. Since motives can be multiple and mixed, that might be one genuine motive among others. Or they might have a social script according to which they are doing what is natural and expected. It can be difficult to realize that what feels good and right, or what feels normal, is actually a resignation of autonomy.

A receptive person is, in the ideal case, free of careless or compulsive expectations, or, what is more attainable, knows how to manage them. Thus, she is willing to face the more difficult problems in the relationship. This means that she is able to confront the ways the relationship threatens autonomy. So, she is able to notice the times autonomy is in danger.

In short, receptivity can protect autonomy because receptivity allows a person to manage her expectations, so that she does not place them carelessly or compulsively either on herself or on the beloved. She can continue to have expectations. Sometimes she should. For instance, she ought to expect her beloved to respect her as a person and to desire her good. Instead of placing such expectations carelessly or compulsively, though, she can place them in a healthy, deliberate way that takes account of the beloved as the beloved is. Receptivity does not remove all expectations; it manages them in a way that promotes the good and dignity of both people.

Conclusion: The Cultivation of Receptivity

There are two threats to autonomy in loving relationships: the risk of resigning autonomy and the risk of paternalism. Receptivity is the kind of disposition that can protect against these risks. But dispositions of character need to be cultivated. I would like to finish by indicating some ways to cultivate receptivity, although I cannot here do all the work needed to address this.

Receptivity involves both noticing and managing one's expectations. So, there are at least two stages that a person normally needs in order to develop receptivity. First, she must become aware of her expectations. Second, she must train herself so that she does not place them carelessly or compulsively.

In order to manage expectations, a person needs to know what the expectations are. If one has a careless expectation that women should be deferential toward one but is unaware of this, perhaps believing mistakenly that one respects women as equals, then one cannot become receptive toward women until one knows that there is a problem. How are people made aware of their expectations? By many means: advice from a good friend, work done with a therapist, guidance from a spiritual director. It is not enough merely to realize that one has an expectation. It is necessary to be aware of when it is being placed, i.e. to develop the habit of recognizing the expectation at the time that it is trying to control one. At first, this often has to be done retroactively. A person can notice patterns in the mistakes they have made in the past. As they continue to accustom themselves to this knowledge, they will find it easier to catch the expectation in the act. When they first begin to notice it in the moment, they might need to slow down, take time to be aware of it, and reflect on it. As time goes by, they will be aware of it more readily, until their awareness becomes a habit.

After a person becomes aware of the expectation, both in general and in the particular moment it is operating, one needs to practice choosing something other than placing the expectation. One must resist doing the thing that the expectation demands. For instance, if one has a deep suspicion that people are untrustworthy and expects betrayal, one might be tempted to engineer a situation in which a loved one will show themselves untrustworthy, such as provoking them to lose their temper. When aware that one has this expectation and thereby recognizes the temptation for what it is, one must resist it by not provoking the loved one. If one repeatedly resists such temptation, one will decrease the expectation's power of determining one's actions. One will be less likely to place the expectation either carelessly or compulsively.

The cultivation of receptivity, then, requires both cognitive and volitional training. This is the outline of a proposal rather than a full program. To have a full understanding of it would require a more detailed account, including empirical work.

Notes

1. Here are the respective references: Bernie Taupin, "Someone Saved My Life Tonight" (as sung by Elton John). Dante, *La Vita Nuova* III, as translated by Musa (1973). What Love says to him in Latin is "I am your master." William Shakespeare, "The Passionate Pilgrim," lines 1–2. William Shakespeare, "The Passionate Pilgrim," lines 1–2.
2. Parental relationships as sites of power struggles are central to Dostoevsky's novel *The Brothers Karamazov*, inspiration for Freud (1955 [1899]).
3. For an influential argument that paternalism is often justified if it is a "nudge" instead of coercion, see Sunstein and Thaler (2003) and Thaler and Sunstein (2008).
4. See also Aboulafia (1983), Meyers (1994), and Oliver (2002).
5. 'Empathy' refers to several mental phenomena, at least including emotional contagion, taking the perspective of another, sharing their emotions, and simulating what might be going on in their mind (see Hoffman 2000; Preston and de Waal 2001; Dullstein 2013). The widespread notion that empathy is a good moral motive is challenged by Prinz (2011) and Bloom (2016) in philosophy and by Decety and Cowell (2015) in neuroscience.

References

Aboulafia, Mitchell. 1983. "From Domination to Recognition." In *Beyond Domination: New Perspectives on Women and Philosophy*, edited by Carol C. Gould, 175–185. Totowa: Roman and Allanheld.

Alaedein, Jehad M. 2008. "Is Bowen Theory Universal? Differentiation of Self among Jordanian Male and Female College Students and between Them and a Sample of American Students through Bowen's Propositions. Dirasat 35: 479–506.

American Psychological Association. 2013. *Diagnostic and Statistical Manual of Mental Disorders*. Arlington: American Psychological Association.

Archard, David. 1990. "Paternalism Defined." *Analysis* 50: 36–42.

Arneson, Richard J. 1980. "Mill versus Paternalism." *Ethics* 90: 470–489.

Bennett, Christopher. 2003. "Liberalism, Autonomy, and Conjugal Love." *Res Publica* 9: 285–301.

Bloom, Paul. 2016. *Against Empathy: The Case for Rational Compassion*. New York: Harper Collins.

Blum, Larry, Marcia Homiak, Judy Housman, and Naomi Scheman. 1973. "Altruism and Women's Oppression." *Philosophical Forum* 5: 222–247.

Bowen, Murray. 1974. *Family Therapy in Clinical Practice*. New York: Jason Aronson.

Bower, Gordon H., John B. Black, and Terrence J. Turner. 1979. "Scripts in Memory for Text." *Cognitive Psychology* 11: 177–220.

Buber, Martin. 1937. In *I and Thou*, translated by Ronald Gregor Smith. Edinburgh: T. and T. Clark [originally published in German in 1923].

Canteras, Newton Sabino. 2018. "Hypothalamic Survival Circuits Related to Social and Predatory Defenses and Their Interactions with Metabolic Control, Reproductive Behaviors and Memory Systems." *Current Opinion in Behavioral Sciences* 24: 7–13.

Card, Claudia. 1990. "Caring and Evil." *Hypatia* 5: 101–108.

Christman, John. 1991. "Autonomy and Personal History." *Canadian Journal of Philosophy* 21: 1–24.
Cudd, Ann E. 2006. *Analyzing Oppression*. New York: Oxford University Press.
Decety, Jean, and Jason M. Cowell. 2015. "Empathy, Justice, and Moral Behavior." *AJOB Neuroscience* 6: 3–14.
de Voogd, Lycia D., Erno J. Hermans, and Elizabeth A. Phelps. 2018. "Regulating Defensive Survival Circuits through Cognitive Demand via Large-Scale Network Reorganization." *Current Opinion in Behavioral Sciences* 24: 124–129.
Dworkin, Gerald. 1972. "Paternalism." *The Monist* 56: 64–84.
Dworkin, Gerald. 2020. "Paternalism." In *The Stanford Encyclopedia of Philosophy* (Spring 2020 Edition), edited by Edward N. Zalta. https://plato.stanford.edu/archives/spr2020/entries/paternalism/.
Dullstein, Monika. 2013. "Direct Perception and Simulation: Stein's Account of Empathy." *Review of Philosophy and Psychology* 4: 333–350.
Elster, John. 1983. *Sour Grapes: Studies in the Subversion of Rationality*. Cambridge: Cambridge University Press.
Fanselow, Michael S. 2018. "The Role of Learning in Threat Imminence and Defensive Behaviors." *Current Opinion in Behavioral Sciences* 24: 44–49.
Fine, Cordelia, Gina Rippon, Rebecca Jordan-Young, and Anelis Kaiser. 2013. "Plasticity, Plasticity, Plasticity...and the Problem of Sex." *Trends in Cognitive Sciences* 17: 550–551.
Frankfurt, Harry. 1999. "On Caring." In *Necessity, Volition, and Love*, 155–180. Cambridge: Cambridge University Press.
Freud, A. 1937. *The Ego and the Mechanisms of Defense*. London: Hogarth Press and Institute of Psycho-Analysis.
Gendler, Tamar Szabó. 2011. "On the Epistemic Costs of Implicit Bias." *Philosophical Studies* 156: 33–63.
Gert, Bernard, and Charles M. Culver. 1976. "Paternalistic Behavior." *Philosophy and Public Affairs* 6: 45–57.
Gilligan, Carol. 1982. *In a Different Voice: Psychological Theory and Women's Development*. Cambridge: Harvard University Press.
Gordon, Linda. 1988. *Heroes of their Own Lives*. New York: Viking Press.
Hegel, G. F. W. 1977. *Phenomenology of Spirit*, translated by A. V. Miller. Oxford: Oxford University Press [originally published in German in 1807].
Hoagland, Sarah Lucia. 1990. "Some Concerns about Nel Noddings's 'Caring'." *Hypatia* 5: 109–114
Hoffman, Martin L. 2000. *Empathy and Moral Development: Implications for Caring and Justice*. Cambridge: Cambridge University Press.
Houston, Barbara. 1990. "Caring and Exploitation." *Hypatia* 5: 115–119.
Jung, C. G. 1959. *Aion: Researches into the Phenomenology of the Self*, translated by R. F. C. Hull. New York: Princeton University Press [originally published in German in 1951].
Kahneman, Daniel and Shane Frederick. 2002. "Representativeness Revisited: Attribute Substitution in Intuitive Judgment." In Thomas Gilovich, Dale Griffin, and Daniel Kahneman, eds. *Heuristics and Biases: The Psychology of Intuitive Judgment*. Cambridge: Cambridge University Press. 49–81.
Kant, Immanuel. 2015. *Critique of Practical Reason*, translated by Mary Gregor. Cambridge: Cambridge University Press [originally published in German in 1788].

Khader, Serene J. 2009. "Adaptive Preferences and Procedural Autonomy." *Journal of Human Development and Capabilities* 10: 169–187.
Kittay, Eva Feder. 1999. *Love's Labor: Essays on Women, Equality, and Dependency*. New York: Routledge.
Kompridis, Nikolas. 2011. "Receptivity, Possibility, and Democratic Politics." *Ethics and Global Politics* 4: 255–272.
Korsgaard, Christine M. 1996. *The Sources of Normativity*. New York: Cambridge University Press.
Krebs, Angelika. 2014. "Between I and Thou: On the Dialogical Nature of Love." In *Love and Its Objects: What Can We Care For?*, edited by Christian Maurer, Tony Milligan, and Kamila Pacovská, 7–24. New York: Palgrave Macmillan.
Lam, Ching Man, and Peggy C. Y. Chan-so. 2013. "Validation of the Chinese Version of Differentiation of Self and Other Inventory (C-DSI)." *Journal of Marital and Family Therapy* 41: 86–101.
Levinas, Emmanuel. 2000. *Entre Nous: On Thinking-of-the-Other*, translated by Barbara Harshav and Michael B. Smith. New York: Columbia University Press [originally published in French in 1993].
Machery, Edouard. 2016. "De-Freuding Implicit Attitudes." In *Implicit Biases Vol 1: Metaphysics and Epistemology*, edited by Michael Brownstein and Jennifer Saul, 104–129. Oxford: Oxford University Press.
Mill, John Stuart. 1859. *On Liberty*. London: John W. Parker and Son, West Strand.
Miller, Richard B., Shayne Anderson, and Davelyne Kaulana Keals. 2007. "Is Bowen Theory Valid? A Review of Basic Research." *Journal of Marital and Family Therapy* 30: 453–466.
Mobbs, Dean, and Joseph LeDoux. 2018. "Survival Behaviors and Circuits." *Current Opinion in Behavioral Sciences* 24: 168–171.
Musa, Mark. 1973. *Dante's Vita Nuova: A Translation and an Essay*. Bloomington: Indiana University Press.
Meyers, Diana T. 1987. "Personal Autonomy and the Paradox of Feminine Socialization." *The Journal of Philosophy* 84: 619–628.
——— 1994. *Subjection and Subjectivity: Psychoanalytic Feminism and Moral Philosophy*. New York: Routledge.
Nedelsky, Jennifer. 2011. "Receptivity and Judgment." *Ethics and Global Politics* 4: 231–254.
Noddings, Nel. 1984. *Caring: A Feminine Approach to Ethics and Moral Education*. Berkeley: University of California Press.
Nussbaum, Martha. 2001. "Adaptive Preferences and Women's Options. *Economics and Philosophy* 17: 67–88.
——— 2013. *Political Emotions: Why Love Matters for Justice*. Cambridge: The Belknap Press.
Okin, Susan. 1989. *Justice, Gender and the Family*. New York: Basic Books.
Oliver, Kelly. 2002. "Subjectivity as Responsivity: The Ethical Implications of Dependency." *The Subject of Care: Feminist Perspectives on Dependency*, edited by Eva Feder Kittay and Ellen K. Feder, 322–333. Lanham: Rowman and Littlefield.
Olsson, Andreas, Oriel Feldman Hall, Jan Haaker, and Tove Hensler. 2018. "Social Regulation of Survival Circuits through Learning." *Current Opinion in Behavioral Sciences* 24: 161–167.

Olver, Rose R., Elizabeth Aries, and Joanna Batgos. 1989. "Self-Other Differentiation and the Mother-Child Relationship: The Effects of Sex and Birth Order." *The Journal of Genetic Psychology* 150: 311–322.

Pohl, Rüdiger F., Ed. 2004. *Cognitive Illusions: A Handbook on Fallacies and Biases in Thinking, Judgement and Memory.* Hove: Taylor and Francis.

Preston, Stephanie D., and Frans B. M. de Waal. 2001. "Empathy: Its Ultimate and Proximate Bases." *Behavioral and Brain Sciences* 25: 1–20.

Prinz, Jesse. 2011. "Against Empathy." *The Southern Journal of Philosophy* 49: 214–233.

Rodríguez-González, Martiño, Elizabeth A. Skowron, Virginia Cagigal de Gregorio, and Isabel Muñoz San Roque. 2015. "Differentiation of Self, Mate Selection, and Marital Adjustment: Validity of Postulates of Bowen Theory in a Spanish Sample." *The American Journal of Family Therapy* 44: 11–23.

Schank, R. C., and R. P. Abelson. 1977. *Scripts, Plans, Goals and Understanding: An Inquiry into Human Knowledge Structures.* New Haven: Yale University Press.

Sen, Amartya, 1989, "Gender and Cooperative Conflict". In *Persistent Inequalities*, edited by Irene Tinker, 123–149. New York: Oxford University Press.

Shiffrin, Seana Valentine. 2000. "Paternalism, Unconscionability Doctrine, and Accommodation." *Philosophy and Public Affairs* 29: 205–250.

Skowron, Elizabeth A., and Myrna L. Friedlander. 1998. "The Differentiation of Self-Inventory: Development and Initial Validation." *Journal of Counseling Psychology* 45: 235–246.

Skowron, Elizabeth A., and Anna K. Dendy. 2004. Differentiation of Self and Attachment in Adulthood: Relational Correlates of Effortful Control. *Contemporary Family Therapy* 26: 337–357.

Skowron, Elizabeth A. 2011. "Differentiation of Self, Personal Adjustment, Problem Solving, and Ethnic Group Belonging among Persons of Color." *Journal of Counseling and Development* 82: 447–456.

Soble, Alan. 1997. "Union, Autonomy, and Concern." In *Love Analyzed*, edited by Roger E. Lamb, 65–92. Boulder: Westview Press.

Spencer, Bernadette, and Jac Brown. 2007. "Fusion or Internalized Homophobia? A Pilot Study of Bowen's Differentiation of Self Hypothesis with Lesbian Couples." *Family Process* 46: 257–268.

Sunstein, Cass R., and Richard H. Thaler. 2003. "Libertarian Paternalism Is Not an Oxymoron." *University of Chicago Law Review* 70: 1159–1202.

Taylor, J. S. 2009. *Practical Autonomy and Bioethics.* New York: Routledge.

Thaler, Richard H., and Cass R. Sunstein. 2008. *Nudge: Improving Decisions about Health, Wealth and Happiness.* New Haven, CT: Yale University Press.

Tronto, Joan. 1998. "An Ethic of Care." *Generations* 22: 15–20.

Tversky, Amos, and Daniel Kahneman. 1974. "Judgment under Uncertainty: Heuristics and Biases." *Science, New Series* 185: 1124–1131.

Yamaguchi, Tagashi, and Dayu Lin. 2018. "Functions of Medial Hypothalamic and Mesolimbic Dopamine Circuitries in Aggression." *Current Opinion in Behavioral Sciences* 24: 104–112.

4 A Minimalist Account of Love

Getty L. Lustila

Introduction

One roadblock to furthering discussions about the moral value of love is the conflation of two different concepts: love and loving relationships. When we construe all discussions about love as being about the value of loving relationships, we not only overlook the variety of ways that love plays a role in how we relate to others, but we thereby mischaracterize the nature of love. The most common victims of this conflation are those *personhood* accounts of love, which hold that we love others in virtue of their *humanity*, as opposed to their particular qualities or the relationship we happen to bear to them. Starting from our commonplace ideas about love, it can be easy to hold that David Velleman's view of love as "attentive suspension," triggered by the recognition of a person's rational will, is laughable (1999, 360). Similarly, when we consider Kieran Setiya's or Kyla Ebels-Duggan's view that love is a sort of "appreciation" of another's personhood, removed from their character traits, we may consider it to be simply false (Setiya 2014; Ebels-Duggan 2019; cf. Bagnoli 2003; Jollimore 2011, 15–18, 25–26).

In contrast, I argue that personhood views are largely right about the phenomenon of love, regardless of whether they accurately describe our commonsense idea of loving relationships. At first blush, this apparent disregard of commonsense may seem like a weakness of these accounts; still, a chief aim of discussions about love is to determine whether love has a *distinct* moral value, separate from the values of commitment, marriage, shared agency, etc. In order to settle these issues, we must then look past cases of loving relationships.

An additional worry about personhood views is that they tie love too closely to respect. We can respect those whom we do not love and can love those whom we do not respect.[1] While each personhood account treats the relationship between love and respect differently, they all consider these two attitudes to be deeply connected. This impulse seems correct to me.[2] Still, I am largely dissatisfied with the existing accounts of how these values intersect.

In this chapter, I will draw upon insights from the writings of the 18th century British moralist Damaris Masham to offer an account of the relation between love and respect.[3] For Masham, love is nothing more than the pleasure felt at perceiving, or considering, the continued existence of another self-subsistent being.[4] Respect connects to love since respecting another person requires, at minimum, that she is not the subject of domination. To respect another is to recognize that they possess a degree of authority, both over themselves and over matters of judgment.[5] Loving another is a precondition of respect. From here, one better appreciates how one's beloved expresses their personhood through thought and action. Masham also gives us the tools to show how autonomy, too, is an outgrowth of love. It is through loving another that we acknowledge their autonomy; without love, respect is merely abstract, possessing few action-guiding qualities and little motivational force.

In the first section of this chapter, I discuss Masham's account of love, which I refer to as a *minimalist account*. In the second section, I consider the extent to which love is a moral achievement. In the third section, I tackle the connections that exist between the minimalist account of love, respect, and autonomy and show how Masham's work supplements other personhood accounts of love. In the fourth section, I examine two objections to the minimalist account of love: first, that all matters of intimacy seem absent from the view; second, that it fails to account for love as, to some extent, a discriminatory attitude. In the last section of the chapter, I end by considering the implications that the minimalist account of love has for how we ought to view our loving relationships.

Love in the 18th Century

Damaris Masham (1658–1708) was an English philosopher. The daughter of Ralph Cudworth, the foremost Cambridge Platonist, Masham received an education not enjoyed by many women at the time. She cut her teeth on the great rationalist philosophy of the period, including works by her father, Henry More, John Norris, and others. Masham also made the acquaintance of John Locke sometime in the early 1680s, which began a lifetime companionship—Locke even resided in her household from 1688 until her death. The details of Masham's education, philosophical or otherwise, are scant, though it is clear that she discussed philosophy with Locke, as there is a record of their correspondence (Broad 2006). Masham also corresponded with Leibniz, initially about her father's *True Intellectual System of the Universe* (1678), and eventually about a number of points in Leibniz's own writings, including his ideas of substance and free will (Sleigh 2005). Masham is best known, however, for publishing two treatises: *A Discourse Concerning the Love of God* (1696) and *Occasional Thoughts in Reference to a Vertuous or*

Christian Life (1705). She offers her account of love in the *Discourse*, which will therefore be my focus here.

The background of the Discourse are the writings of John Norris, who is largely responsible for the introduction of Nicolas Malebranche's philosophy to Britain, and in particular a work titled *Letters Concerning the Love of God* (1695), which featured a published correspondence between Norris and Mary Astell about love and its proper object.[6] In these letters, Norris argues that God is the *only* proper object of love. To make this argument, Norris first draws a distinction between what he calls the "love of desire" and the "love of benevolence"—the former leads us to seek union with the beloved, while the latter leads us to promote the beloved's well-being (Astell and Norris 2005, 100–105). Norris thinks that it is sinful to love God with a spirit of benevolence since God does not require our assistance or charity. More importantly, however, it is improper to seek union with our fellows because God is the ultimate source of our happiness (Norris 1693, 13, 19; Astell and Norris 2005, 70).[7]

Let us say that my friend picks me up from the airport. I might rightly express gratitude at his doing so and return the favor if I can. The goodness, however, that motivated my friend to perform this deed is, according to Norris' view, the product of God. Without my friend receiving the goodness placed in him by God, he would be incapable of such benevolence. And so, after I thank my friend for his generosity and perhaps even buy us dinner, Norris expects me to return home and express my thanks to God for having made my friend and for being responsible for the workaday goodness that exists, even in that limited and inconstant manner in which it does. To the extent that I feel drawn to my friend and find him worthy of love, it is only because of his being the product of God's goodness. Norris warns us that any desire we have to conjoin with our fellow beings inevitably leads us into sin and disrepair.

Masham takes issue with Norris' and Astell's characterization of love and offers the *Discourse* as a reply. Masham argues, first, that it is infelicitous to posit two forms of love: love as desire and love as benevolence, each of which has different proper objects. For her, Norris and Astell tie love and desire too closely together. It may be that when we love someone there is a set of desires which typically follow this love. But one might argue that the connection between love and such desires is tenuous. I love a number of my friends, which causes me to desire their happiness, to seek out joint projects, and motivates me to spend time with them. But I do not always feel this way, regardless of the friend. It is possible that I love one of my friends but avoid the prospect of joint projects and limit the amount of time I spend with him. I may desire his happiness, abstractly, but take issue with many of his choices, even if they issue from his character. It does not follow that I hate my friend.

It is important not to connect desire too closely with love, which gives rise to innumerable types of action. Instead of identifying these actions as expressions of love, thereby overcomplicating the concept or disregarding particular acts of love, we should seek to give an account of love as an emotion, or as an "act of mind," separate from these considerations.[8] In a similar vein, Masham identifies love as complaisance, or a kind of pleasure or pleasing state of mind:

> When I say that I love my Child, or my Friend, I find that my Meaning is, that they are things I am delighted in; Their Being is a Pleasure to me. When I say that I love God above all, I find I would express that he is my chiefest Good, and I delight in him above all things. Again, when I say that I love myself, I likewise mean by it that my Being is dear, and pleasing to me. To say one loves a thing, and that it is that which one has Complaisency in, is just the same: Love being only a Name given to that Disposition, or Act of the Mind, we find in ourselves towards anything we are pleased with.
>
> (Masham 1696, 18)

For Masham, love is the name that we give to the pleasure we experience when considering another as a self-subsistent being, as one who is importantly separate from ourselves. It is important here that in love, we do not seek unity with the beloved or desire to possess them. In either case, to do so would be not to *appreciate* the beloved's being. Instead, Masham claims that "we necessarily annex'd a wishing to it whatever we conceive may either continue, or improve it" (Masham 1696, 22). In love, we wish that the beloved continues to *be itself* in some meaningful sense: to the extent that we interject ourselves into the beloved's nature, we do so only so that they will continue to exist as themselves.[9]

Love as a Moral Achievement

One might think of love as a moral achievement, a view that goes back at least to Plato. As the story goes: in love, we are taken outside of ourselves and led to embrace the other; what begins as a consuming desire develops into an appreciation of the beloved and the ways in which they partake in the form of beauty (Plato 1994, 210a–212a; 2002, 245c–257b, 253c–257a). When we recognize our beloved's approximate perfection, our desire is redirected to the aim of attaining infinity with them, either by reproduction or through the activity of mutual self-discovery (Plato 1994, 206e–208e; 2002, 265a–e). For Plato, love undergoes a transformation by our coming to see the other as they are—a transformation that allows us to treat them as a self-subsistent being (Plato 2002, 251a–252a).[10] On this view, love gives rise to respect only by becoming what it is not.

Consider the view that in order to love someone one must attend to them properly—a view illustrated by Iris Murdoch's example of the mother-in-law coming to appreciate traits possessed by her daughter-in-law that she originally found to be distasteful (Murdoch 2001, 23–24). Murdoch presents this example as a drastic change that takes place in the mother-in-law; by learning to set aside her preconceptions and prejudices, she comes to see the daughter-in-law for "who she is" in some meaningful sense. Murdoch identifies this manner of attention as love. The transformation required to go from looking at another selfishly to considering them lovingly is thought to be the result of a hard-fought battle. As one scholar notes, the "loving look is the upshot of a difficult moral journey," as the obstacles to providing this loving attention are numerous (Bagnoli 2003, 506).

Of course, the difficulty of this transformation can be easily overstated. We often have the experience of *seeing* others. Consider the following example. You leave your office to stretch your legs, intending to take a walk around campus before your next class. On your way out of the building, you pass by a classroom where your colleague happens to be holding a class. The door is open, and you catch a glimpse of them in the middle of coordinating a discussion. You cannot recognize the topic of this discussion, but your colleague is managing the class in a seemingly effortless fashion, exuding both confidence and joy as they field questions, giving the students just enough to whet their curiosity. You walk away with a smile on your face and the thought, "I really loved that." When you go home that evening you might think about your colleague; how you never happened to notice them before and how this one moment has caused you to see them in a new light or, in fact, to really see *them*.

One might respond that your shift in perspective about your colleague's teaching, or even your colleague more generally, is hardly justified by your seeing them in that moment. A momentary glance cannot serve as evidence for thinking your colleague is a skilled lecturer. But this objection misses the point. You might recognize that you do not have insight into what is *really going on* in the classroom; perhaps you caught your colleague in a good moment and that they spent the previous thirty minutes thinking to themselves, "why am I even doing this? I was never meant for this! Perhaps I should just quit." Let us say it was not a good day for them. The students were overwhelmed with the material and lost by your colleague's lectures. None of these observations undercut your stated love at having seen your colleague teach, or even the love you experience when considering them afterward.

What you have recognized in your colleague, and what you love in that moment, is them and the way in which their personhood is expressed in the activity of teaching.[11] You would not feel any differently were you told afterward that your colleague was, in fact, not having a good day.

Now, it is certainly possible that if you were to see your colleague fumble their discussion that you may be less likely to *see them* in that moment. You might think "What an embarrassment!" or "Well, that's awful; I feel terrible for them." In either case, you are too narrowly focused on the activity in which your colleague is engaged as opposed to them, as a person. There may be a similar result if you witnessed them succeeding on a particular day—you may feel jealous or self-conscious of your own abilities. Regardless, it seems as if the actions of others give us a window into their personhood.

Now, one could point out that "love" in this context is merely colloquial: you cannot mean that you love your colleague any more than a person does Yasujirō Ozu or the Bad Brains when they say, "I love Yasujirō Ozu's films" or "I love the Bad Brains." In this case, the critic fails to recognize that, given the difference in objects (person, film, album), what it means to love that thing will depend on its nature. As Masham points out, "our desiring of what we love, or only wishing well to it, or both, follow that act of Love; the Nature of the lov'd Object alone Determines" (Masham 1696, 24–25). If I love Ozu's *An Autumn Afternoon*, I may desire to watch it one evening or to share it with others; if I love my friend, I wish that they continue to be the person I happen to love. The difference lies not in the love but in our proper response to that object of our love. I do not find anything problematic about referring to both cases as love, even though they warrant vastly different responses from us.

I return to these concerns later in the chapter, when considering what I call the *exclusivity objection* in the third section, which targets the permissiveness of the minimalist account of love. For now, I turn to how this account helps explains the connection between love, respect, and autonomy.

Bridging the Gap

On the standard personhood account of love, love is seen as the beginning of moral education. Now, one might argue that we can come to see that human beings possess value in virtue of their humanity by, say, reading Kant's *Groundwork*. From this study, we might recognize that all human beings are worthy of certain treatment, and that their humanity prohibits us from acting in certain ways toward them. It follows that *every human being* deserves respect, which demands that we allow them a degree of autonomy over their deliberations and actions. However, as Ebels-Duggan points out, it is possible to affirm that human beings possess value while also failing to *appreciate* the moral significance of this affirmation (Ebels-Duggan, forthcoming). And so, she claims, in order to transform this affirmation into a sincere moral commitment, we have to come to *directly appreciate* the value of human beings by experiencing love for another person (Ebels-Duggan 2019, 623).[12] Only by our experiencing love for this person can we come face-to-face with their presence and learn to take their value seriously.

While we are not able to love each and every person, we can recognize those we do not love as, nonetheless, actual or potential objects of another person's love. So, the thought goes, we love *some* people and consider them worthy of respect; we recognize others whom we do not love as potential objects of love and as being worthy of respect on these grounds. We must therefore see each and every person as possessing value and as being the proper object of respect. In this way, love is meant to educate us about the humanity and dignity of our fellows, something which cannot be done through reasoning from principles alone.[13]

So, love is based in our recognition of another person's humanity, which provides insistent reasons for respect and also the grounds for the value of autonomy. I agree with the thrust of this argument, though I detect a gap between the love we have for certain individuals and the recognition of others as *someone's* actual or potential beloved and thereby possessors of value. The connection between love and respect is said to be made by our direct appreciation of another's humanity through the experience of love. Without love, we have to settle with the belief that everyone is lovable. But how does this belief compel our respect? Let us say that I find a person to be particularly distasteful. I will assume that others do as well and also see this person as possessing unlovable qualities. The possibility that someone *could* love this person will not compel me to take them or their interests seriously, especially as I will see any person who loves them as mistaken, deluded, or even as unlovable themselves.

The problem with inferring the value of a person from the fact that someone could love them is that we lose the centrality of *attention*, creating the gap between love and respect. We cannot respect another simply on the grounds that someone hypothetically loves them, particularly if we have more salient interests for not doing so. It is here where Masham's account of love can help bridge this gap between love and respect and ground the moral value of autonomy. For Masham, love is the pleasure we feel when we observe, or consider, the existence of a self-subsistent individual (Masham 1696, 18). Our only obstacle to loving others is our not properly attending to them. Overcoming this obstacle is not always the result of great moral fortitude; rather, we often find ourselves attending to others in this manner even when it is least expected (as in the case of seeing your colleague teach a class).

The question, for Masham, is not how we extend the lessons we receive from loving particular individuals to people more generally, but how we cultivate the disposition to attend to our fellows. If we are at least moderately successful in our task, we can love people more often than not, and so see them as the objects of respect, thereby compelling us to recognize their autonomy. To see how Masham's account of love is meant to help us here, we have to look back to the *Discourse*. Here, she takes issue with the idea that God is the only proper object of love. The problem with this position is its unintuitive nature: after all, the fact is that we do love our parents, our children, our friends, our lovers (Masham 1696, 18). Surely, God would not make us capable of such a thing if it were wrong for us to do so. The bigger issue for Masham, however, is the way that this view cuts us off from our fellows. To be detached in this manner means to be unable to answer to those around us.

Masham argues that when we are accountable only to ourselves, we engage in flights of fancy and entertain unsociable views: "the passions where they are strong, argue by a Logic of their own, not that of Reason, which they often and significantly enough, invert to serve their own Purpose. And when Religion is in the case ... they can easily advance this so far, as to dress out an entire System, intelligible only by Sentiment, not to Reason" (1696, 28). When one is severed from others, one risks becoming an enthusiast, thereby adopting principles and systems of belief that are prejudicial and encourage our distrust of others and foment discord. Masham recognizes that this state is one to which we are all disposed. After all, there is little in our common lives that support the precepts of "true religion" and the dictum that one must love one's neighbor as one does oneself (Masham 1696, 29). Given the opportunity, we often find convenient excuses not to extend this love to others.

We see here why the gap exists between appreciating the value of one person by loving them and inferring the value of another by recognizing that they are or could be loved by someone. If we are disposed to find our fellows defective or under suspicion, the inference will be blocked by countervailing factors (i.e., this person associates with X group or enjoys Y as a pastime; is ignorant, insensitive, or morally ugly). We are judging this person to be undeserving of love and therefore of proper consideration, though we recognize that their status as such is largely contingent. Consider the matter of retributive justice. We might hold that causing pain to others, physical or otherwise, is wrong, generally, but fitting in circumstances where individuals *deserve* this treatment. We make a similar determination when we consider a person to be unworthy of our extended love. The problem is, as with retributive justice, that we are often unwarranted in our judgments about the desert of others. Though we all appeal to standards of desert, we, as Aristotle reminds us, are often incorrect in our application.

Because of these considerations, we need to find a way to extend our attention in order to broaden our commitment to the value of others, lest we be left with this gap. But how can this be done? It seems like the only option is to cultivate a disposition to attend to other people. By doing so, we increase the possibility that we end up truly *seeing* others, instead of considering them under the lens of our own self-interest or by ignoring them altogether. One might argue that this solution seems hardly perfect. We cannot maintain undivided attention for all those with whom we encounter. In this manner, such an idea appears foolish, as if we are setting ourselves up to fail, or subjecting ourselves to endless guilt. However, respect for another person does not require our undivided attention. The fact that I have been in a position to *see* this person is enough to institute a shift in my perspective. Consider the example of you having seen your colleague. Your future interactions with your colleague will be altered by the experience of having *seen them*, which laid the seeds of respect. In the next section, I turn to consider two objections to the minimalist account of love.

Intimacy and Exclusivity: Two Objections

There are two significant objections that come to mind when considering the minimalist account of love. The first concerns the lack of intimacy present in the account. When we love another, the objection goes, we are drawn to them in a distinctive manner; we wish to be with them, to express ourselves in a manner we often fail to do, to share in the beloved's woes and victories alike. However, the account of love I have sketched sees our relation to the beloved as detached and cold—as if they were a piece of art or music as opposed to a person. The second objection is connected to the first—when we love another, there is meant to be something special about this attitude. If my partner claims to love me, each of their friends, their entire family, and all their co-workers, there is something lost in their expression of love for me. I might think to myself, "well, this does not mean a whole lot."

These objections are rather serious. I take it that you, the reader, have been in love before and are noting that your experience of having been so is hardly captured by the account sketched above. I concur. When I think of the times that I have uttered "I love you" in a romantic context, there is hardly anything in the minimalist account of love that tracks my experience. At this point, I might remind the reader that this account does not take romantic love as its paradigmatic case of love; I might then remind the reader of our problematic tendency to conflate love and loving relationships. Still, if this account of love that runs roughshod over our experience of romantic love, discounting one of the most significant forms that love takes in our lives, then what is such an account worth? In what follows, I hope to mitigate both of these concerns, serious as they may now appear.

Before confronting these two objections, it is important to point out the problem of drawing on cases of romantic love in these discussions. In this chapter, I aim to give an account of the *distinctive* moral value of love. Like in similar treatments of pride, anger, sadness, and contempt, it is important to differentiate love from similar sets of emotions. In our experiences of romantic love—where we run across lower Manhattan to declare our feelings to our beloved before the opportunity to do so slips through our fingers—there are multiple emotions running through our head (e.g., anticipation, fear, excitement, joy, etc.). It can be difficult to distinguish these emotions from one another because we associate that particular cluster of emotions with romantic love, especially at its early stage. But these cases end up confusing the discussion. Given that we associate these experiences with a certain stage of a loving relationship, they are far from representative of the value of love more generally.

Keeping this in mind, let us return to the question of intimacy, which extends past romantic love, though it is commonly associated with the latter. In the examples that I have given throughout the chapter, there is little talk of intimacy. In the case that I noted above, of seeing a colleague teach a class, there was no desire to be near them, to seek a friendship with them, etc., at least not solely on account of that experience. One might think that this lack of intimacy is enough to disqualify the view. After all, on Velleman's account, a characteristic feature of love is the desire to be vulnerable in the presence of the beloved (1999, 361). One may argue it is intimacy that marks our interactions with beloved as distinctive, and that this reveals the particular significance of romantic love in our lives.

I would avoid making too close a connection between love and vulnerability, as I take the latter to be a fundamental desire of all human beings, one that would be more frequently expressed were we not concerned about rejection. In fact, one can often find it easier to be vulnerable with strangers than with family or loved ones. Though this impulse may appear aberrant, one need only consider the role that a good therapist can play in one's life. An upshot of speaking with a therapist is receiving professional advice; still, we also find it valuable on the level of finding someone with whom to speak. Certain vulnerabilities may put undue stress on those we love, and so it can, at times, be prudent to save our emotional vulnerability for others. Also, complete vulnerability with our beloved can be suffocating. By saving some degree of vulnerability for others, we can resist the urge to abuse the patience of those whom we love, or to engage in emotional warfare with them.

Of course, not all intimacy takes the form of vulnerability. For example, there is the warmth we feel for someone whom we love. One may feel this warmth at unexpected moments. Imagine seeing a woman swaddling a child in a crowded mall, or a couple sharing a falafel and laughing at each other's terrible puns, or a man watching the sunset from his porch while lazily petting his dog. Each of these moments is apt to produce a sense of warmth and overflowing in us, provided we are in a position to experience them. Importantly, our ability to feel at home in these cases is determined by our attention, that is, whether we are attending to the environment and to our fellow inhabitants.

Often, we are not in a position to partake in this experience because we are attending to other matters. This reality is less a vice and more a fact of modern human existence. We are almost always otherwise occupied, which makes it significant when we are not. Notice: the intimacy we feel in those moments I noted above is hardly cold or detached. Like our experiences of art, music, or nature, our experiences of people can be genuinely moving. These experiences, I argue, are nothing less than love. And in those moments, we feel no need to intervene; to greet the woman, to share our favorite pun with the couple, or even to pet the man's dog. Instead, we wish only that these moments persist and become moments for others as well. Rather than lacking room for intimacy, the minimalist account of love provides ample opportunity to feel genuine closeness with our fellow beings, though it, at the same time, recognizes the fragility of this experience and our difficulty of attaining it in any degree.

At this point, the second objection becomes salient: love presumes some degree of exclusivity. On the minimalist account of love, it seems that we may experience love for anyone at any time at all. There seems to be a great fluidity and variability with this attitude. Assuming that the account is true, it is therefore difficult to make sense of how we love a particular person—say, our romantic partner—differently than we do the man watching the sunset with his dog. Further, if we claim that there are particular duties of love, then our obligations will be as fluid and variable as the love itself. This result would no doubt be disastrous. The most pedestrian point to make here is that love comes in degrees, which may well be true. Presumably, we are looking for some feature that type-distinguishes loving my partner from loving a stranger. Here, I argue that the stable basis to which we can refer is commitment, an endorsement of the love that we experience for another, regardless of its degree.

When we make this commitment to the beloved, we are not committing to loving them at each moment or promising never to fall out of love with them; we are committing our attention to them. Knowing the extent to which thoughtlessness and selfishness enters our lives, obscuring the beloved from view, we commit to always remind ourselves of the person that we have seen and loved. While there may be norms for making such a commitment, settling this issue goes beyond the scope of this chapter. One thing that can be noted is that such a commitment typically happens only in the context of a relationship.[14] It would be problematic for me to commit myself to the pun-telling couple or to the woman swaddling her child. My commitment is rightly placed elsewhere, to one who similarly commits to me. In the case of strangers that we happen to love, the most it seems correct for us to do is to wish they will be loved in a committed way by someone else, who sees them as we have.

As we can only reasonably make such a commitment to a small number of people, the worries about exclusivity can be mostly set aside. Those concerned about the promiscuity of love can therefore be helped by the thought that commitments cannot be similarly promiscuous if they are of any weight. Likewise, when it comes to the so-called duties of love, we can see now that they are no different than the duties of partiality. When we commit to attending to a particular person or set of people, there are those who are necessarily overlooked. Given the mutuality condition of this commitment, the relation between us and the beloved will be governed by positional duties. The question of how we fit these duties into a moral view that does right by constraints of impartiality goes beyond the considerations of love. I do not propose to settle this issue. Instead, I can only hope to advance our understanding of the relationship between love, respect, and autonomy, and of the value of love generally.

Let us take stock. According to Masham, our love for another is indicative of our respect for them. We appreciate this person as a self-subsistent being and find joy in their existence. Loving another means that we wish only that the beloved continues to be who they are. Insofar as love compels us to interject ourselves into the beloved's life, it is only to this end. Often, like in the case of seeing your colleague teach a class, this course of action is unnecessary, though love also plays a role in the context of romantic relationships. I turn now to the topic of loving relationships.

Loving Relationships

From what I have sketched above, it may seem that on the minimalist account of love, the majority of our romantic relationships hardly count as loving. Now, I do not find this conclusion to be particularly troubling. Our romantic relationships are largely governed by the norms of partnership. We feel jealous when our partner receives attention from another because we see it as threatening to the commitment made to each other. Love may explain our decision to make such a commitment, but there are countless other factors involved here, which is precisely why romantic love is an object of curiosity. However, these complications make romantic love a poor test case for a theory of love. The deeper we delve, the more we recognize that our romantic relationships are distinctive from more workaday conceptions of love, making romance the exception and not the rule.

Still, there are lessons we can take from the minimalist account of love for our relationships. First, it reminds us to see our partner; second, it teaches us about the contingency of connection; third, it gives us a more realistic view of relationships. Most of us do not *see* the persons with whom we are in a loving relationship. Prudential value is a natural outgrowth of partnerships and joint projects. As such, people begin to see each other as useful in some regard. One person handles the bills, while the other does the shopping; one does the cleaning, while the other does the gardening, etc. At some point the two become a well-oiled machine. While there is beauty to that which is useful—especially a well-ordered household—these two may proceed for years in this manner, into the years of having children, when it is all too easy to disappear into one's roles. They may go days, months, or even years without recognizing anything awry. All the while, each are there, present to the other, ready to be seen.

We will surely lose the appreciation of the way our partner expresses their personhood if we are not in a position to see them. The constraints of the household may even give us reasons to obscure our vision of the beloved, lest we discover anything that threatens the stability of what has been built. We may find ourselves trying to convince our beloved that a particular aim—say, entering a language immersion program—is not worth their time. We might argue it costs too much and requires them to be away from home an abnormal amount. In making our case, we may appeal to the duties of the household, which, we will remind them, outweigh considerations of self-interest, all while not grasping our failure to see our beloved. Though we will surely continue to fall short even with said knowledge, we can perhaps develop strategies to minimize our doing so.

One aspect of seeing the beloved as a person is recognizing the contingency of our connection. This does not require us interacting with our beloved as potentially slipping through our fingers at any moment—such a perspective is unsustainable. We also need not view each moment with them as imbued with great significance. An attitude of radical gratitude is equally unsustainable, if also a bit schmaltzy. Rather, by coming to grips with the contingency of our relationship with the beloved, we appreciate the ways in which, even given the forces and distractions to the contrary, people are able to love one another. Because these experiences of clarity are also temporary, we also know that it will soon pass and can only hope to find ourselves back there in due time. In this way, the minimalist account of love gives us a more realistic view of the scope and limits of our loving relationships.

There have been two recent challenges to our view of traditional, monogamous relationships: one from Carrie Jenkins and another from Julian Savulescu and Brian Earp. Jenkins argues that our traditional views of romantic love are suffocating (Jenkins 2017). Given our nature, it is likely that we can love multiple people at once, even in a romantic sense. Instead of allowing for this possibility, we shame people into accepting a constrained form of pair-bonding that only breeds dishonesty, infidelity, and unhappiness. Jenkins claims that we have to rethink our ideas about love to allow for alternative forms of living. Savluescu and Earp concur, though they see another solution to the problem. They argue that merely allowing for the permissibility of ethical polyamory will not solve the problems that underlie our troubles: namely, that people are prone to jealousy in a manner that cannot be explained by our norms of romantic relationships. For them, the only way out of this mess is to control these darker aspects of our nature through advances in technology (Earp and Savulescu 2020).

I welcome both of these challenges, though I think they fall short in different ways. By allowing for the possibility of ethical polyamory, and by gradually deconstructing those norms responsible for producing cycles of confinement and self-hatred in our romantic lives, we will not necessarily make ourselves better lovers. Savulescu and Earp recognize this shortcoming in Jenkins' positions, noting that the most common obstacles to us having healthy romantic relationships are not social norms, but we ourselves. While we can work to change these norms, the impact will not be felt if we are unwilling to confront the more problematic aspects of our own nature. Setting aside the larger worries associated with the use of biomedical interventions to better our romantic relationships, this strategy also misses the mark. Both of these challenges to traditional romantic relationships assume that we have to place more focus on how to be better romantic lovers. As I have shown throughout this chapter, the only way we can hope to be better romantic lovers is to learn how to love more generally.

Conclusion

I have argued in this chapter, following Masham, that love is nothing more than the pleasure felt at perceiving, or considering, the continued existence of another self-subsistent being. As Simone Weil notes, "belief in the existence of other human beings as such is *love*" (Weil 2002, 64). This account of love chaffs against some of our intuitions: that love should be exclusive, in some sense, and that it involves a degree of intimacy. I have tried to meet these objections and showcase the strengths of this account of love: that it captures our experience of seeing others, and that it explains the connection between love, respect, and autonomy. In doing so, we let go of the idea that romantic relationships are the paradigmatic case of loving, but we have made room for a less celebrated conception of love. This love is not often the subject of books or film: it often goes unseen, being attributed to forces internal and external, from a cheery disposition to the weather. Still, it is this love that binds us.

When we learn to see others, we come to appreciate their humanity, if only for a few moments. If we allow ourselves to live in these moments, we begin to learn the lessons of attention. Only through attention can we become better lovers of people. The difficult part is bringing these insights home, to those with whom we spend most of our time, romantic partners or otherwise. But we cannot learn to be better lovers at home prior to our trying to do so elsewhere, with others we may never see again. Perhaps at some point our romantic relationships will be rid of those most unfortunate aspects of ourselves. Until then, we can remind ourselves of Kurt Vonnegut's plea in *Slapstick*: "I wish that people who are conventionally supposed to love each other would say to each other, when they fight, 'Please—a little less love, and a little more common decency'" (Vonnegut 2010, 3). At least it is a start.[15]

Notes

1. It may be necessary to have *recognition-respect* for another in order to love them. My focus here is on *appraisal-respect*, that is, viewing another with esteem or considering them praiseworthy (Darwall 1977). Certainly we love our children without feeling esteem for them. It would be odd if our love for them was conditioned on whether they were praiseworthy. Further, we need not view our children as valid claim-makers in order for them to be the objects of our love (Darwall 2004, 43, 44).
2. Velleman (1999) is the first recent work to posit a connection between love and respect. He presents the view as building on Murdoch (2001), a claim with which some scholars have taken issue (Millgram 2004; Jollimore 2011). Other scholars (Setiya 2014; Ebels-Duggan 2019) defend modified views of Velleman (1999). I consider my own view to be largely following suit.
3. For more literature on the life and work of Damaris Masham, see Broad (2002, 114-140); Broad (2003, 2006); Hutton (2003); Buickerood (2005); Sleigh (2005); and Hammou (2008).
4. At this point one might reasonably ask, "who are the proper objects and subjects of love?" Masham does not consider this question in her work, though she would likely hold that persons are the only proper objects and subjects of love. I argue that her account of love is more permissive, allowing for the possibility that *any object* is a proper object of love (which is to say that the only constraints on who we can love are psychological as opposed to normative). When it comes to the proper subjects of love, my sense is that the minimalist account of love is more restrictive, though perhaps not to the degree that Masham considers. Any being with the capacity to perceive other beings as self-subsistent and to consider the being of others as a constraint on their conduct (in some manner or another) is properly thought of as a *potential* lover. This being only counts as a lover insofar as they do, in fact, love.
5. My aim in this chapter is not to defend a full-bloodied account of respect. I instead rely on what I take to be two uncontroversial aspects of respect for persons: non-domination and autonomy.
6. The larger intellectual context for this discussion is the debate between John Norris and John Locke about the status of Malebranche's occasionalism. For Locke, the occasionalists were little more than enthusiasts, and dangerous ones at that, a view that was shared by Masham: "If once an unintelligible way of practical religion become the standard of devotion, no men of sense and reason will ever set themselves about it; but leave it to be understood by mad men, and practiced by fools" (1696, 6–7).
7. For more on Norris' argument and its connection to Malebranche, see Mander (2008, 130–145).
8. For a different take on how love can be construed as an emotion, see Abramson and Leite (2011). For a congenial alternative to this view, see Pismenny and Prinz (forthcoming).

9. For more on how we are meant to be an agent to our beloved's interests, see Vellemen (1999, 353) and Ebels-Duggan (2008, 162–163). For different, more open-ended, models of how we are meant to relate to our beloved's interests, see Bagley (2015) and Kreft (forthcoming).
10. Presumably Alcibiades' issue in the *Symposium* is that he cannot stop himself from wanting to *consume* Socrates as opposed to recognizing him as a self-subsistent being. However, as Socrates points out in the *Phaedrus*, being in the grips of love's madness may be necessary for properly appreciating another's autonomy (Plato 2002, 243e7–257b6; cf. Kreft, forthcoming). This chapter is an attempt to make sense of Socrates' seemingly paradoxical claim. I argue that Masham's account of love can get closer to understanding the connection between love and autonomy than have many contemporary views.
11. For more on love as the "appreciation" of someone's personhood, see Gaita (2004, 26–31, 146–156, 211–213). For more on the ethical importance of appreciation, see Brewer (1999, 158–163, 180, 220).
12. Ebels-Duggan notes, "when you appreciate something directly, you may come to embrace a value that you did not grasp prior to the experience in question. Moreover, it seems that in a large and important subset of cases you could not have full appreciated the value absent some experience. In these cases, you could not have come to value the thing as you do merely by considering a report of the reasons or arguments that purport to justify your attitude. It follows that, even in the wake of the experience, you will remain incapable of fully communicating to someone who lacks the experience the reasons grounding your own affirmation of values" (2019, 623).
13. According to Ebels-Duggan, practical reasoning operates on the basis of normative commitments that are grounded in the direct appreciation of the value of a person, object, or end: "The only way to then be fully rationally secure in one's commitments is to trace such a line of reasoning back to commitments that are not subject to any intelligible challenge" (2019, 628).
14. Kolodny (2003) provides an intuitive account of the norms associated with a relationship, though it falls short in offering a plausible account of love. While I agree with the criticisms of the account of love found in Setiya (2014), Kolodny (2003) presents a more reasonable model of what it means to act from considerations of love. Exploring this matter further goes beyond the scope of this chapter.
15. I would like to thank Raja Rosenhagen, Rachel Fedock, and Michael Kühler, for their feedback and for giving me the opportunity to contribute to this volume. I would like to thank Raja Rosenhagen in particular for introducing me to Iris Murdoch's work, which has been rewarding both professionally and personally. I would like to thank Kyla Ebels-Duggan, for a conversation that encouraged me to move forward with my thoughts on Damaris Masham. Thank you to Kieren Setiya, whose writings on love greatly influenced the writing of this chapter. Thank you to Aaron Garrett, for introducing me to the writings of Damaris Masham. Thank you to Lisa Shapiro and Marcy Lascano, for organizing the Intensive Seminar on Early Modern Women Philosophers at Simon Fraser University, which gave me the opportunity to engage with others about Masham's work. Thank you to Charles Griswold, for teaching me that historians of philosophy should contribute to contemporary debates where possible. Thank you to the unnamed colleague, for inspiring the chief examples

in this chapter. Thank you to Alexandria Yen, Malin Lalich, Rebeccah Leiby, Taru Auranne, and others who read and commented on the chapter at various points. This chapter is dedicated to Simone Weil, whose work, *Gravity and Grace*, I was reading nightly during the writing process.

References

Abramson, Kate, and Adam Leite. 2011. "Love as a Reactive Emotion." *The Philosophical Quarterly* 61 (245): 673–699.
Astell, Mary, and John Norris. 2005. *Letters Concerning the Love of God*, edited by E. Derek Taylor and Aldershot: Ashgate.
Bagley, Benjamin. 2015. "Loving Someone in Particular." *Ethics* 125 (2): 477–507.
Bagnoli, Carla. 2003. "Respect and Loving Attention." *Canadian Journal of Philosophy* 33 (4): 483–515.
Brewer, Talbot. 2009. *The Retrieval of Ethics*. New York: Oxford University Press.
Broad, Jacqueline. 2002. *Women Philosophers of the Seventeenth Century*. New York: Cambridge University Press.
Broad, Jacqueline. 2003. "Adversaries or Allies? Occasional Thoughts on the Masham-Astell Exchange." *Eighteenth Century Thought* 1: 123–149.
Broad, Jacqueline. 2006. "A Woman's Influence? John Locke and Damaris Masham on Moral Accountability." *Journal of the History of Ideas* 67: 489–510.
Buickerood, James. 2005. "What Is It with Damaris, Lady Masham? The Historiography of One Early Modern Woman Philosophy." *Locke Studies* 5: 179–214.
Darwall, Stephen. 1977. "Two Kinds of Respect." *Ethics* 88 (1): 36–49.
Darwall, Stephen. 2004. "Respect and the Second Person Standpoint." *Proceedings and Addresses of the American Philosophical Association* 78 (2): 43–59.
Earp, Brian D., and Julian Savulescu. 2020. *Love Drugs: The Chemical Future of Relationships*. Stanford, CA: Redwood Press.
Ebels-Duggan, Kyla. 2008. "Against Beneficence: A Normative Account of Love." *Ethics* 119 (1): 142–170.
Ebels-Duggan, Kyla. 2019. "Beyond Words: Inarticulable Reasons and Reasonable Commitments." *Philosophy and Phenomenological Research* 98 (3): 623–641.
Ebels-Duggan, Kyla. Forthcoming. "Love, Respect and the Value of Humanity." *The Value of Humanity: A Reevaluation*, edited by Nandi Theunissen and Sarah Buss. New York: Oxford University Press.
Gaita, Raimond. 2004 [1991]. *Good and Evil: An Absolute Conception*. New York: Routledge.
Hammou, Philippe. 2008. "Enthousiasme et Nature Humaine: A Propos d'une Lettre de Locke à Damaris Cudworth." *Revue de Métaphysique et Morale* 3: 337–350.
Hutton, Sarah. 1993. "Damaris Cudworth, Lady Masham: Between Platonism and Enlightenment." *British Journal for the History of Philosophy* (1): 29–54.
Jenkins, Carrie. 2017. *What Love Is*. New York: Basic Books.
Jollimore, Troy. 2011. *Love's Vision*. Princeton, NJ: Princeton University Press.
Mander, W. J. 2008. *The Philosophy of John Norris*. New York: Oxford University Press.

Masham, Damaris Cudworth. 1696. *A Discourse Concerning the Love of God.* London: Awnsham and John Churchill.
Millgram, Elijah. 2004. "Kantian Crystallization." *Ethics* 114 (3): 511–513.
Murdoch, Iris. 2001 [1970]. *The Sovereignty of the Good.* New York: Routledge Classics.
Norris, John. 1693. *Practical Discourses upon Several Divine Subjects,* 3 vols. London: S. Manship.
Kolodny, Niko. 2003. "Love as a Valuing Relationship." *The Philosophical Review* 112 (2): 135–189.
Kreft, Nora Isolde. Forthcoming. "Love and Autonomy." *The Oxford Handbook of Philosophy of Love*, edited by Christopher Grau and Aaron Smuts. New York: Oxford University Press.
Pismenny, Arina, and Jesse Prinz. Forthcoming. "Is Love an Emotion?" *The Oxford Handbook of Philosophy of Love*, edited by Christopher Grau and Aaron Smuts. New York: Oxford University Press.
Plato. 2002. *Phaedrus,* translated by Robin Waterfield. New York: Oxford University Press.
Plato. 1994. *Symposium,* translated by Robin Waterfield. New York: Oxford University Press.
Setiya, Kieran. 2014. "Love and the Value of a Life." *Philosophical Review* 123 (3): 251–280.
Sleigh, Robert. 2005. "Reflections on the Masham-Leibniz Correspondence." *Early Modern Philosophy: Mind, Matter, and Metaphysics*, edited by Christia Mercer and Eileen O'Neil. New York: Oxford University Press.
Weil, Simone. 2002. *Gravity and Grace.* New York: Routledge.
Velleman, David. 1999. "Love as a Moral Emotion." *Ethics* 109 (2): 338–374.
Vonnegut, Kurt. 2010 [1976]. *Slapstick or Lonesome No More!.* New York: Dial Press Trade.

5 "Someone I Would Have Hated to Be"
The Threat of Love in *Rear Window* and *Vertigo*

Troy Jollimore

> Tell me everything you saw, and what you think it means.
> Lisa (Grace Kelly), in *Rear Window*

Introduction

Both *Rear Window* and *Vertigo* center on the image of a dangling man. In *Rear Window* the image comes at the film's climax, as R. B. Jefferies, the protagonist, grips the windowsill of his apartment for a few moments before falling to the ground below. But this is only the visual literalization of Jefferies' existential predicament: he has, in fact, spent the entire film in a state of spiritual suspension—a suspension that centers on romantic love and his fears, hesitations and anxieties regarding such love. *Vertigo* finds its protagonist, John "Scottie" Ferguson, dangling over a void just a few minutes into the film. Scottie avoids falling to his death in this scene but will soon find himself plunged into a chaos of impassioned infatuation and irrational obsession. In the process, he will suffer and endure many of the things Jefferies feared. Since these protagonists are, in a significant sense, our stand-ins, our onscreen representatives, we can say that he ends up realizing many of *our* fears about love as well.

This chapter explores these two films' treatment of some of our ideas, feelings, and anxieties about romantic love. The image of the dangling man—high-up, indecisive, detached, and removed from life—is central, as are the symbols of falling (which connotes death, of course, but also falling in love, and at the same time a loss of freedom and a lack of control over one's body) and the existential void over which we are suspended and into which we risk plunging.

Romantic love causes considerable anxiety. In part this is because we worry about not having it, about not being loved. But the thought of loving, and being loved, can also be frightening. We may feel that we stand to lose our independence, our autonomy, our sense of what matters to us, of what we want. Because love can invite or provoke radical change, we might fear that it will cost us our identities, our very selves. We may feel possessed when we love, or are loved, as if we belonged to someone other than ourselves. *Rear Window* and *Vertigo* explore and dramatize these worries, giving us ways to think and feel more adequately, sensitively, and deeply about essential elements of what it means to live a human life.

Rear Window: The Threat of Marriage

> One of the clearest forms [American thinking about autonomy] takes is the idea that individual autonomy is to be achieved by erecting a wall of rights between the individual and those around him. [...] The logic of this is that the most perfectly autonomous man is thus the most perfectly isolated.
>
> Jennifer Nedelsky (2011), *Law's Relations*

Let us start by noting a similarity between these two films that I take to be crucial: both *Rear Window* and *Vertigo* revolve around an act of violence against women. In particular, each film revolves around a murder plot in which a man kills his wife. In both films, moreover, the protagonist is a kind of detective figure whose work is centered on *seeing*—a magazine photographer, in the former case, and a police detective turned private eye in the latter. This character is anxious about his autonomy in the way mentioned above: he is tempted by the enticing possibilities of a romantic or sexual entanglement but concerned that in giving in to temptation he might lose his independence. Both films, indeed, foreground and literalize the issue of freedom by placing that protagonist (portrayed by James Stewart in both cases!) in a state of physical bondage at or near the start of the film: *Rear Window*'s Jefferies with a broken leg in a cast, and confined to a wheelchair; *Vertigo*'s Scottie in a "corset," and also burdened with a debilitating case of vertigo that afflicts him whenever he ascends to heights.

Rear Window's plot can be summarized briefly. The protagonist, L. B. Jefferies, temporarily confined to a wheelchair as the result of an accident, whiles away his hours observing his neighbors, whose apartments he can see across the courtyard of his building. He begins to suspect, and eventually becomes convinced, that one of those neighbors—a salesman named Thorwald—has murdered his wife and disposed of her body. Jefferies' associates, in particular his girlfriend, Lisa Fremont, are at first skeptical, but in the end they are drawn in and help him investigate. Thorwald, after becoming aware of Jefferies' surveillance, confronts him directly and throws him out the window; but he survives and is vindicated, as it is proved that his suspicions were correct.

What this brief summary leaves out is as important—indeed, more so—as what it includes. (In particular, it says little about Jefferies' relationship with Lisa, which will be my main concern; in my view, the investigation plot is in a sense secondary.) Jefferies' identity as an independent, an adventurer, indeed a bit of a rogue, is communicated to the audience before we even hear him speak. In a visual tour of his apartment, conducted while he is asleep in his wheelchair, we see a set of photographs he has taken in the course of his career. They depict exciting subjects (fire, explosions, a car flipping on a racetrack) in exotic locales, suggesting a life of intrepid escapades. His current situation, trapped in a wheelchair, and hence in his apartment, on a sweltering day in New York City, offers a stark contrast. His apartment's "rear window" faces the courtyard of his building, and through it, he can see his neighbors in their various domiciles; observing them seems to have become his primary source of entertainment in his confinement. As for genuine interactions, there is the occasional telephone conversation, and there are two people, both women, who visit him on a regular basis. Stella (Thelma Ritter), a nurse hired by the insurance company, comes to give him massages and opinions. Lisa Fremont, a model and socialite, comes because she is in love with Jefferies and wants to marry him.

The contours of Jefferies' predicament with Lisa are outlined in a series of three conversations: the first, by phone, with his editor, Gunnison; the second with Stella; and the third with Lisa herself. Gunnison, having mixed up the dates of Scottie's release from his cast, is calling to offer him an assignment. Jefferies insists that he be given the assignment despite the obvious impracticability of this; then, on being denied, he insists that Gunnison give him something:

JEFFERIES: Listen if you don't pull me out of this swamp of boredom, I'll do something drastic.
GUNNISON: Like what?
JEFFERIES: I'll get married. Then I'll never be able to go anywhere.
GUNNISON: it's about time you got married, before you turn into a lonesome and bitter old man.
JEFFERIES: Yeah, can you see me, rushing home to a hot apartment to listen to the automatic laundry, the electric dishwasher, the garbage disposal, and a nagging wife.
GUNNISON: Jeff, wives don't nag anymore. They discuss.
JEFFERIES: Is that so? Is that so? Well maybe in the high rent district they discuss. In my neighborhood they still nag.

To a degree this comes across as typical misogynistic masculine banter; and on a first viewing, in particular, it is likely to be taken as such. In fact, Jefferies is expressing some deep anxieties. It is worth noting that the first words we hear in the film are not spoken by an onscreen character, but by a radio announcer; as the camera conducts an initial circuit of the courtyard, giving us glimpses of Jefferies' various neighbors, the voice, emitted by a radio in a neighbor's apartment, intones: "Men, are you over forty? When you wake up in the morning do you feel tired and run-down? Do you have that listless feeling?"

Anxiety about aging, then—about settling down, becoming complacent, losing one's youth, one's powers, and one's freedom—is quite literally in the air. (Moreover, for audiences at the time Stewart would have brought with him shades of certain *earlier* roles—that of George Bailey in Frank Capra's *It's a Wonderful Life* (1946), for instance, another male character who wanted travel and adventure but who ended up trapped, in this case in the little town of Bedford Falls, by marriage, children, and the family business.) Jefferies' characterization of marriage as a "drastic" action, then, speaks to a deep concern, as does Gunnison's warning that, at his age, he is risking becoming a "lonesome and bitter old man." These concerns, about the fading strengths of one's energetic and masculine youth, and the increasing difficulty of remaining independent and self-sufficient, are only exacerbated by the state of stasis and isolation Jefferies' recent accident has placed him in—a state in which, being himself rendered inactive, he is resigned to passing his days by watching the activities of others.

Two things are worth observing about Jefferies' accident. The first is that it was, by Jefferies' own admission, the result of his becoming too directly involved in his work. (Gunnison says to Jefferies: "I didn't ask you to stand in the middle of that automobile race track"—to which Jefferies defensively responds: "You asked for something dramatically different! You got it!") Jefferies' current incapacitation, then, is the result of his having momentarily abandoned his typical role, that of the detached observer who, rather than plunging himself into the thick of life, stands apart from life, contemplating it and making images of it from a safe distance. Now he is a detached observer again, watching his neighbors carry out their romantic lives while attempting to hold his own as motionless as possible. Having once made the mistake of eschewing the safety of detachment in favor of active participation in life—and having learned the hard way that the result of such boldness can be a state of *enforced* non-participation, one which offers little in the way of interesting, diverting entertainments—Jefferies is, perhaps, more reluctant than usual to make the same mistake again, and thus even more resistant to Lisa's enticements of marriage and a life together.

The neighbors observed by Jefferies include a young attractive single woman, a newlywed couple, and the Thorwalds, the long-married couple whose marital strife will culminate in the wife's murder at her husband's hands. It is if Jefferies were a movie viewer being offered a panoply of stills and short sequences depicting all the various stages of married life—with the notable exception, that is, of a couple that has remained happy and in love while growing older with each other. And this relates to our second observation about Jefferies' accident and its aftermath—one that is likely fairly obvious by now: there is a strong sense in which the state of dependence caused by Jefferies' injuries serves, for him, as a kind of trial marriage. It gives him the chance, that is, to learn what it means to stay home, to be taken care of, to be tamed, and to a certain degree to be trapped; to see only a few people, to not be in the habit of keeping a bag packed and being ready to dash to the airport at a moment's notice.

Since Lisa has been pressing Jefferies to marry her, this trial run possesses a certain gravity. His anxiety at being more or less caged in his apartment is thus not only closely tied to but is emblematic of the tapestry of anxieties about committed romantic love that *Rear Window* and *Vertigo* set out to explore. As suggested earlier, the salient anxiety here is the fear that such love, particularly once it is institutionally solidified by marriage, is by nature constraining, requiring one to limit one's activities and pursuits, to abide by conventional rules, to give up much of what one desires, and thus to sacrifice a good deal of one's freedom.

Jefferies' Dilemma

> The essence of being human is that one does not seek perfection; that one is sometimes willing to commit sins for the sake of loyalty ... and that one is prepared in the end to be defeated and broken up by life, which is the inevitable price of fastening one's love upon other human individuals.
>
> George Orwell, "Reflections on Gandhi"

Does this anxiety, so characterized, exhaust the sources of Jefferies' reluctance to marry Lisa? On the one hand, it is surely a significant part of it. It is doubtful, however, that it comprehensively captures Jefferies' concerns—a fact that is made more evident over the course of the ensuing conversations, first with Stella, then with Lisa herself. Stella seems largely to represent the voice of conventional thought about romantic matters: in her view, men and women are meant to get married, it is good for men to settle down, and Lisa is the perfect partner for Jefferies. None of this is unexpected, but the mention of Lisa's perfection provokes an interesting response from Jefferies:

JEFFERIES: She's just not the girl for me.
STELLA: She's only perfect.
JEFFERIES: *Too* perfect. Too beautiful, too talented, too sophisticated, too everything—but what I want.

The most obvious reading of this exchange would take Jefferies' claim that Lisa is "perfect" as ironic, trading on an ambiguity between being perfect according to widely accepted conventional standards and being a perfect match for his desires. This reading is surely not wholly wrong, and it fits with Jefferies' comment, which follows shortly, that Lisa "belongs in that rarefied atmosphere of Park Avenue, expensive restaurants, and literary cocktail parties." But it faces two serious objections. First, it implies, implausibly, that Jefferies does not himself desire a romantic partner who is beautiful, talented, or sophisticated. This is an implausible position to attribute to anyone, but particularly so in Jefferies' case, given that he *is* already romantically involved with Lisa and clearly has strong feelings for her. Second, the suggested interpretation leaves unanswered a significant question: if Jefferies knows that Lisa is not perfect for him, then why does he seem to regard himself as facing a dilemma? If the situation represented mere disagreement between conventional attitudes and Jefferies' own views, it is unlikely he would find himself very troubled. What does a man like Jefferies care about conventional views? He could dispose of Lisa, knowing that she was not what he wanted, and be done with it.

A more promising interpretation distinguishes two kinds of reason that are relevant to love. Following Sara Protasi, we can identify reasons that speak in favor of "social relationships"—including marriage—and distinguish these from "love's reasons"—that is, those reasons that speak in favor of love itself. "There are all sorts of reasons," Protasi writes, "to enter into a social relationship with someone: social duty, interest, kindness, desire to fall in love, and so forth. These reasons are, however, distinct from *love's* reasons" (Protasi 2014, 217). Making this distinction helps us preserve the thought that Jefferies faces a painful dilemma: he has strong reasons for loving Lisa—she is, from the perspective of love, "perfect"—but also has strong reasons for refusing to commit more thoroughly to a romantic relationship with her. From that perspective, she is deeply imperfect. (Indeed, it might be—for reasons that should become clearer as we proceed—that he is worried that in becoming as involved with her as he has, he has already acted against some very important reasons.) Moreover—and here we begin to get at the true root of Jefferies' painful dilemma—the things about Lisa that inspire Jefferies' passionate love for her are the very things that would make it impossible for the two of them to achieve a happy marriage. (Or at least, Jefferies takes this to be the case. Lisa presumably disagrees; perhaps she would say that this whole way of thinking about love and its reasons is deeply wrongheaded.)

Jefferies' claim that Lisa is "perfect" is not ironic but entirely sincere. As a desirable woman, she is perfect: beautiful, talented, sophisticated, and a thousand other attractive things. And his comment about "that rarefied atmosphere of Park Avenue, expensive restaurants, and literary cocktail parties" need not and should not be read as mocking or scoffing. It is not *his* world, perhaps, but it is a world, one that has real value, and one in which Lisa has risen in virtue of her beauty, grace, and intelligence, to a kind of pre-eminence. The problem is not that Jeffries sees no value in her or in what she does. The problem rather is that he cannot see how she can continue to live a life governed by such values while also somehow accommodating herself to him—unless, of course, he were to change in order to accommodate her; and this does not seem desirable either.

"Can you see her tramping around the world with a camera bum who never has more than a week's salary in the bank?" he asks Stella. And then adds: "If only she was ordinary." This comment is also not as ironic as it might at first appear. Such irony as it contains gestures toward Jeffries' dilemma, the paradox that drives his impossible situation. An ordinary woman, after all, would not present the problem he is faced with. An ordinary woman might be willing to adapt to him, to accommodate his unconventional life, to alter or even give up her identity so as to make a life together possible. And because she began as "ordinary," this would be no great loss. Indeed, it would not be a bad thing to ask an "ordinary" person to change in this way; nor would it make one a bad person to want this. The hitch is that Jeffries would not have fallen passionately in love with an ordinary person. It takes an extraordinary woman—a "perfect" person, a Lisa—to make him fall in love. (He is, again, an independent, detached man, one who prefers to observe rather than participate.) And one can't ask a perfect person to change; one can't even desire that, not consistently anyway, for that would be to desire that what one loves just as it is cease to be as it is. Indeed, when we turn to our discussion of Jeffries' counterpart, Scottie, in *Vertigo*, we will find a person who is willing, indeed driven to force his beloved to undergo a revision and reconstruction process of just this sort; and we will see, there, just how ugly such a thing can be. If the possibility that Lisa might refuse to change for him—that her professions of willingness to do precisely that are false or represent a kind of ignorance of her own abilities to change—makes Jeffries fearful, he is even more afraid that staying with Lisa might in fact change her; for he does not *want* her to change, and he certainly does not to be the one who changes her.

Have we put our finger on a general problem, dilemma, or paradox with respect to love? It is not, we may perhaps reassure ourselves, a universal one: that is, we could imagine people who manage to avoid it, if not through wisdom and stratagem then through luck. One might, after all, fall in love with a person whose lifestyle is already compatible with yours. Jeffries might have fallen in love with a fellow independent adventurer. Of course, it is quite possible that Jeffries would never, in fact, have been strongly attracted to such a person. Perhaps he would have found such a woman too masculine, too "mannish," or simply too much like him. (Who wants to marry, or take to bed, a mirror image of oneself?) For all we know, Lisa might meet Jeffries' peculiar preferences, proclivities, kinks, and quirks in various other ways as well. Kant's observation that "out of the crooked timber of humanity nothing straight was ever made" is nowhere more true than with respect to what we are sexually and romantically attracted to—a fact which undermines Stella's somewhat naïve view that, given Lisa's attractions and perfections, *any* man would be out of his mind to pass up the chance to marry her.

Thus, even if we suppose that Jefferies would in principle be open to being with a woman who was not a model or socialite, who enjoyed sleeping on hard ground and subjecting herself to physical discomfort and danger, who enjoyed eating fish heads and rice as much as (or more than!) a fine dinner at 21—a woman, that is to say, very much like him—there would remain the practical difficulty of finding such a woman, who was available, and to whom he was attracted, and who was attracted to and willing to be with *him*. And of course *he* would need to be available too—which, in *Rear Window*, given his emotional bonds with Lisa (as complex and unstable as they may be) he most certainly is not. These pragmatic considerations may fall short of constituting *in principle* impediments to marriage, but they do not fall as far short as one might like. The fact is that a great many of us, indeed probably most of us, will end up at some point attracted to and romantically involved with a person who is sufficiently perfect (from the perspective of love) and sufficiently imperfect (from the standpoint of social relationships) to pose a version of the problem. Jefferies' particular traits and quirks may exacerbate the issue in his case, which is part of what makes his situation a useful illustration for our purposes; but it only exemplifies and clarifies a predicament that many of us, in some way, find ourselves in.

Jefferies' dilemma, then, is not straightforwardly reducible to the conflict between the perspective of love (which involves considering a person almost aesthetically, as a thing in itself, a bearer of intrinsic values) and the perspective of social relationships (which invite an assessment in terms of pragmatic and even somewhat utilitarian considerations: will the two of us *work* together as a couple?). There is a deeper reason—or rather, a deeper set of reasons—for Jefferies to fear getting (more) involved with Lisa. Because he loves Lisa, and sees her as perfect, Jefferies strongly desires that Lisa not change. And because he is happy with himself as a person, he also desires that he himself not change. But love, by its very nature, has a tendency to change people. Perhaps some people are romantically drawn to those they regard as highly imperfect, with the hope of "fixing" them. (Scottie's attraction to Madeleine in *Vertigo* is clearly pertinent in this connection.) They may avoid the problem I am sketching here (though they no doubt face significant problems of their own). But for others—those who are attracted to people they see as already inherently attractive, and not needing to be "fixed"—the fact that lovers tend to be changed as the result of romantic love may well suggest that there is a deep tension, and indeed a kind of self-defeating element, in such love. Some of our most powerful reasons for avoiding love, it turns out, seem to arise from love itself.

Love, Union, and Transformation

> But however much I loved her, it seems I continually wanted to conceal from myself how much she actually affected me, which really does not seem appropriate to erotic love.
>
> Kierkegaard's (1978) journals

It is worth reminding ourselves that Jefferies' fear is not merely the fear that being in a love relationship would require lifestyle changes that might prove to be constraining, and hence that he might stand to lose a certain degree of his freedom. People sometimes speak of such losses in terms of autonomy, but if we think of autonomy, as is common, as primarily an internal matter—a matter of how one's personality is organized, and of how much control one has over one's own decision-making powers and the capacity to act on one's decisions—then we will likely not see changes in the external circumstances of one's life as threatening autonomy in a deep sense. Thus, while Jefferies surely fears that his life will be changed by marriage, his deeper fear is that *he* will be changed. It is himself that Jefferies stands to lose. To fall in love is to open oneself (or to be opened, since it often feels that one has little choice in the matter) to becoming a different person. That said, it is worth saying—and recognizing this will, presumably, only strengthen the grounds for Jefferies' anxiety—that the two phenomena are not unrelated; agreeing to changes in the external conditions of one's life can, over time, enable and lead to unintended yet quite radical changes in one's very self. Margaret Gilbert's description of the process makes it fairly clear how easily such a transition can take place:

> Marriage, I suggested, is a fruitful field for fusion. [...] [O]ver time negotiations take place and agreements are reached on a multitude of issues, major and minor, such as whether we can afford to buy a house, who is the best babysitter, and how often we should eat fish. Such agreements arise in part in the course of carrying out joint projects. There are also many random conversations that result in joint acceptance of some proposition, value, or principle. [...] In any case, the parties come continuously jointly to accept numerous beliefs, values, and principles of action. [...] What I call *stable* fusion has its own special import. Even when difficult compromises have been made over an opinion or a principle of action there is some likelihood that when a couple continuously cohabits and interacts, personal preferences will pale or get converted. The couple's practices may, as a psychological matter, so predominate that the individual has no countervailing tendencies any longer. Being committed to acting and speaking a certain view in Mr. Jones's presence, Ms. Jones may

eventually lose some of her own original view: it may cease to be her personal view. Indeed, there is some normative pressure upon her to let this happen. For each party will probably better sustain "our view" in being if they have no countervailing tendencies, and they are committed to sustaining that view as best they can. There is some likelihood, then, that stable fusion will also be *untrammeled*. There will be no countervailing tendencies within the individuals concerned.

(Gilbert 2015, 266–267)

Gilbert, it should be noted, views the forging of this kind of joint agency in a mostly positive light. (Whether and to what extent one shares this view depends on a number of matters, including how much one tends to regard love as a kind of union between the lovers—a topic to which I will return—and how much one tends to identify with one's own "countervailing tendencies.") And after all, this is precisely what some people long for from love: to be changed, improved, saved. The hitch, though, is that from the perspective of someone who is happy with himself the way he is—and, moreover, happy with his lover the way *she* is—love's promise to erode, erase, or transform the boundaries of the self (and, along with them, the self) can seem less like a promise and more like a threat. One would like, perhaps, to be able to accommodate one's partner on an external level but hold one's self separate in order to preserve its integrity and maintain one's autonomy. But while one may intend, and even promise (whether to one's partner or to oneself) to do precisely that—this seems to be the intention and promise Lisa articulates in her somewhat tense post-dinner conversation with Jefferies—the realities of the constant process of negotiation Gilbert describes, and indeed of the very nature of friendship and love, imply that such a resolution will likely be far more difficult than one might suppose to carry out successfully. There are, at any rate, no guarantees:

[T]he forward-looking element in friendship makes every relationship risky. When I approach you in friendship my hope is that you will make me wish for things I couldn't even have thought to wish for without you. I give you power over myself and trust you not to exploit it. I put my identity at risk because, despite the certainty that love inspires, it is impossible for me to know what our relationship will ultimately mean for me and whether it will be for good or bad. Nothing ensures that my feeling or my judgment is right [...] Worse, nothing ensures that our relationship won't harm and degrade my judgment itself, making me feel happy to have become someone I would have hated to be, perhaps rightly, had you not come into my life.

(Nehamas 2016, 136–137)

I do not think it matters much, if at all, that Alexander Nehamas is speaking in this passage of friendship and not specifically of romantic love. Romantic love shares many features of friendship, including this element of risk; and if anything it will pose an even greater risk than ordinary friendships, for a variety of reasons. Not the least of these reasons is people's tendency to lose their heads while infatuated—a tendency that is central to Scottie's tragic story in *Vertigo*. There is, too, the fact that we tend to think of romantic love as involving, to use Gilbert's word, a kind of "fusion"—that is, we often think of romantic love as a matter of unification between two people, in which their individual boundaries are to some degree, or perhaps entirely, erased. Genesis 2:24 tells us that in marriage, "a man shall leave his father and his mother and hold fast to his wife, and they shall become one flesh." In Plato's *Symposium* Aristophanes tells the symposium guests that the desire "to make one out of two and [thus] heal the wound of human nature" is "the source of our desire to love each other" (Plato 1989: 27). And in *Civilization and its Discontents*, Freud observes:

> Towards the outside, the ego seems to maintain clear and sharp lines of demarcation. There is only one state [...] in which it does not do this. At the height of being in love the boundary between ego and object threatens to melt away. Against all the evidence of his senses, a man who is in love declares that 'I' and 'you' are one, and is prepared to behave as if it were a fact.
> (Freud 1995, 66)

Even those philosophers who stop short of the claim that love unites distinct individuals or dissolves their boundaries frequently allow that the characters and identities of the individuals involved are changed through love. Dean Cocking and Jeanette Kennett's "drawing view" sees friendship as involving a "process of mutual drawing [...that] clearly shows how the self in friendship is, in part, a relational thing that is developed and molded through the friendship" (Cocking and Kennett 2000, 284–285). In a related vein, John Armstrong notes that goals, desires, and values a person has previously regarded as fixed and perhaps even fundamental may be altered by being in a love relationship:

> [P]riorities change through a relationship. A woman who has—as she thinks—no interest in having children may, from within a loving relationship, come to have a different view. And here, the ground of the change is the relationship itself. She may have learned, with her partner, to recognize capacities and concerns she did not know she had. [...] [A] relationship [is not] a kind of garment which merely goes on top of, and does not in any way change, the inner person.
> (Armstrong 2002, 35)

The changes prompted by love can be, and I believe often are, positive; and it is at least possible that they might leave one's self, or large parts of it, intact. But neither of these is guaranteed. Being prompted to recognize capacities and concerns one already possesses hardly sounds threatening. But if this is all that love involved, then it would look somewhat superficial, a mere garment that covered or revealed but did not alter one's "inner person." Nehamas comes closer to the source of Jefferies' anxiety when he notes that in loving, I "put my identity at risk" and that "nothing ensures that our relationship won't harm and degrade my judgment itself, making me feel happy to have become someone I would have hated to be, perhaps rightly, had you not come into my life."

Indeed we should refer to Jefferies' *anxieties* rather than his anxiety, for this recognition may ground several species of fear. There are, after all, multitudinous ways in which Jefferies might be changed for the worse. (There are also multiple ways in which he might be changed for the better. But since Jefferies does not feel that he needs to be improved, the possibilities of improvement speak less persuasively here.) He might become less adventurous, less open to new experience, more settled, weaker, softer. He might come to hate travel or learn to enjoy dining at 21 every night and wonder how he ever managed to choke down fish heads and rice. These are perhaps the first possibilities that spring to mind, but they are not the most threatening ones. For these possibilities are, at least, compatible with Jefferies' maintaining a highly significant part of his current identity: the part that loves, values, indeed cherishes Lisa.

In the darker transformations, Jefferies loses that as well. We know that such possibilities are on his mind because of the amount of his attention that he focuses on Thorwald; for it is precisely these possibilities that Thorwald represents. If the newlyweds across the courtyard seem to symbolize the mostly pleasant, mostly happy initial stages of wedded life, Thorwald exerts his particular fascination by symbolizing a considerably more ominous later stage, the stage at which love has somehow managed to transform the lover into his very opposite: the person who hates the person he once loved. Of course, Jefferies is presumably aware that this does not happen in every case. But when he looks at the various apartments across the way—the array of miniaturized urban dioramas presented for his, and our, contemplation—a happily married older couple is the one thing he pointedly does not see. It is almost as if the "happily ever after" so often spoken of in stories and Hollywood films is the one possibility that Jefferies cannot, in fact, imagine.

So to the extent that Jefferies values *himself*, and conceives of himself as (among other things) one who loves Lisa, he has something real to fear from love. Moreover, to the extent that he is concerned about *Lisa*, he has further reason to fear. For Jefferies' being transformed from someone who loves Lisa into someone who hates her would be a terrible thing, not only for him, but for Lisa as well. This is true even if their marriage does not follow the lead of the Thorwalds and devolve into uxoricide (though all the more true, of course, should it prove to do so). And since Jefferies *does* care about Lisa—again, he loves her—the fact that this imagined future threatens her as well as him must be taken seriously. If it is true, as Nehamas suggests, that love's changes cannot be predicted or controlled, then Jefferies is at the very least not entirely wrong to take himself to have some quite powerful reasons to try to avoid committing fully to his love for Lisa. And ironically enough, the more he loves Lisa, the stronger these reasons are.

Moreover, as was briefly alluded to above, the fact is that *both* lovers are subject to being transformed by love; and thus, everything we have said to this point about Jefferies could be said about Lisa as well. That is, the risk is not only that he will come to hate her, but that she will come to hate him; or, more generally, that she will be changed by love into someone her current self (not to mention Jefferies' current self) would not love, or like, or even perhaps recognize. (To anyone who gazes into the Thorwalds' apartment, it is clear that he has no love for her; but she doesn't seem to like *him* very much either.) Keeping this in mind helps us understand why at times Jefferies seems so distressed by the fact that Lisa is so "perfect." It is not *merely* the fact that the more perfect she is, the less likely she is to change in order to adapt to him. He does not *want* her to change, for he loves her, truly and sincerely, as she is. And what love promises—or threatens—is, precisely, change. To dismiss Jefferies' anxieties about marriage, then, as nothing more than a shallow or immature desire to refuse to commit or settle down in order to hold on to the pleasures and convenient freedoms of his single life would be to badly misunderstand him, and to refuse to take his situation as seriously as it warrants. Jefferies' dilemma is both genuine and deep.

Vertigo: The Power and the Freedom

> [H]uman love is normally too profoundly possessive and also too 'mechanical' to be a place of vision.
>
> Iris Murdoch (1970)

Although *Rear Window* takes Jefferies' dilemma seriously, it does not seem to suggest that well-intentioned lovers cannot, in some cases, overcome it. Rather, it seems to end with the suggestion that Jefferies and Lisa will indeed go on to establish a successful romantic relationship—though not, presumably a frictionless one, and not one entirely free of deception. The final scene finds Jefferies asleep once again in his wheelchair, with both legs now broken as the result of his confrontation with Thorwald. Despite this, his face displays a contented smile. Lisa, reclining near him, is casually dressed and reading William Douglas's *Beyond the High Himalayas*. This is, we are meant to understand, the new, more adventurous Lisa, whom love has already changed, and who will be able to fit into Jefferies' life. Almost immediately, however, after confirming that he is indeed asleep, and that she is unobserved (for the first time in the film), she replaces her book with an issue of *Bazaar*, a fashion magazine (The "Beauty Issue," as it happens!).

Is Jefferies still afraid of changing Lisa, or of being changed? One assumes, from the placid and comic tone of the film's conclusion, that his fear has at the very least been lessened. He has if nothing else learned that Lisa really is more adventurous than she might have seemed, that life in New York might be more exciting than it might have seemed (there are murders and other crimes to be dealt with, and one doesn't even need to leave one's apartment to find them), and that he and Lisa have the ability to work together to confront and deal with the challenges posed by this life. All of this might suggest to him that at the very least it is not at all inevitable that their being together will change either of them into persons their former selves would have found either unrecognizable or intolerable.[1] And Lisa's swapping out of *Beyond the High Himalayas* for *Bazaar* surely suggests that she has not entirely given herself up but has rather retained a core of herself; while her triumphant smile, the fact that she gets the film's final shot and the fact that Jefferies (who in this shot is seen essentially from Lisa's point of view), has been returned to a state in which he depends on her, all suggest both that she is pleased with the outcome and that, in her view—which we seem meant to share— she was right all along in maintaining that it would be possible for the two of them to live together without betraying themselves. The scene is, indeed, a simultaneously ironic and affectionate symbolic portrayal of married life, a life in which the man is somewhat constrained, and in which both partners have to adapt their identities to the other to a reasonable degree, but in which none of this forestalls the possibility and promise of further future adventures.

Of course it is also surely true that seeing Lisa in danger, and thus being faced with the possibility of losing her, has forced Jefferies to realize how much he cares for her. Indeed, both the experience of witnessing her vulnerability and that of working on a joint project with her have likely taught him to see Lisa, for the first time, as genuinely her own person, and in doing so reminded him of an important truth about love: that it is a *person*, and not a set of attractive (but changeable) qualities, that a lover is committed to. Here we have slid into *Vertigo* territory— or perhaps we have been there all along. If, as previously noted, the two films have a great deal in common, it is at the same time true that *Vertigo* offers a far darker vision. In many ways, indeed, *Vertigo* may strike us as the actualization of Jefferies' worst fears. (Some have suggested that everything following the opening sequence of *Vertigo* might be considered a hallucination experienced by Scottie as he hangs from the precipice at the start of the film. An equally interesting possibility, it seems to me, is that the entire film is a nightmare Jefferies might have had while dozing in his wheelchair in the sweltering heat of summer.[2]) Unlike Jefferies, who remains detached for much of his film, Scottie is rapidly sucked into the whirling vortex of his passion for Madeleine Elster and is, ultimately, destroyed. *Vertigo*, moreover, goes farther than *Rear Window* in dramatizing some of the extreme depersonalizing effects of romantic love in its more malignant forms. This theme appears in a variety of contexts: Scottie's dramatic loss of identity and autonomy following Madeleine's death, Judy's treatment as an object at the hands of both Elster and Scottie, and, of course, the rich metaphor of possession, which runs throughout the film.

The film's plot is complex and, moreover, implausible. For our purposes, it will be enough to say the following: John "Scottie" Ferguson, formerly a police detective, is hired by a wealthy man, Gavin Elster (Tom Helmore), to watch his wife, Madeleine (Kim Novak), who is behaving oddly. Scottie falls in love with Madeleine and begins an affair with her, which ends tragically when, under his watch, she throws herself off a tower to her death. Scottie is shattered by this event and apparently unable to recover from it until he meets Judy Barton, who reminds him of Madeleine. They begin a relationship and he tries to make her over into a replica of Madeleine. The remarkable success of this endeavor is explained by the fact—revealed to the viewer in a flashback from Judy's point of view—that Scottie has been deceived: Elster, plotting to murder his actual wife (whom Scottie never met), hired Judy to pretend to be her, so that Scottie could function as a "made to order witness." Scottie's discovery of the deception and subsequent confrontation with Judy leads, tragically, to Judy's accidental death in a fall from the same tower from which the actual Madeleine had fallen.

As in *Rear Window*, the central crime plot concerns a man who murders his wife; and as in *Rear Window*, the murderer functions as a possible future version of the protagonist. (Here, though, he is not recognized as such until Scottie has already begun to resemble him.) Its main protagonist (James Stewart again!) is a kind of observer: in this case, a former police detective and private eye, a man who, once again, begins the main part of the film in a state of constraint (he wears a "corset," which he, like Jefferies, looks forward to getting free of). This is, again, the result of an injury sustained while taking an active role in his work: Scottie fell while chasing a suspect across the rooftops of San Francisco. In *Vertigo* we see the events leading up to the injury, as the opening scene depicts the chase, and it is significant, surely, that the first person we see in this film is a man escaping to his freedom—a man who, moreover, escapes so successfully that he disappears from the film altogether, so that we in the audience never learn what his name was, what his crime was, or anything else about him. (Watching this sequence, we might well recall that Camus writes that "existential philosophies [...] without exception suggest escape." (Camus 1955, 33).) As the film progresses we will see multiple failed escape attempts, including Scottie attempting to leave Elster's office, but turning around to stay; Judy in her hotel room, packing her things to flee Scottie, but changing her mind; and Judy, still later, in the midst of Scottie's transforming project, expressing the wish to leave him, then saying she can't because she doesn't want to.

This dreamlike opening sequence, which functions almost as a mythological backstory against which the remainder of the film's action plays out, is followed immediately by a much more sedate scene, set in the apartment of Scottie's friend, Midge (Barbara Bel Geddes).[3] Here, in addition to learning about Scottie's corset and his vertigo, we learn a bit about his life and past. He is single, but was once engaged to Midge, who still, it seems, desires him. We begin to sense that he, like Jefferies, is a man who values his independence, perhaps to his own detriment, and that his secret wish—again, like Jefferies—is to view the world from a detached perspective, as if from on high, in order to be safe from the risks and threats posed by a genuine engagement with life. But Scottie is incapacitated for such a task in a way that Jefferies is not: the end of this scene provides a vivid symbolic representation of its impossibility, as Scottie climbs up a small step stool in an attempt to overcome his vertigo and then, when he looks down at the streets far below, is instead overcome by it. He collapses, falling into the arms of Midge, the woman he rejected years ago but still keeps around as, apparently, a safe alternative to an actual romantic relationship. Scottie, then, much as he might like to, lacks Jefferies' ability to keep himself detached from life, to stay safe by standing above the fray. When Madeleine appears he will plunge almost immediately into a passionate and ultimately ruinous pursuit.

As in *Rear Window*, the murderer—Gavin Elster—represents a possible future for Scottie, someone he might well become. Like Thorwald, Elster is what Jefferies fears: a man trapped by his life and marriage, who escapes by betraying and destroying the person he presumably once loved (and in doing so, betrays his former self as well). Scottie's meeting with Elster finds the latter, who comes across as a somewhat sophisticated and romantic gentleman, longing for "the power and the freedom" of the old days in San Francisco, while confessing that he "married into" the shipbuilding business, a business he does not enjoy. When Scottie says "You don't have to do it for a living," Elster replies, "No. But one assumes obligations." We do not yet know, and will not learn for some time, that Elster is planning to deal with his assumed obligations by disposing of his wife, and that the power and freedom he envies is largely that of free, powerful men to deal with inconvenient women in this manner. Nor have we yet realized what is apt to become apparent on later reflection, that every time the coupling of the words "power" and "freedom" appears in the film (it will occur twice more), it is in connection with the disposal of a female victim. The words are next uttered by Pop Leibel, a local historian, who tells Scottie and Midge the tragic story of Carlotta Valdez. (*Vertigo* is, among other things, a compendium of stories about women, some of them told by the characters, others enacted. The told stories are told, mostly, by men, with the exception of the true story about herself Judy writes in a letter to Scottie, before tearing it up.) Valdez is connected to several spots Madeleine has visited, and Scottie begins to wonder whether her spirit is possessing Madeleine. This is, of course, part of Elster's plan, and his choice of this particular story seems emblematic both of his own personality and of the film's concerns.[4] For Carlotta, Leibel tells us, was used and then abandoned by her husband, causing her to go mad. He then says:

> I cannot tell you how much time passed, or how much happiness there was. But then he threw her away. He had no other children; his wife had no children. He kept the child and threw her away. Men could do that in those days. They had the power ... and the freedom. And she became the Sad Carlotta. Alone in the great house ... walking the streets alone, her clothes becoming old and patched and dirty ... the Mad Carlotta ... stopping people in the streets to ask, "Where is my child? ... have you seen my child?" [...] There are many such stories.

There are, indeed, many such stories, though on a first viewing it will not yet have occurred to us that we are watching yet another one. The third utterance of "power" and "freedom" comes later, spoken by Scottie himself, who has finally discovered Judy and Elster's deception. "Oh, Judy!!" he says to her. "When [Elster] had all her money, and the freedom, and the power, he ditched you? What a shame!" In his anger at her, his rage at his having been betrayed, he is being ironic, but not, one suspects, entirely ironic; there remains, after everything, a dimension of his character that is, in fact, capable of feeling compassion for her at the way she has been treated. Like Carlotta—and like Scottie himself—she, too, has been used by a man who commanded enough power and freedom to treat other people as mere means to his ends and get away with it.

It becomes apparent through the course of the film that Elster treats woman as his possessions, and possession is indeed one of the central metaphors in *Vertigo*, and perhaps the key to its dark vision.[5] Like the historical Carlotta, of whom Leibel says, "she was found ... by that man, and he took her [...] But then he threw her away," and like the actual Madeleine to whom Elster was married, who was also, literally, thrown away when she became inconveniently constraining, Judy has been treated as a tool, an object to be utilized and then "ditched." (And Scottie, too, has been manipulated in ways highly damaging to him, and hence treated as a mere means.) But more than being treated as a possession, she has been viewed as one, not only by Scottie, and of course Elster, but by the film's audience. For we have not only bought Elster's claim that Judy is Madeleine, we have also at least partly swallowed the implausible idea, planted by Elster, that his wife is possessed by the spirit of Carlotta Valdez; and as a result we have found ourselves not only seeing Judy as someone she is not, mistaking an actor for her role and taking Elster's creation for a real woman; we have constantly scrutinized the woman we thought we were seeing for signs that she was not really herself, that she was being controlled by an outside force, and that this would explain her odd behavior. In all of this, we are deceived like Scottie and respond to what we see much as he does. (The irony of all this, of course, was that the story was true—Madeleine *was* possessed—but not in the way we were led to believe.) Of course, we are released from our deception sooner than Scottie, via Judy's confessional flashback, with the result that when *he* finally learns the truth we are able fully to appreciate, and to feel, the sick horror of his realization.

It is in the interim between the audience's learning of Elster's plot and Scottie's discovery of it that Scottie himself seems to become possessed, in a different sense, by Elster. (Here, too, he seems to realize Jefferies' fear that falling in love will compromise one's autonomy.) Seeing the resemblance between Judy and Madeleine, he takes control of Judy and forces her to alter her appearance to become, as much as possible, a duplicate of his lost love. Once again directed and possessed by a controlling man, once again treated like a possessed object, a mere thing, Judy can only plead, "Couldn't you like me, just me, the way I am?" The disturbing and downright creepy scenes that depict Judy's forced transformation at Scottie's hands—scenes in which Scottie wrests control over Judy's physical appearance away from her, insisting that it is more important to him than it could possibly be to her—put his delusional obsessiveness blatantly on display:

SCOTTIE: The color of your hair ...
JUDY: No!
SCOTTIE: Judy, please, it can't matter to you.
JUDY: If ... if I let you change me, will that do it? If I do what you tell me, will you love me?

Indeed, just prior to this Judy herself has admitted, in another of the film's abortive escapes, that although she could protest her treatment and put a stop to it by simply leaving, she cannot bring herself to do it:

JUDY: I wish you'd leave me alone. I want to go away.
SCOTTIE: You can, you know.
JUDY: No, you wouldn't let me. And ... I don't want to go.

Is it Scottie's grip, or Judy's lack of will to escape, that keeps her in place? The two have so merged, perhaps, that one cannot really distinguish them. It is no more clear whether Judy knows how to relate to a man other than by becoming his object than it is clear that she knows whether she really is Madeleine or someone else, and if someone else, who. Scottie, meanwhile, shattered by Madeleine's death, has barely started to rebuild an identity of his own, and what he has now is constructed around the delusional hope of going back in time to (re)possess (another) Madeleine. It is frequent for viewers of *Vertigo* to conclude that Scottie cannot really love, but from a certain perspective his problem is that he loves too well: he is so devoted to Madeleine that he cannot leave her behind, cannot imagine a life without her. Viewed in this way, Scottie represents the ideal of monogamy pushed nearly to its logical extreme, from the perspective of which the idea that a lost lover might be replaced by someone else is objectionable, even offensive. As spoken by the narrator of Jeanette Winterson's *Written on the Body*,

> To lose someone you love is to alter your life forever. You don't get over it because 'it' is the person you loved. The pain stops, there are new people, but the gap never closes. How could it? The particularness of someone who mattered enough to grieve over is not made anodyne by death. This hole in my heart is in the shape of you and no-one else can fit.
> (Winterson 1993, 155)

Scottie, who would have rejected the idea that a "new" person could have filled the hole in his heart, has experienced the miracle of finding another person with the same exact shape as his lost Madeleine; it is as if she were not a new person at all. The irony, of course, is that Judy *is* Madeleine, and so not a new person; but we know that before Scottie does—indeed, we know it through the entire process of his attempt to convert Judy *into* Madeleine—and so we can see, as he can't, that his belief that an exact replica of Madeleine would *be* Madeleine proves not how profound his attachment is but that it is attached to the wrong object. Then again, from Scottie's perspective, his eventual discovery that Madeleine was Judy all along might seem to vindicate his mad project. Madeleine, it turns out, was Elster's creation. Why could she not also be Scottie's?

Love, Self-Knowledge, and the Future

> Anxiety has a similar effect to vertigo: it is the "dizziness of freedom," and "he whose eye happens to look down into the yawning abyss becomes dizzy." Yet it is not the abyss (the possibility) that creates the anxiety but rather the individual who looks upon it: some do not look down, subjective perceptions about the size of the chasm

differ, and the passion with which individuals approach the abyss and leap differs enormously.

(Skye Cleary 2015, *Existentialism and Romantic Love*)[6]

Perhaps the most threatening aspect of love is that it makes our well-being and our identity contingent on the actions and continued well-being of another vulnerable human subject. In the months following Madeleine's death, Scottie is devastated, a shell of a man. For some time he is nearly comatose and confined to a psychiatric hospital, suffering from "acute melancholia together with a guilt complex." Even after his release he is barely functional. Aimless, afflicted by terrifying nightmares, he can think of nothing to do with himself but return to sites where he once went with his lover, or else wander San Francisco at random. Watching him, we recall that when she was first seducing him Madeleine had said, "Only one is a wanderer. Two, together, are always going somewhere." Here, too, he represents the realization of one of Jefferies' deep fears: that love, by demanding that our identity be re-forged with the beloved at the center, makes us entirely dependent on that beloved, so that if they were lost we would be left with no identity at all. We might be reminded, here, of Harry Frankfurt's view that all values and reasons are ultimately grounded in love. "Love is the originating source of terminal value. If we loved nothing, then nothing would possess for us any definitive and inherent worth" (Frankfurt 2004, 55–56). Thus, if we had no final ends—if we loved nothing—"it is more than desire that would be empty and vain. It is life itself. For living without goals or purposes is living with nothing to do" (Frankfurt 1999, 84). The Scottie Ferguson of this period is clearly a man for whom nothing possesses "any definitive and inherent worth," whose life is "empty and vain," and thus someone who is "living with nothing to do." He has no reason to do anything, other than to hope against hope that the world can somehow be magically restored to what it once was.

Why does Jefferies fare so much better than Scottie? To some degree he is simply lucky. Scottie loses Madeleine—twice—while Jefferies, despite his reluctance to commit, does not lose Lisa. And Scottie is the victim of a plot, whereas the murderer in *Rear Window* is barely aware of Jefferies and does not attempt to make him part of his machinations. But Scottie also has a less firm grip on his own identity than Jefferies does; he merges with Madeleine, reconstructing his life around his desire for her. As we have noted, his vertigo is, among other things, a symbol of his (excessive) inability to remain detached. (Jefferies, by contrast, excels at detachment.) Scottie is more of a romantic than Jefferies, more willing to sacrifice his identity and autonomy in love, less able to hold himself apart in order to preserve an integral core in a love relationship, and hence less able, one presumes, to recover from love's loss. Although Scottie sometimes appears diffident, particularly in the first part of the film, that appearance seems to conceal and protect a man for whom nothing is more important than the possibility of impassioned love.

But there is one more significant difference between their narratives. I have suggested that Thorwald represents a possible future for Jefferies—someone that he might become—and that Elster does the same for Scottie. If this is so, then the timing of the meetings between the protagonists and their possible future selves, and the nature of those meetings, is important and indeed decisive. Scottie meets Elster three times in the film, before he has any reason to suspect him. By the time he has learned the truth about his situation, Elster, like the fleeing man we glimpsed in the opening shots, has escaped from the film, and the only person who remains whom Scottie can confront about the deception and manipulation he has suffered is Judy. Jefferies, by contrast, is in possession of most of the story when he finally meets Thorwald in person. Thus he, unlike Scottie, has the chance to confront, and so symbolically vanquish, his undesired possible future self. Jefferies literally struggles with that possible future self and essentially delivers him into the hands of the police; in doing so, he decisively rejects that aspect of his own identity. In the process, he sees this version of himself up close (using his flashbulb not only to momentarily paralyze him, but more importantly, to shed light on him) and so obtains a kind of self-knowledge. Self-knowledge, indeed, is the answer to the question Thorwald confronts him with in this scene: "What do you want from me?"

Early on in the film Stella had said to Jefferies, "People need to get outside their own house and look in for a change. How's that for homespun philosophy?" Since he represents a possible future version of Jefferies, getting outside of himself and looking in is exactly what Thorwald allows Jefferies to do; it is, in a sense, what he has been doing all along. And the confrontation with Thorwald ends, of course, with Jefferies literally getting what Stella said he needed—that is, getting outside of his own home. Thus, although he is injured in the struggle, being thrown out the window by Thorwald, this should not be seen as a defeat; rather, Jefferies' ejection from the apartment where he has been able to live in isolation and play the detached observer represents his re-entry into life—which is why the next time we see him, in the film's final scene, he is no longer dangling suspended over an existential void, or living vicariously through voyeurism, and he and Lisa seem to have achieved a genuine relationship.

In rejecting Thorwald, Jefferies is liberated from his fear of becoming "someone [he] would have hated to be," and finds the strength and courage to overcome his resistance to commitment and to join with Lisa. She is, of course, a changed Lisa, having discovered, with Jefferies' encouragement, interests and capacities that had previously been latent within her. But Lisa has changed less than Jefferies, or at any rate is less surprised by the changes: she suspected all along, and had even tried to assure him, that she could become such a person. The prospect of change is threatening, but also promising. Of course, the final shots of any film, particularly those that suggest a happy ending, indulge in a pleasant fiction: *this is how things will be from now on*. Obviously, we cannot say with certainty what Jefferies and Lisa's future will be like. Indeed, if my reading is correct, the idea that we *cannot* know—that where true love is involved, the only thing we can predict is that we may well be changed in ways we cannot control or predict—is central to these two films' thinking about love and its place in human life.

Notes

1. Moreover—and more important than any of this, I suspect—there is the fact that by the end of the film, Jefferies has directly confronted his feared future self and, by bringing him to justice, vanquished him. I return to this point in the final section.
2. Which would mean, of course, that Scottie's nightmare, suffered just past the halfway point of the film, is a nightmare within a nightmare.
3. Sadly, limited space prevents me from discussing the Midge character at any length. This is a real loss, for Midge is in fact quite important to what the film has to say about love.
4. Since Elster is, as many commentators have pointed out, a kind of stand-in for Hitchcock (who makes a cameo appearance directly outside Elster's office, as if the two had just switched places), it makes sense that the story would be emblematic of the director's concerns as well.
5. The connection of autonomy with property in American political thought is highly significant. A fuller version of the quotation from Jennifer Nedelsky used as the epigraph to section 2 reads as follows: "One of the clearest forms [American thinking about autonomy] takes is the idea that individual autonomy is to be achieved by erecting a wall of rights between the individual and those around him. Property [...] is, not surprisingly, the central symbol for this vision of autonomy. The logic of this is that the most perfectly autonomous man is thus the most perfectly isolated."
6. The quotations in the passage are from Kierkegaard (1980), 61.

References

Armstrong, John. 2002. *Conditions of Love*. New York: Norton.

Camus, Albert. 1955. *The Myth of Sisyphus*, translated by Justin O'Brien. New York: Knopf.

Cleary, Skye. 2015. *Existentialism and Romantic Love*. New York: Palgrave-Macmillan.

Cocking, Dean, and Jeannette Kennett. 2000. "Friendship and Moral Danger." *Journal of Philosophy* 97 (5): 278–296.

Frankfurt, Harry. 1999. "On the Usefulness of Final Ends." In *Necessity, Volition, and Love*. Cambridge, UK: Cambridge University Press.

Frankfurt, Harry. 2004. *The Reasons of Love*. Princeton, NJ: Princeton University Press.

Freud, Sigmund. 1995. "Civilization and Its Discontents." In *The Standard Edition of the Complete Psychological Works of Sigmund Freud*, Vol. 21, edited and translated by James E. Strachey. London: Hogarth Press.
Gilbert, Margaret. 2015. "Fusion: Sketch of a 'Contractual' Model." In *Joint Commitment: How We Make the Social World*. Oxford: Oxford University Press.
Kierkegaard, Soren, 1978. *Soren Kierkegaard's Journals and Papers* (Vol. 6), edited by Howard Hong and Edna Hong. Bloomington: Indiana University Press.
Kierkegaard, Soren. 1980. *The Concept of Anxiety*, translated by Reidar Thomte and Albert B. Anderson. Princeton, NJ: Princeton University Press.
Murdoch, Iris. 1970. *The Sovereignty of Good*. New York: Schocken Books.
Nedelsky, Jennifer. 2011. *Law's Relations: A Relational Theory of Self, Autonomy, and Law*. New York: Oxford University Press.
Nehamas, Alexander. 2016. *On Friendship*. New York: Basic Books.
Plato. 1989. *Symposium, translated by Alexander Nehamas and Paul Woodruff. Indianapolis*, IN: Hackett Publishing Company.
Protasi, Sarah. 2014. "Loving People for Who They Are (Even When They Don't Love You Back). *European Journal of Philosophy* 24 (1): 214–234.
Sartre, Jean-Paul. 1993. *Being and Nothingness,* translated by Hazel Barnes. New York: Washington Square Press.
Winterson, Jeanette. 1993. *Written on the Body*. New York: Alfred A. Knopf, 1993.

6 Murdochian Presentationalism, Autonomy, and the Ideal Lovers' Pledge

Raja Rosenhagen

Introduction

When lovers forge loving unions, union theorists think, their identities merge into a *we-identity*. Henceforth, the lovers' future decisions depend no longer on their individual outlooks, but on the fused outlook they are taken to share. In a merger, one may suspect, individual autonomy is diminished or lost.[1] But shouldn't just love preserve and foster individual autonomy? In the context of her rejection of the so-called love-justice dichotomy, Rachel Fedock considers something quite like this line of thought (cf. Fedock 2020). Here is a gloss:

> P1: Love, on union theories, diminishes individual autonomy.
> P2: To be just, love must preserve or foster, not diminish individual autonomy.
>
> C: On union theories, love is unjust.

Union theorists may accept P2 yet insist that maintaining loving unions is a practical task, one that lovers can execute justly (cf. Kühler 2011). Call this *Kühler's contention*. If it is right, if C ought thus to be resisted, and provided that the above argument is valid, P1 must be wrong. Some hold that it is. Consider, for example, the following passage by Neil Delaney:

> It's not as if your wishes for consolidation and identification on the one hand, which are after all simply aspects of the profound psychological merging sought after in romance, and the desire to preserve the integrity of your personal boundaries on the other, are hopelessly irreconcil[i]able [sic!] aims.
>
> (Delaney 1996, 341)

Delaney, too, accepting the union theorists' basic idea, talks about love in terms of psychological merging. That romantic lovers want to form a distinctive form of *we* with their beloved, he grants, is "pretty generally accepted" (Delaney 1996, 340). In the paper cited, he does not use the word 'autonomy.' Yet arguably, his reference to the desire to preserve the integrity of one's personal boundaries points to exactly that: a desire for the preservation of one's individual autonomy. So construed, Delaney denies, as we saw above, that the romantic lovers' desire to psychologically merge and the desire for the preservation of individual autonomy are hopelessly irreconcilable. Love, he thinks, construed (with union theorists) as a kind of merger, and the preservation of individual autonomy are compatible.[2] Delaney, thus, denies P1.

I agree with Fedock: there is no dichotomy between love and justice. I also sympathize with *Kühler's contention*: maintaining loving unions is a practical task that can be executed justly. Delaney is right, too: no principled tension links love and the preservation of autonomy. But if Delaney is right and P1 false, we should set our argument aside. Resting on a false premise, it doesn't establish its conclusion.

Note that in setting the argument aside I don't wish to save union theories. My qualms about them will transpire near the end of this chapter but are anyway mostly tangential to this paper. P2 of the above argument, however, is independently interesting. The normative ideal to which it points has implications that go beyond what I have so far attributed to any of my interlocutors. If we take 'just love' to be a non-empty term, P2 will entail a general version of *Kühler's contention*, viz. that (maintaining) love (is a task that) can be (executed) just(ly). On this view, at least in its more ideal forms, love does not just form no dichotomy with, but *au contraire conforms* with justice. But endorsing P2 involves more than accepting this. As we saw, Delaney, too, thinks that love and the preservation of autonomy are reconcilable. P2 goes further, as it suggests that there is a positive link between just love and individual autonomy: love that is just—and *ipso facto* aligned with virtue—is supportive and protective of individual autonomy. With this interpretation on the table we can ask: *why* is just love a matter of preserving and fostering individual autonomy? Against the backdrop of *what* notion of just love and on *what* conception of individual autonomy is P2 a good claim to make?

In what follows, I work toward providing answers to these questions. In part, I do this by drawing on and developing aspects of Iris Murdoch's work, which I in turn motivate by taking my cues from the debate on experience's rational role. Before I begin, allow me some preliminary remarks. First, Murdoch, following Simone Weil, characterizes love as a quality of attention.[3] Love, she takes it, ideally involves what she calls *just attention*. Paying just attention to another is a way of doing justice to them and their perspective as one looks at them and actively imagines[4] what they are like and what may underlie and make intelligible their actions. Such looking is undistorted by selfish desires or fears about how others should or might be (or act) to serve or threaten one's ego and its selfish ends. Refraining, for now, from further examining the specifics of the notion of *just attention*, let us place the following on record: as for Fedock, for Murdoch, too, the idea of a fundamental dichotomy between love and justice must be misguided. Surely, a lover's love may be selfish, misguided, misdirected, and tainted in various ways. "Love is the general name of the quality of attachment," Murdoch says, "and it is capable of infinite degradation and is the source of our greatest errors."[5] And yes, some of the mistakes we commit in the name of love will be errors of injustice. Yet if the conflict between love and justice is proposed to be fundamental, then for Murdoch, such a proposal must rest on mistaking love's degraded varieties as exhausting what love is, i.e., on a failure to comprehend what love is ideally.

Second, the Murdochian account that I will develop, while friendly toward *Kühler's contention*, also points beyond it. With Murdoch, I take it that loving is at least also a matter of attending to our beloved justly. We attend to others and their surroundings continually—indeed near-continuously—and such attention co-determines what we see and how we subsequently act. Arguably, attention is at least to some extent responsive to the will—we can partly control, modify, and adjust it. That we can willingly snap out of a particular way of attending to things is familiar enough. Just think of a situation in which you catch yourself casting things in a light that is too pessimistic—under the influence perhaps of being frustrated about something quite unrelated. If you realize that your brooding colors your overall perception of the situation, you may readjust and look again. Similarly, the way we attend to a beloved is something we *do* and at least partly control. Emphasizing that attention responds to the will may thus tempt us to construe maintaining love as involving a (near-)continuous *practical* activity—attending to one's beloved—which yields subsequent actions that accord with and respond to what we see (or imagine). Just love, we may then think, is a practical ideal governing this activity. Though this seems apt, for Murdoch—as will transpire—just attention is a *theoretical* task, too; it requires getting one's moral concepts right and deploying and developing them on subsequent occasions of attention to increase one's freedom from selfish fantasy, in ways geared toward what is good and real. Maintaining love justly, so construed, is both: a practical and a theoretical achievement.

Recall, third, that I am interested in a conception that sustains P2, i.e., one on which just and ideal lovers, *qua* just lovers, recognize and foster their beloved's individual autonomy (in a sense to be spelled out). Following Murdoch's lead, I propose that excelling at the latter requires the lover's continuous acknowledgment of and response to the fact that their respective beloved, *qua* individual, differs from them. But if this is accepted, the initial portrayal of the union view begins to look skewed. For if just love requires the acknowledgment of and response to the fact that our beloved differs from us, then in love so construed, our identities cannot and do not merge. If asked to provide an image of ideal romantic lovers, respondents typically provide a description of a couple that has formed some sort of deep physical or psychological union,[6] a union in which some common goals may be found and jointly pursued, while others will (and indeed should) be pursued individually, but with the support from one's beloved. With a few minor caveats, something quite like this is surely acceptable.[7] Also, to say this is not to make a bold metaphysical claim. There is a completely innocuous sense in which such unions do exist—derivatively and metaphysically grounded in the existence of the individuals forming them and, e.g., their attitudes and commitments toward each other.[8] To characterize the notion of loving relationships, I suggest, it is worth exploring what attitudes and commitments they might ideally involve and how these may sustain the claim that such relationships preserve and foster autonomy. I do this by looking at the Murdochian equation of love with just attention and by developing the conception of a mutual commitment that I will dub *the ideal lovers' pledge*.

On this note, a caveat: love, even just the romantic sort, comes in many varieties. '*The ideal lovers' pledge*' labels a commitment that, I believe, should appeal to those who like me endorse P2. But the label's determinate article is not meant to convey that the ideal it picks out is universal (or prescriptive). It need not pick out the only way in which a commitment people make toward each other *qua* lovers may be ideal as there may just not be only one such way. And yet I trust that a large variety of romantic relationships can be understood as aiming toward something much like what it picks out.

In the next two sections, I sketch a view I dub *Murdochian presentationalism*. To motivate it, I look, in the next section, at a debate within contemporary philosophy of mind and epistemology and show how presentationalism escapes difficult problems that beset its more prominent contenders. Doing this, I think, pays off.[9] For I believe that presentationalism provides an interesting model of empirical reasoning which can be fruitfully extended to specifically moral reasoning (see Rosenhagen ms). Presentationalism and Murdoch's account of love, I think, are a natural fit. In the section that follows the next one, I thus use presentationalism to motivate certain crucial aspects of Murdoch's view, show how conversely, the latter supports the former, and blend the two by giving presentationalism a Murdochian twist. After that, I outline the Murdochian (presentationalist's) notion of freedom and add to the mix a broadly Kantian notion of individual autonomy. With this in hand, I show, in the last section, how the view thus arrived at sustains P2 and close by presenting the *ideal lovers' pledge* and by drawing attention to the kind of metaphor Murdochian presentationalism suggests for thinking about loving relationships more generally.

Motivating Presentationalism

As my approach is informed by recent debates on the rational role of experience, this section supplies the requisite background. If asked how to conceptualize perceptual experience, most philosophers affiliate with either of two camps—representationalism or relationalism. *Presentationalism*, my preferred view, belongs to neither. To introduce it, I will sketch the two alternative views and then show how presentationalism differs from them and escapes some pressing problems they face.

Representationalism

The number of representationalist accounts is legion. As the label indicates, their characteristic tenet is that experience is fundamentally a matter of representation; like thought and belief, it has representational content.[10] Representationalists disagree on various issues. One set of issues concerns what content is, another how it relates to the so-called phenomenal character of experience—often glossed as *what it's like* to have an experience. Bracketing these, let us note that the content claim invites a temptingly simple account of the rational role of experience, along with a general story of how experience can play it. On it, if things go well and are as they seem, experiential content supplies experiential premises. These enable experience to play its rational role: justifying beliefs.[11]

Representationalism faces serious problems. Here is one: representationalism about experience naturally combines with foundationalism, according to which experiential content serves as a regress stopper at which the demand for justification comes to an end.[12] It is, however, far from clear in virtue of what experiential (or better: perceptual)[13] content is to have such impressive justificatory powers.

Second, suppose that at least sometimes, perceptual content provides grounds for justification. For these to be fertile, the subject's conceptual apparatus would need to be such as to enable her to properly exploit that resource. If the subject's view is wrong or irrational, or her conceptual apparatus muddled,[14] so may be the inferences she draws from her experiential content—even if the latter possesses unabated justificatory power. Representationalists leaning toward foundationalism who believe that experiences (must)[15] provide potential grounds for justification must therefore also provide this: an account of what a subject's view and concepts must be like for the subject to be able to exploit the goods that perceptual experience is said to deliver—at least in the good case.

Note, third, that these challenges become harder if experiential content can be determined, at least partly, by not just the external mind-independent items it purports to represent, but also the subject's beliefs, conceptional capacities, or other internal factors. One way to think of such subject-born determination is in terms of muddled concepts affecting experiential content, another in terms of top-down effects on experience from background states, e.g., beliefs, hopes, expectations, desires, fears, biases, even moods. Perhaps experiential content is often affected by either muddled concepts or background states. And if it is, then plausibly, such effects are often outside the subject's ken. This creates trouble. For if experiential content may be so affected, why and when are we to rely on it for justification?[16]

Representationalists, then, must answer at least three queries: if (as is natural) they endorse foundationalism, how does experience get its justificatory power? What must a subject's view and concepts be like to allow them to harness such power? How to rule out that one's experience is co-determined by muddled concepts or background states in such a way that experience is robbed of its justificatory power? Without answers to these questions, representationalists must fear that experience may often fail to execute its alleged rational role or execute it poorly.[17]

Relationalism

Relationalism, or *naïve realism*, is explicitly opposed to representationalism, since as per one of its three main tenets, experience lacks content.[18] Second, experience is taken to be fundamentally a relation, often called *acquaintance*, between subjects and mind-independent worldly items[19] that obtains in further specifiable circumstances (e.g., lighting conditions, the subject's visual acuity, physical location vis-à-vis items, distribution of attention, etc.). Typically, the third tenet is this: acquaintance with worldly items constitutes experience's phenomenal character, the *what it's like* to undergo it. Experience, relationalists think, plays two main roles. For one, it presents mind-independent objects to subjects, thus making them available for reference and demonstrative thought.[20] The second role, again, is that of serving to justify perceptual beliefs. Like representationalists, relationalists face some well-known problems. I mention just a few: first, relationalists have a hard time providing a positive account of some illusions and hallucinations—especially if in them, the individual is not related to suitable mind-independent items. Second, their notion of acquaintance is notoriously difficult to characterize. Third, it is hard to explain how content-less experience can justify beliefs.[21] Fourth, if relationalists take the subjective dimension of experience to be exhausted by its phenomenal character and if they take it to be constituted by what worldly items experience relates its subject to, it seems that they must rule out direct effects of background states on experience as impossible.[22]

Relationalism is still in the making, but these issues must be addressed.[23] Here is one more, familiar from above: experiences must hook up with concepts and beliefs somehow. And if the subject's concepts are muddled, so may be the way their experiences, concepts, and beliefs hook up. If so, the already difficult problem as to how experience can play its rational role gets even harder.

In the next subsection, I sketch a conception of experience and its rational role developed and defended by Anil Gupta: *Reformed Empiricism*, or *presentationalism*. As will transpire, presentationalism dodges many of the problems discussed as it offers a more general conception of the rational role of experience, one experience can play come what may. This makes it an independently attractive view. It is more appealing even, I think, once we realize that it combines well with and in fact serves to motivate the view Iris Murdoch defends with respect to how we may improve the evaluative practices characteristically involved in our morally relevant interactions with others, including those we love.

Presentationalism

In experience, presentationalists hold, items presented to consciousness manifest *appearances*. 'Appearances,' as they use the term, denotes the experience's subjective aspect—what experiences of items are if considered from the subject's point of view. What manifests appearances can be environing mind-independent items, yet appearances may also result from other factors, e.g., environmental conditions and subjective features, including the subject's constitution, her mental states, even brain states. Appearances, presentationalists insist, are *multiply factorizable* (see Gupta 2006, ch. 1): there are various ways the world and the experiencing subject could be, each of which would jointly manifest appearances that from the subject's viewpoint are identical. Different factors, that is, can generate *subjectively identical* appearances. Accordingly, appearances, considered in isolation, don't reveal what they are *of*. Pace representationalism, they thus don't have, *qua* experience, any representational content, so that experience alone does not provide subjects with anything to endorse or reject (though content may be associated with it).[24] Experience by itself thus cannot serve to justify anything. Instead, presentationalists hold, the rational role of experience is this: having an experience makes rational certain *transitions*—transitions, *inter alia*, to perceptual judgments. Which transitions to which judgments? This crucially depends on what background view one inhabits.[25] Different views, if combined with the same experience, may make rational different transitions. How? Roughly, thus: views contain beliefs, yet also, crucially, linkages that rationally link each possible experience with view-specific transitions to, e.g., perceptual judgments that it would be rational to transition to were that experience had.[26] Accordingly, whenever some appearance manifests in a subject's consciousness, then in light of her view, some transitions to (*inter alia*) perceptual judgments become rational.

To illustrate, consider Pia. Pia, suppose, is unfamiliar with the Müller-Lyer illusion. Upon seeing it, certain appearances manifest in her consciousness. As Pia has no reason to suspect funny business, having this experience, in light of her view, makes it rational for her to transition to the following judgment: "These two lines differ in length."[27] Contrast Mia, Pia's twin. Unlike Pia, Mia is familiar with the illusion. But it is robust; knowing it neither undoes it nor does it alter its appearance. Indeed, we may suppose that Mia is being appeared to exactly like Pia. However, conjoined with Mia's view, having an experience involving that exact same appearance makes it rational for Mia to transition to a *different* judgment—to wit: "These two lines are the same length."

Presentationalists dodge issues that beset representationalism and relationalism. They have no need for the notion of acquaintance, nor do they insist that the phenomenology of experience, i.e., the set of the appearances it comprises, is constituted by mind-independent items. On Gupta's presentationalism, experience lacks content, and what does not exist cannot be distorted by background states. Such states could also affect appearances, though.[28] But crucially, even if they did, the rational role of experience as presentationalists construe it would remain completely unhampered. For any experience *e*, having *e* against the backdrop of any view will make some transitions to, e.g., judgments rational—regardless of how *e* is generated, whether it is an illusion, hallucination, or neither.

Note also that if experience lacks content, one cannot assign it an inappropriate justificatory weight.[29] Of course, on presentationalism, too, things can go wrong in familiar ways. Note two: first, upon having an experience *e*, we may fail to transition to anything that it would, upon having *e* and in light of our view, be rational to transition to. Second, we might, upon having *e*, rationally transition to perceptual judgments that are ill-justified, false, even irrational. In the first kind of case, we behave irrationally conditional on our view. Surely, this is possible and may even happen frequently. In the second kind of case, we are also rationally off-target, but differently. For if our view is such that against the backdrop of it, upon having *e*, we rationally transition to judgments that are false, ill-justified, or irrational, then our view must at least in part be false, ill-justified, or irrational as well. Nevertheless, relative to that view, transitioning to the judgments as we do, upon having *e*, may be perfectly rational.

Scientific theories should be falsifiable and scientists be able to specify experiences that are incompatible with their pet theory.[30] Analogously, a view should contain linkages from possible experiences to judgments that are at odds with it. Judgments one transitions to rationally, upon having such experiences, will create rational pressure to suspend judgment or revise one's view (along with the beliefs and concepts it contains). Such revisions may lead to improved views—less irrational, more justified, and more knowledgeable. But if we revise our view in the wrong direction (perhaps rationally so), it may get worse. Future experience, the idea goes, will tell. Importantly: even if our views are partly false, ill-justified, or irrational, and our conceptual apparatus partly muddled, the rational role of experience will not be undermined.[31] For against the backdrop of *any* view, even muddled ones, having experiences will make it rational to engage in some transitions (and not others).[32] Accordingly, this conception of the rational role of experience is completely general. Provided that experience is combined with a view, experience cannot fail to play it.[33] And as long as our view contains linkages such that having certain experiences would make rational transitions to judgments that are at odds with it, our experience can provide the friction required for us to be rationally compelled to change, perhaps improve our views in response to it.[34] Ideally, things go well and eventually, possibly after many detours, we may get things right.

This completes my sketch of presentationalism. I have argued that presentationalism escapes a number of serious problems that beset its most prominent contenders. For this reason alone it is worth pursuing. As we will see, presentationalism is also appealing as a way of thinking about moral reasoning, especially the Murdochian kind. Let us move on, then, and add to it a Murdochian twist.

Murdochian Presentationalism

Iris Murdoch's central tenet is that in morality, love is a central notion (see, e.g., Murdoch 1970, 2, 30, 46). According to her, moral progress and acting well—i.e., in ways that are attuned to what is real, aim at what is truly good and truly benefits others—require love, construed as *just attention*. "Love," she famously says, "is the perception of individuals, [...] the extremely difficult realisation that something other than oneself is real" (Murdoch 1959, 51). Love requires that we avert our attention away from the self—that "dazzling object that [is such that] if one looks *there* one may see nothing else" (Murdoch 1970, 31)—and direct it at others. Truly seeing them, not caricatures that serve the enemy of moral life: the fat relentless ego (Murdoch 1970, 52), requires attending to them unselfishly, looking at and imagining them (and their actions) in ways that do justice to who they are.

To illustrate, consider selfish Sid. To Sid, others matter only as they promote or impede the pursuit of his goals. How he characterizes others reflects his selfish needs: *useful, influential, yet exploitable, weak, threateningly smart*, or *worthlessly stupid*, say. In characterizing others, we must use *some* labels. Yet Sid's coarse categorization transforms the people he interacts with into shallow and distorted caricatures of who they are. To him, they appear as shadows cast by the dim light of his needs, not as the complex characters they are, driven by individual motives, desires, and ideas, and as who they might be revealed through the loving gaze of just attention. For our characterizations of others and their actions to become better attuned to what is real and particular, Murdoch urges, and for our moral concepts to improve through subsequent occasions of judicious application, we must *look* and *imagine*. But Sid, being the sorry selfish lad we imagine him to be, has little intrinsic motivation to attend to who others really are or to imagine how their own actions may look to them. To him, doing this seems like a waste of time. Forfeiting opportunities to attend and improve, his concepts remain coarse and blunt instruments. They cover up rather than reveal, deform his experience of the people he meets rather than help him appreciate the subtle shape of their characters. As a result, his vision remains distorted, distracted, and unrefined.

Let us blend Murdochian language with that of presentationalism: first, selfish attention to others may distort how they appear to us and may determine what evaluative assessments of them we are rational to transition to as we characterize them and their actions. Second, our experience of others, if combined with a view that is selfish as it contains selfish beliefs, may make it rational for us to transition to ways of judging and acting toward others that respond—rather than to who they are, what they do, and why—to what pleasure or utility we seek to derive from them. As we make such transitions, we are likely to judge and act in ways that fail to do them justice. If conjoined with experience, a selfish view may thus make rational transitions to unjust beliefs, judgments, and actions.

Both of the above may apply to Sid. First, his selfishness may prevent him from seeing others justly, his appearances may be distorted; he doesn't care enough to look. Yet the transitions to the evaluative judgments and actions he offers in response to his experience may be completely rational, given his view. Second, even if his appearances are unaffected, his view may be so selfish that upon having experiences, he rationally transitions to judgments and actions that serve his needs, but fail to be responsive to who the people he interacts with are, to what they think, need, and intend. Here is a third possibility: Sid's view may combine with strong dispositions to act selfishly, dispositions that prevent Sid from transitioning to actions that are rational in light of his view.

I return to the topic of dispositions below. For now, let us observe that in the first two cases, we will find fault with Sid. We will take his appearances to be selfishly distorted and his view overly egocentric. Even so, the judgments and actions Sid transitions to may still be perfectly rational, conditional on his experiences and his view. In the third scenario, however, Sid is not even conditionally rational. Instead of judging and acting in line with what is rational in light of his view and experience, selfish dispositions interfere. The anxious avaricious tentacles of the self (cf. Murdoch 1970, 103) may hide in various places. Of Sid, who here appears only as an illustrative caricature, we cannot say where they do. If we met him, we might find out, if we *looked at* and *imagined* him justly.

Note, parenthetically, that Sid himself may eventually have occasion to revise his view. For if his vision is indeed distorted and his actions indeed unjust, they will be unresponsive to reality and blind to the needs, hopes, intentions, and legitimate demands of others. This in turn will create the kind of friction mentioned in the last section. It may build up, thwart Sid's selfish plans, force him to revise his views, even compel him to *look*. Such revisions may of course make things worse, simply make Sid more shrewd, or, if more attentive to others, then just enough to serve his selfish aims better. But since this would not remove, only modify the friction, friction may still build up and eventually yield changes toward the less selfish. In our compassionate moods, we feel for those in whom such changes never occur, whose lives seem untouched by the light that (we imagine) guides us, and for whom friction never turns into the rock bottom of conversion. Of course, if changes do occur, they need not, typically *will* not, be as profound (let alone dramatic) as the conversion of Dickens' Scrooge or the redemption of Lucas' Darth Vader. Life is subtler than *that* kind of fiction and moral progress is slow, difficult, and piecemeal. Observers may not notice it (or may have long since stopped looking).

Returning to the good case, recall that unselfish, loving attention is geared at doing justice to who others are, involves imagining realistically what they believe, what options they can see, how they characterize these options, and how they differ from us. Such attention, if it springs from a suitable view, may make rational transitions to evaluations that are appropriate and fair, perhaps to actions that are directed at the common good. Doing this well is extremely difficult. Often we fail. Moral progress, Murdoch would submit, requires humility and compassion. 'Humility' in this context translates into 'readiness to learn.' Others' perspectives may be blurred, too, yet clearer where ours are murky. If they disagree with us, we may benefit and learn from them by looking at and imagining them—unselfishly and justly. Compassion, on the other hand, arises from the realization that actions may look comparatively bad to us, yet good to others who evaluatively characterize them and the people they affect differently. Ideally, attending to others justly engenders understanding, which in turn facilitates attempts to help them improve, if, on closer inspection, their understanding seems deficient. This may fail and what looks like compassion (to us, too) can be self-serving paternalism in disguise. But attempts to help others may also be truly compassionate, empathetic responses to them, their outlooks, and their idiosyncratic features—actions that serve not selfish ends but the common good. In short: seeing others and imagining how things look to them realistically will make us reevaluate and recharacterize the options for action open to us and may make rational transitions to actions that are better not just for us, but for them also.

Above, we saw that presentationalists can handle cases that trouble both representationalists and relationalists: cases in which our views and concepts are muddled and cases in which background states affect our view and experience. Self-conscious presentationalists must entertain the possibility that others understand and apply evaluative concepts differently and that subjects in identical environing circumstances may face different appearances.[35] Moreover, they will acknowledge that different responses to identical circumstances can be equally rational, conditional on the responding subjects' views. If so, however, presentationalists should embrace Murdoch's appeal to humility and compassion. Presentationalism entails that others may rationally transition to judgments and actions I disapprove of. When facing such judgments and actions, I should humbly consider that the other may have acted rationally. Perhaps my own view is deficient, my selfish ego may surreptitiously interfere with what I see and imagine, my appearances may be distorted. If I find that I disagree with others or their actions, this must not be an *automatic* reason for me to blame them (though reasons for blame may of course exist). Instead, disagreement with others may well motivate me to attend to them more closely, to learn more about how things really stand with them and the situation at hand, or to act compassionately, depending on what circumstances require or allow, and on what I can do.[36]

We thus arrive at *Murdochian Presentationalism*. There is much more to be explored than what I can here provide, but *in nuce*, I will say this: Murdochian presentationalism takes the theoretical insight of presentationalism—the realization that against the backdrop of differing views, different responses to identical circumstances can be equally (conditionally) rational—as motivating the Murdochian practical insight that acting well toward others requires that we transcend the constraints of our subjective rationality by opening ourselves up to being affected by our attempts to attend and imagine others and their actions justly. Support relations go both ways. Murdoch is a realist. For her, looking at others justly and freeing oneself from selfish fantasy are part and parcel not merely of the attempt to morally better oneself. They are also part of the quest for truth and understanding—the attempt to get better attuned to what is real. Indeed, moral progress aims for knowledge of the individual and once we accept the importance of just and unselfish attention in obtaining such knowledge, we should also accept that the *practical* pursuit of moral progress and the *theoretical* pursuit of rationality, truth, and knowledge of what else is real belong to one and the same project as two sides of one coin.

The "quiet constant work of attention" (Murdoch 1998, p. 200), Murdoch says, slowly builds up the world which we confront, see, and in which we can thus choose, "a world upon which our imagination has, at any given moment, already worked" (Murdoch 1998, 199). Murdoch's suggestion here is that the options we take to be available for action, along with the people and things we see, are always and inevitably present to us in terms that are shaped by our idiosyncratic histories. As the presentationalist would say, they depend on the specifics of our view and the shape of the concepts it contains. Such histories will crucially involve prior occasions of attention, applications of (evaluative and other) concepts, interactions with others, and ways in which our beliefs about how concepts relate to one another have grown out of them. Such histories, as per the presentationalist, concern how our views have been shaped and revised through the continuous pressure of experience. Let us suppose that rather than merely looking (the neutral word), one can pay conscious attention (the good word) to others (see Murdoch 1970, 37). Let us assume, further, that such attention can be just. Furthermore, let us entertain, with Murdoch, that just attention yields clear and realistic vision. Now, if presentationalism is ultimately geared at arriving at views that are subsequently more rational, more coherent, and more accurate, and if practical and theoretical pursuits are as closely related to one another as the discussion in the previous paragraph suggests, then engaging in increasingly just attention emerges as a habit that presentationalists should strive to cultivate—if only for instrumental reasons: it is broadly conducive to conceptual progress and potentially essential to the project of advancing their theoretical pursuits.[37]

According to presentationalism, we saw above, views (and the beliefs and concepts they comprise) develop, in part,[38] under the pressure of experience, through subsequent applications of empirical concepts, e.g., in perceptual judgments, through which we may learn and enrich our view or realize that there is need for revision. Murdoch concurs. As our concepts develop, she claims, "a deepening process, at any rate an altering and complicating process, takes place" and "since we are human historical individuals the movement of understanding is onward into increasing privacy, in the direction of the ideal limit" (Murdoch 1970, 29).[39] In making these remarks, Murdoch's focus is specifically on value concepts. However, she also hints at the possibility that such a process of complication and development toward an ideal limit could be one that *all* concepts undergo, even so-called ordinary empirical concepts such as color terms (Murdoch 1970, 29). Presentationalists purport to provide a general account of how views can change under the pressure of experience. And if for views to change frequently entails that the beliefs and concepts they contain change along with them, we can see how presentationalists might flesh out the story of conceptual change toward an ideal limit that Murdoch hints at—not just regarding the ordinary empirical concepts and theories that *presentationalists* focus on, but regarding the evaluative concepts *Murdoch* focuses on as well.

This concludes my sketch of Murdochian presentationalism, which blends the language of presentationalism with Murdoch's language of just attention, clear vision, and unselfing. Presentationalism, I suggested, invites and serves to motivate the plea to treat others with humility and compassion that is implied in Murdoch's focus on just attention. I argued that Murdoch's account of just attention in turn complements the project of presentationalism, suggested, more generally, that theoretical and practical pursuits are inextricably intertwined, and proposed that presentationalism may help flesh out Murdoch's claims about how our moral (and other) concepts develop. Next, I will integrate two further pieces required to articulate the view I take to sustain P2: a clarification of what freedom is *not* and a broadly Kantian notion of individual autonomy.

Freedom and Autonomy

Freedom to Versus Freedom from

What is individual autonomy? The freedom, perhaps, to deliberately choose between publicly available options for action? To Murdochian presentationalists, this proposal must be doubly implausible. First, suppose I consider some action, φ. Assume, further, that φ seems attractive to me, yet unfathomable to you. Perhaps we can overcome our differences. After talking and mutual attending, you may adopt my characterization of φ-ing, or I may modify mine, based on what I can now see.[40] Yet perhaps not. Resolving differences in how we understand concepts and how we apply them can be complicated, a life-long task.[41] As we have come to understand already, paying just attention is difficult. Consequently, Murdochian presentationalists must hold that given (perhaps subtle) individual differences in views and, perhaps, appearances, options for action are typically *not* publicly available, not under the evaluative characterizations that matter to the agent. Some morally relevant actions may be available *only* to me. My reflecting with the aim of reevaluating others and their actions, for example, is a rather private affair. It involves replacing one idiosyncratically framed and understood evaluative characterization with another, updated one. Who, except me, could possibly engage in *this* activity?[42]

Here is a second problem with the proposal: in moments of choice, Murdochian presentationalists will hold, most of the morally important work has already been done. Recall the following passage: "The world which we confront is a world upon which our imagination has, at any given moment, already worked. [...] we evaluate [...] largely, by the constant quiet work of attention and imagination" (Murdoch 1998, 199–200). To Murdochian presentationalists, what matters most morally are not isolated moments of choice. Instead, most important is the way in which we continuously attend and imagine others and the situations in which we find ourselves:

> [I]f we consider what the work of attention is like, how continuously it goes on, and how imperceptibly it builds up structures of value round about us, we shall not be surprised that at crucial moments of choice most of the business of choosing is already over.
>
> (Murdoch 1970, 37)

This is not to deny, of course, that choosing a path of action—especially under duress or time constraints—can require serious moral reflection, but to insist that such situations are no good models for moral activity in general.[43] Moral activity is ongoing and how we have come to characterize our options, through constant and quiet attention, often wears on its sleeves which one is best, so that we pursue it almost automatically.

> A mediocre man who achieves what he intends is not the ideal of a free man. To be free is something like this: to exist sanely without fear and to perceive what is real. I would be prepared to imply that one who perceives what is real will also act rightly.
>
> (Murdoch 1998, 201)

Selfish Sid, too, chooses. But as per this passage, such choosing does not by itself reveal his freedom. To Murdochian presentationalists, Sid's freedom must seem severely hampered. He cannot make out what his options really are. The good he aims to materialize is conceptualized in too narrow and selfish a fashion and lacking the discernment that just attention affords, the way he characterizes his options remains unrealistic and distorted. He transitions, even rationally, to judgments and actions which are based on bad vision and often unjust, which leads to friction and may leave his selfish plans at risk of being thwarted—though this need not be so, as we saw already.

To Murdochian presentationalist, freedom is not freedom *to* choose, but freedom *from* whatever distorts our views and blurs our vision—notably: selfishness and the fear that arises from entertaining the possibility that one might not obtain or keep what the ego desires. Freedom tethers us and our vision to reality, allows us to see and evaluate options clearly, and enables us to do what may in fact be good in a sense that transcends what may initially have seemed good to us. Let us next combine this view with a take on individual autonomy as resting, in part, on the capacity to bind oneself by norms.

Autonomy

Being bound by norms—at least implicitly—is essential to intelligibly having views at all. Any view must be intelligible as a practice governed by various implicit—and, perhaps, explicit—norms that specify which inferential moves between concept applications, judgments, and actions are appropriate (or not). Within such a structure concepts acquire their specific shape and determinate (or determinable) content.[44] As Murdochian presentationalists will insist, such a structure must also contain linkages that rationally link views, perceptual judgments, and actions via possible experiences.[45]

Views so construed could be characterized in a number of ways. In principle, one way could be by specifying the norms that the agent *should* comply with, given what they believe. But this introduces complications, for even if we set aside pragmatic limitations, such a task raises the issue of competence. The bird's eye view from which what in fact follows from what can be seen must elude us: judgments concerning such issues cannot but happen against the backdrop of our own normative practice.

A different way of characterizing a view is by referring to rules that subjects who inhabit the practice sustaining it are *de facto* disposed to comply with. Many such rules will also be specified in normative terms. After all, an important part of the practice that sustains a view will be that of treating certain items (e.g., utterances and other actions) as correct (or not). Importantly, focusing on rules characterizing dispositions that inhabitants of a view *de facto* exhibit makes the characterization of a view more realistic. It lets in a set of factors that are especially pertinent to the topic at hand. For we may note that the rules characterizing *de facto* dispositions may well be at odds with the norms by which those who inhabit the view take themselves to be bound. After all, *de facto* dispositions will be shaped only in part by the respective inhabitants' explicit and implicit normative commitments. They will also reflect unconscious motives, drives, emotions, hopes, etc.—i.e., the complex psychological mechanism of those whose view is under consideration.

Clearly, rules that govern a subject's *de facto* dispositions need not, typically will not be explicitly available to those who comply with them. Some may be.[46] Probably most, though, will govern the subject's judgments and actions implicitly, manifest, *inter alia*, in how they understand, relate, and apply moral and other notions and act. In a community, self-conscious clarity on such issues is likely to be distributed unevenly and is probably best increased not from some fictitious external point of view, but by processes of collective explication and negotiation.

Again, rules governing our *de facto* dispositions can and often will be co-determined by conscious and unconscious motives and may differ from the norms by which we *think* we are bound. In this context, it is natural to draw on a common interpretation of Kantian autonomy. According to it, autonomy is the capacity to impose a form of rational self-constraint: the capacity to deliberate and bind oneself by norms (moral, but also other ones). On this notion, selfish psychological factors that co-determine *de facto* rules but do not appear as either implicit or self-conscious commitments to norms introduce an element of heteronomy: to the extent that our actions and thoughts are determined by such factors, we are not autonomous. We can rephrase this in terms of Murdochian presentationalism: selfishness and fear may distort what we see, surreptitiously shape our view and how we characterize others and our options for action, and thus hamper our freedom. Improvement in individual autonomy then appears as an improvement of Murdochian freedom and, more generally, as a modification of how we exercise (and follow through on) our capacity to bind ourselves by norms—one that minimizes selfishness regarding both what we bind ourselves by and whether we truly act on what we take our commitments to be or in line with what it is rational to transition to, given our view. Such improvement is naturally fostered by explication (though explication is not the only way to foster it—modeling behavior is another).[47]

Explicating norms by which we are—or take ourselves to be—bound and explicating heteronomous factors that co-determine how we are *de facto* disposed to act serves to increase our semantic, moral, and psychological self-consciousness. Here are three ways in which such explication can increase autonomy. First, some of the norms that shape our dispositions to act and think are socially inherited and implicit in how we act. Explicating them makes them available for conscious endorsement. To transition from simply complying with an implicit norm—as it were passively and automatically—to willingly binding oneself by it is to move toward a more self-conscious and autonomous exercise of the appurtenant capacity. Second, and relatedly, explication makes implicit norms available for rejection and for individual or intersubjective refinement and negotiation—e.g., as one considers their applicability on occasions of (joint) attention. Third, explicating heteronomous factors increases self-awareness and can allow one to work toward changing one's dispositions in familiar ways. Consider the kind of self-awareness that enables you to stop yourself from getting upset about something that somebody says to you. Such self-awareness may, e.g., involve the following realization: the utterance in question may not be directed at you, or not be meant the way you notice you are inclined to take it. You may even understand why you are so inclined. The utterance of your present interlocutor, B, may for instance remind you of what a past interlocutor, A, may have said to you—something that back then you may have found very hurtful. It is because you transfer what you take to be A's past adversarial intentions onto B that you incline toward a specific response. An increase in awareness and understanding can change our dispositions' manifestation conditions and, thus, the dispositions themselves. Awareness clarifies vision and enables us to counteract transference. It removes an illusion and increases our ability to attend to what is really there—in this case: B, who differs from A—and makes us more free.

Plausibly, many rules that characterize the dispositions we *de facto* comply with are largely due to our psychological and socio-cultural upbringing. Explicating them is a social task which requires reciprocal recognition, attribution of motives and reasons, and, where appropriate, criticism. What our norms *ought* to be, too, must be socially negotiated. In such activities, Murdochian presentationalists insist, just attention matters. It allows us to truly see others, to incorporate the valid points they may be raising, to issue just criticism, and to render compassionate assistance. And the smallest arena for such negotiations, one in which intimacy makes such negotiations particularly powerful, is that provided by romantic love.

The increasingly autonomous subject, then, consciously binds herself by decreasingly selfish norms, becomes more aware of and finds ways to excise ways in which heteronomous factors suffuse the fabric of her being, attends to others justly, recognizes them as trying to pursue the good they can see, and responds to them humbly and compassionately. To her, disagreement with others invites attention and provides opportunities for testing and refining the norms she embraces. She may welcome disagreement as potentially revelatory of subtle distortions of her own view, as an opportunity for detecting and overcoming residual selfishness, or as an opportunity for compassionate action geared toward assisting others in explicating and refining the norms that bind them, in turning them into norms they bind themselves by, and thus in increasing their individual autonomy. Full individual autonomy, so construed, is a distant ideal, one that we may not reach and that we may need to work toward together. With it in hand, we can finally return to P2.

Just Love and the Ideal Lovers' Pledge

P2, Expanding Outlooks, and the Ideal Lovers' Pledge

As per P2, recall, to be just, love must preserve or foster, not diminish individual autonomy. In light of the previous section (and inserting appropriate agentive terms) we can now gloss P2 as follows: a just lover must preserve or foster the beloved's individual autonomy. To do this is to preserve or foster the beloved's ability to self-consciously bind themselves by norms, to assist them in their endeavors to see and imagine others clearly, and, relatedly, to help them reduce the influence of heteronomous factors that may affect their view, distort their vision, and co-determine their dispositions to act.

According to Murdochian presentationalism, this is precisely what just lovers do. Whether it be preserving or fostering the beloved's autonomy, efforts geared toward these aims cannot succeed until the lover knows and understands the beloved well. We have seen that such knowledge, while difficult to obtain, is what just attention delivers. Seeing clearly who the beloved is and what options for action they see requires a certain amount of selflessness. To truly see their beloved, a lover must acknowledge that their beloved, *qua* individual, is different from them. As lovers get to see and imagine their beloved better, they get a sense of what they value, what vision of the good underlies and motivates their actions, and how heteronomous aspects may undermine their autonomy. *Qua* lover, lovers will wish their beloved well. They will consider the vision of the good that they imagine their beloved aims for and try to appreciate its value (if it is not already obvious to them). They will support the beloved in their attempts to materialize that good, may strive to continuously explicate and negotiate individual and joint commitments,[48] and gently and compassionately help the beloved explicate and excise heteronomous factors. They will also, and this matters, allow the beloved to reciprocate and in turn help the lover in corresponding ways.[49]

As lovers reevaluate their own options for action in light of what they see and what strikes them as good for both themselves and the beloved, there is a sense in which the lover's outlook expands and begins to incorporate the beloved's outlook—to the extent that they can see it. But doing this need not mean that all of the beloved's goals properly become the lover's goals, too. There may well be projects my beloved pursues the point of which I fail to see. But I may decide to promote and support them anyway. For even if I cannot fully see their point, I may be able to see and appreciate that for my beloved, undertaking the commitment to pursuing such projects is an expression of their individual autonomy—something that matters to them deeply, is an important part of how they see themselves and of what they see themselves as moving toward.[50] I need not want to move *there* or move there *that way*, but as a just lover, it may well be essential for the pursuit of the vision of good that attracts me that my beloved be able to pursue theirs as well.

Just attention to the beloved may modify the *range* of the lover's options for action, but also, and crucially, what the lover perceives these options to be and entail. Just attention enables doing well by our beloved and, as I put it above, transcends the lover's subjective rationality. One way in which this happens is that the characterizations of the lover's options for action get reframed by their knowledge of the beloved. Love expands, suffuses, and reorients the lover's outlook. Such reshaping need not always prioritize actions that the lover takes to be most rational, based on what they now see. Being compassionate toward one's beloved may sometimes require that one refrain from pursuing what strikes one as the most rational option. Perhaps the beloved cannot imagine what merit one attributes to that option, would feel hurt were one to pursue it. Imaginatively anticipating the beloved's response to one's actions will both affect one's evaluative characterization of these options and may draw one toward responding to the beloved's otherness compassionately, i.e., in ways they can accept or that may help them see one's preferred option in a different light. But humility requires that one be open to the possibility that the beloved sees things better than one does—just love has room for faith and trust in the beloved and their vision, even against one's reason.

Here, then, is what I call the *ideal lovers' pledge*. As I see it, it is the undertaking of a commitment to try and justly attend and humbly and compassionately respond to one another, to acknowledge and respect one's differences, to mutually assist one another in explicating, clarifying, and developing one's views, joint and individual projects, to explicate the norms that characterize one's dispositions to act, to foster the beloved's autonomy by promoting their ends, helping them excise heteronomous factors, and letting them help one do the same. Taking this pledge, I contend, is itself an exercise of individual autonomy. It is a conscious, unselfish exercise of our capacity to bind ourselves by norms and involves a commitment to making continuous attempts to bind oneself by norms that are less selfish and thus, if acted upon, beneficial to both lovers (and, perhaps, to others more generally)[51].

Since this commitment is fairly abstract, lovers will need to continually negotiate, in practice, how it ought to be understood and applied, always with a view to benefiting both lovers and making them more autonomous, by making their views and outlooks less selfish and better attuned to what is real. Such negotiations will typically rest on the mutual recognition of the lovers as capable of exercising their autonomy, and as being both able and entitled to hold each other accountable. At the same time, just lovers remain ever-ready to look again, to compassionately support each other when they fail, and to see their respective otherness as an opportunity to learn. Doing this well may well be an infinite task; injustice and heteronomy can enter in numerous and surreptitious ways. But preventing it from doing so by attending to and by responding to the beloved justly surely is worth striving for.

Loving Unions—Shifting the Imagery

Throughout, I have argued for a position that makes it intelligible how to think of just love as preserving or maintaining individual autonomy. The view I promoted—*Murdochian presentationalism*—is epistemologically motivated and interesting in various ways—not least in that, through its focus on attention and clear vision, it suggests that those pursuing theoretical ends need to take seriously moral and practical concerns to achieve their aims. It is productive, too, e.g., in that it allows fruitful communication between philosophy and psychology (as some of the examples bring out). If Murdochian presentationalism is false, it is false in interesting ways.

Just love, we saw, must be and remain sensitive to the fact that our beloved is different from us and that they may well remain partly unintelligible; we may forever fail to see exactly what they do or what they strive for. Put differently, the just lover should expect that although there may be convergence of outlooks, such convergence need not be total. But just lovers may rejoice in their beloved's otherness, not least because in engaging with and discovering it, they continue to find out more about their beloved, but also about themselves.

In Helm (2017), Bennett Helm claims that for union theorists, a central task is that of spelling out just what the *we* of (ideal) loving unions comes to. In closing, let me briefly return to my qualms with the union view: I have no strong objection against them, but to the extent that union theorists think of loving unions in terms of a merger, I am unconvinced. For if Murdochian presentationalism is correct, the imagery of merging is misleading: in just love, neither identities nor ends merge—though ends may of course be shared and outlooks converge.[52] A more helpful notion to characterize ideal loving relationships, I think, is the notion of *harmony*. In the tradition Murdochian presentationalism stands in, this is not a new suggestion. For example, one can find references to harmony in Weil's remarks on friendship: "Friendship," she says, "is a supernatural harmony, a union of opposites" (Weil 1977, 367).[53] In fact, the tradition of conceptually linking love and harmony goes back much further. As Aditi Chaturvedi, commenting on the Empedoclean fragment B96, points out,

> *harmonia* stands for mixing in a particular proportion - there is balance and not complete unity or merging [...]. It entails a proper fitting together of discrete entities that nonetheless retain their original identity and don't simply blend into one another.
> (Chaturvedi 2016, 49)[54]

The notion of harmony—understood as a well-ordered and balanced fitting together of heterogeneous elements—provides an apt metaphor, I submit, a helpful image as we think about ideal loving relationships. In them, I argued, lovers retain and mutually foster their respective individuality—their harmonious relationship accommodates and acknowledges the lovers' respective otherness. Such harmony is created and sustained by just love, which appreciates and supports the individuality, otherness, and individual autonomy of the lovers, aims at implementing a continuous commitment that I explicated in terms of the *ideal lovers' pledge*, leads to an expansion of the lovers' respective outlooks, and reorients them towards the good and the real.

Notes

1. See Kühler (2020, section 3), for a fuller overview, references, and a useful classification of union views.
2. Note that Delaney characterizes the merging involved in romantic unions as *psychological*. He also emphasizes that people want their love to generate and sustain a commitment to them of a certain type (cf. Delaney 1996, 40). While I wish to remain neutral with respect to the former, I fully agree with the latter. Later, I will have more to say about what I take such a commitment ideally to involve.

3. For a very helpful discussion of Weil and Murdoch, see Broackes (2012, esp. 19ff.) and Broackes (2019).
4. Murdoch on the importance of imagination: "The formulation of beliefs about other people often proceeds and must proceed imaginatively and under a direct pressure of will. We have to attend to people, we may have to have *faith* in them, and here justice and realism may demand the inhibition of certain pictures, the promotion of others. [...] To be a human being is to know more than one can prove [...]" (Murdoch 1998, 199). Importantly, then, as we interact with others, we take them to *be* some specific way and to *act* out of some motives (not others), go beyond the facts, may exhibit faith in them, succeed or fail to do them justice and, thus, be more or less attuned to reality.
5. The passage continues, "when it is even partially refined it [i.e. love] is the energy and passion of the soul in its search for Good, the force that joins us to Good and joins us to the world through Good." (Murdoch 1970, 103). That Murdoch's notion of love borrows from the Platonic *eros* is obvious. For an exploration of this topic, see Hopwood (2017). In Rosenhagen (2019a), I suggest that laying her notion of love alongside Aristotle's *philia* is instructive as well.
6. I take no stance on whether romantic love is essentially physical, with respect neither to (a) what kind of relation it is, nor (b) what occasions it. As for (a), like Jollimore, I hesitate to assert or endorse necessity claims regarding romantic love (see Jollimore 2019, 67). As for (b), the question what occasions love is causal and though reasons may be causes, not all causes for love need to be reasons. In discussions about love, this point is sometimes missed. Hurka (2017) thinks that reasons for romantic love are both normative and non-normative. Engels Kroeker (2019), like Martin (2015), holds that one's reasons for love may be *just* a-rational, *just* rational, or hybrid. Though I am sympathetic to the latter, I take issue with talk of a-rational reasons. I prefer to say that in forming bonds of romantic love, some of the properties lovers possess or attribute to one another are causes for love. These may, but need not also serve as reasons.
7. One caveat: couples provide just the simplest and most common kind of case. We need not embrace the (false) claim that relationships of romantic love are confined to couples, nor the prescription that they should be.
8. I adopt the notion of grounding and the permissive metaphysical stance implied here from Schaffer (2009).
9. According to Sellars, the "aim of philosophy, abstractly formulated, is to understand how things in the broadest possible sense of the term hang together in the broadest possible sense of the term." (Sellars 1963, 1). Below, I suggest that practical and theoretical pursuits hang together more tightly than standard disciplinary divisions would suggest.
10. I henceforth drop the qualifier "representational."
11. Representationalists favoring different notions of content will vary in how they fill in the story. For this chapter, the specifics don't matter—I just need to provide a generic version.
12. It is notoriously difficult for coherentists to accommodate the foundationalist intuition that experiential contents or the beliefs associated with experience carry special justificatory weight.
13. Typically, "perceptual experience" is used as the broader term and "perceive" is used factively. On this usage, one can have a *perceptual experience* as of p even if p is not the case but cannot *perceive* that p unless p is the case.

14. It cannot be *completely* muddled. The idea of a concept with respect to which *every* belief we could possible hold is false is the (absurd) idea of a concept that lacks determinate content (cf. Rosenhagen 2019b).
15. Any epistemology worth its name, McDowell insists, must accommodate receptive knowledge lest it make empirical rationality unintelligible (cf. McDowell 2009, 468, citing Rödl 2007, ch. 3 for support). Rejecting foundationalist pictures according to which "the knowledge experience makes available to us constitutes the foundation of *all* our discursive activities," he claims that the subject's ability to know through perception "is intelligibly only as an element in an ongoing condition of being rationally at home in the world – so only in a context in which our discursive activities are already under way" (McDowell 2019, 394, *emphasis added*). My point is that McDowell must put flesh on the bones of what he gestures at when he helps himself to the expression "being rationally at home in the world."
16. Are such effects pervasive? Some philosophers (e.g., Siegel) and cognitive neuroscientists affirm this (e.g., Hohwy 2014), many entertain it at least as possible and thus potentially worrisome. For dissent, see Firestone & Scholl 2016.
17. Representationalists could accommodate such effects by holding that experience has a rational standing that is modifiable by background states (cf. Siegel 2017). In Rosenhagen (2018), I argue that this is unsatisfactory. It yields a highly revisionary view of experience, leaves it unclear how representational content and the phenomenology of experience relate, leaves what is rational for subjects to do, upon having a certain experience, opaque to them, and fails to capture the important rational role experience plays both in individual reasoning and in empirical debate.
18. Some maintain that one should retain and combine relationalist and representationalist insights. Examples are Schellenberg (2014, 2018) and McDowell (2013). However, to the extent that these philosophers also hold that experience does have content, staunch relationalists cannot agree with them (see Nanay 2014).
19. Depending on individual relationalists' ontological proclivities, the mind-independent worldly items are variously construed as objects, as properties, or as facts (i.e., sets of objects and properties). Examples are Brewer (2011, 2018, 2019a, 2019b) (objects), Genone (2014, 2016) (appearance properties), and Fish (2009) (facts). I discuss various challenges that I take these views to face at length in Rosenhagen (2018).
20. As Campbell puts it, experience brings the environing items and their qualitative features, "into the subjective life of the perceiver" (Campbell and Cassam 2014, 33).
21. These problems relate to an issue Jonathan Kvanvig identifies as *Sellars's problem* According to it, it is hard to see how experience that lacks propositional—or, for that matter, *any*—content could serve to justify beliefs, but also hard to see how, on the view that experiences do have content, one is to determine which ones can generate justification (cf. Kvanvig 2007, 169–170). As we saw above, representationalists face the latter kind of issue, whereas the former poses a challenge to relationalists.
22. The word 'directly' indicates that such effects are not mediated via attention. Genone (2016), too, notes the problem.
23. To address some of the challenges listed, people have begun to develop relationalist positions that jointly form what is now sometimes dubbed *New Wave Relationalism*. Some of those who are busy developing

interesting new versions of relationalism are Ori Beck, Craig French, Heather Logue, Farid Masrour, Ian Philips, Umrao Sethi, and my colleague Kranti Saran.
24. Gupta eschews the idea that experience has content as otiose, but that move is optional (cf. Gupta 2019, 243, fn. 31; also Rosenhagen 2018, ch. 10).
25. Henceforth, I drop the qualifier 'background' and just talk about views.
26. Views may also contain linkages to other activities, such as referential activities or ostensive definitions (see Gupta 2019) or to suspension of judgment. Indeed, I think presentationalists can broaden this idea and allow that a view can also contain linkages to all sorts of actions (cf. Rosenhagen ms).
27. One may wish to insist that there must be an absolute sense in which one cannot be fully rational if upon having a certain experience, against the backdrop of a certain view, one transitions to a perceptual judgment that is false or even irrational. This point can be granted. However, one can be irrational in this absolute sense while at the same time being completely rational in another: how one transitions from a partly incomplete, false, or even irrational view, if confronted with a given experience, to perceptual judgments can be perfectly rational, conditional on the view.
28. Non-Gauptik versions of presentationalism may keep a notion of content, which could then be co-determined by background states.
29. On versions of presentationalism on which an experience *is* associated with some content, the specifics of such association are view-dependent, too. On them, too, experience in and of itself cannot be assigned justificatory weight.
30. If there were none, the theory would be useless for explanatory and predictive purposes and lack empirical content.
31. Again, there are limits to how muddled views can be. There must also be limits to how irrational something can be and still count as a view that contains determinate rational linkages between experiences and perceptual judgments. Details concerning such issues become interesting quickly, but also more complicated than it is useful to explore here.
32. Views can be poor and rational transitions can lead to uninteresting judgments, e.g., "I (seem to) see something blue."
33. Presentationalism is compatible both with the relationalist claim that experience serves to bring subjects in touch with mind-independent items and with a claim both representationalists and relationalists endorse: experience may help justify beliefs. But neither claim, presentationalists will insist, properly captures experience's fundamental rational role.
34. Like Popper rejected unfalsifiable theories as metaphysical (meant pejoratively, see, e.g., Churchland 1975), a view v on which *any* possible experience makes rational transitions to judgments in line with v should be rejected as pathologically insensitive to experience. For a discussion of such pathologies, (see Gupta 2006, ch. 4, and Gupta 2019, ch. 4).
35. For presentationalists who keep a notion of content, further possibilities arise: another, B, could be appeared to in the same way as oneself, A, while B's appearances are associated with contents that differ from those associated with the same appearances for A; also, for B, both the appearances and the associated contents could differ from A's, etc.
36. Two remarks: (1) One can be mistaken about who one is and about what one is able to do. But if paying just attention is already difficult, it is even more difficult as something one engages in with respect to oneself (on this, both Aristotle 2014, IX.9, and Murdoch agree). (2) How far compassion

toward those who act in ways that strike as us as cruel may go, and to what extent, if any, we are morally obliged to attend to them is a difficult question.

37. To the extent that selfish dispositions are treated as separate from views, just attention should appear attractive as a method to reduce discrepancies between how, in light of their view, agents *should* act and how they in fact *do*.

38. Changes in views, beliefs, and concepts can of course also be triggered by purely logical reflection.

39. *Qua* realist, Murdoch must take the ideal limit to be an accurate view on which agents who embark on their moral quest for truth from different starting points would eventually converge. The reference to privacy shows that to her, the development of views, concepts, and beliefs is a highly idiosyncratic affair. Whether Murdoch underestimates the role empirical debate about objects of joint attention can play with respect to expanding common conceptual ground regarding moral (and other) concepts is an interesting question.

40. I might, e.g., realize that φ-ing is unacceptable for me, too, as on my modified characterization, it conflicts with what else I deem good. I may not fully succeed in understanding your characterization—my attention may be flawed or I may use the terms figuring in it differently. I may also disagree with you and still act the way you suggest. Were you to experience an untoward consequence of my acting this way—one I anticipate, while you do not—you might learn from this more than by my repeatedly telling you. This is a standard tool in the parent's toolbox. I might also anticipate that acting as you suggest will make *me* experience an untoward consequence. If I care about your learning, I may be ready to face the untoward consequence and doing so may be an act of loving compassion. However, I might also just care about the expected pampering of my ego that I derive from my being able to tell you that *I told you so*. As always, in interpersonal interactions, there is room for compassion and selfishness and what one's actions and their underlying motives are can be opaque not just to others, but also to oneself.

41. For an illustration of how such difficulties can arise not in moral contexts, but in the context of scientific classification, see the opening example in Hanson (1965 [1958], ch. 1).

42. This is one of the points Murdoch's famous M&D example drives home (see Murdoch 1970, 17ff., esp. 23).

43. As Murdoch puts it, what is required is a shift in imagery. She thinks that we should not understand moral activity primarily in terms of movement, in terms of discontinuous leaps of the isolated will, but in terms of the metaphor of vision that emerges from (and, we may add, *is directed at*) the continuous fabric of being (cf. Murdoch 1970, 22).

44. It is an interesting question, not to be pursued here, what the normative structure of a view must minimally be. Certainly, some minimal coherence constraint must be met. Arguably, norms must also hang together in a sufficiently dense way to confer conceptual content on the concepts whose conditions and consequences of application they govern. An account of the kinds of structures necessary for a practice to be discursive is provided in Brandom (2008).

45. This emphasis on experience sets apart Murdochian presentationalism from a view like, e.g., Brandom's inferentialism that eschews the notion of experience entirely and tries to do just with the concept of reliably differentiated dispositions to respond to observable stimuli (see, e.g., Brandom 1994; for criticism: McDowell 2010).

46. One might imagine a community of speakers in which no such norms are explicitly available as their language lacks the expressive power to explicate them. Brandom (1994) discusses a related possibility. For doubts, see McDowell (2005).
47. If, like Murdoch, we want to make room for the virtuous peasant, explication cannot be *necessary* for moral progress. Perhaps moral excellence can result from a naturally virtuous and unselfish disposition or from learning by intuitively imitating the virtuous. Lambert (2020) provides an interesting account of the potential importance that modeling appropriate behavior may take on in the public sphere, developed against the backdrop of Confucian ethics.
48. Again, explication, albeit a powerful tool to increase autonomy, may not be a necessary tool.
49. Providing unilateral assistance without accepting any in return may create dependence and be a way of surreptitiously inflating the assisting lover's ego.
50. For a nuanced discussion of how to think about the distinction between *sharing ends with the beloved* and (unselfishly) *sharing in the beloved's ends*—a discussion that is also sensitive to the need to allocate the authority to decide how to pursue ends in ways that respect whose ends they primarily are—see Fahmy (2016).
51. For an exploration of how Murdoch's notions of just attention may affect notions of freedom in the broader realm of the political—one that betrays in more than one way a shared interest and interpretative agreement with respect to some of the Murdochian topics discussed here, see Forsberg (2020).
52. See Delaney (1996) and, again, Fahmy (2016), for why merging and sharing are very different.
53. The opposites Weil has in mind: on the one hand, our friend is something as necessary to us as food; on the other hand, they are someone whose autonomy and freedom, despite the affectionate bond of necessity that ties us to them, we are committed to preserve.
54. I have benefited from a serendipitous reading of this paper by Chaturvedi, my colleague at Ashoka, who also generously provided me with a very helpful manuscript on her interpretation of Empedoclean harmony (Chaturvedi ms.). In it, she revises a remark that in the passage quoted in the text is omitted and in which she distinguishes harmony from love. In the manuscript, she argues, to my mind convincingly, that harmony, the appropriate fitting together of disparate entities, is precisely characteristic of Empledoclean Love (which, *inter alia*, is responsible for the creation of a harmonious, well-ordered cosmos).

References

Aristotle (2014). *Nicomachean Ethics*, translated with introduction and notes by C. D. C. Reeve. Indianapolis: Hackett.
Brandom, R. (1994). *Making it Explicit. Reasoning, Representing, and Discursive Commitment*. Cambridge (Mass.)/London: Harvard University Press.
Brandom, R. (2008). *Between Saying and Doing: Toward an Analytic Pragmatism*. Oxford: Oxford University Press.
Brewer, B. (2011). *Perception & Its Objects*. Oxford: Oxford University Press.
Brewer, B. (2018). "Perceptual Experience and Empirical Reason," in: *Analytic Philosophy* 59 (1), 1–18.

Brewer, B. (2019a). "Empirical Reason: Questions for Gupta, McDowell, and Siegel," in: *Philosophical Issues* 29, 311–323.
Brewer, B. (2019b). "Empirical Reason: Answers to Gupta, McDowell, and Siegel," in: *Philosophical Issues* 29, 366–377.
Broackes, J. (2012). "Introduction," in: Broackes, J. (ed.). *Iris Murdoch, Philosopher. A Collection of Essays*. Oxford: Oxford University Press, 1–92.
Broackes, J. (2019). "Iris Murdoch and Simone Weil," *Talk at the Royal Institute of Philosophy*, uploaded to YouTube on Jan 28, 2019. https://www.youtube.com/watch?v=LmCRWqkOiqs [last access: 06/30/2020].
Campbell, J., and Q. Cassam. (2014). *Berkeley's Puzzle: What Does Experience Teach Us?* Oxford: Oxford University Press.
Chaturvedi, A. (2016). "*Harmonia* and *Rta*," in: Seaford, R. (ed.). *Universe and Inner Self in Early Indian and Early Greek Thought*. Edinburgh: Edinburgh University Press, 40–54.
Chaturvedi, A. (ms.). "*Empedocleian Harmony.*"
Churchland, P. M. (1975). "Karl Popper's Philosophy of Science," in: *Canadian Journal of Philosophy* 5 (1), 145–156.
Delaney, N. (1996). "Romantic Love and Loving Commitment: Articulating a Modern Ideal," in: *American Philosophical Quarterly* 33 (4), 339–356.
Engels Kroeker, E. (2019). "Reasons for Love," in: Martin, A., 277–287.
Fahmy, M. S. (2016). "Love's Reasons," in: *Journal of Value Inquiry* 50, 153–168. https://doi.org/10.1007/s10790-015-9504-y.
Fedock, R. (2020). "Dissolving the Illusion of the Love and Justice Dichotomy," in: *this volume*.
Firestone, C., and B. Scholl. (2016). "Cognition Does Not Affect Perception: Evaluating the Evidence for 'Top-down' Effects," in: *Behavioral and Brain Sciences* 39. https://doi.org/10.1017/s0140525x15000965
Fish, W. (2009). *Perception, Illusion, and Hallucination*. Oxford: Oxford University Press.
Forsberg, N. (2020). "The Freedom that Comes with Love," in: *this volume*.
Genone, J. (2014). "Appearance and Illusion," in: *Mind* 123 (490), 339–376.
Genone, J. (2016). "Recent Work on Naïve Realism," in: *American Philosophical Quarterly* 53 (1), 1–25.
Gupta, A. (2006). *Empiricism and Experience*. Oxford: Oxford University Press.
Gupta, A. (2019). *Conscious Experience. A Logical Inquiry*. Cambridge (Mass.): Harvard University Press.
Hanson, N. R. (1965 [1958]). *Patterns of Discovery. An Inquiry into the Conceptual Foundations of Science*. Cambridge (Mass.): Cambridge University Press. [First published in 1958, edition cited: first paperback edition from 1965.]
Helm, B. (2017). "Love," in: Zalta, E. N. (ed.). *The Stanford Encyclopedia of Philosophy* (Fall 2017 Edition). https://plato.stanford.edu/archives/fall2017/entries/love/ [last access: 06/30/2020].
Hohwy, J. (2014). *The Predictive Mind*. Oxford: Oxford University Press.
Hopwood, M. (2018). "'The Extremely Difficult Realization That Something Other Than Oneself Is Real': Iris Murdoch on Love and Moral Agency," in: *European Journal of Philosophy* 26 (1), 477–501.
Hurka, T. (2017). "Love and Reason, The Many Relationship," in: E. Engels Kroeker & L. Schaubroeck (eds.). *Love, Reason, and Morality*. London: Routledge, 1–19.

Jollimore, T. (2019). "Love, Romance, and Sex," in: Martin *(2019)*, 61–71.
Kühler, Michael. (2011). "Love as Union vs. Personal Autonomy," in: Farghaly, N. & C. T. Toralba (eds.). *Love on Trial: Adjusting and Assigning Relationships.* Brill, 91–104. https://doi.org/10.1163/9781848880764_010.
Kühler, Michael. (2020). "Love as Union and Political Liberalism," in: *this volume.*
Kvanvig, J. (2007). "Propositionalism and the Metaphysics of Experience," in: *Philosophical Issues* 17 (1), 165–178.
Lambert (2020). "Love's Extension: Confucian familial love and the challenge of impartiality," in: *this volume.*
Martin, A. (2015). "Love, Incorporated," in: *Ethical Theory and Moral Practice* 18 (4), 691–702.
Martin, A. (ed.) (2019). *The Routledge Handbook of Love in Philosophy.* New York: Routledge.
McDowell, J. (2005). "Motivating Inferentialism. Comments on *Making it Explicit* (Ch. 2)," in: *Pragmatics & Cognition* 13 (1), 121–140.
McDowell, J. (2009). "The Given in Experience: Comment on Gupta," in: *Philosophy and Phenomenological Research* 79 (2), 468–474.
McDowell, J. (2010). "Brandom on Observation," in: B. Weiss & J. Wanderer (eds.). *Reading Brandom: On Making It Explicit.* New York: Routledge, 129–144.
McDowell, J. (2013). "Perceptual Experience: Both Relational and Contentful," in: *European Journal of Philosophy* 21, 144–157.
McDowell, J. (2019). "Responses to Brewer, Gupta, and Siegel," in: *Philosophical Issues* 29 (1), 390–402.
Murdoch, I. (1959). "The Sublime and the Good," in: *The Chicago Review* 13 (3), 42–55.
Murdoch, I. (1970). *The Sovereignty of Good.* London: Routledge & Kegan Paul.
Murdoch, I. (1998). *Existentialists and Mystics: Writings on Philosophy and Literature,* edited and with a preface by P. Conradi, foreword by G. Steiner. New York: Allen Lane The Penguin Press.
Nanay, B. (2014). "The Representationalism versus Relationalism Debate: Explanatory Contextualism about Perception," in: *European Journal of Philosophy.* https://doi.org/10.1111/ejop.12085.
Rödl, S. (2007). *Self-Consciousness.* Cambridge (Mass.): Harvard University Press.
Rosenhagen, R. (2018). *Experience and Belief: An Inquiry into the Doxastic Variability of Experience.* Doctoral Dissertation, University of Pittsburgh. http://d-scholarship.pitt.edu/id/eprint/35163.
Rosenhagen, R. (2019a). "Toward Virtue: Moral Progress through Love, Just Attention, and Friendship," in: I. Dalferth & T. Kimball (eds.). *Love and Justice. Consonance or Dissonance (=Religion in Philosophy and Theology, Book* 101). Tübingen: Mohr Siebeck, 217–240.
Rosenhagen, R. (2019b). "Norwood Russell Hanson's Account of Experience: An Untimely Defense," in: *Synthese.* https://doi.org/10.1007/s11229-019-02395-3.
Rosenhagen, R. (ms). "Reformed Empiricism, Rational Linkages, and Rational Contribution". Talk presented on February 15, 2020, at the *Reformed Empiricism and Its Prospects* Conference at the IIC in New Delhi, India.

Schaffer, J. (2009). "On What Grounds What," in: Manley, D., D. J. Chalmers, & R. Wasserman (eds.). *Metametaphysics: New Essays on the Foundations of Ontology.* Oxford: Oxford University Press, 347–383.

Schellenberg, S. (2014). "The Relational and Representational Character of Perceptual Experience," in: Brogaard, B. (ed.). *Does Perception Have Content?* Oxford: Oxford University Press, 199–219.

Schellenberg, S. (2018). *The Unity of Perception.* Oxford: Oxford University Press.

Sellars, W. (1963). "Philosophy and the Scientific Image of Man," reprinted in: Sellars, W. *Science, Perception and Reality.* London: Routledge & Kegan Paul Ltd., and New York: The Humanities Press, 1–40.

Siegel, S. (2017). *The Rationality of Perception.* Oxford: Oxford University Press.

Weil, S. (1977). *The Simone Weil Reader*, edited by G. A. Panichas. Wakefield, Rode Island/London: Moyer Bell.

7 Dialogical Love and Its Internal Normative Fabric

Angelika Krebs

Romantic lovers *share* what is important in their lives and are *internally*, that is, by virtue of their love, committed to contribute to and respect the other's autonomy and good life, or so I will claim. In order to understand romantic love, we thus need to understand how two people can truly share feelings and actions and what kind of obligations go along with this. Max Scheler and Edith Stein offer us some valuable insights on this issue.

In the first section, I will introduce three major models of romantic love: the fusion model, the care model, and the dialogue model. I will argue in support of the third model, which views romantic love essentially as a form of sharing.

The thoughts of Max Scheler and Edith Stein about sharing are reconstructed in the second section. I will hold that Edith Stein's perceptions, which in turn are extensions of Max Scheler's work, constitute a convincing account of collective feeling and acting, and thus of what lies at the heart of romantic love.

The third and last section will update this account on the basis of current philosophical understandings of emotion and the contemporary debate on collective intentionality.

Three Models of Romantic Love

Whether we turn to the history of ideas or look at the contemporary philosophical field, we encounter three models of love. The first sees love mainly as fusion, the second mainly as care, and the third mainly as dialogue.

According to the first, the *fusion* model, lovers seek to merge into one. A classic version of this model is found in Plato's *Symposium*. Here, Aristophanes recounts the myth of *eros*, according to which all human beings are halves searching for their other missing half in order to become whole and one again. The American philosopher of emotion, Robert Solomon, defends a modern version of this model in his book *About Love* (Solomon 1988), noting however that our need to become whole and one again conflicts with our need for autonomy, so that the romantic urge for fusion can only lead to despair. And this is precisely the problem with the fusion model: fusion and autonomy don't sit well together.

The main intuition behind the second—the *curative*—model is that lovers want to care for each other's flourishing. *Philia*, as Aristotle characterizes it in Books eight and nine of his *Nicomachean Ethics*, is a traditional example of this form of love. In *philia* you care about the other's good in life and try to do all you can to make her flourish. The best-known recent proponent of this model is Harry Frankfurt (see *The Reasons of Love* 2004). However, while parental love might indeed be mainly curative in kind, romantic love seems to be more demanding; it aims to achieve a dialogue with the other. Unrequited romantic love is a disaster!

According to the third model, the *dialogical* model, lovers wish to share their lives. This model can be traced back to Aristotle too, if we take into account that his *philia*, in contrast to *agapé*, is decidedly reciprocal and consists mainly in living together and sharing your favorite pastimes. Another classic proponent of this model is Martin Buber. In *I and Thou*, he claims that love is *between* the partners; it resides in their connection: "Love does not cling to the *I* in such a way as to have the *Thou* only for its 'content', its object; but love is *between I* and *Thou*" (Buber 1958, 14–15). Contemporary versions of this model are to be found in Roger Scruton (1986), Bennett Helm (2010), and Angelika Krebs (2015).

The dialogical model incorporates what is most plausible in the other two models: first, that love aims at a kind of union (as the fusion model has it), but one that builds upon and celebrates the autonomy of the other; second and relatedly, that love includes care for the other's good life (as the curative model has it), but primarily to safeguard the other's autonomy as a prerequisite for sharing. Dialogical love is not only the most fulfilling type of romantic love; it is also the most demanding. It needs time to develop and mature. This is not at all the case for fusion love, which is usually best when it is fresh, and even less the case for curative love.[1]

Romantic lovers *share* activities like playing music, hiking, or traveling, and feelings such as being angry or in flow. They share them not for one hour or two, but for the longer term. Furthermore, they share them *intrinsically*; that is to say, for their own sake. This kind of sharing is *essential* to human flourishing, as human nature is social and fulfills itself by sharing (among other things). Or, as Aristotle famously puts it in his *Politics*, man is a political creature and one whose nature is to live with others. Like all intrinsic activities, sharing for its own sake usually goes along with *pleasure*. Thus there is some truth in the saying that a shared joy is a double joy (as the pleasure of sharing is added to the original joy) and a shared sorrow halves a sorrow (as the pleasure of sharing reduces the original sorrow).

Dialogical love and normative fabric

To be sure, it is not only lovers who share activities and feelings. Yet in romantic love, the sharing is of a special kind. It is not only intrinsic (and pleasant, essential, and for the longer term); it is also *comprehensive* and *personal*, directed at the full individuality of the other. In contrast, think of two strangers who together carry a heavy wardrobe up the stairs; their sharing is mainly instrumental and without much regard for the particularity of the other.

Sharing is to be contrasted with, first, acting and feeling in parallel; second, mutual contagion; and third, sympathy with each other. Acting and feeling *in parallel* is doing or experiencing the same side by side, in the I-mode. *Contagion* is being causally infected or swayed by what the other feels or does. *Sympathy* differs from contagion in being intentional; it is directed at the other, but like contagion it is in the I-mode, even when it is reciprocal.

In *sharing*, the participants follow practical and affective schemes that are essentially schemes for two or more people. Think of waltzing, having a philosophical discussion, or grieving together. In contributing, the participants are directed both to the schemes (of how to waltz, etc.) and to each other, constantly attuning their respective inputs. Thus, the structure of sharing is triadic (see Figure 7.1 below).

Each participant understands her input as contributions to something *we* do or feel; accordingly, each feels responsible not only for her own input but also for the joint venture. Sharing is in the We-mode.

Let us turn to the writings of Max Scheler and Edith Stein in order to better understand how this feeling and acting in the We-mode operates.

Max Scheler and Edtih Stein on Sharing

In Scheler's *The Nature of Sympathy*, written in 1913, he introduces the idea of emotional sharing (*Miteinanderfühlen*) with his now famous example of two parents standing beside the dead body of their child and experiencing their grief together. Scheler distinguishes this shared feeling from three other types of sympathy.

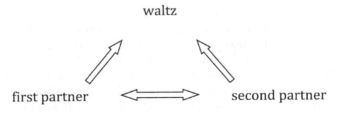

Figure 7.1

Max Scheler's Four Forms of Fellow-Feeling

The four forms of sympathy or fellow-feeling Scheler distinguishes are:

1. *shared feeling*;
2. *fellow-feeling with someone* (the "caring" form, noted above);
3. *emotional infection*;
4. *emotional identification* (the "fusion" form, noted above).

A fifth category that Scheler employs is that of *empathy* or reproduced feeling; it is not a form of fellow-feeling itself, but functions in Scheler's typology as the basis of all true fellow-feeling. True fellow-feeling includes both shared feeling and also fellow-feeling with someone; it excludes emotional infection and emotional identification. The chart below presents, in quotation marks, the definitions of these five phenomena as given in *The Nature of Sympathy* as well as the examples Scheler cites for each of them. Most importantly, however, the chart notes how Scheler analyzes his five categories with the help of three criteria, namely, first, whether the respective phenomenon is directed at the feeling of the other; second, whether it recognizes the feeling of the other; and, third, whether it participates in the feeling of the other.[2]

Although Scheler initially strictly distinguishes between empathy and the four forms of fellow-feeling, he does see certain connections between them. Accordingly, in his opinion, emotional identification both genetically and logically underlies the reproduction of feeling in empathy, which, in turn, underlies true fellow-feeling in both of its forms. These *dependence laws* are also recorded in the chart, but space prevents us from exploring them here.

The central passage about shared feeling is only half a page long. It starts with the example already mentioned of two parents mourning their dead child and goes on to contrast their community of feeling with feeling in parallel on the one hand and fellow-feeling with someone on the other. The assertion (quoted from Scheler 2009, 13 in the chart) that the parents feel their grief "in common" is specified, first, as the parents' directedness at the same value-content, and, second, as the parents' possession of the same kind of emotional keenness or functional relation. "Value-content" refers to the painful loss of the child, that is, not only the death of the child (as a value-neutral reference), but the death in terms of its meaning for the parents' flourishing (in an evaluative sense). "Emotional keenness" refers to the suffering caused by this loss. Scheler calls this keenness a "function," because for him mental feelings (or emotions) such as grief are not just states of feeling, which do not refer to anything outside of themselves, such as physical pain. Rather, Scheler understands mental feelings as "intentionally" directed

Dialogical love and normative fabric 135

Scheler's four forms of fellow-feeling and reproduced feeling	Definitions, quoted from *The Nature of Sympathy* (Scheler 2009)	Criteria: • Directed at the feeling of the other (1) • Knowledge of the feeling of the other (2) • Participation in the feeling of the other (3)	Examples
Reproduced/vicarious feeling (*Nachfühlen, Einfühlen*)	"The reproduction of feeling or experience must therefore be sharply distinguished from fellow-feeling. It is indeed a case of feeling the other's feeling, not just knowing of it, nor judging that the other has it; but it is not the same as going through the experience itself. In reproduced feeling we sense the *quality* of the other's feeling, without it being transmitted to us, or evoking a similar real emotion in us." (9)	1. intentionally directed at the other's feeling 2. perception of the other's feeling directly from their expression and not through an inference or imitation; depends on emotional identification and underlies true fellow-feeling (community of feeling and feeling "about something") 3. no participation in the other's feeling (only its quality and not its reality is grasped; does not preclude indifference, even cruelty)	- what novelists are able to do - our capacity to feel empathy with a dying bird
Community of feeling/shared feeling (*Miteinanderfühlen*)	"A's sorrow is in no way an 'external' matter for B here, as it is, e.g. for their friend C, who joins them, and commiserates 'with them' or 'upon their sorrow'. On the contrary, they feel it together, in the sense that they feel and experience in common, not only the self-same value-situation, but also the same keenness of emotion in regard to it." (13)	1. intentionally directed at the other's feeling 2. reproduced feeling (as the grasping of the quality of the other's feeling) and fellow-feeling (as the grasping of the reality of the other's feeling) are interwoven 3. participation in the other's feeling as one and the same feeling (as value-content, as functional quality, but not as function, i.e., consciousness of the different individual starting points); of utmost ethical value	- shared parental grief: father and mother mourning over the dead body of their beloved child
Fellow-feeling with someone (*Mitfühlen mit jemandem*)	"But here A's suffering is first presented *as* A's in an act of understanding or 'vicarious' feeling experienced as such, and it is to this material that B's primary commiseration is directed. That is, *my* commiseration and *his* suffering are phenomenologically *two different facts*, not *one* fact, as in the first case [the community of feeling]." (13)	1. intentionally directed at the other's feeling 2. reproduced feeling precedes fellow-feeling as a separate act 3. participation in the other's feeling as a reaction to the other's feeling, therefore involving two feeling facts (as value-content, functional quality, and function); in ethical value, inferior to that of shared feeling	- sympathy with grieving parents: friend C who joins the parents and commiserates with them in their sorrow

Figure 7.2

136 *Angelika Krebs*

Scheler's four forms of fellow-feeling and reproduced feeling	Definitions, quoted from *The Nature of Sympathy* (Scheler 2009)	Criteria: • Directed at the feeling of the other (1) • Knowledge of the feeling of the other (2) • Participation in the feeling of the other (3)	Examples
Emotional infection (*Gefühlsansteckung*)	"Here there is neither a *directing* of feeling towards the other's joy or suffering, nor any participation in her experience. On the contrary, it is characteristic of emotional infection that it occurs only as a transference of the *state* of feeling, and does *not* presuppose any sort of *knowledge* of the joy which others feel." (15)	1. not intentionally directed at the other's feeling, but unconsciously and involuntarily (with mechanical causality, but can be put in service of conscious will) 2. does not presuppose knowledge of the other's feeling 3. no participation in the other's feeling, but a flow with its own laws (that sweeps everyone along and makes them do things nobody wants to do or would take the responsibility for); of negative ethical value	- gaiety at a party - laughter of children - lamenting tone of voice of old women - cheeriness of a spring landscape - dreariness of rainy weather - plaintiveness of a room - wanting to see cheerful faces - fear infection in an animal herd - folie à deux - mass panic - revolutionary mass
Emotional identification (*Einsfühlen*)	"The true sense of *emotional unity*, the act of identifying one's own self with that of another, is only a heightened form, a limiting case as it were, of infection. It represents a limit in that here it is not only the separate process of feeling in another that is unconsciously taken as one's own, but his self (in all its basic attitudes), that is identified with one's own self." (18)	1. not intentionally directed at the other's feeling, but unconsciously and involuntarily (however, not with mechanical, but with vital causality); located in the vital I (affects, drives, passions) between body and person 2. as instinctive knowledge of others, underlies reproduced feeling and through it true fellow-feeling 3. no participation in the other's feeling and thus not true fellow-feeling, but an I-Thou undifferentiated flow; if not pathological (as in hysteria or obsession) or dumbing (as in a mass); of positive ethical value	- primitive thinking - mysteries of antiquity - hypnosis - hysteria - child's play with a doll - obsession - truly loving sexual intercourse (as gate to the life-stream) - mass (as a bad, dumbing down substitute for it) - unity of mother and baby - targeted wasp sting for the purpose of paralyzing the caterpillar in order to lay eggs in it

Figure 7.2 (Continued)

at something in the world; they "mean" something in the world, as they have a value-content, and are not just caused by something in the world.

According to Scheler, the parents' suffering is of one and the same functional quality but not one and the same function; that is, there are two functions with an identical quality. Thus, we can say that there is a sense in which there are two feelings present, namely, as two functions. In this sense, there is only a type-identity between the parents' feelings, and not a token-identity. But Scheler himself emphasizes the other meaning, in which there is only one feeling in shared feeling, as a shared value-content and a shared quality of emotional keenness. He makes this point more explicitly later on in his book. He writes:

> Even in the first-mentioned example above [shared feeling], the process of feeling in the father and the mother is given separately in each case; only *what* they feel—the *one* sorrow—and its value-content, is immediately present to them as identical.
> (Scheler 2009, 37)

How can Scheler hold that two people react with an identical—and not only in some respects the same kind—of emotional keenness toward an identical—and not only in some respects the same—situation in the world? "Identity" is, after all, sameness in every respect! To clarify this, we need to examine Scheler's view of personal community, as opposed to the three other forms of the social unit.

Scheler's Four Forms of the Social Unit

Three years after *The Nature of Sympathy*, Scheler published his main work, *Formalism in Ethics and Non-Formal Ethics of Values*. Toward the end of this volume, Scheler differentiates between four forms of the social unit:

1. the *mass*: constituted in infection and imitation;
2. the *life-community* (e.g., a family, a local commune, or a people): characterized by original coexperiencing;
3. the *society*: comparably distanced and existing through promises and contracts;
4. the *personal community* or collective person (e.g., a culture, a church, or a state): constituted in shared experience of individual people.

In differentiating these four forms, Scheler explicitly builds upon the distinction of the four forms of fellow-feeling delineated in *The Nature of Sympathy*, while also revising some aspects of his arguments in that book ("in conformity with the detailed, but not quite sufficient, preliminary work, *Zur Phänomenologie und Theorie der Sympathiegefühle*, especially its appendix"; Scheler 1973, 526). It is not easy to compare the two lots of four distinctions with each other, and Scheler himself is not much help.

Scheler names two principles for differentiating the four forms of the social unit. The first is the *"kinds of being with one another* and experiencing one another" (from the *Sympathy* book) on the one hand, and second is the "rank of *values* in whose direction the member-persons of a social unit see 'with one another'" (Scheler 1973, 525) on the other hand. The *Formalism* book distinguishes the higher ranking personal values (like the being of the person and virtue values) from the lower ranking thing-values (such as in ascending order: the useful, the pleasant, and the noble). Scheler produces this ranking of values using criteria such as divisibility, durability, dependence on other values, and the depth of satisfaction (for closer treatment, cf. Scheler 1973, 100–104).

Scheler does not doubt, for example, that the values are higher the less divisible they are. Sharing material goods (a piece of cloth or a loaf of bread) among several people is only possible through a division of these goods, for the bodily sensations (warmth or satiation) that correspond to these are located in the body. In this way, a piece of cloth is worth approximately double than the half of the cloth is. This is entirely different with spiritual values, for example, art works. These are intrinsically indivisible; there can be no "partial piece" of an art work. Art works can be discerned and felt and their value can be enjoyed by any number of people at the same time. Sensible values "divide" the individuals that feel them, while spiritual values "unite" them (Scheler 1973, 94).

The following chart reproduces as concisely as possible Scheler's complex system of distinguishing the four kinds of the social unit. The chart also marks the connections between the categories, as did its predecessor on the four forms of fellow-feeling. For Scheler, the life-community genetically and logically underlies society, which in turn both underlie the personal community.

How do Scheler's two sets of four distinctions relate to each other? This is relatively straightforward in the cases of *mass* and *emotional infection*. Both of these play practically no role in the dependence laws, but it makes sense to correlate life-community with emotional identification, society with reproduced feeling or fellow-feeling with someone, and personal community with shared feeling. Both dependence chains start with an original unity (the I-Thou indifferent stream of experience), followed by a distancing process that provides the precondition for the formation of a higher unity, a unity appropriate to human beings in terms of their autonomous or personal nature.

A detailed analysis of Scheler's definition of *life-community* confirms this reading. What is decisive here is that in the life-community, the

Dialogical love and normative fabric 139

Scheler's four forms of the social unit	Definition, quoted from *Formalism in Ethics and Non-Formal Ethics of Values* (Scheler 1973)	Criteria: • Kinds of being with one another: constitution (1), existence of individual (2), reality of the unity (3), and solidarity (4) • Kinds and ranks of values (5) • Spatial extension (6) • Temporality (7)
Mass (*Masse*)	"A social unit is constituted (simultaneously) in so-called contagion and involuntary imitation devoid of understanding. Such a unit of animals is called the *herd*, of men, the *mass*." (526)	1. constituted via infection without understanding and involuntary imitation, so that it is mechanical through sense stimulation 2. the individual is not existing as an experience 3. has its own reality and laws apart from its members 4. no solidarity whatsoever 5. no personal values, only thing-values, therefore of lower rank 6. without a fixed location 7. of only short duration
Life-community (*Lebensgemeinschaft*)	"A social unit is constituted in *that* kind of coexperiencing or reliving (cofeeling, costriving, cothinking, cojudging, etc.) which reveals some '*understanding*' of the members of this unit (distinguishing it from the mass). However, this understanding is not that which would precede this coexperiencing as a separate act, but that which occurs *in* coexperiencing *itself*. In particular, here there is no 'understanding' in whose acts a member coexperiences his individual *egoness* as the starting point of such acts; still less is the other being *objectified* (which distinguishes this unit from society). It is in this immediate experience and understanding, in which (as I have shown in the work mentioned) there is *no division* of any kind between the experience of self and that of the other or between bodily expression and experience in the comprehension of member *A* and that of member *B*, that the basic social unit which I call the *life-community* (in the pregnant sense) is constituted." (526)	1. constituted in coexperiencing (with understanding), therefore a-mechanical 2. the individual I does not exist primarily as an experienced vantage point, but rather only secondarily, through an act of singularisation; there is understanding here, but without inference and it does not precede coexperiencing; the other's being is not objectified; identical content stream of experience with its own laws and with a unified striving and counter-striving (however, with no real will, no ethos, just conventions and customs) 3. the reality of the community as primary focus of responsibility, with the individuals' co-responsibility preceding self-responsibility; therefore only representable solidarity is present (within a position in the social structure, e.g. social standing) 5. no personal values, only thing-values (welfare and the noble); therefore of lower rank 6. spatial extension of, e.g., marriage/family (including underage members and pets): dwelling-place, of the local commune: home, of the people: fatherland, and of humanity: Earth; overlapping of spatiality is possible 7. the temporality of the life-community outlasts that of the life of individual members

Figure 7.3

Society (*Gesellschaft*)	"The social unit of the *society* is basically different from the essential social unit of the life-community. First, the society, as opposed to the *natural* unit of the life-community, is to be defined as an *artificial* unit of individuals having *no original* 'living-with-one-another' in the sense described above. Rather, *all relations among individuals are established by specific conscious acts* that are experienced by each as coming from his *individual* ego, which is experientially given *first in this case*, as directed to someone else as 'another'." (528)	1. constituted in conscious acts of the mature and self-conscious individual (e.g. through promises and contracts) 2. the individual exists, understanding of others is mediated through analogical inferences (dependent on unmediated understanding of the life-community); common cognition mediated through criteria and artificial terminologies (dependent on the unmediated shared natural language of the life-community); common will mediated through promises and contracts (dependent on the unmediated common striving and solidarity of the life-community) 3. no independent reality of the unity (only artificial unity); common will only through fiction and violence (the principle of the majority) 4. exclusive self-responsibility and no solidarity whatsoever (even baseless distrust) 5. thing-values (the pleasant, like sociability, and the useful, like civilization) 6. no own space, or rather with the Earth as space of the life-communities, from which the elements of society come 7. no prolonged duration, only contemporaneity of the living
Personal community/ collective person (*Personale Gemeinschaft/ Gesamtperson*)	"We must designate as *collective persons* the various *centers of experiencing* [Er-lebens] in this endless totality of living with one another, insofar as these centers fully correspond to the definitions of the person which we gave earlier." (520) "[T]he unity of independent, spiritual, and individual single persons 'in', an independent, spiritual, and individual collective person." (533) "[T]he idea of a solidary realm of love of individual, independent spiritual persons in a plurality of collective persons of the same character (this unity of collective persons among themselves, as well as the unity of the individual person and the collective person, is possible in God alone)." (538)	1. constituted in shared experience 2. individuals are experienced, therefore dependent on society 3. the unity has its own reality (↔ sum, synthesis, construction, interaction) 4. unrepresentable solidarity, single person and collective person, each self-responsible and co-responsible, no final responsibility to the collective person (like in life-community) or to the single persons (like in society); co-responsibility of the collective person also to other collective persons beside and over it (but there is responsibility to a higher instance, e.g. God) 5. personal values (the holy and the spiritual) and in sovereign rule over life-communities (as their collective body) and through them indirectly also over society and its thing-values; collective person as highest form of the social unit; each real existing social unit is a mixture of all four forms, tendency for historical development from predominant existence in masses, to predominant existence in life-communities, to predominant existence in society, to predominant existence in the collective person 6. spatiality, e.g., of the state (as a mixed spiritual-vital, imperfect collective person; only perfect in form of nation-state): territory (overlaps not possible), of culture-nation and cultural group (as purely spiritual, imperfect collective person): culture area as a playground of influence (overlaps possible) and of church (as purely spiritual, perfect collective person): supra-spatial and intra-spatial; elevates everything 7. temporality, e.g., of the state: more durable than the people; of culture (nation and culture group): more durable than the state; of the church: eternal

Figure 7.4

individual I-being of each member is not coexperienced as a starting point (cf. the long quotation in the chart from page 526). But it is precisely this coexperiencing of the individual starting points that is constitutive of shared feeling. Shared feeling is only possible because it is based upon the distance between people, which is given in reproduced feeling. That is why—and as opposed to what is often claimed in secondary literature (e.g., Frings 1997, 101; Spader 2006, 164; Schlossberger 2016)—life-community cannot contain shared feeling. The "understanding" that Scheler emphasizes in the life-community is probably a transitional phenomenon ranging somewhere between the instinctive understanding of identification and reproduced feeling.

The *personal community* can certainly be matched to shared feeling (although feeling is more passive than free action, which is typical of the personal community). As in his analysis of shared feeling, in his analysis of the collective person, Scheler emphasizes that the communal does not result from an addition of parallel individuals, but that it represents its own reality:

> The collective or group person is not composed of individual persons in the sense that it derives its existence from such a composition; nor is the collective person a result of the merely reciprocal agency of individual persons or (subjectively and in cognition) a result of a synthesis of arbitrary additions. It is an experienced *reality*.
> (Scheler 1973, 522)

The collective person is not a collective soul substance, which Scheler maintains would be absurd; rather, it is a unity of being of acts of different kind—like an individual person—but these acts are distributed among various people. Examples of such distributed acts are questions, love or orders that, in order to be complete, demand counter acts, like answers, that the love be requited or obedience. Scheler characterizes these *social acts* in terms of their unity of sense:

> ...the ideal *unity of sense* of these acts as acts of the *essence* of love, esteem, promising, giving orders, etc., acts that require as ideal correlates responses of love, esteem, accepting, obeying, etc., in order to bring about a fact of uniform sense.
> (Scheler 1973, 536)

The Unity of Feeling in Shared Feeling

In shared feeling, the participants feel "one and the same" feeling. How should we imagine such unity of feeling in shared feeling, and how does it occur? Three answers in the Schelerian spirit are possible. The first answer refers to Scheler's idea of the I-Thou indifferent stream of experience. The second answer has the supra-individual accessibility of certain value-contents as its starting point. The third and most promising answer is oriented toward Scheler's statements on social acts and transfers these statements out of the context of the collective person into shared feeling.

According to the first answer, the participants in shared feeling fall back into the *I-Thou indifferent stream of experience*. It is the stream that creates the necessary unity (cf. Schmitz 1998; Schmid 2008). Yet for Scheler, the distance that is achieved in reproduced feeling is constitutive of shared feeling. His whole *Sympathy* book is written as a counter to monistic metaphysical attempts to remove this distance, attempts that he identifies as such in, for example, Hegel and Schopenhauer (cf. Scheler 2009, 64).

As we have seen, for Scheler reproduced feeling and with it shared feeling are in fact logically and genetically dependent on identification. But what is only a precondition or a basis for something else cannot at the same time be essential for it. After all, fellow-feeling with someone and reproduced feeling are also dependent on identification, without being in themselves identification or shared feeling. Shared feeling is more than reproduced feeling and is something other than fellow-feeling with someone. What is this more and this something other? The participants in shared feeling feel one and the same sorrow or joy, but not because they have forgotten that they are two people.

The second answer to the question after the unity in shared feeling retains the separation of the Is and focuses on the *supra-individual accessibility of certain value-contents*. In contrast to bodily pain, which is only directly accessible to the person who experiences it, spiritual value-contents, like the death of a person or the sublimity of a piece of music, are accessible to everyone who is open to the value. The lower bodily values divide us and the higher spiritual values unite us. Those listening to a piece of music at a concert are united in this good (cf. Van Hooft 1994; Guerrero 2020).

The problem with this answer is that it also takes something to be essential to shared feeling that is only its precondition. For feelings to be shared, the value-content at which they are directed has to be accessible supra-individually. Therefore, bodily feelings cannot be shared (cf. Scheler 2009, 13). But the lonely, and also the parallel and consciously parallel, and even the enjoyed consciously parallel, accesses to something supra-individually accessible is still not a shared access. If it were so, it would be hard to feel anything alone, apart from bodily sensations and idiosyncratic responses. In this second answer, shared feeling does not collapse into identification like in the first answer, but into parallel feeling. But the participants in shared feeling are not sharing one and the same sorrow or joy just because they are directed at the same value-content.

According to the third answer, shared feeling is a feeling in which the participants intend their feelings as a contribution to a joint feeling and understand the feelings of the others in the same way. A shared feeling is the *unity of sense* of different feeling contributions. It is not the sum of separately intelligible feelings plus everybody's knowledge about the feelings of the others. Shared feeling cannot be achieved in this summative fashion. Shared feeling is an irreducible category of feeling, like joint action is in question and answer or in order and obedience. The participants in shared feeling feel one and the same sorrow or joy because their feelings are contributions to a single coherence of sense. This third and most fruitful way of understanding the unity of shared feelings can be further explicated by reference to the work of Edith Stein.

Edith Stein's Development of Scheler's Approach

In *Individual and Community*, published in 1922, Edith Stein explores an example that is reminiscent of Scheler's case of the grieving parents, namely, that of a troop mourning the death of its leader. Stein distinguishes three phenomena with respect to her example:

1. *personal feeling*: a member of the troop mourns for the leader as a personal friend;
2. *membership feeling*: a member of the troop mourns for the leader as the leader of the troop;
3. *community* feeling: the troop mourns for its leader.

The third phenomenon is the one that is of interest to us and to Stein. The second phenomenon supplies the essential material for it. The first phenomenon does not play any role in it—Stein introduces it only for the sake of distinction.

Stein begins her analysis with the second phenomenon, membership mourning. According to her, the member's mourning is directed at the importance for the group of their leader's death. The member has *an intention toward the object*, which can more or less do justice to the object. We know this objective intention from Scheler, who names it as directedness to a value-object. Yet Stein goes beyond Scheler and claims that, apart from this objective intention, the mourning member also has *"an intention toward the communal experience"* (Stein 2000, 137); his mourning is also aimed at the troop's mourning as it is constituted by the individual members' contributions. This intention, too, can be more or less successful. The most we find in Scheler in this regard is that *"All* fellow-feeling involves *intentional reference* of the feeling of joy or sorrow to the other person's experience" (Scheler 2009, 13).

Stein explains, and here she is again in perfect agreement with Scheler, the manner in which community mourning is constituted by the individual members' contributions. She uses biography as an analogy. The biography of an individual is more than the sum total of all that happened in the individual's life. It is a coherence of sense in which some events are more important than others. This is true, too, in community mourning. Some individuals' contributions are more important than others'. It is the unity or coherence of sense that holds the members' contributions together and makes for the unity of community mourning:

> The relationship of the communal experience to the individual experience is constitution, not summation. If you were capable of compiling within yourself all the coalescing experiences, but you united them as a mere aggregate without inner coherence in themselves, you wouldn't be in possession of the full communal experience, any more than you get the unity of an object by merely stringing together the sensory data. You don't have a new whole instead of an aggregate of components until the multiple contributions, governed by the unity of one sense, have integrated themselves into a structure of a higher kind.
>
> (Stein 2000, 144)

More explicitly than Scheler, Stein notes two presuppositions for community feeling. The first is that the members understand each other, that they are able to reproduce the feelings of the others. The second is that the object toward which their feelings are directed is supra-individually accessible. With regard to the second presupposition, Stein even goes so far as to call the unity of all who are united in a generally accessible object but do not interact with each other a weak form of social unit. This weak form of social unit she calls "the unity of structure of experience." Stein contrasts it with mass, society, and true community, all of which she understands more or less along Schelerian lines. Stein's two presuppositions roughly correspond to the two options of understanding the unity of feeling distinguished in the last section. By making clear that both interpersonal understanding and supra-individual accessibility are mere presuppositions of shared feeling, Stein rejects these first two options.

With Edith Stein on Max Scheler's shoulders, we finally get a convincing account of shared feeling: The participants in shared feeling feel the same sorrow or joy because they both aim, first, at the same value object and, second, at their community with each other. That is, they both try to do justice, first, to the importance of their loss or gain and, second, to their common sorrow or joy, as it is constituted by all of their contributions.

Shared Feeling and Its Normative Fabric Today

The account of shared feeling presented in the last section can be updated on the basis of contemporary philosophy of emotion and the present debate on collective intentionality.[3]

Emotional Sharing

The dominant philosophical theory of emotion today is the so-called cognitive theory (e.g., Ben-Ze'ev 2000). It usually distinguishes analytically between at least three components in the unified experience of emotions:

1. *bodily feeling*;
2. *evaluative judgment* (in the wide sense, including non-propositional seeing as);
3. *expressive behavior*.
   The narrative variant of the cognitive theory (e.g., Goldie 2000 or Voss 2004) adds:
4. binding together the various components into a *narrative* that is in turn superseded by a feeling tone (or "feeling towards").

Actualizing the cognitive Schelerian account on this basis, we may say that different people share an emotion:

1. if they are similarly affected in their *bodily sensations* by a certain state of affairs;
2. if they *realize* that the others are also so affected;
3. if they *together evaluate* the state of affairs;
4. if they *together act* out their emotion;
5. if they *together "write"* a narrative with a feeling tone that transforms the irredeemably individual or parallel bodily sensations into parts of the shared emotion.
   "Together" refers to the *holist* sense of collective intentionality, already the hallmark in Scheler and Stein, and defended currently by Margaret Gilbert (1989), John Searle (1990), and Ulrich Baltzer (1999) against the reductionist camp of the We-intentionality debate that includes Michael Bratman (1999) and Philip Pettit (2003).
   While conditions 1–5 are necessary and jointly sufficient for emotional sharing, the following conditions are only typical of it:
6. that the participants *infect* each other emotionally;
7. that they together *regulate* the course of their emotion.
   In advance of the emotional episode, we often but not always find:
8. that the participants have *together built a world-view* and a language—think, for example, of the shortcuts and pet names in lovers' talk;

9. that they have *together developed emotional patterns*—think of family rituals;
10. that they have *together furnished their life* (thus inviting some moods and emotions and excluding others)—think of national styles of interior decorating like German "Gemütlichkeit";
11. that they have *together embarked on projects*—think of partners in crime and their guilt.

If this account of emotional sharing is on the right lines, strangers can also feel an emotion together. It is not necessary that they have a common history as spelled out in points 8–11, although a common history facilitates this. With a common history, sometimes one word, one look, one little gesture is enough to make sure of the shared narrative.

For an example of emotional sharing among strangers, take Otto Friedrich Bollnow's story about an audience at a lecture where everyone tries to keep their distance from each other. Yet, when the speaker happens to make a really good joke, the ice is broken. Everyone looks at her neighbour to see whether she appreciates the joke as well. And they all join together in their applause (cf. Bollnow 1995, 103).

Points 8–11 are not only unnecessary for emotional sharing; they are also not sufficient for it. Think of two lovers with a common history staying in different countries and unable to communicate with each other, when they learn about some catastrophe that has struck them, like the death of a dear friend or the burning down of their house. Their emotions will be impregnated with their common history, but they will not be shared. For emotional sharing requires real interaction between the participants. This need not be face to face. Telephone or e-mail would suffice. Merely imagined interaction, however, does not suffice. You cannot have a shared feeling alone.

The Normative Fabric of Sharing

Sharing has an *internal* normative fabric. Every participant is required to contribute his share and to respect the autonomy of the others. If he does not, he can be reproached for free-riding and domination and thus for undermining true sharing. The rules of sharing are *internal* and not external, for example, moral, like human rights that you have to respect no matter what. You are bound by the rules of sharing because you are involved in a joint practice. If, for example, you play chess together, you are bound by the rules of chess. The "oughts" of your moves on the chess board are first and foremost *not* moral oughts (although moral oughts apply in chess as well—they apply everywhere!—and can point in the same direction extensionally).

Margaret Gilbert calls these internal rules of sharing "political" (Gilbert 1989, 411). She believes that the participants in a joint practice are obliged to contribute *equal* shares. There might be social conventions, she admits, that are accepted by all participants and that transform the originally equal obligations into unequal obligations—for example, if women in sexist societies are expected to do the lion's share when it comes to emotional labor.

Gilbert is right to claim that in joint practice *all* participants are required to do their share. Yet when you reformulate this requirement as an "equal" requirement for all participants, you can easily slip into seeing it as a requirement for all to do an *equal share*, that is, to contribute equal amounts. The following example shows that this slip from equality as universality to distributive equality is unfounded: From "all people are hungry," it is fine to move to "all people, equally, are hungry" but not to "all people are equally hungry," as surely some people will be hungrier than others. Similarly, the requirement that each contribute an equal amount to the joint practice does not follow from the requirement that each has to contribute something.[4]

Rather, it all depends, first, on the type of joint practice; second, on the respective competence of the participants; and third, on how much each is interested in it. If, for example, one person invests more because he is more interested than the others, this must be possible. The others cannot be reproached for free-riding on him as long as they do not fall below the minimal or fair share required for this type of joint practice.

This also holds true for romantic love. Nevertheless, Gilbert is correct in criticizing the exploitation of female emotional work in joint practice. The normative basis for this criticism is, however, not to be found in the idea of sharing itself, with its allegedly inbuilt requirement for distributive equality. Rather, the basis might lie in the type of joint practice at hand, say, an equal partnership in heterosexual relations of women and men, or, if the type is itself discriminatory like the patriarchal marriage, then the basis is a moral criticism of this type of joint practice.

Without a broad typology of kinds of joint practice, there is always the danger of idealizing joint practice as such. For instance, Michael Bratman distinguishes between cooperative and non-cooperative types. In the non-cooperative joint practice of playing chess, for example, you act together against each other, and it goes without saying that you do not help each other out. In contrast, romantic love is cooperative and helping each other out is part of it.

In fact, the internal rules of dialogical romantic love are maximal compared to the rules of all other forms of sharing. Unlike in the example cited above of two strangers cooperatively carrying a wardrobe up the stairs, romantic sharing is intended for the long term and engaged in for its own sake, to enjoy the rich individuality of the other. The rules of romantic love include, for example, careful listening to the other and deep thinking from the We-perspective. If a lover in a mature love relationship violates these rules of love not once, by mistake, but repeatedly, he harms the other and the love that is between them. Even if he professes the best intentions and claims that his behavior does not express his inner loving attitude, he is not living up to the rules of love and therefore is unloving to a certain degree (depending on the extent and character of the violation). His lack of fairness in sharing amounts to a lack of dialogical love.

Mature dialogical love has a kind of *objectivity* that young dialogical love (as well as all care and fusion love) lack. In young dialogical love, much of the sharing is as yet only intended and thus subjective, not yet fully manifest in actual sharing behavior, which in turn is not in the hands of the individual lover. Actual sharing behavior depends, first, on the willingness of the other person and, second, on the success of their common venture. Sharing might go wrong despite best intentions on both sides. We all know this or should know it. Therefore, it is problematic to attribute to someone a loving desire to share without evidence of actual sharing behavior. Dialogical love is complete only when this behavior is in evidence. In this sense, it is, as Martin Buber formulates it, *between* the lovers and not just in the individuals themselves.

Notes

1. Cf. Krebs (2015) for a fuller presentation and critique of the three models, as well as Ben-Ze'ev and Krebs (2018) for the role of time in love.
2. For a useful survey of Scheler's distinctions, cf. Goldie's Chapter 7 (2000), which, however, fails to fully capture the phenomenon of shared feeling. For Stein's related distinctions, see *On the Problem of Empathy* (1989).
3. Cf. Ben-Ze'ev and Krebs (2017).
4. See, e.g., Krebs (2002) for further analysis of the concept of equality versus justice, and for the exploitation of female care work.

References

Baltzer, Ulrich. 1999. *Gemeinschaftshandeln*. Freiburg: Alber.
Ben-Ze'ev, Aaron. 2000. *The Subtlety of Emotions*. Cambridge: MIT Press.
Ben-Ze'ev, Aaron, and Krebs, Angelika (eds.). 2017. *Philosophy of Emotion I–IV*. London: Routledge.
Ben-Ze'ev, Aaron, and Krebs, Angelika (eds.). 2018. "Love and Time. Is Love Best When It Is Fresh?" In *Oxford Handbook on Love*, edited *by* Chr. Grau *and* A. Smuts. Oxford: Oxford University Press.
Bollnow, Otto Friedrich. 1995. *Das Wesen der Stimmungen*. Frankfurt: Klostermann.
Bratman, Michael. 1999. *Faces of Intention*, 93–161. Cambridge: Cambridge University Press.
Buber, Martin. 1958. *I and Thou*. New York: Charles Scribner's Sons.
Frankfurt, Harry. 2004. *The Reasons of Love*. Princeton: Princeton University Press.

Frings, Manfred. 1997. *The Mind of Max Scheler*. Milwaukee: Marquette University Press.
Gilbert, Margaret. 1989. *On Social Facts*. Princeton: Princeton University Press.
Goldie, Peter. 2000. *The Emotions*. Oxford: Clarendon Press.
Guerrero, H. Andrés Sanchéz. 2020 "Joint Feeling." In *Handbook of Phenomenology of Emotions*, edited by H. Landweer and Thomas Szanto. London: Routledge, 466–477.
Helm, Bennett. 2010. *Love, Friendship, and the Self*. New York: Oxford University Press.
Krebs, Angelika. 2002. *Arbeit und Liebe*. Frankfurt: Suhrkamp.
Krebs, Angelika. 2015. *Zwischen Ich und Du. Eine dialogische Philosophie der Liebe*. Frankfurt: Suhrkamp.
Pettit, Philip. 2003. "Groups with Minds of Their Own." In *Socializing Metaphysics*, edited by F. Schmitt. New York: Rowman and Littlefield, 167–192.
Scheler, Max. 2009. *The Nature of Sympathy*, translated by P. Heath. London: Routledge.
Scheler, Max. 1973. *Formalism in Ethics and Non-Formal Ethics of Value*, translated by M. Frings and R. Funk. Evanston: Northwestern University Press.
Schlossberger, Matthias. 2016. "The Varieties of Togetherness. Scheler on Collective Affective Intentionality." In *The Phenomenological Approach to Social Reality*, 173–195, edited by A. Salice and H. B. Schmid. Berlin: Springer.
Schmid, Hans Bernhard. 2008. "Shared Feelings—Towards a Phenomenology of Affective Intentionality." In *Concepts of Sharedness*, 59–86, edited by H. B. Schmid, K. Schulte-Ostermann, and N. Parros. Frankfurt: Ontos.
Schmitz, Hermann. 1998. *Der Raum, der Leib und die Gefühle*. Ost Fildern: Ed. Tertium.
Scruton, Roger. 1986. *Sexual Desire*. New York: The Free Press.
Searle, John. 1990. "Collective Intentions and Actions." In *Intentions in Communication*, 401–415, edited by Ph. Cohen, J. Morgan, and M. Pollack. Cambridge: MIT Press.
Solomon, Robert. 1988. *About Love*. New York: Simon and Schuster.
Spader, Peter. 2006. "Scheler's Moral Solidarity and the Essential Nature of the Person." In *Solidarität. Person und Soziale Welt*, 157–168, edited by Chr. Bermes, W. Henckmann, and H. Leonardy. Würzburg: Königshausen and Neumann.
Stein, Edith. 1989. *On the Problem of Empathy*, translated by W. Stein. Washington: Institute of Carmelite Studies.
Stein, Edith. 2000. "Second Treatise: Individual and Community." In *Philosophy of Psychology and the Humanities*, 129–314. Washington: Institute of Carmelite Studies.
Van Hooft, Stan. 1994. "Scheler on Sharing Emotions." *Philosophy Today* 38, 18–28.
Voss, Christiane. 2004. *Narrative Emotionen*. Berlin: De Gruyter.

8 Tolerance, Love, and Justice

Christian Maurer

Tolerance, Justice, and Autonomy

It seems just unavoidable that as imperfect human beings or, in other words, as weak agents, who live in society with other imperfect human beings, we will sooner or later be confronted with differences in values. Some of these differences, which may manifest themselves in opinions or practices we more or less strongly disagree with, we will judge to be somewhat disturbing features of the other—they will not pose, however any serious challenges to sharing society with her. We may be annoyed by her choices in fashion, or by her uncivil ways of behaving and expressing herself, but we may think of such differences as relatively unimportant and negligible. In such cases, we may resolve to adopt an attitude of indifference, thus overcoming our initial irritation.

Other differences in values we encounter, however, we may deem to be more important, more deeply objectionable, maybe even morally problematic and risking to undermine the very idea of sharing society with the other. We may be scandalized by what we see as her utterly egoistic attitudes and behavior, by her religious convictions which deny equal moral status to non-believers, by her racist and sexist comments, by her occasionally demeaning and disrespectful ways of treating others. Some of those differences in our values, which we see appearing in such behavior, we may indeed also see as conflicting with ideals of justice and equality, and as the sources of some really significant division among us. If such differences are furthermore seen as grounded in deeply held convictions, which are autonomously adopted and stubbornly defended against criticism, and not in merely irritating quirks that can be explained as the consequences of an awkward upbringing or of some bad temper, then we may ask ourselves hard questions, such as whether we really want to respect the autonomy of the other, whether we want to intervene in one way or another, or whether we want to cut off our relationship and thereby avoid the presence of the other—even if the differences in values in question may not have produced any actual harm (yet).

Under certain conditions, and within certain limits, adopting the attitude of tolerance in reaction to features which manifest deeply objectionable differences in value with others may be an appropriate, and maybe even a virtuous, albeit difficult response.[1] In the present essay, I shall argue that this is not just true in the realm of non-intimate relations among, say, citizens but also in intimate relations of love. There, tolerance is sometimes criticized to be misplaced, since it is thought to be incompatible with properly caring for the good of the other, or since it is said to involve a demeaning vision of the other which is incompatible with the vision of love.

More generally, the core of tolerance has been described as "the refusal, where one has the power to do so, to prohibit or seriously interfere with conduct that one finds objectionable" (Horton 1996, 28). Insofar as tolerance is treated as a *virtue*, it has been recently characterized as a form of "patient endurance [...] in response to some difference that divides one person from another" (Bowlin 2016, 206). Whether it be a principle of political prudence or a moral virtue, for tolerance to be an appropriate attitude, the difference in value must have, first, some minimal importance—it must reflect some normatively substantial tensions, ethical or otherwise.[2] The proper object of tolerance are not mere quirks or superficial social conventions, and tolerance is misplaced where, upon due consideration, indifference would really be appropriate. Second, however, the difference in values which is the target of tolerance must not be too deep either: tolerance or patient endurance is equally misplaced when its objects are values which are connected to practices which cause an enormous deal of unjust harm, for example. These would require active intervention, not tolerance. Where to precisely draw the limits between the tolerable and the indifferent on the one hand, and between the tolerable and the intolerable on the other hand, is a matter of never-ending debates in politics and morals.

Why be tolerant in the first place? A tolerant attitude regarding deep and objectionable differences in values may have various grounds of justification. Tolerance as a practice of non-intervention may be grounded in purely pragmatic considerations, such as an egoistic ponderation of the costs and benefits of violent intervention, or in a preference for avoiding a Hobbesian state of war, and for maintaining an admittedly imperfect, yet at least more or less pacified society. Furthermore, one could adduce epistemic reasons acknowledging the fallibility of one's own convictions and values.[3] Yet tolerance may also be conceived as a virtue if grounded in some principled respect for the wrong, yet autonomous decisions of those who live as my equals in the same society, or in considerations of justice, which are judged to outweigh the reasons for objecting and, possibly, intervening regarding the deep differences in values. Within certain limits, I may see tolerance regarding such differences as appropriate or even morally required since if I attempted to impose my own values on the other (in other ways than simply by trying to convince her that she is wrong), I would seriously disrespect her autonomy—even if I consider her values as morally objectionable. And ultimately, I may not want to live in a society where morally objectionable yet autonomously taken decisions are suppressed. Obviously, there are limits to tolerance, for example, if a great deal of unjust harm is thereby permitted: tolerating also means having a sense of the line between the tolerable and the intolerable.

Tolerance implies that there be some factor which outweighs the objectionable difference. Such may be the mentioned considerations regarding justice, or my respect for the other's autonomy. This factor does however not eradicate my representation of the difference in question as a deeply objectionable one—in other words, tolerance is not meant to collapse into indifference, and the tolerating person is not meant to bring herself to seeing the difference in question as unimportant. Rather, tolerance implies that the difference is continuously seen as deeply objectionable—and so tolerance remains an inherently difficult attitude in that it includes some persisting inner tension. The tolerant agent sees a difference as deeply objectionable yet resolves not to intervene, for reasons she deems more important. One might be tempted to think that were the tolerating person to stop tolerating and instead resolve to work herself toward adopting the attitude of indifference, drop some of her deeply held convictions, or chose to actively intervene, her life might be somehow easier since freed from the inner tension inherent in tolerance.[4]

Tolerance and Justice, Forbearance and Love?

The paradigmatic setting for discussions of tolerance by philosophers and political theorists regards deeply objectionable differences with more or less distant others. They are members of my own society, and persons whom I thus cannot completely avoid, but with whom I am also not connected with an intimate bond of love—love here taken in a broad sense, encompassing friendship, romantic love, and familial love. In the following sections, I want to shift attention to cases where we encounter deep differences in values with people we *love*—that is with people we typically know very well, we neither can nor want to avoid easily, and with whom we have bonds of intimacy which we are usually committed to keep and cultivate, even if there are some problems.

How to react if we encounter deeply objectionable differences in values with our loved ones? Can and should we patiently endure such differences, try paternalistic intervention, or end our relationships? In this essay, I want to examine patient endurance in loving relationships. At this point, we may distinguish between tolerance and forbearance ("indulgence" in French, "Nachsicht" in German). Since the concept of

Tolerance, love, and justice 153

forbearance is nowadays rather uncommon, it will require some introductory remarks, and for this I shall turn to John Bowlin's recent book *Tolerance Among the Virtues*.[5] Bowlin, an American theologian and philosopher, attempts to make sense of tolerance as a genuine virtue, and not just as one of virtue's "semblances"—that is as something that looks like a virtue but in reality isn't one.[6]

Bowlin develops his defense of tolerance as a virtue partly in critical dialogue with Paul's and Aquinas' treatment of charity, forbearance, and tolerance. In the *Epistles to the Romans*, the Apostle Paul recommends a form of patient endurance of those members of the Christian community who obstinately persist in their doctrinal errors, yet who nevertheless remain included in the circle of those we love, and want to continue loving (in some not further specified sense of the word "to love"). *Romans* 15:1 states (in the King James Version): "We then that are strong ought to bear the infirmities of the weak, and not to please ourselves." For Paul, forbearance as a human act is ultimately part of the process of fraternal correction (which may be conceived as some sort of paternalistically motivated temporary non-intervention): its ultimate goal is to bring the beloved yet erring other into the inner circles of the beloved and converted ones.

Aquinas gives us a systematic exegesis and reformulation of the Pauline Epistles, and he prepares the terrain for discussing the similarities and differences between forbearance and tolerance. Bowlin reconstructs Aquinas' position as follows:

> Tolerance and forbearance, like siblings in a family, resemble each other in important ways. Both assume a shared society of some sort and both act in response to members or to those, like strangers, who lack full standing and yet nevertheless occupy a designated role within the society. [...] Both produce acts of patient endurance in response to objectionable difference, both accent the goodness of this act, the value and respect it expresses apart from its effects, and both offer this act for the sake of the society shared with those endured and the autonomy enjoyed with respect to their differences. At the same time, these are distinct perfections; tolerance belongs to justice while forbearance either belongs to divine charity or resides in ordinary friendships.
>
> (Bowlin 2016, 212)

Setting the theological background aside, on such a reading tolerance and forbearance strongly resemble each other in that they both produce acts of patient endurance of deeply objectionable differences with other members of our societies. The two attitudes differ, however, in that tolerance is treated as an attitude that is *due*, given considerations of justice, and in that forbearance is treated as something that is a *gift*, since it is motivated by love—either by divine charity, or by some sort of natural human love (Bowlin 2016, 207). I will thus tolerate some differences out of considerations of justice and forbear others out of love. As Bowlin puts it, if both forbearance and tolerance involve an act of patient endurance, then "for the tolerant, this act comes as right and due, for the forbearing as love's endurance." (Bowlin 2016, 5)

Tolerance and forbearance furthermore differ in that the tolerant are concerned with the good of society at large, and are not motivated by the hope "that the differences that divide them from those they endure might dissolve" (Bowlin 2016, 215). The forbearant, by contrast,

> are not content with a relatively modest union of judgment and love, one that admits of distance and difference. Rather, they assume a more substantive union at the start, one constituted by mutual love and well-wishing, the shared life and common projects, that distinguish friendships, and they hope their endurance will eventually yield an ever more perfect union, one that eliminates the need for their act [of patient endurance, Ch.M.].
> (Bowlin 2016, 215)

This may suggest that tolerance and forbearance are acts of patient endurance of objectionable differences adapted to distinct realms in our lives: tolerance is for the public realm and for those we do not love, and forbearance is for the private realm and for those we love. The two forms of patient endurance also crucially differ in their goals: a state of peace, in spite of persisting deep differences, in the case tolerance, and in the case of forbearance a deeper union (somehow connected to love), where the differences are hoped to be finally overcome. For Aquinas, then, tolerance is not a real virtue, whereas forbearance is—this latter is ultimately motivated by charity or friendship-love.[7]

Bowlin himself suggests to overcome this strong division between tolerance and forbearance, a division on the basis of which some thinkers criticize tolerance as a mere "semblance" of virtue. He insists that things are more complicated than in the suggested picture. For example, friendships and other forms of love may constitute settings which generate norms that really *require* acts of patient endurance, rather than just have such endurance as a free gift (Bowlin 2016, 219–221). Furthermore, the division between private and public looks misplaced in that some so-called public relationships may well be friendship-like and thus not only require acts of tolerance but also acts of forbearance (Bowlin 2016, 221–222).

Like Bowlin, I think that a division of labor between, on the one hand, tolerance as patient endurance of objectionable difference in the non-intimate realm of non-loving and public relationships and, on the other hand, forbearance as patient endurance of objectionable difference in the intimate realm of loving relationships, suggests a dichotomy that is too strong. Especially, it diverts from the question of whether and to what extent tolerance is psychologically and morally compatible with loving relationships. In the following sections, I want to expand on these points, yet from a more specific conception of love than Bowlin.

Robust-Yet-Fragile Love

In the following, I want to sketch out a conception of love as a both robust and at the same time fragile phenomenon which is experienced by weak and imperfect agents—not by moral saints or sages. This closely ties my discussion to something which human beings may experience and try to cultivate. In the subsequent sections, then, I want to look at the potential roles of tolerance and forbearance in the context of such love. Once again, I want to think of love in a broad sense, covering the so-called romantic variety as well as the kinds of love we find in friendships and in families.

It is quite generally acknowledged that love is a deeply enriching phenomenon, from the psychological as well as from the moral point of view, yet that it also comes with specific risks, from the psychological and from the moral point of view.[8] In connection with this point, present-day philosophers often insist that loving someone is different from merely liking her in that love exhibits some exemplary depth.[9] To explain the metaphor of depth, one may point at factors such as love's selective focus (the objects of love are few or very few persons), love's robust and positive evaluation of the beloved persons and of their qualities (the persons we love and their traits are typically seen as loveable, and this evaluation is tenaciously held and defended by the lover, amongst other things by her reluctance to compare and rank the beloved one with others), as well as, especially, the profound caring about the well-being and flourishing of the beloved persons.[10]

The mentioned features strongly suggest that such love is quite a *robust* phenomenon. Love is of crucial importance for the lover, who may even treat it as constitutive for herself, and who may be committed to defend her love and her loved ones against external and internal threats. Yet love in this sense is still *fragile*. Unlike, say, "unconditional" love, "agapic" love or divine charity, it is not immune to all changes in the lover, the beloved, and their context. Robust-yet-fragile love is typically bound to reasons in the sense that at least in principle, it could be justified, and that it looks thus to the lover—if her love stroke her as completely irrational or immoral, she would typically start to question herself.[11] More generally, reasons for love may disappear or be undermined by developments in the lover, the beloved and their relationship and thus force the lover to reassess her attitude toward the other.

In spite of being a deeply enriching phenomenon, robust-yet-fragile love undoubtedly comes with psychological and moral dangers. Its selective focus, for example, may engender blindness regarding the justified concerns of others, who are outside the narrow focus of my love. Love's robust persistence may silence very reasonable doubts concerning the continuation of love, and its partiality may engender conflicts with the norms of justice.[12] Furthermore, robust-yet-fragile human love engenders vulnerabilities for those involved, on at least two accounts: first, the fact that the lover cares deeply about the physical and moral well-being of the beloved makes her vulnerable to circumstances affecting the beloved. Second, the lover, by admitting various dimensions of intimacy in different degrees, renders herself vulnerable to wrongdoing by the beloved herself. This may suggest that robust-yet-fragile love comes with moral obligations adapted to the intimate and fragile context it creates.

Deep Disagreements in Values in the Context of Robust-Yet-Fragile Love

It may happen that within the context of relationships grounded in such robust-yet-fragile love, we discover differences in values we consider deeply objectionable. This will at minimum perturb our relationships with our beloved ones, maybe alienate us from them to some degree, and possibly push us toward ending our relationships with them. We may also try to paternalistically intervene, or try to persuade ourselves that the differences in question are in reality indifferent. In yet other cases, we may resolve to patiently endure the deeply objectionable differences in values with our loved ones and ask ourselves whether robust-yet-fragile love is psychologically and morally compatible not only with forbearing objectionable differences in value (as suggested by Paul, Aquinas, and Bowlin), yet also with tolerating them (as suggested by Bowlin)? And how do forbearance and tolerance affect robust-yet-fragile love?

Consider human relationships which are grounded in robust-yet-fragile love—friendship, romantic love, love within the family. Such relationships constitute special contexts which differ from those we have with other members of the larger society—whether we do not know them at all, or do know and maybe even like them, without however loving them. An important difference between friendship and romantic love on the one hand and parental and filial love on the other should be noted: the former two kinds of love are (typically, but not exclusively) connected to relationships between equals in which choice (the choice to enter, to continue, or to end the relationship) and reciprocity play a considerable role. By contrast, the latter are (typically, but not exclusively) connected to relationships between unequals marked by differences in authority and power. Choice plays a comparatively marginal role, and ending a relationship by simply avoiding the other is not an option that is readily at hand—for psychological, moral, and legal reasons.

The mentioned robust-yet-fragile forms of love between imperfect human beings are often going to be put to the test by adversities in circumstances, and by transformations in the beloved, in the lover herself, and in the relationship. Due to the intimacy of love, and due to the physical, emotional, and moral proximity of the lovers, deep differences in values in the context of love may be significantly more pressing than they are in non-loving relationships, and situations of conflict may arise with a virulence that is not usually reached in non-loving relationships, where avoiding an irritating other is often an easier option. A beloved person, say, may develop deeply objectionable character traits or reveal hitherto hidden ones, the lover herself may transform and come to reassess her former values, the relationship may morally corrode and become harmful to both parties, or a changing social context may make the relationship and the values upon which it is grounded appear in a different light. All of these dimensions may overlap and occur together.

Crucially, these and similar transformations, which deeply affect intimate loving relationships, defy rapid and one-sided analyses. Given the nature of the relationships, such transformations must be immensely complex, and they typically give rise to very different, if equally coherent interpretations of "what really happened." Moral responsibility and guilt cannot be easily and one-sidedly attributed—loving relationships typically exist over the course of substantive time-spans and involve numerous episodes of actions and reactions, which in turn shape the persons, their relationship, their perceptions of the relationship, their perception of the other and of themselves. All this complicates the picture of deeply objectionable differences in values in the context of robust-yet-fragile love.

Deep Disagreement in Values in Robust-Yet-Fragile Love: Imagining an Example

Deeply objectionable differences in values with our loved ones may pose a serious challenge for robust-yet-fragile love. Within certain limits,[13] patient endurance of such differences may be psychologically and morally compatible with love and required if the loving relationship is to continue. For a richer discussion of this theme, I want to propose an example of a deep disagreement in values in a loving relationship—an example which is not too far-fetched and rich enough to illustrate the intricate relations between robust-yet-fragile love, forbearance and tolerance. Intergenerational constellations may well serve the purpose here, since these often combine love with value differences, some of which may be really deep.

Imagine you have grandparents you deeply love—and you know how much they love you, and have been loving you ever since your earliest childhood. You feel immense gratitude and care deeply about them and about your relationship, partly (but not exclusively) because of your shared history. However, when you grow up and your political self awakens, you start experiencing some deep differences in values with them, differences which risk affecting your "vision" of them and your feelings for them.[14] Say that several discussions have made you realize how deeply you disagree on the matter of abortion. Whereas you strongly defend a right to abortion, your grandparents strongly oppose it—maybe on religious grounds. You come to understand that this disagreement reflects some deep differences in your values. For some time, you successfully manage to focus away from it, but you sense that it could threaten your relationship. Love's inherent robustness will keep your relationship going, and you may manage to partly "explain away" the tensions in your values by invoking different contexts and individual histories, and by referring to something like the "intergenerational gap." Yet after additional discussions on the topic, you start feeling increasingly irritated, and you see a genuine risk of further alienation—your formerly wholehearted love for your grandparents has now become perturbed. You know that on the flipside, they may have analogous feelings regarding the topic and your opinions. Maybe there are even connected difficult topics which suddenly gain weight: different ideas about gender roles, about same-sex-marriage, and so on.

So here you are: you say that you are still loving your grandparents, but now—to use the parlance of our times—"it's complicated." In some of your more tired moments, you ask yourself how much you are already alienated, and you may ask yourself whether the deep differences in values, which are now in the open, are still compatible with your mutual love and with the continuation of a loving relationship. How much alienation, how much tensions and perturbation can you and your love bear? At this point, the question may arise: how much and how long can and should you patiently endure such differences in values? Are they psychologically and morally compatible with forbearance? And are they psychologically and morally compatible with tolerance? The following sections address these questions.

Forbearance and Tolerance in Loving Relationships

Imagine you adopt a simplified "Aristotelian" conception of *philia*, which is a form of love for a virtuous person that is conditional upon the virtuous qualities of the beloved. Once her virtuous qualities have disappeared or have been "washed away" by troubling discoveries concerning deep differences in values, and once you have done all that is in your power to bring your friend back on the path of virtue, you may consider it impossible and inappropriate to continue loving the person, since "not everything can be loved, but only what is good" (Aristotle, *Nicomachean Ethics* IX.3). If such a simplified "Aristotelian" account may make us conclude that continuing to love the other in the sense of *philia* is inappropriate when deep differences in values have appeared, then by the same token it tells us that *philia* is incompatible with tolerating such a deep difference within a continuing loving context.

Should you to stop loving your grandparents because of the deep difference in value? For reasons to be further spelled out, that would certainly be too radical a conclusion. However, if you take seriously the conception of robust-yet-fragile love (as opposed to a conception of love as an unconditional gift), then you may make a general concession to the simplified "Aristotelian" account of love: insofar as the virtuous qualities of the beloved are rightly said to be among the various reasons which ground your love, then the other's loss of these qualities may make you think about your loving relationship.

Now, it seems inevitable that in most lasting loving relationships between weak and imperfect humans, beloved persons will typically *not* be seen as moral saints—sooner or later, a lover will discover frailties, imperfections, and faults in the beloved. (The same applies to any non-self-deceived lover herself, of course!) In loving relationships between humans, wrongs of different kinds and degrees are likely to occur, problematic character traits are likely to be discovered, and even if love may engender an overly optimistic vision of the beloved, such "blindness" will typically not be so complete as to render all problematic acts and character traits of the beloved invisible to the lover.[15] This holds equally for loving relationships in the family, between friends, and between romantic lovers. Some (but not all) wrongs, then, may indeed be perceived as making manifest deep differences in values, and it is in these cases that the questions may arise of whether these latter are compatible with continuing to love, and whether forbearance or tolerance, within certain limits, are psychologically and morally appropriate reactions, and thus viable alternatives to ending the loving relationship.

It may be elucidating to compare the respective roles of forbearance and tolerance in loving relationships to that of forgiveness. Forgiveness is a complex moral process, the primary focus of which is an *act* of wrongdoing, rather than a continuous deep difference in values. (In many cases of wrongdoing, however, an act may be construed as exemplifying deep differences in values—rightly or wrongly so.) The aim of the process of forgiveness is for a victim to come to terms with the wrongdoing in order to become "open for the future" again—with or without the company of the wrongdoer. In the context of love in particular, forgiveness may be required to render possible the continuation of a relationship with an imperfect yet still beloved human other, if such a continuation is desired and seen as appropriate. Like robust-yet-fragile human love, human forgiveness is a fragile process during which many things may go wrong, and during which the forgiving person and the wrongdoer have to make certain steps for the moral act to properly succeed.[16]

For an example, consider two romantic lovers who both consider sexual encounters outside the romantic couple as a wrongdoing, as "adultery", and not as an indifferent act. Now one of them has committed the act, and the other resolves to forgive her. For forgiveness to succeed, at least something like regret or the willingness to change is typically required on the side of the person who has committed the wrongdoing, and on the side of the wronged there must be a willingness to see the wrongdoer not fully determined by her act.[17] Crucially, as in tolerance and forbearance, the forgiving person will not represent adultery as indifferent, but she will integrate the wrong done *qua* wrong into a vision that does not block her from going into the future. Forgiveness is one possible reaction to wrongdoing in a loving relationship, and it may be offered for the sake of that relationship, and for the still-beloved person—in case the wronged person resolves not to stop loving. Love may thus both be connected to the wrong, for example because of the vulnerability it engenders, but it may also be part of the remedy to it, for example in virtue of the relationship it creates, which provides grounds for forgiveness—within limits.

But what about the imagined example with your grandparents? Things look more complex when it comes to deep disagreements about values, where a loving relationship is seen as threatened not primarily by an *act* of wrongdoing, but by a deep and persistent value difference. Here, you may have to ask yourself the question of whether or not to patiently endure what you consider a deeply problematic attitude—either in the form of forbearance or in the form of tolerance (and maybe in combination with forgiveness).

Forbearance in Love

Under certain conditions, and within certain limits, forbearance may be a psychologically bearable and morally appropriate option to deal with deeply objectionable differences in values affecting a loving relationship. Say your grandparents do not *behave* in ways which would be beyond the limits of the patiently endurable, for example, by going out to hospitals to shame and blame women who plan to have an abortion, thus directly causing immense distress to very vulnerable persons. But they stick to their opinions and values and defend them in private discussions—as you do. The disagreement is manifest, and it is likely to endure: you are as deeply convinced that you are right as they are, and none of you are willing to change your views. You see that the resulting tensions pose a real threat to your loving relationship, and you have already felt moments of alienation. Yet you continue valuing both your grandparents and your

Tolerance, love, and justice 161

relationship, partly—but not exclusively—because of your shared history, and in spite of that occasional feeling of alienation.

If, in spite of your deep disagreement, you resolve to forbear their views (whether or not you will be successful in this), you seem to thereby assume that these are within the psychological and moral limits of what is patiently endurable. Part and parcel of your forbearing the difference is your hope that there will be a persisting and potentially again deeper relationship or union with your still beloved grandparents, in spite of the present division. You may not ask yourself how realistic this hope is, but you are willing to take regular efforts to see the loveable features in your grandparents. In analogy to forgiveness, you may resolve to see your grandparents as not fully determined by their deeply objectionable views—you try to "hate the sin, yet love the sinner," as it were. The immediate object of your forbearance will be some morally problematic opinions or character traits, which you will take efforts to distinguish from their character and person as a whole. Your efforts to forbear the deep difference in values with your grandparents may be motivated by the fact that you love and value them and your relationship, and it is your love for them that keeps you sticking with this relationship. You do not forbear because you feel under some obligation to do so, but because you still love them and care about them. In addition, you may harbor some hope that your continuing your loving relationship may make them change their views, and that there may be an again deeper union between you. Maybe the fact that you continue your loving relationship will make it easier for them to see the human faces behind the target of their strong rejection?

Of course, your love is not going to be as easy, wholehearted and untroubled as it was before your discovery of the dividing differences. But you also know that few if any robust-yet-fragile human loves are ever untroubled. Continuing to love someone while forbearing some of their flaws is difficult and engenders potential for conflicts, partly because deeply objectionable differences in values may acquire more weight in intimate loving contexts than in impersonal ones, and because these differences also endanger something of special value to the lover—a loving relationship. Still, forbearing such differences may be an attitude we adopt for the sake of a beloved person and for a loving relationship, out of a loving commitment, and in this way love's robustness may provide us with its own resources to cope with tensions that occur within the context of love.

It may be suggested that in terms of patient endurance, forbearance is better adapted to the context of loving relationships than tolerance.[18] Our forbearance is grounded in love for a somewhat estranged but still beloved other, not in impartial considerations of justice or in an abstract respect for the other's autonomy, and it comes with the hope that the loving relationship will deepen again. But now imagine that you face deeply objectionable differences in values with a loved one and you feel that you have abandoned your hope for a renewed deeper union. Adopting the attitude of forbearance is thus not an option—but is adopting the attitude of tolerance, and is this psychologically and morally compatible with continuing to love? I want to suggest that it can be—again, within limits.

Tolerance in Love

It may be doubted that tolerance is compatible with love in the first place: in virtue of its objection component, tolerance may be said to involve a view of the other as morally inferior, which is incompatible with properly caring for her. However, this doubt seems too general, if only because different conceptions of tolerance emphasize different facets of this form of patient endurance. Tolerance has, for example, been conceived in a more specific and, say, optimistic version as respecting the other person plus appreciating her different ways of life in view of the enrichment this engenders for society as a whole.[19] However, I think it is crucial to keep the idea that there are deep differences in values to which we rightly continue to object—and it is precisely here that the attitude of tolerance in a less "optimistic" version may have its place. Furthermore, the present chapter wants to specifically explore the possible roles in love of those forms of tolerance which treat certain differences in values as a moral flaw. I want to argue that robust-yet-fragile love, within limits, is psychologically robust enough to encompass tolerance (in this sense) of at least *some* deep differences, and that such tolerance (and not only forbearance) is morally compatible with robust-yet-fragile love.

Once again, the paradigm setting for philosophical discussions of tolerance (as opposed to forbearance) concerns the realm of non-loving distant relationships, where the goal is living peacefully in society with others. Here, tolerance may be said to be motivated by purely pragmatic considerations, or by principled considerations regarding justice or respect for the other's autonomy. But what about tolerance in the context of robust-yet-fragile love? According to the description above, tolerance does not include the hope that deeply objectionable differences in values will be overcome—rather, you believe that the divide will continuously exist, yet that some form of arrangement must be found.[20] Also, tolerance is not offered out of love, but primarily out of considerations of justice, or out of respect for the autonomy of the other, and it is not primarily concerned with the other's good or flourishing, but with the good of the larger society. Is this attitude psychologically and morally compatible with love?

I think that robust-yet-fragile love can be psychologically robust enough to encompass tolerating (rather than forbearing) *some* deep differences in values—complicated, unsatisfactory and risky as this may be. Tolerating such differences, unsupported by the hope that the other will change, may require more considerable efforts to see certain morally problematic aspects of the person as not fully determining her (again, along the lines of "hate the sin, love the sinner"), as well as efforts to see other loveable aspects in her. As in forbearance, you will be required to distinguish the tolerated traits from the overall moral character of a person. Given the intricacies of the situation, you may indeed be primarily motivated to make such efforts out of respect for the other's autonomy, or out of considerations of justice, and not out of love. You may feel under a certain obligation to make these efforts, and you may make them not because the other's well-being would be your primary concern, but because you think of the good of a larger group (e.g., the bigger family).

Within certain psychological limits, however, you may still be able to see the other as loveable, *in spite* of these problematic features. The danger of increasing alienation, however, is real, and something like "wholehearted", unreserved love may not be possible anymore. You will experience your love as being complicated by tolerance, and that may mean to love with a sometimes nagging awareness of the deeply objectionable differences in question—your love will not simply "blind" you to those features. But then again, you know that in virtue of the intimacy it creates, love engenders encounters with other human beings in a depth, both positive and negative, that would not be possible outside the context of love. It engenders coming to know the other more deeply, and thus also to possibly see character traits one might prefer not to see. Nevertheless, one aspect of love's robustness is precisely its capacity to cope with problematic features of the beloved by integrating them into a complex and malleable vision of the other.

The psychological and moral limits for tolerance in robust-yet-fragile love are likely to be quite narrow. The description above suggests that such love will neither bear too deep differences nor to many of them. But if such love is to some degree psychologically compatible with tolerance, is it also morally *right* to tolerate in love? Would it not be morally preferable to end relationships marked by deep differences in values, because they engender risks such as moral contagion and flawed compromises? I think that this point reminds us that there are moral limits to tolerance. However, it should not be taken to morally delegitimize loving relationships which encompass with tolerance some deep differences in values. Sometimes, robust-yet-fragile love for real human beings may simply mean having to deal with deep differences in values, and insofar as love itself is of value to us, we may not terminate a loving relationship because of the presence of such differences. In extreme cases, this tenacity of love may become morally problematic, but in other cases, we may prefer love to survive and consider as less important the fact that, therefore, we have to tolerate a moral flaw.

Robust-yet-fragile love, if its objects are real humans, will rarely ever be unclouded—but maybe that's just love. And insofar as such love has a value of its own, preserving it may sometimes not just be morally acceptable, but also desirable. Within limits.

Conclusion

I have adopted a distinction between forbearance and tolerance as two forms of patient endurance of deeply objectionable difference in values, thereby following Bowlin's analysis of Paul and Aquinas. I have also argued against a strict division of labor between the two, with forbearance reserved for the realm of intimacy (insofar as it is connected to love and personal union), and with tolerance reserved for non-intimate contexts (insofar as it is connected to justice and the good of society): adopting a conception of love as a robust-yet-fragile phenomenon, I have argued that not just forbearance, but also tolerance is psychologically and morally compatible with such love. In tolerance, we may encounter deep differences in values we can nevertheless psychologically bear without hoping to overcome them—love's capacity to integrate at least *some* such deeply objectionable differences will make us go on. And within certain limits, combining love and tolerance will be morally acceptable and, insofar as love has its own value, desirable.[21]

Notes

1. I shall here not distinguish between tolerance and toleration. Sometimes, the former is reserved for a pragmatic or virtuous attitude adopted by individuals, and the latter for a political principle adopted by institutions. In this essay, the former cases are in the foreground. On Peter Balint's distinction between toleration and tolerance as forbearance, see Note 7.
2. In this and the following passages, the treatment of toleration in Forst (2013) has been most useful—on the present point especially, see Forst (2013, 18).
3. On the reasons for tolerance, see Williams (1996, 19–23), Forst (2013, 20–23), as well as the extensive discussion in Bowlin (2016, 18–59). Kühler (forthcoming) offers a systematic discussion specifically focussing on toleration in close personal relationships.
4. It is thus not surprising that tolerance has often been discussed as a notoriously difficult attitude to adopt and cultivate—see again Williams (1996) and Forst (2013).
5. For a first description of this distinction, see Bowlin (2016, 5), and then throughout his book.
6. This is one of the criticisms Bowlin sees addressed to tolerance by various philosophers and theologians, see Bowlin (2016, 20–34).
7. Peter Balint has recently proposed a distinction between toleration and "tolerance as forbearance," which differs from Aquinas' distinction. For Aquinas, both tolerance and forbearance necessarily involve an objection component, whereas for Balint, only forbearance does, since toleration can be understood in a more neutral way. See Balint (2017, 5f).

Tolerance, love, and justice 165

8. Troy Jollimore, in his book *Love's Vision*, has suggested to treat love as "something in between," highlighting its psychological and moral resources as well as its risks. (Jollimore 2011, 23–27) Given the present chapter's focus on weak and imperfect human persons, Jollimore's approach is fruitful in that it allows to analyze different dimensions of the experience of love by such persons.
9. See, in particular, Helm (2010, 1–2; 2017).
10. For the metaphor of depth, see also Milligan (2011, 29–50). Discussions of these and similar frequently mentioned features of love can be found for example in Velleman (1999), Frankfurt (2004), Jollimore (2011).
11. This does not mean that the lover must be able to provide a list of reasons or features which "objectively" justify her love. Jollimore (2011, 26), describes love's being bound to reasons as follows: "Love is thus a matter of reason, insofar as it is a response to something external that attempts to be adequate to the nature of its object. And there is, at least in principle, the possibility of failure."
12. Jollimore highlights this point in his discussion of love, suggesting that there are two distinct and irreducible attitudes toward the value of human beings: an impersonal one, which is grounded in the impartial standards of justice, and a personal one, which is grounded in love. These are two complementary ways of seeing the value of other beings. See especially Jollimore (2011, 157–161).
13. Beyond merely pointing at examples that suggest that there *are* limits of patient endurance of deeply objectionable differences in values, I shall refrain from attempting to define these limits more precisely. As in the case of tolerance in the political realm, the precise limits of patient endurance in a loving context will be a matter of ever renewed assessment.
14. The metaphor of "vision" in love owes much to Iris Murdoch's work—see esp. Murdoch's description of the stepmother-example in Murdoch (1971, 16–19). The ideas on vision in Jollimore (2011) are however more directly pertinent to my conception of robust-yet-fragile love.
15. See especially the discussion in Jollimore (2011, ch. 3).
16. I shall here think of forgiveness roughly in terms of Griswold 2007, (62–69 and 47–59). Griswold lists several arguments for treating forgiveness not as an unconditional gift, but as a moral act which, like human robust-yet-fragile love, is subject to certain conditions of success.
17. On this last condition, see Griswold (2007, 54), on what has been termed "reframing," that is, the adopting of a specific vision of the wrongdoer by the wronged.
18. On this topic, see also the critical in discussion in Bowlin (2016, esp. Ch. 6).
19. See for example the discussion in Forst (2013, 29–32).
20. See again the similar discussion in Bowlin (2016, 232).
21. I wish to thank John Bowlin, Sarah Stewart-Kroeker, Donna Delacoste and Giovanni Gellera, as well as the editors of the present volume for their valuable feedback on earlier versions of this chapter. This paper has benefitted from the support by the Swiss National Science Foundation (SNSF), grant number PP00P1_163751.

References

Aristotle. 1966. *The Nicomachean Ethics,* translated by Sir David Ross. Oxford: Oxford University Press.

Balint, Peter. 2017. *Respecting Toleration. Traditional Liberalism and Contemporary Diversity*. Oxford: Oxford University Press.
Bowlin, John. 2016. *Tolerance among the Virtues*. Princeton: Princeton University Press.
Forst, Rainer. 2013. *Toleration in Conflict. Past and Present*. Cambridge: Cambridge University Press.
Frankfurt, Harry. 2004. *The Reasons of Love*. Princeton: Princeton University Press.
Griswold, Charles. 2007. *Forgiveness. A Philosophical Exploration*. Cambridge: Cambridge University Press.
Helm, Bennett. 2010. *Love, Friendship and the Self. Intimacy, Identification, and the Social Nature of Persons*. Oxford: Oxford University Press.
Helm, Bennett. 2017. "Love." In *The Stanford Encyclopedia of Philosophy*, edited by Edward N. Zalta. https://plato.stanford.edu/archives/fall2017/entries/love/.
Horton, John. 1996. "Toleration as a Virtue." In *Toleration: An Elusive Virtue*, edited by D. Heyd, 28–43. Princeton: Princeton University Press.
Jollimore, Troy. 2011. *Love's Vision*. Princeton: Princeton University Press.
Kühler, Michael. Forthcoming. "Toleration and Close Personal Relationships." In *The Palgrave Handbook of Toleration*, edited by Mitja Sardoč. Basingstoke: Palgrave Macmillan.
Milligan, Tony. 2011. *Love*. Durham: Acumen.
Murdoch, Iris. 1971. *The Sovereignty of Good*. Oxford: Routledge & Kegan Paul.
Velleman, David. 1999. "Love as a Moral Emotion." *Ethics* 109: 338–374.
Williams, Bernard. 1996. "Toleration: An Impossible Virtue?" In *Toleration: An Elusive Virtue*, edited by D. Heyd, 18–27. Princeton: Princeton University Press.

9 Abandonment and the Egalitarianism of Love

Tony Milligan

Introduction

In what follows I focus upon love as an emotion and do so upon the assumption that while love itself need not be thought of as a religious emotion, it is nonetheless an emotion which is often central to religion and which occupies a privileged place within Christianity. It may even be just as central to religious experience as "awe" or less flatteringly, "oceanic feeling," concepts which form part of the familiar discussions of the emotional dimensions of religious life (e.g., in Heschel 1976, 77–78). With Howard Wettstein (2015, 6–7), I will take it that love under some guise (*ahimsa*, *metta*, etc.) is equally part of the picture. This is a point about religious experience, but one which draws us rapidly into the domain of the political, given the prominent role that power relations play within religion and how they may be reinforced or undermined by religious conceptions of the rules governing "how we ought to feel." (More formally, the "normative" dimension of religious talk about love, and emotion in general.) And here I reach beyond the Christian tradition quite deliberately in order to suggest that it has no monopoly on situating love at the heart of religious life or, more ambiguously, spirituality. Even so, there is a special kind of explicit textual and liturgical prominence which Christianity gives to love, a "hypervaluation of love," in the terms favored by John Corrigan (2004, 19), with a certain kind of unconditional and constant love taken as the model. It is a model which casts a shadow over abandonment and the ending of love. Love which is love of the right sort, or an admirable sort, once begun, ought to go on.

This is a position which raises concerns about possible complicity in the continuation of relations of dominance, especially so if one ought to remain constant in the face of serious moral transgressions and a realization that the other person "is not who I thought they were." Yet it is easy here to slip from a simple critique of the way in which love's unconditionality really *can* be problematic (both personally and politically) into some more generalized hostility toward Christianity as such. The latter is not at all my aim. Although, here I write from outside of this tradition, as a stranger to it. A stranger who is perplexed by it but not, I hope, hostile. Instead, I want to suggest, and to some extent argue, that appeals to love's unconditionality and to constancy which are at home within Christian discourse, and which may be well placed there, should not be territorially ambitious. There are areas of life and love where such appeals ought not to go. In line with this, the primary focus here will be upon the normativity of talk about love rather than upon the phenomenology of experiencing love. However, it is not obvious that the one can be understood without the other. A sense of *what it is like* to be a religiously engaged agent, subject to disciplining norms and traditions, will be at work throughout.

A feeling of abandonment is one of our great fears and simultaneously one of the risks that we enter into through the love of another human. Even the love of a god, or the idea that we may be loved in turn by a god, does not escape from this danger. The few final words attributed to Jesus which appearing in more than one of the canonical gospels (Matthew 27.46; Mark 15:34) are a lament for, and questioning of abandonment by, God. Such a sense of abandonment, the definite sense of a loss of love, is familiarly associated with certain aspects of a crisis of faith and with feelings of "void" of the sort described in successively less Christian terms by St. John of the Cross, Simone Weil and Iris Murdoch (Milligan 2014). Nothing, not even the faith of Jesus, protects a religious agent from a terrible sense that love has been withdrawn. Indeed, vulnerability of this sort, coupled with a desire for constancy, seems to be integral to an openness to love such that we cannot have one without the other. Openness to love is a virtue, or a moral accomplishment, precisely because it comes at such a high risk.

In and out of religious orders, we desire to love and to be loved constantly, with no transfer or removal of affection. It is love of this lasting sort which figures in St. Paul, a love which hopes all things, bears all things, and never fails (I Corinthians 13.4). But what happens when we try (as some commentators have done) to shift the idea of such constancy over from a clearly Pauline or *agapic* love to love of a more intimate, sexualized or erotic, sort? And here I will take it that the relation between these two loves (the agapic and the erotic) is complex rather than a matter of exclusion in all cases (Milligan 2011, 59–72). I want to narrow my claim, and make it more precise, by suggesting that the shift from religious contexts in which love's unconditional constancy seems admirable, to more intimate erotic contexts, is a move which carries too many problems. And these are not simply a matter of acknowledging that talk of unconditionality is perhaps more figurative than literal. What I want to say is that if unconditional love belongs anywhere, then it still belongs elsewhere than intimate relationships. Here, I use "intimate" in a familiar sense which typically involves or, at times, tends toward physical, sexual engagement. There are other senses of intimacy, including those associated with the life of religious devotion, or notions of a personal relation to a god, which are not in play.

I will suggest that a love which is not unconditional and does *not* bear or forgive all, is *normatively* more appropriate as an exemplar of such intimate love. In our personal love lives, few of us, perhaps none of us, can truly be saints. (As much as I admire him politically, Gandhi was a terrible husband, and even worse as a father.) The attempt to spread the proper bounds of love's figurative unconditionality is liable to result in harm to others, harm to self, and block our pathway to better gender relations than those we have enjoyed in recent times. Yet, the idea of constancy which may be in place elsewhere, as a piece of spiritual imagery, haunts our understanding of intimate love such that the ending of a genuinely intimate love, even when appropriate, may well be a reasonable source of regret, something to be mourned. In practice, the ending of any love is also liable to be influenced by less-than-admirable considerations. Loving well is difficult, ending love well may be entirely out of reach.

Love's Egalitarian Constancy

Familiar articulations of Christianity do not simply hold out the promise of an affective connection to the transcendent (however understood) they also tell us how we *ought* to feel in relation to that which is worldly. Although, an attitude toward the worldly can itself be read as, *indirectly*, an orientation toward the divine. Kierkegaard's *Works of Love* (1847) and Simone Weil's *Waiting for God* (1951) advance precisely this view, with Weil drawing upon Kierkegaard. Both extend this in a way which threatens to make the indirect love of God more genuine than the love for the intermediary. "The world can never get through its head that God in this way not only becomes the third party in every relationship of love but essentially becomes the only loved object, so that it is not the husband who is the wife's beloved, but it is God" (Kierkegaard 2009, 125). This exclusivity is, however, uncharacteristic of Christian approaches, which also *require* a genuineness of felt love for other humans. The relevant Christian norms for feeling include a generalized requirement for love. To lend plausibility to the case for such a conception of love, I will treat it as (1) something which can be at least partially disentangled from any heavy ontological commitments; and as (2) a requirement which can, up to a point, be fused with liberal sensibilities in the best sense of the latter, a sense which is consistent with the acceptance that there are moral truths. In particular, it can be fused with a valuing of others *as equals*, as equally worthy recipients of love.

While the sheer generality of the requirement to love others may suggest that it is best understood as a non-cognitive response, perhaps expressive rather than a way of tracking some properties of the world, the Christian tradition provides narratives which suggest (and perhaps entail) that this is not so. Love is embraced as a *recognition* that self and others are part of God's creation, indeed that we are *equally* a part of God's creation or, more figuratively still, that we are *all* God's children. Yet even with such narratives in place, the lack of variability, the very fact that the requirement for love does not change from situation to situation, meshes poorly with our familiar experience of feeling and caring. Our regular patterning of emotional experience, and especially of love, is context sensitive, partial, and particularistic. We feel in very different ways toward different individuals on different occasions. Phenomenologically, loving x does not feel quite the same as loving y, even if x and y are both loved as close friends, or as one's children or as others with whom we are sexually engaged. It would be odd, even a little unwelcome, if my love for the friend from university, who still sends me Christmas cards, felt the same as my love for a lost friend, someone from primary school, someone now dead but still loved. And the difference here is not only the presence of grief in the one case and its absence in the other. The feeling of love itself alters with contingency and circumstance. And so, while the Christian injunction to love may be uniform, love itself feels anything but uniform. Of course, the phenomenology of love may differ, while the love remains the same. Anger too feels very different from case to case without ceasing to be anger. The whole point of appealing to a cognitive component of emotions is so that we do not have to segment them by appeal to the sameness of feeling. However, with other emotions, such as anger, we are not called upon to feel it toward everyone. Nobody says "be angry at everybody." There are bounds to the different sorts of anger that we may feel toward others, and how we experience it. When love follows this same pattern of seeming very different from case to case, we may expect it to be similarly bounded and linked to contingency and circumstance, also, perhaps, vulnerable to changes in the latter.

Yet there is something beautifully appealing about the Christian vision of love's unwavering constancy. It offers a guarantee that we may all remain suitable recipients for love, no matter what we do, and no matter how far we may fall from grace. The appeal of such constancy is all the stronger when we see what it looks like in generously constructed exemplars, which situate love in ordinary, everyday, contexts. Rai Gaita, in an example which is regularly cited in discussions of the philosophy of love, and which draws upon a modified Christian paradigm of love, recalls his early years as a hospital porter. He watched in the background while medical staff treated patients with respect, but such respect did not entirely or fully exclude a sense of personal superiority (2002, 17–24). Gaita's suggestion is not that the doctors were callous. Many of us have felt much the same when visiting a dementia ward. Our respectful care is mingled with something else: relief, apartness, a sense of the world of the dying as thankfully alien. And here, the respect for the other and the reassuring apartness of our belonging to the world of the living are not easily disentangled.

In the Gaita case, such a respectful response, with its attendant sense of apartness, compares poorly with the attitude of a hospital visitor, a nun whose love for the patients carried no trace of condescension or superiority, no sense of *ressentiment*, or *being better than they*. Hers was, in each instance, a response to an equal, a reassurance of care no matter what, a love which was "unconditional" (Gaita 2002, 22). The story is agapic, with an acknowledged connection to Christian theology, but secularized by Gaita via the idea that such love is a response to, and recognition of, a common humanity rather than a mode of relating to God (Gaita 2002, 20–21). However, the dominant line of religious influence upon this conception of love is clear and it might be argued, with Kierkegaard and Weil, that such love has a mixed intentionality, that it is partly about the humanity of the other and partly an implicit attitude toward God. Alternatively, we may even rethink or demythologize accounts of Christian agape in the light of this approach, not as an impossible desexualized ideal, but as attempts to tell a tale about our shared humanity, or at least about the shared and apparently egalitarian lovability which each of us retains when all else is gone, and when all other hope is lost. And here, talk about our all being God's children may seem to capture matters better or "more naturally" than forced talk about our "lovability." We may then understand why direct talk about love and humanity sometimes fails, and why a more indirect route may be preferable.

While it requires no worrying ontological commitments, the loving response of Gaita's nun still points in the direction of a peculiarly saintly conception of love even if it is not itself love of this sort, love of the most absolutely demanding kind. We might even be tempted to wonder about whether it is appropriate to think of it as love at all, rather than some proximate emotional response such as compassion. What, after all, is there to connect such a felt identification with virtual strangers in hospital beds to our familiar understanding of love as a response to a history which is usually shared, a response which is inseparable from a genuine grief upon the death of the other? Perhaps we might grant that Gaita's nun was very good with the patients and had a better bedside manner than any of the doctors. Perhaps she was compassionate and truly egalitarian toward them, but it would be odd to imagine that she would have experienced a genuine sense of bereavement upon their death. Sadness yes and a reminder of her own standing as equally mortal. But there is a significant difference between feeling sad over the death of a stranger or acquaintance and experiencing the terrible void of grief upon the loss of someone we love. Yet here, we may argue that the love of the nun is, in a sense, a love of humanity (with which we all have a long history) rather than a more or less sudden love of the stranger in the bed. The price that we would pay for such a move is the loss of some of the admirable particularity of the nun's loving response, the sense that it is not simply a *response to* an individual but also *about* that individual more than it is about anything else. Love's recipient fuses instead into the democratic mass of humanity where they become more anonymous.

Let us now suppose we shift the focus of our own attention away from anything so directly, outwardly, spiritual as the nun's love. Let us do what Gaita does not do and shift it toward a kind of love which is altogether more intimate (in the specified paradigmatically sexualized sense) yet tries to retain the same sense of absolute unconditionality. This may seem to take us not only beyond Gaita's nun, but beyond the bounds of St Paul and into the erotic, an arena in which a Christian or Christian-influenced conceptions of love are not always comfortable. This is, of course, a subject on which a great deal of ink has been spilt, and so I shall simply affirm what has been said many times before: that an overly strong separation of eros and agape presents an entirely implausible, ungenerous, and unlivable account of Christian love (Benedict 2006, 24). Those, such as myself, who are in some sense outside of the Christian tradition, not by standing (impossibly) outside of its influence but in the sense of rejecting core doctrines or (in my case) feeling unmoved or hopelessly confused by some of its imagery, do the tradition a disservice and do not understand it if we latch onto this as an easy line of attack. Yet there are contexts (such as the love of Gaita's caring nun) which are more clearly agapic, in the Pauline sense, than intimately erotic. And what is involved here is not simply a matter of bodily engagement, or spiritual love versus a flesh-bound longing. True, the nun may be ready to take the patients' place, but she does not want to climb into bed with them. However, there is more to the difference between her love and intimate sexualized love than this. At the risk of presupposing "what we all know," the boundary here is a familiar matter of different ways of being emotionally engaged, and differences in the lived-experience of love more generally.

Transferring Spiritual Constancy into the Intimate Domain

Gaita's nun loves admirably and well. Or, at least she does so if she truly loves at all. There is a great deal to be said for loving in this way, however difficult it may be to accomplish. It seems far beyond me, but still a real possibility. What I regard as problematic is not this, but rather the temptation to make sense of love in the domain of a more intimate love in a way which mirrors the unconditionality of love in Gaita's more religiously shaped exemplar. The best, or at least clearest, example of this is a move which Kamila Pacovská has made in a paper on "Loving Villains: Virtue in Response to Wrongdoing" which extends Gaita's love

Abandonment and the egalitarianism of love 173

into the intimate domain in order to argue that a more saintly agent will defensibly respond to others as equals through an unconditional *intimate* love, even where the beloved has been guilty of some dreadful transgression. "What enables saintly characters to treat such people as equals, without superiority of condescension, is a belief in equal human worth that doesn't derive from deserts and a conception of themselves as equals and fellows even of the least deserving" (Pacovská 2014, 138). I will take it that Pacovská is tapping into a more widely held intuition about how Christianity might inform a conception of intimate love, and doing so in an effective way. Indeed, St. Paul's guidance on love often seems to be read in just this way, as a guide to how we ought to treat our nearest and dearest rather than a guide to human conduct more generally.

Drawing upon the Christian-influenced account of love set out by Gaita, Pacovská has tried to bring the demanding idea of a saintly or near-saintly *intimate* love into sharper focus. Love, of the relevant sort, must persist even in situations of disillusionment about the other. It is patient and does not abandon even the most dreadful of criminals, even those who have been guilty of awful transgressions up to and including moral evil. Instead, it recognizes the flawed, imperfect but abiding humanity or lovability of the other. Pacovská's examples are literary and my response will draw upon the same literature. Such love is approximated by the patient and forgiving wife of Banker Bullstrode in *Middlemarch*, a woman who has to cope with the disclosure that her very proper and religious husband made his money by criminal means. (She must also cope with the suspicion that he may have, in some sense, permitted a former accomplice to die.) Such unconditional, or at least unwavering, love is approximated even more closely by another of Pacovská's examples: the long-suffering Sonia in Dostoevsky's *Crime and Punishment*. The man she loves, Raskolnikov, has killed a money-lender and he has killed Sonia's only friend at the scene of the crime in order to cover up the first dreadful deed. He has done something terrible to his own life and, in the process, has wounded Sonia dreadfully. Yet Sonia continues to love Raskolnikov, even in his failure to repent and even though, in her case, the wounding is deeper and more personal than it is with Bullstrode and his wife. Sonia does not know how to love distantly. There is a raw immediacy to her pattern of care.

The more such characters have to understand or to forgive, the more saintly their love has to be. When each in turn finds out that the person they love has transgressed, they do not withdraw their affection. They do not cease to love. Nor is the continuity of their affective response simply a matter of propriety, even in the case of Bullstrode's wife, Harriet. They do not continue with an outwardly correct but inwardly cold attitude toward the transgressor. Rather, love's passion deepens as they embrace a joint suffering with their beloved. Such sharing is expressed in all manner of simple ways. This is a love which seems to endure a great deal, understand a great deal, and forgive a great deal. And, notwithstanding a certain fear about romanticization, how could we not admire such a love? Yet Iris Murdoch, who we expect always to be on the side of love, suggests something which, very pragmatically, points in a quite different direction: "Falling out of love (with a person, possession or activity) is a skill we should all have access to" and in her own novels we see this skill regularly deployed (Murdoch 1993, 331). But how could we not admire something more constant than a love which permits (perhaps requires) inconstancy or even abandonment? The very possibility of the latter may seem to suggest that what we may have regarded as love has been, all along, flawed in its intentionality, mistakenly attached to something inessential, to a quality such as good looks which may easily be lost (Vlastos 1981). There is, after all, something suspect about at least some loves which are withdrawn after changes to the beloved, or after the disclosure of new information.

To see what such a flawed attitude might involve in practice, Pacovská contrasts the above, differing, examples of loving constancy with the shifting affections of Miss Elizabeth Bennett in *Pride and Prejudice*. Elizabeth begins to have feelings for the charming Mr. Wickham when he is well regarded by all around him but then abandons those feelings as soon as she finds out his true, that is, manipulative, cunning, self-serving and dishonest, character. Elizabeth's inconstancy, upon the discovery of Mr. Wickham's true character, although it carries no overtones of betrayal, looks suspiciously like an instance of what has been called "*trading-up*" in the literature on the philosophy of love. That is, abandonment of an emerging attachment in favor of a better deal, a love object which is more worthy (Jollimore 2011, 17). Yet, curiously, this may serve as an example of a transferal of affections *at its best*, in a case where our sympathies are utterly engaged. We, the reader, tend to think that Elizabeth has made the right move. She ought not to be with Wickham, but with someone else. Perhaps even the much-misunderstood and rather handsome Mr. D'Arcy. However, the example is used by Pacovská to highlight the greater accomplishments of the constant lover. In particular, the accomplishment of seeing the wrongdoer as an equal. The valuation of the other does not waver upon the discovery of a great fault.

Instead, I want to suggest that while there really *is* an illuminating shortfall in Elizabeth's affections, it is *not* a shortfall which involves any lack of saintly persistence. Elizabeth is *quite right* to shift her affections, even though what motivates her to do so is arguably mixed, and not entirely admirable. But I also want to concede that there is a problem here, a gray area involving cases of very different sorts. It makes perfectly good sense to say that there is *often* something bad about no longer loving someone in an erotic way when one finds out a new piece of information or even if they undergo certain kinds of character change or identity change. If someone asks about the small green prayer book on the bookshelves, then says "I could never love a Jew," and promptly leaves their partner, something has gone badly wrong. Or, if someone can no longer love their spouse because the latter has come out as transsexual and they happen to hold to some rather unpleasant views about gender, then the end of the love is surely reprehensible. The *reasons for no longer loving* in both cases are bad reasons. If, on the other hand, someone takes steps to end an intimate love or perhaps to change it into love of another sort, because of their own sexuality and the fact that the kind of desirable intimacy which is integral to their contentment can no longer be achieved under new conditions, that is, a different matter. The heart wants what the heart wants. Under changed conditions, it may not want what we or a previously loved other have to offer. The changes need not involve moral transgression, although they do need to be major enough to change the way that one sees the other. (If Suzanne leaves me because I have watched Australian rules football more often than Gaelic football, that would be odd. Or, if she leaves me because a new book has been badly received by critics, that would be odd as well.) My point here is *not* however, about the value of constancy in the face of certain kinds of alteration, even alterations which are bound together with transgression. Rather, it is about a problematic transfer of saintliness into the intimate domain. The transgender case just mentioned relates to a major change of identity but does not call for saintliness. Similarly, there would be something very worrying about any attempted saintly response by Elizabeth Bennett. She should not be in the business of "saving" Mr. Wickham nor should she endure his dishonesty with love intact.

Articulating Concern about a Saintly Intimate Love

There are significant reasons for concern about the kind of saintly, or near-saintly, love which Miss Bennett conspicuously fails to show. Most obviously, it is all very well for a character in a novel to love in this unconditional and egalitarian way, but we might not want anyone we truly cared for to do so in real life. This familiar point, from Susan Wolf (1982), is an objection to the pursuit of moral saintliness more generally, although it does not detract from our admiration for moral saints, but only from the *promotion* or *pursuit* of such saintliness. The fact that a certain pattering of affective response is simply too demanding to be either recommended or required need not, after all, detract from the accomplishment of those who, somehow and against all odds, make the grade. We might not want a loved one to lead such a life of sacrifice, even though such a life could itself be admirable. Other concerns may lead us to believe that Iris Murdoch may be right about the deep importance of learning how to fall out of love, a standpoint which happens to be convenient for Elizabeth Bennett. It would, after all, be deeply egocentric to desire that someone we love should continue to love us even if we should betray ourselves by becoming morally monstrous. It is tempting to say that we *ought* to want them to protectively cease their loving, or at least cease to love us in the same intimate erotic way, if such a thing should ever occur. This may even be integral to intimate love, as it is ordinarily understood. Part of my loving my wife Suzanne, in the intimate erotic way, is that I desire her well-being and do so in a deep manner. But if I truly desire her well-being, then there are counterfactual circumstances under which I would desire her to walk away for her own sake. (Even if my desires might also conflict if such a moment were ever to arrive: I would want her to, and not want her to. My heart would be so unsure.)

Considerations of this sort can, of course, be used to suggest a self/other asymmetry: Suzanne should not love a monstrous me, but perhaps I should still love a monstrous she. The reader admires Sonia for continuing to loving Raskolnikov, but our opinion of Raskolnikov would not be improved if, at the end of the novel, he felt that he was still entitled to her love. However, perhaps this option, of lifting a self/other asymmetry from such imagined scenarios, runs too great a risk of a slippage toward a self-aggrandizing conception of what we expect ourselves to deliver in comparison to the imperfections of others. And this may lead us to lean more in the direction of regarding an unconditional constancy, on the part of either party to an intimate relationship, as a commitment of the wrong sort. We may then suspect that a continuing intimate love, upon the disclosure of some terrible transgression, is often inappropriate because (1) the transgressing agent simply ceases to be an appropriate object for the *kind* of love in question, although a shift toward something less personal and more akin to the agapic love of Gaita's nun may still be possible (even if its wisdom is a contingent matter); or (2) the transgressing agent remains a suitable object for such love *but perhaps not from the person in question*. The very attempt to sustain an intimate love with the transgressing agent could involve hubris, a reaching beyond our limited erotic capabilities. Instead, and in love of the intimate sort, perhaps we should respond *at* or *close to* what Murdoch intermittently refers to as our own moral level. Just as Elizabeth Bennett does, although her attachment to the rogue Mr. Wickham may be weaker than a true intimacy of sufficient depth for the problem to fully arise.

Does this introduction of conditionality within intimate love leave us only with a love that is second rate, unstable or otherwise unreliable? This is one way of picturing matters, but not necessarily the most generous way. Alternatively, we may embrace the fact that a love which is continually renewed even though it carries no ultimate guarantees, and does not promise everything, has its own kind of fragile beauty. I may not want Suzanne to love me unconditionally, but I certainly want her to continue to love me indefinitely, into a shared future in which I give her no great reason to walk away, beyond the ordinary reasons that humans give to one another on a daily basis. I may even suspect that any love which was structured otherwise, any truly unconditional love, of Suzanne for me, was not really about me at all, the me who changes significantly over the course of time, and often within a single afternoon. "There is," as Martha Nussbaum points out, "a beauty in the willingness to love someone in the face of love's instability that is absent from a completely trustworthy love" (Nussbaum 1986, 420). Here, we may again run an argument that risk is the price of accomplishment, an intimate and personal love without risks, with guaranteed constancy, may then seem to be the kind of love which is actually lacking in an important way.

Something of this sort may be true, but even these considerations do not entirely go to the heart of what is *most obviously* worrying about cases like those of the admirable, forgiving and sacrificial Mrs. Bullstrode and Sonia. They do not go to the heart of concerns about gender, which the image of loving feminine sacrifice raises. It is, first, notable that all the obvious exemplars of such a sacrificial love, even Gaita's nun who contrasts with the male doctors, are female. Their kind of constancy may then look worryingly like a license for the continuation of abusive relationships. Constancy of this sort may even lend itself to a strong "feeling rules" reading of love as a religiously informed emotion where the feeling rule in question is that *thou shalt stand by thy man*, and where the formulaic language of "feeling rules" itself seems appropriate because it carries overtones of an affective subservience to authority: the authority of institutions, the authority of God, the authority of a husband, the authority of love itself (Hochschild 2003, 56–75). The role of women within such a picture of loving agency is pivotal, not marginal, but it is captured by the pieta and by dolorous resignation. Again, this may be good imagery for a novel, we may like Sonia more than Elizabeth Bennett, but that is not enough to turn her way of loving into a good design for life, at least not for those we love (in any sense).

Less obviously, a concern may be raised about equality and about the extent to which such a love can truly be married to liberal egalitarian norms. This is, perhaps, a problem of a deeper sort. One which strikes at the heart of secularized versions of any attempt to take an agapic, Gaita-style love out of the place where it is at home and use it as the model for loving intimately. Unlike the situation for Gaita's nun where equality with the other is absolutely pivotal, in cases such as that of Mrs. Bullstrode and Sonia, there are senses in which the possibility of a genuine relationship of equals has been irretrievably lost. (Unless they too have evil-doing histories about which their authors say nothing.) In these texts, love may continue, and it may continue as intimate love and not the *agape* accorded to strangers, but the nature of the love *does* change and must change in order for the texts to remain exercises of the imagination rather than sheer fantasy. There is a shift into the relation of lover to loved as something maternal, albeit paradoxically so. Paradoxically, because, in the case of Sonia, the sacrifice also expresses something child-like (although perhaps not anything innocent). Here, as parallel cases, we may think also of the prominent late-19th and early 20th century French exemplars of spiritual and erotically charged female sacrifice: the images of Bernadette Soubirous and Theresa of Lisieux, true unto death, simultaneously childlike and maternal, with the model of Joan of Arc at no great distance in the background. Similarly, the forgiving Harriet Bullstrode is strictly maternal but the more complex, saintly and childlike Sonia, who has herself endured so much, *becomes* the "little mother" both to Raskolnikov and to his fellow offenders.

This retains an appealingly sacrificial dimension, but it does not look at all close to the best way for intimate relationships to go. It does not look like the kind of love which anyone ought to recommend or cultivate as the best of its kind. Instead, it is what is left when one of the partners fails to grow up, or else when something goes dreadfully wrong and a great imbalance is then introduced. Egalitarianism may be a great strength of the Christian influenced agapic loving response of Gaita's nun, but it turns out to be far more problematic with an intimate love whose unconditionality is brought into the open as a result of some manner of radical moral failure.

These critical points about gender and equality are simultaneously ethical and political. They may jar with an outlook which seeks to keep intimate love and politics rigidly apart from one another, or which is altogether more suspicious of the idea that a broadly liberal outlook upon life constitutes the right kind of politics. They also clash with a deep level of admiration for the saintly Sonia, and for the long-suffering Mrs. Bullstrode, which is there because their authors tap so effectively into our attitudes. Not only our attitudes toward femininity and sacrifice, but also our own personal abhorrence of (and no doubt also our fears of) abandonment. In a sense, it is easy for us to admire Sonia more than we admire the sensible Elizabeth Bennett (who has been less challenged by life), but this may say more about what it is to fear abandonment than it does about what is involved in loving intimately and in the best way. The very thought of abandonment is so terrible a prospect that we hesitate always to endorse its legitimacy. In this sense, ideas of constancy from more agapic images of love and devotion exercise their force. We are even familiar with narratives, perhaps even personal experiences, in which a former partner, the one who has *actually* walked out, nonetheless feels drawn to say "You left me years ago," or "Our marriage was over long before I went," in order to avoid the impression of deserting a living relationship, or abandoning another who remains worthy of love. And when someone, again someone awkward like Murdoch, someone with the power to slip a little sand under our shells, asserts that "Heavenly love is unlike Earthly love. Christ broke up families" (Murdoch 1993, 144), that the apostles effectively *walked out on* their loved ones in order to follow a spiritual leader, we insist that the texts be read otherwise, in a more generous manner. It is abhorrent that this should be, in any straightforward sense, simply true. Similar tales of Buddha's abandonment of his wife and child cannot be allowed to stand on their own, they must be rescued, redeemed by the supplementary narrative device of a later encounter where both heartily endorse his wise decision. My point here is not to say that this was the wrong thing to do in either of these very special cases, and there is certainly a better argument in favor of these instances of abandonment than there is for someone leaving their family to go off to a tropical island in order to paint and make merry with the locals. Even so, the harsh side of *moving on* is difficult to come to terms with. Abandonment of any sort has a bad reputation, and we might wonder how the curtailment or redirecting of love away from those we love in an intimate manner could ever escape from such worries.

The Trouble with Elizabeth

As a partial, incomplete, response to such concern, I will suggest that we need to distinguish between the ending, or redirecting, of love and its regular disreputable accompaniments. That is, false narratives, misrepresentation, recrimination, defensive hostility, and dubious motives. A sensitivity to the latter can constitute a strong line of defense for saintly constancy even in the face of situations of disillusionment. It is, I want to suggest, sensitivity of this sort, rather than love's inconstancy per se, which warrants concern even in the Elizabeth Bennett case. If we begin to suspect that the constant, loving Mrs. Bullstrode and Sonia (who loves not just a flawed being, but an axe murderer) really are dangerous exemplars, and that Elizabeth Bennett was quite right to curtail her emerging love for a mere scoundrel, what then? Does it follow that Elizabeth's motives for curtailment were necessarily of the right sort, that she was implicitly or explicitly following a better set of norms or (more narrowly) rules for feeling, or in some way escaping from the constraint of such rules? This is far less obvious. Perhaps what drives our sense that, in this contrast, the constant and saintly lovers are *more* to be admired is the recognition that in a case such as that of Miss Bennett, a problematic pattern of affective response really is in play.

More specifically, I want to suggest that a disturbing parallel may be drawn between her affective responsiveness and a similarly problematic pattern of affective responsiveness identified by John Corrigan in his classic study of feeling rules among the mid-19th-century Bostonian Protestant elite (Corrigan, 2002). Corrigan draws out the respects, in which an ideology and practice of emotionally charged religiosity was shaped by the model of the stock exchange, with the enthusiasm of the black revivalist congregations constituting a dangerous threat of speculative boom and bust, while the dissipation of the Irish Catholics threatened stability. Within this order of things, love of the right, moderate and rewarding sort, constituted a suitable investment of one's limited emotional currency. To marry well was to make a good investment in one's future. To marry badly was to slide from a reasonable risk-taking into sheer gambling. This is a far cry from our familiar shaping of preferences in line with a conception of what, and who, can make us happy. Instead, the market is a model for morality. Again, the lines between norms of intimacy and political critique of societal norms become blurred.

Does any of this critique sound familiar in the case of Miss Elizabeth Bennett? There is certainly nothing so crude as the financial calculations of surrounding characters: friends, relatives, acquaintances. Guidance by explicit financial projection would be too obvious and cut-rate. It would involve one or several thoughts too many. Deliberation of the sort that her mother continuously and rather too openly makes. Instead, Elizabeth follows her heart, but exactly what does her heart follow? Partly, her heart tracks virtue, or at least good looks and virtue. But this alone does not remove suspicion. The hearts of agents often look for love in places which still give us reasonable grounds for concern. We may think here of those who sincerely and wholeheartedly come to love others who look suspiciously like themselves, or like younger versions of a favored parent. We may be inclined to suspect that although she follows her heart, and the heart wants what the heart wants, there is nonetheless a deep level at which Elizabeth remains mired in the same affective predicament as the novel's other financially insecure agents. Hers is not a marriage of convenience, but it is nonetheless a very convenient marriage. Indeed, this too is an aspect of Austin's novel as social critique. It is part of her genius that she shows us a character who falls in love with precisely the person that we, the reader, want her to fall in love with but who, in doing so, shows a keen appreciation of the rules of the game.

There are even tell-tale points in the novel where a disturbing set of rules for emotional engagement seems very close to the surface: in Elizabeth's resistance to her mother's favored ordering of a good match followed by love afterward; in her response to her sister about *when* she first realized that she loved D'Arcy, she replies, jokingly, that it was upon seeing his grounds at Pemberly (respectively in Chapters 6 and 59). We may also note the reasonable concern of her father after she finally accepts D'Arcy's proposal, concern that she really is sacrificing herself nobly for the good of the family by marrying someone proud, disagreeable but well-off (Chapter 59). Austin repeatedly directs our attention to the fact that Elizabeth has done exactly what the socio-economic realities of the day tell her to do, and exactly what other characters see her as doing. She has genuinely and wholeheartedly fallen in love with the best and happiest of all investments in the future. Her prior inconstancy may be justified, and she does get the right man in the end, but a deep level of her motivation remains open to question. This, I suggest, is an utterly familiar phenomenon, a justified redirecting of love from here to there, from one person to another, which is accomplished in a way that brings ordinary and familiar human flaws into play.

There are, of course, all manner of problems which might be raised with the example. We can reflect that Elizabeth's earlier attachment to the wrong man was only in its early stages when it was nipped in the bud, and that she did not abandon a life partner of many years standing. But can we not just as readily think of cases where "staying the course" is also destructive? Are we not familiar with loves which can do no good for those involved, and old loves with which ourselves could do nothing good? Loves which stood no chance of leading anyone upwards? Destructive attachments, loves that agents like us are not obviously equipped to turn into something better, attachments in which agents like us may even become addicted to the suffering. Less generous readings of Sonia's love may lean in this direction: she wants to punish herself for the way in which she has been forced to earn her living. In such cases, the sharing of a protracted history may even make matters worse, more bound to inertia, and less likely to succeed. There may be people who can only hurt or only be hurt by us because of the way in which the relationship has become sedimented over time. And here, while it may always seem open to us to continue to love only from a safe distance, the love itself can tend to draw agents together. The least harmful option which is also workable may then be to follow something much closer to Murdoch's approach and to fall out of love, or rather give ourselves the opportunity to do so, and not to resist so much if, over the course of time, the bonds of love begin noticeably to dissolve.

Acknowledgements

The publication was supported within the project of Operational Programme Research, Development and Education (OP VVV/OP RDE), "Centre for Ethics as Study in Human Value," registration no. CZ.02.1.01/0.0/0.0/15_003/0000425, co-financed by the European Regional Development Fund and the state budget of the Czech Republic. An earlier version was delivered at the 2015 Christian Philosopher's Conference, St. John's Seminar Wonersh. Thanks go to Kamila Pacovská for comments at earlier presentations of the chapter and to Rai Gaita for clarification of the scope of his account of love.

References

Benedict. [1996] 2006. *Deus Caritas Est*. San Francisco: St. Ignatius Press.
Corrigan, John. 2002. *Business of the Heart*. Berkeley: University of California Press.
Corrigan, John, ed. 2004. *Religion and Emotion: Approaches and Interpretation*. New York: Oxford University Press.
Gaita, Raimond. 2002. *A Common Humanity: Thinking about Love and Truth and Justice*. New York: Routledge.
Heschel, Abraham Joshua. 1976. *God in Search of Man: A Philosophy of Judaism*. New York: Farrar, Strauss and Giroux.
Hochschild, Arlie Russell. 2003. *The Managed Heart: Commercialization of Human Feeling*. University of California Press.
Jollimore, Troy. 2011. *Love's Vision*. Princeton, NJ: Princeton University Press.
Kierkegaard, Søren. [1847] 2009. *Works of Love*. H. Hong and E. Hong (trans). New York: Harper Perennial.
Milligan, Tony. 2011. *Love*. Durham: Acumen.
Milligan, Tony. 2014 ."Love in Dark Times," *Religious Studies* 50.1: 87–100.
Murdoch, Iris. 1993. *Metaphysics as a Guide to Morals*. London: Penguin.
Nussbaum, Martha. 1986. *The Fragility of Goodness: Luck and Ethics in Greek Tragedy and Philosophy*. New York: Cambridge University Press.
Pacovská, Kamila. 2014. "Loving Villains: Virtue in Response to Wrongdoing." In Maurer, Christian, Tony Milligan and Pacovská, *Love and Its Objects: What Can We Care For?* Houndsmill: Palgrave Macmillan, 125–139.
Vlastos, Gregory. 1981. "The Individual as an Object of Love in Plato." In *Platonic Studies*, 2nd edition. Princeton, NJ: Princeton University Press, 3–42.
Weil, Simone. 1951. *Waiting for God*. E. Crawford (trans). London: Routledge.
Wettstein, Howard. 2015. *The Significance of Religious Experience*. Oxford: Oxford University Press.
Wolf, Susan. 1982. "Moral Saints," *The Journal of Philosophy* 79.8: 419–439.

Section II
Loving Partiality and Moral Impartiality

10 Dissolving the Illusion of the Love and Justice Dichotomy

Rachel Fedock

Introduction

I will argue that justice and love are not *as* distinct as purported by some theorists (Carol Gilligan 1982, 1987; Nel Noddings 1984; Annette Baier 1991; Virginia Held 2006).[1] Justice and love, I claim, are interconnected, where one makes little sense in isolation from the other. In other words, love and justice are different, but closely related features of the normative world. Love and justice have often been conceived as not only sharply distinct, but divergent in their aims and sometimes conflicting in their demands. Justice and its values have been seen as irrelevant within loving relations or even incompatible. Furthermore, the compatibility between loving relations and moral impartiality has been questioned. I refer to this perceived contrast as the "love and justice dichotomy," LJD. First, I will briefly introduce a few theories of love and care to illustrate some of the history of the LJD. I will then explore those theorists whose work challenges the LJD, including Iris Murdoch's (1970), but particularly David Velleman's (1999).[2] On his theory, love is inherently just, and hence compatible with moral impartiality, validating my claim that the LJD is an illusion. Finally, I sketch the beginnings of in what a feminist-focused theory love[3] consists, resulting in a further break down of the LJD. Where Velleman and Murdoch focus upon the concept of love, I describe how to love the beloved in relations (in terms of care), further demonstrating the necessity of justice within loving relations and that love and moral impartiality are compatible. Furthermore, I argue that loving relations may involve a fight for justice. This could imply that loving is a political act in some cases, promoting the beloved's standing in society, perhaps facilitating their agency.[4] Drawing upon these challenging works and my own description of loving relations, I conclude that the LJD is an illusion.

History of the LJD

I view the care and justice dichotomy as playing a central role in solidifying the LJD.[5] An ethic of care tends to emphasize both the tension between caring and moral impartiality,[6] and the incompatibility of justice within caring relations, similar to the LJD. Care and love are not identical concepts; however, when discussing caring relations, care ethicists refer to intimate relations with children, partners, family, and friends, often also, relations of love. For instance, Baier's (1991), Noddings' (1984), and Held's (2006) work focuses on caring in the context of mothering, and while they recognize these relations as loving, developing an account of love is not their aim. Hence, I take much of the care and justice dichotomy to directly translate to the LJD, although 'care' is a broader concept than 'love'.

As my account of loving relations involves care, I shall briefly clarify their differences now, expanding upon them later. I do not have the space to argue for the distinctions between love and care here, but I will describe what I have in mind. Although I may claim to "love" pizza, I take such expressions to be hyperbolic, where love is reserved for, perhaps a small inner circle of friends and/or family. In agreement with Velleman that love requires suspended attention, we simply do not have the cognitive capacity to love many persons (1999, 360–361).[7] However, caring about black lives or dismantling the patriarchy is no exaggeration. Our capacity to care about things, to value them, is vast. With respect to minimal care, we may be able to care about all of humanity, feeling sympathy and concern, but relations of intense care (or maximal care) with whom we are close to may be few, just as with love, where we invest in the cared-for's well-being. Intermediate care may involve caring for persons where needs are met, but love may be absent. Elsewhere, I argue that love involves at least minimal caring, where one would prevent harm if possible (Fedock 2018). So, love involves at least minimal care, but perhaps even more intense care, and while we can care about and for many things and persons, love and care overlap only in limited cases, those with whom we are in special relations.

Care theorists emphasize and often reinforce the tension between care and justice, claiming that their values are incompatible, such as moral impartiality and partiality in caring relations (Gilligan 1982, 1987; Noddings 1984; Baier 1991; Held 2006). The care and justice dichotomy has its roots in the work of Carol Gilligan (1982, 1987). Gilligan challenged Lawrence Kohlberg's work on moral development (1984). He theorized that one's morality develops in a hierarchical way, where one first begins with concern for one's self, and then others (involving caring), culminating in acts based on principles of justice, the highest and most sophisticated stage of moral development and reasoning, broadly speaking. Gilligan rejected this hierarchy and alternatively proposed that two ethics obtain rather than one, a care perspective and a justice perspective, entirely distinct, utilizing different moral tools. She *defined* an ethic of care in opposition to an ethic of justice, solidifying the dichotomy. Not only does justice and its values have no place in caring relations, but so too, caring values are incompatible with justice. The duck/rabbit illusion became Gilligan's most famous illustration of her proposal. Just as one cannot see the duck and rabbit simultaneously, and must switch their perspective, so too, care and justice are distinct perspectives; switching is required. In other words, care is incompatible with justice, and justice is incompatible with care.

According to care theorists, when making decisions based upon justice, derived from Kantian and contractarian sources, the use of abstract concepts, universal rules, and reason are deemed the traditional tools, accompanied by the value of impartiality. When making decisions based upon love or care, care and love theorists tend to see concrete situations and experiences, contextual details, and emotions as required, while many view love as constitutively an exercise in partiality. Persons are viewed as independent and autonomous individuals through the eyes of justice, while relations of love and care often highlight the dependence or the interdependence of persons, seeing them as relational or embedded in relations. Finally, justice requires that people are treated with respect, whereas love often involves treating the beloved with tenderness, care, and compassion, aiming to preserve the well-being of the beloved. The concepts of love and care are incompatible with justice, while justice has no place in loving relations.

Within the literature on love, I have found the conflicts between love and justice less discussed, but implicitly present.[8] Velleman succinctly summarizes a perceived general tension between love and morality.

> Love and morality are generally assumed to differ in spirit. The moral point of view is impartial and favors no particular individual, whereas favoring someone in particular seems like the very essence of love. Love and morality are therefore thought to place conflicting demands on our attention, requiring us to look at things differently, whether or not they ultimately require us to do different things (1999, 388–389).

Here, he draws particular attention to the supposed tensions between the impartiality of morality and the partiality of love. On *relations* views of love, conflicts between love and justice arise because the primary bearers of value are the relationships themselves, not the individuals (Velleman 1999; Niko Kolodny 2003; Held 2006). On such views, relations provide reasons for partiality, in direct conflict with justice, particularly equitable universality, where we are required to treat all persons equally. In addition, the value of the relation may take precedence over the individuals in relations, likely diminishing personal autonomy.

Theories of love tend to emphasize the importance and role of desires, emotions, caring, and concern for the beloved (Frankfurt 1982, 1999a, 1999b, 2004; Friedman 1998; Helm 2009, 2010). Most theories do not emphasize respect nor recognize that impartiality, universality, or objectivity could have any place in love, similar to the care ethical framework previously described.[9] Such theories imply that justice has little or no place in loving relations.

The conflict between love and autonomy has received significant attention. In my use of 'autonomy,' I borrow Narayan's conception where, "a person's choice should be considered autonomous as long as the person was a 'normal adult' with no serious cognitive or emotional impairments, and was not subject to literal or outright coercion from others" (Narayan 2002, 429). I would add that this involves, broadly speaking, a procedural criterion, where the agent has engaged in critically reflective deliberation to make their choice, although I resist adopting a specific procedural account. I add this procedural dimension because it seems implicitly present in Narayan's discussion. She argues that women often "bargain with patriarchy," an exercise in agency which involves negotiating with patriarchal systems. One example she describes is women's choice to wear a burqa from the conservative Sufi Pirzada community in Old Delhi (Narayan 2002, 420). The women interviewed expressed a complexity of reasons why they both did and did not want to wear it. Some disliked that fact that it made them look like "water buffaloes," but liked the anonymity it provided in public, for instance. I think we can infer that critically reflective deliberation is a prerequisite for such expressions of autonomy.

Respecting autonomy is an essential aspect of justice (for Kant) and hence reveals a point of tension between love and justice: when loving involves diminished personal autonomy for the sake of the relation or union. The popular *union* view proposes some variant of the idea that two selves, identities, souls, etc. "merge" creating a joint identity and autonomy, while retaining some degree of individual identity and autonomy in some cases (Solomon 1981, 1988; Scruton 1986, Nozick 1989; Fisher 1990; Delany 1996; Friedman 1998). Solomon, for instance, directly admits this "paradox of love," how one can retain personal autonomy in love, failing to address the conflict (1988, 64). Others recognize varying degrees of union on their views, where all personal autonomy may be lost, or some is retained. However, individual autonomy seems to diminish on such theories, directly conflicting with the principle of justice to respect personal autonomy, perpetuating the LJD. As the 'we' may often take precedence over the 'I' on union views, an agent may cease to critically reflect on choices with respect to the 'I.' Union views do not typically provide protections against such possible diminishments of individual autonomy.

To conclude this section, although values of justice have often been absent in theories of love, I believe the solidification of the LJD can be traced to the care and justice dichotomy, where justice has no place in caring relations and moral impartiality is at odds with maintaining caring relations. Similarly, love and morality have often been assumed to "differ in spirit," as Velleman puts the point, where special relations of love, inherently partial, conflict with moral impartiality. Furthermore, both relations and union views of love result in at least some loss, but at worst, a full loss of personal autonomy. Although this history is substantial, I intend to demonstrate that the LJD is an illusion.

Challenges to the LJD

Throughout Velleman's analysis of love, he illustrates ways in which the LJD comes apart, providing an understanding of love that involves aspects of justice, where love is an exercise in moral impartiality. He reveals the interdependence of supposedly oppositional concepts, such as respect versus love, universal, impartial morality versus the particularity and contextuality of love, and rationality versus care and love, supporting my claim that love and justice are interconnected concepts. For the sake of brevity, I will focus on his account of the attitude toward the beloved, which involves respect, universality, particularity, and incomparability (Velleman 1999, 360–361).[10]

Velleman's account of love is Kantian at its core, but also influenced by Murdoch (1970). He sees respect and love as along the same continuum, where respect is the "required minimum" and love is the "optimal maximum" response to the same value: the dignity of persons (1999, 336). As love and respect are along the same continuum, they are no longer in conflict, revealing the fallacy of the supposed tension between love and care on the one hand, and respect on the other. Hence, respect is a prerequisite to love.[11] As respect is central to justice, and respect is essential in love, I claim that respect hence is essential in loving relations. Love, then, requires justice.

Although love is particularistic, focused on valuing the individual, the universality of morality is maintained in the sense that all persons possess the same value and that value derives from dignity. One does not value their beloved more than others on Velleman's account. All persons are valued equally and, hence love and moral impartiality are not in tension. Likewise, Velleman goes on to note that we appreciate the universal value of persons through particular persons and contextual experiences; we appreciate the value of all persons through appreciating the value of those with whom we are in special relations, recognizing all have the same value, namely, dignity (1999, 373). So we learn how to respect all persons by first learning to respect those with whom we are in loving relations. Moral impartiality (justice) needs love (loving relations) in order to be properly conceived.

Velleman does, however, veer from the traditional Kantian interpretation of dignity in terms of the rational will. Alternatively, he claims that rational nature is not the intellect, not even the practical intellect; it's a capacity of appreciation or valuation — a capacity to care about things in that reflective way which is distinctive of self-conscious creatures like us. Think of a person's rational nature as his core of reflective concern, and the idea of loving him for it will no longer seem odd (1999, 365).

For Velleman, rationality involves the ability to value ends, and since persons are ends in themselves, the rational will is "a capacity to care about things" in a reflective way. This understanding of valuing persons illustrates the interdependence of supposedly incompatible concepts; rationality and care come together here as rationality is defined as a caring capacity. Theories of love, which perpetuate the LJD, may view love as irrational; however, Velleman demonstrates that rationality, a caring capacity, is at love's core.

'Incomparability' is another aspect of Velleman's conception of the attitude toward the beloved, which involves multiple layers, both Kantian and Murdochian. Persons whom we love possess incomparable value because persons do not have a price; they have dignity and that which has no price cannot be compared, as first delineated by Kant (Velleman, 1999, 366). Contrary to any theory of love and care that recognizes relations as the prime bearers of value, Velleman claims that we do not treat those with whom we are in special relations differently because our *relations* with them are more valuable than other relations. On the contrary, *individuals* with whom we are in special relations are the source of value for Velleman, and their value cannot be compared to the value of other individuals. Relations theorists hence struggle to explain how such a view can be consistent with moral impartiality, whereas Velleman's theory directly solves this conundrum, while still appreciating how the beloved maintains incomparable value (Kolodny 2003; Held 2006). So again, his account calls into question the supposed tension between valuing a particular person and valuing all persons equally. Loving relations and moral impartiality are not in conflict.

As for the Murdochian components of incomparability, Velleman describes her account of love as impersonal and objective, an exercise in detachment, as she puts it, "really looking" (Murdoch 1970, 15). "Really looking," for Murdoch, involves attention and respect. When we love a person, we see them for who they really are, their true self, achieved only through an unbiased and objective perspective, at a distance, detached from the beloved. Murdoch's conception of love is impartial in a sense, an unbiased perspective, but focusing on a particular person. Her described exercise of love invokes traditional aspects of justice: impartiality, objectivity, and respect. As such, her account further challenges the LJD, as I claim these features are necessary in loving relations. In addition, as love is an exercise in impartiality, it is an exercise in morality, not in conflict with it.

"Really looking" and seeing a person, according to Velleman, brings about feelings of awe and wonder toward the beloved, a kind of suspended attention, where one is simultaneously close to, yet distant from the beloved (1999, 360–361). We become emotionally vulnerable to the beloved, letting down our emotional defenses. As he claims that minimal respect "arrests" our tendency toward self-love, love "arrests our" tendency "toward emotional self-protection" and we become receptive to and affected by the beloved (1999, 360–361). But this raises the question: if all persons possess the same value, why do we love some but not others or why do we not love everyone? Velleman argues that everyone expresses their dignity differently and we are only receptive to particular ways in which particular persons express their dignity. So one loves another because they respond to the way in which the other expresses their dignity, but one does not respond in the same way to others' expressions of dignity. Loving relations, I claim, involve a rational perspective, "really looking" at the beloved from an unbiased perspective with attention and respect, giving rise to emotions such as awe and wonder, letting down our guard, becoming vulnerable to the beloved, again, intertwining features of the supposed LJD.

Velleman demonstrates that the LJD is an illusion. He presents a particularistic conception of love; the beloved is incomparable, yet this is consistent with moral impartiality, constitutively involving aspects of impartiality such as respect, unbiased and objective attention, and valuation, and yet all persons are valued equally. Collectively, these aspects of love and justice demonstrate the interconnectedness between them, revealing they cannot be easily disassociated from one another. Hence, I take it that neither love nor justice can stand alone. Each needs the other, as in isolation, they are both incomplete. Love needs justice as love requires respect, and hence loving relations require justice. Justice needs love because we appreciate the values of justice (respecting others' dignity) first through those with whom we are in special relations, those we love. In recognizing our beloved's dignity, we recognize all persons have dignity. And, as love requires justice and we do not value our beloved more than others, loving is compatible with impartial morality. In addition, Velleman leaves significant space for the preservation and promotion of personal autonomy on his account due to an emphasis on respect, making his theory inherently just.

Love: A Fight for Justice

My account is feminist-focused as it aims to eliminate some forms of patriarchal oppression, but I do not assume that women suffering from oppression *necessarily* are deficient in autonomy. Some may be and some may not. In agreement with Serene Khader (2011), I contend that those who are oppressed may still maintain autonomy. I argue that feminist-focused, maximal caring, loving relations empower the beloved, promote their autonomy (a fight for justice), and go above and beyond what is required for basic flourishing (when possible). Basic flourishing includes things like adequate shelter, healthcare, nutrition, etc., whereas going above and beyond basic flourishing, non-basic flourishing, I understand to involve things like pursuing personal projects. As Velleman and Murdoch dissolve the LJD in their conception of love, I add to this by describing loving relations as just relations in practice, further demonstrating that love requires justice. In addition, if we ought to aim at eliminating the oppression of our fellow citizens (when we are able), we ought to eliminate oppressive structures experienced by those whom we love as well. This action could be conceived as a political act, and if so, the personal is political.

I have proposed elsewhere that *good* care is the following: minimally, 'care' means (a) to prevent uncontroversial impending harm,[12] in the intermediate case, meeting fundamental needs, maximally, promoting the flourishing of the object of care, which includes empowering them (promoting autonomy and eliminating inappropriate adaptive preferences, IAP), while *always* (b) respecting the me-ness of both the care-giver and care-receiver (Fedock 2016).[13] I borrow the language of "me-ness" from Robin Dillon (1992). Me-ness has the advantage of not "fetishizing autonomy," as Khader might put the point (2016). Autonomy is neither necessary nor the primary marker of personhood on Dillon's account.

> Me-ness encompasses characteristics such as being reflectively self-conscious, having an historical experience of unity, continuity, and trajectory, having a plan of life and a conception of one's own good, being always engaged (though never single handedly) in the tasks of self-construction and self-interpretation as well as world-construction and world-interpretation and so having one's own particular perspective on oneself and the world…care respect values these characteristics only insofar as they are dimensions of or conditions of each person's being the particular person she is. Autonomy, while one path to becoming a "me," is not on this account viewed as either necessary or as especially important for being a person deserving of respect. This has the satisfactory consequence that even a manifestly and profoundly non-autonomous human being has intrinsic value and dignity…not, of course to deny the moral and personal value of autonomy (118–119).

So none of these characteristics are necessary, but one is sufficient for personhood (me-ness for Dillon), while additional characteristics are contingent. I borrow and expand upon Khader's definition of "empowerment," which is "the process of overcoming one or many IAP through processes that enhance some element of a persons' concept of self-entitlement and increase her capacity to pursue her own flourishing" (2011, 176). Inappropriate adaptive preferences (IAP) are preferences that are

> (1) inconsistent with basic flourishing (2) that are formed under conditions non-conducive to basic flourishing and (3) that we believe people might be persuaded to transform upon normative scrutiny of their preferences and exposure to conditions more conducive to flourishing (2011, 42, 51).

I expand upon her notion of IAP to include non-basic flourishing as well. Combining Velleman's theory of love with my theory of care, a matter of degree, yields different kinds of loving relations, depending on the degree of care present: minimal, intermediate, and maximal. To be clear, love itself does not come in degrees, but as caring does, loving relations are differentiated via the degree of care present. I do not claim that meeting needs nor empowering the beloved are necessary features of love. They are contingent as Velleman's theory leaves room for benefitting the beloved, but does not require it. For instance, his example of loving one's cranky grandfather illustrates such a case (1999, 353). One can love their cranky grandfather and yet have no desire to benefit him, meeting his needs or empowering him. One could "really see" their cranky grandfather and be emotionally vulnerable to him, but may have experienced harm from him in the relationship, and hence may not feel compelled to empower him, or provide frequent companionship (a need), but would always ensure that he is safe, a case of loving, minimal care. Perhaps another's grandfather is also loved, but a little less cranky, and experienced less harm, but still some in the relationship. And in this case, the person does provide companionship at times, yet does not empower him; this would be a case of loving, intermediate care. However, these features are necessary in cases of maximal caring love, my focus here. In sum, maximal caring, loving relations involve promoting the flourishing of the beloved, which includes empowering them, aiming to maintain the autonomy of the beloved and promote their autonomy when possible, facilitating the elimination of IAP, and respecting their me-ness.[14]

This account, hence, is feminist-focused because it aligns with a central concern of feminism: concerns about women's flourishing and capacities for autonomy affected by patriarchal oppression.[15] Of course, feminism recognizes that oppression is interconnected: classism, heteronormativity, racism, ableism, etc. However, limits on individual autonomy and/or flourishing are not exclusive to women, as men and other genders experience oppression too. The expansion of autonomy, flourishing, and empowerment ought to be the aim for *any individual* in a loving relationship, regardless of gender, I assume here, argued for elsewhere, (Fedock 2016). What flourishing looks like cross-culturally may vary to a significant degree. So although my initial motivations are rooted in feminist concerns, the resulting theory should be understood as a theory of love (for all) in application, but feminist-focused in production. As hooks would say, "feminism is for everybody" (hooks 2000).

Velleman's theory is progressive, leaving significant room for the promotion of autonomy, flourishing, and empowerment, due to his emphasis on respect and other aspects of justice, challenging the LJD, but does not go as far as to argue for it. My account requires the promotion of autonomy to attain non-basic flourishing (when possible), as well as attempting to eliminate IAP in cases of maximal caring love, a fight for justice. Two crucial criteria for a feminist-focused theory of love, I argue, are the promotion of autonomy of each individual in the loving relation, while also attempting to facilitate the elimination of the beloved's IAP, empowering them. Feminists have argued that relations of love can be oppressive to women, such as Mary Wollstonecraft (1996 [1792]), Simone de Beauvoir (1984), and Marilyn Friedman (1998); however, I urge that not only can a feminist-focused theory of love avoid oppression, it can combat oppression, which may possibly be construed as a political act.

One may wonder why we need to include the promotion of autonomy. In short, to fight oppression (of all genders), but more specifically to promote *non-basic flourishing*—above and beyond securing shelter, nutrition, etc.,—personal projects when possible. Might not eliminating IAP accomplish all of our goals? I argue that the promotion of autonomy (Narayan's conception, understood as procedural, a critically reflective, deliberative process) is required to promote at least some aspects of non-basic flourishing. To elaborate, Khader makes a distinction between having a choice (and what those choices are) and making a choice (a deliberative process) in her discussion of empowerment, a distinction which is at times conjoined or conflated with respect to different conceptions of autonomy (Friedman 1998; Stoljar 2000; Khader 2011, 183). This distinction seems to identify two ways in which one can be(come) disempowered: not having a range of acceptable options to choose from or not engaging in a deliberative process. If basic flourishing obtains, then according to Khader's theory, presumably the agent has a range of acceptable options to choose from, so the agent "has a choice." The remaining option left, which could explain an impediment on non-basic flourishing may lie in a lack of deliberation (a lack of autonomy), where the agent makes a choice (consciously or unconsciously) not to deliberate about available options, conceiving of them as unacceptable options. In cases of oppression or gaslighting, the agent may not even see herself as being able or worthy of making a choice in the first place.[16]

Dissolving illusion of love and justice 195

Imagine a case where a woman's basic flourishing obtains, and that she may even enjoy some aspects of non-basic flourishing, such as having more than adequate material resources, experiencing significant privilege. But let's further imagine that she does not enjoy some aspects of non-basic flourishing, specifically, the pursuit of personal projects.[17] Let's further imagine that this woman is a mother and accepts that the role of being a "good mother" involves devoting all of her time to her children, attempting to create a Pinterest perfect life, chauffeuring them to numerous activities, creating perfect, healthy, elaborate dinners, crafting intricate bedroom décor for them, etc. (an American trend). Further, let's assume that the mother does not enjoy activities like cooking or decorating and is quite aware of other options: not allowing her children to get involved in too many activities, giving up crafting, and giving up creating elaborate meals and asking her partner for help. However, considering her conception of what a "good mother" is, she does not perceive these acceptable options and refuses to deliberate (consciously or unconsciously) as to whether or not she should give up some of the time spent on her children and, instead, devote that time to herself. This hypothetical could illustrate a lack of autonomy: refusing to critically reflect and deliberate about various options (consciously or unconsciously), thereby diminishing non-basic flourishing.[18]

If the lover does not promote the autonomy of the beloved (in this case, the woman), feminist-focused maximal caring love does not obtain; the promotion of autonomy is not simple encouragement to pursue her own projects, but to encourage critical and reflective deliberation about pursuing activities for the sake of her children and pursuing activities for herself. But, if the lover does promote autonomy in the way described, maximal caring love can obtain because again, doing so facilitates the battle against oppression, promoting empowerment, a fight for justice—a fight against oppressive norms regarding what it means to be a "good mother." Although I do not have enough space to make an argument here, such action could possibly be construed as a political act, enhancing the beloved's standing in society (Rawls 2001). So as maximal caring love requires a fight for justice: the personal is political.

To recall, this account of maximal caring love is feminist-focused by virtue of attempting to alleviate feminist concerns in loving relationships with respect to threats to women's (and men's and other genders') autonomy, flourishing, and empowerment. Hence, I have argued that requiring the promotion of autonomy of individuals in loving relations to attain non-basic flourishing can alleviate some of these concerns, as well as attempting to eliminate the beloved's IAP, empowering them. Requiring lovers to promote the autonomy of their beloved dismantles the LJD because maximal caring love, as I have argued, requires fighting for justice for the sake of the beloved. Hence again, loving relations need justice. Possibly my account might further imply that fighting oppression within relations may be a political act. In this case, loving relations can facilitate political justice. And Velleman leaves the most room for the promotion of autonomy in his theory due to his emphasis on respect, making his theory the most conducive to a feminist-focused theory of love.

The Illusion Dissolved

To recap, the LJD has a long-standing history, and admittedly, intuitive appeal. Phenomenologically, conceptually, psychologically, and methodologically love and justice, prime facie, appear at direct odds with one another. Where love is typically felt, associated with emotions and desires, justice is cognitively conceived, thought to require the elimination of emotions, while utilizing reason. We think of love as applying to a few particular persons in our lives, where partiality is expected and may be required, but justice applies to all equally and impartially. These initial intuitions, regarding love and justice, have understandably translated into a long-standing tradition of their divide.

However, examining the nuances involved in love and justice reveals otherwise, I have hoped to show. The most glaring division, between love, autonomy, and justice, perhaps surprisingly reveals necessary connections between them, where loving relations constitutively involve respecting the beloved's autonomy. As I have argued above, maximal caring love requires justice in as far as lovers are required to promote each other's capacities for autonomy and attempting to eliminate IAP, empowering each other. Love, in essence, requires a fight for justice. Furthermore, theorists such as Murdoch and Velleman reveal the interwoven aspects of love and justice, dismantling numerous other dimensions of the supposed dichotomy, where love is just and consistent with impartial morality. The combined evidence here dissolves the LJD altogether, revealing the interconnections between love and justice. We understand and value justice by first learning how to love, while love requires a fight for justice.

Notes

1. Although Held, Gilligan, and Noddings focus on care, I take their analyses to fall under the studies of love as the caring relations they often discuss are relations of love as well. Within the domain of love studies, Robert Solomon (1988), Bennett Helm (2009, 2010), Marilyn Friedman (1998), and Harry Frankfurt (1982, 1999a, 199b, 2004) perpetuate the divide between love and justice by virtue of how their theories are structured, I suggest. I would like to thank the members of NYSWIP (2015), who provided insightful and valuable feedback on parts of this chapter, particularly the section, "Love: a Fight for Justice." Your contributions have led to numerous, critical revisions, Serene, Khader, Virginia Held, Amy

Dissolving illusion of love and justice 197

Baehr, Gina Campelia, and Carolyn Plunkett for which I am extremely grateful. I would also like to thank Raja Rosenhagen for his invaluable commentary at the Thirty-Seventh Annual Philosophy of Religion Conference, Claremont Graduate University. And finally, I must thank my co-editors for their invaluable feedback on numerous drafts, Michael Kühler and Raja Rosenhagen. Any errors are my own.

2. For further discussions of Murdoch and Velleman, see Arina Pismenny's, Raja Rosenhagen's, Nora Kreft's, and Niklas Forsberg's contributions in this volume (2021).
3. To clarify, in this chapter, I am concerned with loving relationships between adults, including friendship and romance, which may include adult familial relations as well.
4. For a more extensive discussion of the political implications of loving in a similar vein, see Barrett Emerick's and Niklas Forsberg's contributions in this volume (2021).
5. We can certainly trace its origins back to Greek conceptions of love, such as *eros*, where love constitutively involves passion and desire, absent of justice.
6. Although moral impartiality could include Kantian or utilitarian theories, here, I will focus up on Kantian theories of justice.
7. I do diverge from Velleman's conception of persons to include non-human animals. So, I do not think it is a mistake to say that I love my dog (2008, 203–204).
8. Of course, the practical conflicts between love and justice have been widely discussed, i.e., when one must choose between duties to one's country and family. The practical conflict, however, is not my focus here, rather the supposed conceptual and psychological incompatibility.
9. Where Singer (1994), Velleman (1999), and Murdoch (1970) are exceptions. Other theorists do recognize the necessity of respect in their theories, but respect is not a central feature (Friedman 1998; Helm 2010).
10. Velleman's account pertains to adult relationships of love.
11. I argue elsewhere in "The Moral Phenomenon of Care" for the interdependence between care and respect (unpublished).
12. By this I only refer to cases upon which, I think, most would agree, such as preventing death, physical abuse, sexual abuse, and verbal abuse.
13. This definition was largely inspired by the work of Joan Tronto (1993), Karen Warren (1990, 2000), Sibyl Schwarzenbach (2009), and Held (2006). As for the autonomy clause, others also recognize its importance within a theory of care, such as Carol Gould (1990). 'Autonomy' ought not to be understood in a political sense, conflicting with caring values, but rather a practical sense, where both the caregiver and receiver respect and are attentive to the other's wants and needs. I diverge from Khader in including the promotion of autonomy as an element of empowerment (2011); however, I take it to be a contingent feature and not necessary.
14. I present a case below to illustrate what I have in mind. In "Love, Care, and Respect: a Feminist Perspective" (2018), I argue that there are several necessary features of maximal love, the promotion of autonomy being one of them. Here I will focus on the promotion of autonomy, leaving aside the requirement to maintain the autonomy of the beloved for the sake of brevity.
15. Including, but not limited to overt or implicit sexism, institutional sexism, or sexist/oppressive gender conceptions.
16. Thanks to Michael Kühler for making this point.

17. Non-basic flourishing parameters vary dramatically across cultures, so here I am assuming a mother in Western culture, which presumably values the pursuit of personal projects for flourishing.
18. I am not claiming that a mother cannot enjoy these activities. In the case that a mother does enjoy these activities (with or without autonomous deliberation), she achieves some aspects of non-basic flourishing. We may think of this mother as adopting the care of her children as a personal project.

References

Baier, Annette. 1991. "Unsafe Loves." In *The Philosophy of (Erotic) Love*, edited by Robert Solomon and Kathleen Higgins, 433–450. Lawrence, KS: University Press of Kansas.

Beauvoir, Simone de. 1984. *The Second Sex*, translated by H.M. Pashley. Harmondsworth: Penguin.

Delany, Neil. 1996. "Romantic Love and Loving Commitment: Articulating a Modern Ideal." *American Philosophical Quarterly* 33: 375–405.

Dillon, Robin S. 1992. "Respect and Care: Toward Moral Integration." *Canadian Journal of Philosophy* 22: 105–132.

Emerick, Barrett. 2020. "Love, Activism, and Social Justice." In *Love, Justice, an Autonomy: Philosophical Perspectives*, edited by Rachel Fedock, Michael Kühler, and Raja Rosenhagen. New York: Routledge Press.

Fedock, Rachel. 2016. *The Theoretical and Psychological Foundations of Care in Environmental Ethics*. Doctoral Dissertation, City University of New York, Graduate Center.

Fedock, Rachel. "Love, Care, and Respect: a Feminist Perspective." paper presented at the Philosophy Forum, SUNY Potsdam, Potsdam, NY, May 2018.

Fisher, M. 1990. *Personal Love*. London: Duckworth.

Forsberg, Niklas. 2020. "The Freedom that Comes with Love." In *Love, Justice, an Autonomy: Philosophical Perspectives*, edited by Rachel Fedock, Michael Kühler, and Raja Rosenhagen. New York: Routledge Press.

Frankfurt, Harry. 1982. "The Importance of What We Care About." *Synthesis* 53 (2): 257–272.

Frankfurt, Harry. 1999a. "Autonomy, Necessity, and Love." In *Necessity, Volition, and Love*, 129–141. Cambridge: Cambridge University Press.

Frankfurt, Harry. 1999b. "On Caring." In *Necessity, Volition, and Love*. Cambridge: Cambridge University Press.

Frankfurt, Harry. 2004. "On Love, and Its Reasons." In *The Reasons of Love*. Princeton: Princeton University Press.

Friedman, Marilyn. 1998. "Romantic Love and Personal Autonomy." *Midwest Studies Philosophy* 22 (1): 162–181.

Gilligan, Carol. 1982. *In a Different Voice: Psychological Theory and Women's Development*. Cambridge, MA: Harvard University Press.

Gilligan, Carol. 1987. "Moral Orientation and Moral Development." In *Women in Moral Theory*, edited by Eva Kittay and Diana Meyers, 19–33. Totowa, NJ: Rowman & Littlefield.

Gould, Carol. 1990. "Philosophical Dichotomies and Feminist Thought: Towards a Critical Feminism." In *Feministische Philosophie*, edited by Nagl Herta, 184–190. Wiener Reihe Band 4. Vienna: R. Oldenbourg Verlag.

Held, Virginia. 2006. *The Ethics of Care: Personal, Political and Global*. New York: Oxford University Press.
Helm, Bennett. 2009. "Love, Identification, and the Emotions." *American Philosophical Quarterly* 46: 39–59.
Helm, Bennett. 2010. *Love, Friendship, and the Self: Intimacy, Identification, and the Social Nature of Persons*. New York: Oxford University Press.
hooks, bell. 2000. *Feminism Is for Everybody*. Cambridge: South End Press.
Khader, Serene J. 2011. *Adaptive Preferences and Women's Empowerment*. New York: Oxford University Press.
Khader, Serene. 2016. "Beyond Autonomy Fetishism: Affiliation with Autonomy in Women's Empowerment." *Journal of Human Development and Capabilities* 17 (1): 125–139
Kohlberg, Lawrence. 1984. *The Psychology of Moral Development: Moral Stages and Life Cycles*, Vol. 2. Essays on Moral Development. San Francisco: Harper & Row.
Kolodny, Niko. 2003. "Love as Valuing a Relationship." *The Philosophical Review* 112: 135–189.
Kreft, Nora. 2020. "Love and Our Moral Relations with Others." In *Love, Justice, an Autonomy: Philosophical Perspectives*, edited by Rachel Fedock, Michael Kühler, and Raja Rosenhagen. New York: Routledge Press.
Murdoch, Iris. 1970. *The Sovereignty of the Good*. New York: Routledge & Kegan Paul.
Narayan, Uma. 2002. "Minds of Their Own: Choices, Autonomy, Cultural Practices, and Other Women." In *Mind of One's Own: Feminist Essays on Reason and Objectivity*, edited by Louise Antony and Charlotte Witt, 418–432. Boulder: Westview Press.
Noddings, Nel. 1984. *Caring: A Feminist Approach to Ethics and Moral Education*. Berkeley: University of California Press.
Nozick, Robert. 1989. "Love's Bond." In *The Examined Life: Philosophical Meditations*, 68–86. New York: Simon & Schuster.
Pismenny, Arina. 2020. "The Amorality of Romantic Love." In *Love, Justice, an Autonomy: Philosophical Perspectives*, edited by Rachel Fedock, Michael Kühler, and Raja Rosenhagen. New York: Routledge Press.
Rawls, John. 2001. *Justice as Fairness: A Restatement*. Cambridge: Harvard University Press.
Rosenhagen, Raja. 2020. "Murdochian Perspectivalism." In *Love, Justice, an Autonomy: Philosophical Perspectives*, edited by Rachel Fedock, Michael Kühler, and Raja Rosenhagen. New York: Routledge Press.
Schwarzenbach, Sibyl. 2009. *On Civic Friendship: Including Women in the State*. New York: Columbia University Press.
Scruton, Roger. 1986. *Sexual Desire: A Moral Philosophy of the Erotic*. New York: Free Press.
Singer, I. 1994. *The Pursuit of Love*. Baltimore, MD: Johns Hopkins University Press.
Solomon, R.C. 1981. *Love: Emotion, Myth, and Metaphor*. New York: Anchor Press.
Solomon, R.C. 1988. *About Love: Reinventing Romance for Our Times*. New York: Simon & Schuster.

Stoljar, Natalie. 2000. "Autonomy and Feminist Intuition." In *Relational Autonomy: Feminist Perspectives on Automony, Agency, and the Social Self*, edited by Mackenzie, Catriona, and *Natalie* Stoljar. Oxford University Press.
Tronto, Joan. 1993. *Moral Boundaries: A Political Argument for an Ethic of Care*. New York: Routledge.
Velleman, David. 2008. "Beyond Price." *Ethics* 118: 191–212.
Velleman, David. 1999. "Love as a Moral Emotion." *Ethics* 109: 338–374.
Warren, Karen. 1990. "The Promise and Power of Ecofeminism." *Environmental Ethics* 12 (2): 125–146.
Warren, Karen. 2000. *Ecofeminist Philosophy: A Western Perspective on What It Is and Why It Matters*. Lanham: Rowman & Littlefield.
Wollstonecraft, Mary. 1996. *A Vindication of the Rights of Woman*, 2nd ed. Dover Thrift Editions. Mineola, NY: Dover Publications.

11 Love and Our Moral Relations with Others

Nora Kreft

Introduction

In the first chapter of *The Robust Demands of the Good* (2015), Philip Pettit develops his idea of love as robust care. He argues that if A loves B, then A provides care for B not only in all actual scenarios, given certain prompts or triggers, but also over a certain range of hypothetical scenarios. A does not just provide care for B as things stand but would provide care for B even if B lost all of his money, or his social status, and also in situations in which providing care for B would inconvenience A to some extent. So love is best understood (at least in part) as a disposition to provide care in a variety of possible scenarios, whether or not they become actual.

Further, according to Pettit, being thus disposed does not just mean being motivated to provide care, but also having reason to do so. There is a sense in which, as a lover, one *ought* to provide care for one's beloved, given the right prompts. This "ought" is not necessarily a moral ought, but a constitutive one: it captures the rationale of love. Among other things, this means that when you ask A why she would provide care for B in a variety of different cases, A's response "Because I love B" is intelligible and satisfactory.

Pettit goes on to say that the reasons of love—the reasons to provide care for the beloved—can be outweighed by other reasons. He discusses an example in which a person has to decide between consoling her beloved who just lost his pet and assisting some stranger on the street in a life-and-death situation. If she decides to help the stranger here—which is what she has most reason to do, especially if we assume that she is the only one around who can help—it does not undermine her status as a genuine lover. In other words, the range of possible scenarios in which a lover would provide care for her beloved is not unlimited, and it is compatible with love not to support one's beloved in cases such as this.[1]

In the next two sections, I focus on this case. I agree with Pettit that the lover should help the stranger instead of consoling her beloved in this scenario, and I also agree that this would not undermine her status as a genuine lover. But I disagree that the situation is correctly analyzed as the reasons of love being outweighed by the reasons to help the stranger. I argue that love itself gives us a reason to help the stranger here. So that in helping the stranger, the lover is in fact (also) acting out of love for her beloved, not in spite of her love. More generally speaking, I defend the position that love gives us reasons to respect and care not only for the beloved but also for *other* human beings, at least to some, further specifiable extent and in certain, further specifiable situations. I hereby invoke a long tradition in philosophy to view love as a morally virtuous attitude—an attitude that has the potential to change our moral relations not just with our beloved, but to a certain degree with everyone.

In the final section, I relate my points to what Pettit calls the "guidance problem": the question, inspired by Williams' famous "one-thought-too-many" scenario, how (if at all) love's partiality is compatible with the demands of an impartial morality.

When I speak of "love" here, I am referring to all types of interpersonal love, including romantic love, love within the family and friendship. Of course, these are distinct ways of loving people, but for my current purposes, the differences are not relevant.

Korsgaard's Organ Case

What if the lover in Pettit's example actually decides against helping the stranger in order to support her beloved? While she is making tea for her beloved and holding his hand while he is crying over his dead cat, she is letting the stranger die. Pettit calls this a case of "ruthless love"—love that provides care even when the reasons of love are outweighed by stronger reasons and in particular, by moral ones. Ruthless love might fail to deliver what Pettit says is "the good of love," i.e., what we value about love, but according to him, it is love nevertheless.[2] That is why the lover is still acting on *reasons of love* when she lets the stranger die and makes tea for her beloved. She is doing something wrong as a moral agent here, but not as a lover.

Unlike Pettit, I believe that her decision is not only morally wrong, but also in tension with her love for her beloved. To explain, I want to start with an example Christine Korsgaard mentions briefly in a different context. She imagines a father who is waiting for an organ donation for his sick daughter. Without the organ, his daughter will soon die, and the chances for the donation to come in time are slim. The father then decides to kill another child to get the organ for his daughter.

Korsgaard writes that "if I were prepared to kill other people's children to get their organs in order to save the life of my child, that would reveal something amiss, not merely with my general moral character and my attitude towards the other children, but with my attitude toward my own child. (...) it would be as if I felt that my child's right to her own organs derived from my love for her, and that would be the wrong way of caring about *her*." And later she adds: "If I love (...) a person, I regard his humanity – his autonomy and his interests – as something of universal and public value. (...) As the case of stealing organs shows, if I am to be respectful of the value of humanity in my beloved, then I must be respectful of that value generally."[3]

For the father in the example, love makes the difference between being prepared to kill a child and protecting it. He protects whom he happens to love but is prepared to kill whom he does not love in the same way. The fact that the other children are human beings just like his own child does not seem to impress him much: he either does not consider their humanity as giving him any reasons for protecting their lives at all, or it is a reason that he considers to be outweighed by the reasons to save his daughter that he takes his love to give him.[4]

Korsgaard thinks that this is not only a morally problematic attitude toward the other children but shows that something is "amiss" with his love for his daughter. By disregarding the other children's humanity as he does, he shows disregard for humanity in general, including the humanity of his daughter. But this is incompatible with love, according to Korsgaard: a lover does not disregard their beloved's humanity in this way but regards it as "something of universal and public value."

On one reading, something of "public value" is objectively valuable; and something of "universal value" is not just contingently valuable or only in certain situations, but across the board, in all possible sorts of situations, it is an end in itself. So, another way of putting it would be to say that something of both public and universal value is an objective end in itself—something that ought to be pursued or protected not just for some other sake, but also for its own sake.[5] If that is right, Korsgaard seems to be saying that lovers *qua* lovers regard their beloveds as objective ends in themselves on account of their humanity, and since their beloveds share their humanity with all other human beings, lovers *qua* lovers also regard other people as objective ends in themselves on account of their humanity.

I come back to this last move from one's own beloved to all human beings below. But first, what does this mean for the father in the example? I said that he does not take the humanity of the other children to give him any reason not to kill them, or at least not a reason that could not be outweighed by the reasons he takes himself to have to save his beloved in particular. Is this compatible with regarding the other children as objective ends in themselves on account of their humanity? Might it not be possible that he regards them as such and yet takes himself to have no overriding reason not to kill them in the situation he is in?

I think not. As mentioned, I assume that regarding them as such means believing that they—or better, their existence and flourishing—ought to be protected and pursued for their own sakes. This does not necessarily imply that one takes *oneself* to have reason to protect and pursue their existence and flourishing, at least not actively and not as long as someone else is protecting and pursuing it. That someone does not have to be oneself.[6] But I think it *does* imply that one takes oneself to have reason to at least *not stand in the way* of their existence and flourishing being actively pursued and protected. And it also implies that one considers this to be a strong reason in the sense that it is not easily outweighed, especially not by reasons that flow from non-publically and non-universally valuable things such as one's own contingent desires.[7] In fact, it is a *prima facie* overriding reason.

If that is right, the fact that the father in the example does not take himself to have these kinds of overriding reasons not to kill other children suggests that he does not regard his daughter as an objective end in herself on account of her humanity. Korsgaard's point is that this reveals that something is "amiss" with his love for his daughter—it makes us doubt the sincerity of his love.

One might wonder whether her point relies on a questionable norm of consistency for lovers. Is she saying that lovers have to also think of other people as objective ends in themselves on pain of consistency? In a certain sense of "on pain of consistency," this would not be very convincing: if the problem is supposed to be that lovers who do not regard all instantiations of humanity as equally valuable are irrational, then we would have to show that lovers *qua* lovers are bound by norms of rationality. But why should they be? Or rather: why should it not be compatible with love to be irrational in this way? Why should this kind of irrationality be a reason to doubt the sincerity of someone's love?

In this context, there is another sense of "on pain of consistency," however. It might simply be psychologically implausible that someone regards their beloved as an objective end in themselves on account of their humanity but does not regard what they recognize to be other instantiations of humanity in the same way. Why would they have such different reactions to what they recognized to be the same thing? Since it would be so hard to make psychological sense of this, it would make us question whether they *actually* regarded their beloved in the way Korsgaard claims is required of them *qua* lovers. Of course, this leaves open the possibility that they do not recognize other human beings as humans—maybe they simply misidentify them. But similarly, we might doubt that someone could be entirely blind to and misidentify other people's humanity when they regard their beloved's humanity as an objective end in itself. Again, it would make us wonder whether they really do regard their beloved in this way. So the thought would be that someone who regarded their beloved's humanity as an objective end in itself would be sufficiently aware of and sensitized to what it means to be human that they would not (or at least would be very unlikely to) make these sorts of mistakes.

In the following section, I defend a similar line of thought. In particular, I defend the idea that lovers *qua* lovers regard their beloved's existence and flourishing as an objective end in itself and that they do so on account of their beloved's humanity. And I agree with Korsgaard that this means that they value other human beings similarly, again, *qua* lovers and not just *qua* moral agents. I relate this back to Pettit's cat case in the end, and to the reasons lovers have *qua* lovers. I do not mean to say that love *generates* these reasons. On the picture I defend, love does not itself generate a reason not to kill other human beings to save one's own beloved (to stick to Korsgaard's example), but love makes lovers recognize this as their reason. I come back to this distinction.

Everyone's Humanity

Lovers desire to pursue and protect their beloved's existence and flourishing for its own sake and not merely as a means to some further end (or some other kind of relative end). In that sense, they value the beloved's existence and flourishing as an end in itself. Do they also believe that their beloved's existence and flourishing really *is* an end in itself, objectively speaking and independently of their desire?

According to Harry Frankfurt, the answer is no, not necessarily. For him, believing that the beloved's existence and flourishing is an objective end in itself is neither sufficient nor necessary for love. It is compatible with love and with desiring the beloved's existence and flourishing for its own sake that one takes their existence and flourishing to be objectively valueless, or that one does not have any beliefs about its value at all.[8]

I agree with the sufficiency-claim: it is possible to believe that something is an end in itself, objectively speaking, without loving it. More narrowly, it is possible to believe that something is an objective end in itself and not desire and pursue it as one's *own* end. For example, one might believe that studying art is an objective end in itself, but neither want to study art oneself nor believe that one ought to study art. All it commits one to, arguably, is believing that *somebody* ought to study art, but that somebody can be someone else.[9] I made a similar point in the previous section.

However, I disagree with Frankfurt that the belief is not necessary for love. If at some time t1, a lover imagines a time t2 in which they have ceased being in the psychological state that constitutes their love—for instance, because they (the lover) are dead at t2—they still, at t1, desire their beloved's existence and flourishing for its own sake at t2. Put slightly differently: if a lover imagines that for whatever reason their beloved's existence and flourishing will not be an end in itself for them anymore at some future time, they will now, when they are still lovers, want it to be the case that their beloved continues to exist and flourish at that future time, and they will still want this for its own sake. They will hope at t1 that their beloved's existence and flourishing will be someone else's end and/or that it is ensured in some way at t2.[10]

If this was not the case—i.e., if someone at t1 was indifferent to what happened to their beloved at t2 when the beloved's existence and flourishing was not their own end anymore—I think we would doubt that they truly loved their beloved at t1. If that is right, it seems that lovers take their beloved's existence and flourishing to be an end in itself even independently of it being an end in itself for them in particular. Otherwise, it would not make any sense to be concerned with it for its own sake when they imagine hypothetical scenarios in which it is not an end in itself for them anymore. The argument can be extended to other people's ends: a lover would want their beloved's existence and flourishing to be ensured not just independently of this being their own end, but independently of it happening to be *anyone's* end in particular. The most plausible explanation for this is that lovers (rightly or wrongly) consider their beloved's existence and flourishing to really be an end in itself, objectively speaking.[11]

So my claim is that lovers *qua* lovers believe that their beloved's existence and flourishing is an objective end in itself—something that ought to be protected and pursued even independently of their own love and of the fact that it happens to be an end in itself for them. This belief, whether correct or not, is part of the attitude of love.

Further, even though the belief is not sufficient for the lover's desire to pursue the beloved's existence and flourishing for its own sake, the desire is at least in part explained by the belief. It is not as if these are just unconnected parts of love, in other words. Instead, the desire is partly a response to what the lover takes to be the objective worth of the beloved's existence and flourishing. Or at least, it is how the lover *experiences* their desire. This is not always the case: we can want to pursue gardening, say, for its own sake and also believe that gardening is an objective end in itself but experience our desire as independent from this belief. We might think that we would want to continue gardening for its own sake even if it turned out not to be an objective end in itself after all. It might just be a personal hobby for us and as such, we do not really care whether it is objectively worthy in any way (even though we certainly believe that it is). Nothing hangs on it for us. But desiring and pursuing the beloved's existence and flourishing for its own sake is not just a personal hobby for the lover. At least in the lover's own narrative, it is deeply connected to what the lover takes to be the objective worthiness of this pursuit.

What does it mean to believe that someone's existence and flourishing is an objective end in itself, however? One thing it implies is that the beloved's existence and flourishing—or simply, the beloved—is considered to be valuable in an irreplaceable way: since it ought to be protected and pursued for its own sake (at least by *someone*, as mentioned), nothing could take its place and be protected and pursued in its stead. By contrast, something we consider to be a mere means to a further end we take to be valuable in a replaceable way: it ought to be protected and pursued not for its own sake, but only insofar and for as long as it is effective in reaching the end in question, and we are willing to replace it for anything that is as good or better in reaching the end. So if lovers believe that their beloved is an objective end in themselves, they also believe that the beloved is irreplaceably valuable.[12]

In turn, this means that lovers do not consider their beloveds to be valuable merely on account of instantiating certain valuable qualities such as beauty, say, or wisdom and so on. Even if such qualities are *also* objective ends in themselves, that would not necessarily turn particular instantiations of them into objective ends in themselves. It is compatible with considering beauty to be an objective end in itself that we take the particular instantiations of beauty to be replaceable for each other. So the source of the beloved's objective end-hood and irreplaceability must lie elsewhere.

If we take a step back, this is actually a remarkable way of valuing something: as an objectively irreplaceable concrete individual. To make sense of it, we would need to identify a type of value that turns its particular instantiations into objective ends in themselves. What could this be?

Interestingly, if we were talking about the attitude of respect rather than love, the answer would suggest itself quite naturally: we would point to humanity itself, or to personhood (I use these two terms interchangeably here).[13] At least, this is how we commonly understand respect: it is to value another human being as an objective end in themselves and irreplaceable as a result, simply on account of their humanity. A lot of our every day practices reflect this way of relating to other human beings—respect is not necessarily a rare and high-minded attitude, but something that comes to us quite naturally (which is not to say that it is not often absent, of course). For instance, our funeral practices could be seen as reflecting the belief that when a human being dies, something of value has been lost that not even an exact copy could fully replace.

It is unclear what, if anything, could justify this way of valuing human beings. Perhaps it is their capacity for autonomous agency, or (self-)consciousness, or having a special kind of self-conception. The details are not important here. For my current purposes, it is more important what *explains* our valuing other human beings this way. According to David Velleman, what explains it is a certain kind of experience we can have with others: "Some people just strike us as there in their faces, as if the lights are on and there is somebody home."[14] I think this is right: the experience of someone as a *somebody*, with a perspective on the world and with an inner life, explains why we value them in ways we do not value anything else. Or, put differently, it explains why we take respect to be a fitting attitude toward human beings in particular (as well as toward other beings we experience in a relevantly similar way).

Now, the claim is that this experience is also central to the attitude of love. For Velleman, this is just what love *is*, namely, seeing the beloved *as* a person.[15] For reasons I come back to in the next section, I disagree with identifying love with this experience. But I agree that this experience is a central part of love, because it explains how lovers come to value their beloveds as objective ends in themselves and as irreplaceable in the first place.

Let's briefly take stock. I argued that it is part of the attitude of love that lovers consider their beloveds to be objective ends in themselves (in fact, this partly explains their desire to pursue the beloved's existence and flourishing for its own sake). As such, they consider them to be irreplaceably valuable—which means, in turn, that they consider them to be valuable on account of more than their valuable qualities alone. I suggested that they consider them to be objective ends in themselves on account of their humanity, similarly to Korsgaard's claim in the passage cited earlier. This is because experiencing them as human beings explains *why* they consider them to be valuable in this special way, just as it explains why they consider anyone to be valuable in this particular way.

Again, this experience is not sufficient for love. We often experience and value others in this way without loving them—respect seems to be the right term for that attitude. Also, as I argued earlier, it is compatible with respecting someone that we do not actively protect and pursue (or take ourselves to have reason to actively protect and pursue) their existence and flourishing, as long as we do not stand in the way of someone else doing so, and as long as we are not the only ones who can ensure their existence and flourishing. But this kind of passivity is not compatible with love: when we love someone, we want to actively protect and pursue their existence and flourishing. This is not only something we take to be *an* objective end in itself, but *our* end in particular. Still, the experience of the beloved as a human being and thus as valuable in this special way is a necessary and central part of love, as it partly explains the desire for their existence and flourishing.[16]

What follows from this for the lover's relation to other human beings? I think Korsgaard is right that if lovers value their beloved in this special way on account of their humanity, they also value other human beings this way. As I argued in the previous section, the point is not that they should value others in this way on pain of consistency. Even if the charge of inconsistency is right, lovers are not necessarily bound by norms of consistency *qua* lovers (that is not necessarily part of what we might call the *rationale* of love). Rather, the point is that lovers *would* value other human beings in this way because it would be psychologically implausible if they did not. Just as it would be odd if we recognized a striking piece of music that we listened to intensely many times only when it is played on a record player but not when it is played in a concert hall, it would be strange if we valued our beloved on account of their humanity, but were completely blind and desensitized to the humanity of others.

Let's go back to Pettit's cat case. I said that if X values Y's existence and flourishing as an objective end in itself, X takes themselves to have a *prima facie* overriding reason to at least not stand in the way of *someone* protecting and pursuing Y's existence and flourishing. That someone does not necessarily have to be X themselves. In a situation, however, in which X is the only one who can guarantee Y's existence and flourishing, X takes themselves to have a *prima facie* overriding reason to protect and pursue Y's existence and flourishing. If lovers *qua* lovers take other human beings to be objective ends in themselves, then a lover in the situation Pettit envisages would take themselves to have a *prima facie* overriding reason to help the stranger instead of consoling their beloved. As mentioned before, this reason is not generated by their love—it is generated by the stranger's humanity. But still, it is part of the attitude of love that lovers take themselves to have this reason (just as it is part of the attitude of respect).

This conclusion might strike us as too strong, because it means that we should doubt anyone's love for their children, partners, close friends, siblings, and so on, if they do not take themselves to have a *prima facie* overriding reason to help others who need their help. This does follow from the conclusion, but here are two points in defense: first, it does not necessarily mean that we should doubt someone's love if they do not *in fact* help others who need their help. It is possible to act contrary to the reasons one takes oneself to have, even when one considers them to be overriding. It is a difficult question how much *akrasia* is compatible with sincerely taking oneself to have certain overriding reasons to do something. But at least some *akrasia* seems to be compatible with this. As someone who feels the normative weight of these reasons, however, one would feel remorse about this kind of *akrasia*, and one would try to improve. So what I am saying is that a lover who does not live up to their reasons to assist others in need (or to not stand in the way of their existence and flourishing being protected and pursued) would feel guilt. It would not leave them "cold," so to speak, especially in the face of their beloveds. (People often say that had they refused assistance to someone in need, they could not have looked their beloved in the eye anymore. This suits the view I am defending here.)

Second, what I am saying does not imply that love is incompatible with any sort of immorality. It is just incompatible with violating or disregarding someone else's humanity, in the way the father does in Korsgaard's example or the lover in Pettit's cat case.

In the introduction, I mentioned that according to Pettit there is a range of possible scenarios in which a lover would provide care for their beloved, given certain prompts.[17] I have argued that there is also a range of possible scenarios in which a lover would provide care to people other than the beloved—not just as a moral agent, but as a lover. Perhaps we could even put it in this way: caring for the beloved can sometimes take the form of also caring for others. In a way, in Pettit's cat case, assisting the stranger is a greater expression of care for the beloved than holding the beloved's hand while letting the stranger die.

One Thought Too Few

In the above, I distinguished between believing of something that it is an objective end in itself and something being one's own end in itself. Lovers believe that their beloved's existence and flourishing is an objective end in itself, but it is also *their* end in itself: *they* want to pursue and protect their beloved's continued existence and flourishing for its own sake, they are personally invested in it. Loving their beloved thus makes them care for their beloved in ways they do not care for others, and they also take themselves to have reasons to care for for their beloved that they do not have to care for others. They are partial toward their beloveds in this sense.[18]

The fact that, *qua* lovers, they also take themselves to have *prima facie* overriding reasons not to stand in the way of other people's existence and flourishing being protected and pursued (and to assist other people if no one else can guarantee their existence and flourishing) is compatible with that. At least in most situations, luckily, caring for our beloveds does not conflict with not standing in the way of other people's existence and flourishing being protected and pursued, or with helping them in situations of acute need. In fact, sometimes, helping others in acute need can be an indirect way of also caring for our beloveds, as I said. So in most situations, being partial toward their beloveds in some ways does not conflict with the reasons lovers take themselves to have to also care for others.

What about the rare situations in which they do conflict, however? What if two people are drowning in a lake, someone is passing by, realizes that she can only save one of them and then recognizes one of them as her daughter? As a loving mother, what would she do and what reasons would she take herself to have for rescuing either one of them?

According to Velleman, as a lover, the mother would not be able to choose between her daughter and the stranger in this case. Since he conceives of love as seeing the beloved *as* a person, as mentioned, love is just a more intense form of respect. As such, it is not inherently partial toward the beloved. He does believe that the mother should in fact rescue her daughter, but this is not because of her love for her daughter, but because of the specific kind of interpersonal relationship they have. Their relationship will involve implicit or explicit promises to care for each other in times of need, and it gives her a reason to choose her daughter over the stranger in this example.[19]

By contrast, according to Pettit, the mother would choose her daughter because she loves her. She would act partially here, in other words. If the mother is also a moral agent, then she will have a kind of moral alarm system in place, meaning: she will be partial toward her beloved only in situations in which it does not conflict with morality; when it does conflict with morality, her inner alarm bells will be ringing, preventing her from simply following love's lead. But here, since most moral theories would agree that it is morally permitted to rescue one's beloved in situations such as these (e.g., because of the implicit promises that are part of relationships), her alarm system would stay quiet.[20]

Neither response seems quite right to me. I turn to Velleman first. It just strikes me as implausible that, as a lover, the mother would not take herself to have any more reason to rescue her daughter than to rescue the stranger. When she jumps in to rescue her daughter, which she will inevitably do, with panic welling up inside of her, hurrying for her life to make it in time, she is also acting on reasons she takes herself to have *qua* lover and not just *qua* promiser. The mother's loving desires for her daughter that make her daughter's existence and flourishing an end in itself for her in particular (rather than just an objective end in itself) give her reason to rescue her daughter instead of the stranger.

This does not mean that she does not recognize the plight of the stranger, however, and feel the weight of what is happening to them. As a lover, she does take herself to have reason to assist the stranger after all—it is just that given that she has more reason overall to assist her daughter here, the reasons to assist the stranger are ultimately outweighed. Being outweighed does not mean they are gone. Rather, as a lover and not just as a moral agent, she is aware of and feels their normative pull.

While Pettit does not have to rule out the possibility of a lover also being concerned with the stranger, it is compatible with his account that the mother is entirely indifferent to the stranger (according to his account, this is true even if she is also a moral agent). This also strikes me as odd, and I agree with Velleman when he writes that "although I may be insensitive to suffering until I see it in people I love, I cannot then remain insensitive to it in their fellow sufferers. (...) The idea that someone could show love for his own children by having less compassion for other children strikes me as bizarre."[21]

What is the difference between the lake-scenario and Korsgaard's organ case above? One might worry that they are structurally similar. How come lovers take themselves to have reasons not to kill other children to save their own, if they take themselves to have reasons to rescue their own child instead of the stranger? In the organ-case, if the father had not been there, the other child (the child he kills to save his own) would not have died. By contrast, in the lake-scenario, if the mother had not been there, the stranger would have died anyway. In fact, both the stranger and her daughter would have died—they are both in the same life-and-death-situation. Since the mother is morally obliged to rescue as many as she can, and she can only save one of them, she is morally obliged to somehow choose between the stranger and her daughter here. Given this, it seems that choosing in this situation is not necessarily an expression of putting one above the other, i.e., of taking the existence and flourishing of either one of them to be more or less valuable than that of the respective other—even if in choosing she is taking into account her loving desires for her daughter.

The father in the organ-case does not face this choice, however, since the other child is not in the same life-and-death situation. So his actions do reveal that he regards the existence and flourishing of the other child as less valuable than his own (in the sense spelled out before), and I argued that this was in tension with his love for his own child.

When I say that the mother in the lake-scenario feels the pull of the reasons she takes herself to have to rescue the stranger, does she have one thought too many in Bernard Williams' sense of the term? Williams thinks that lovers in the lake-scenario who are partially motivated to rescue their beloveds by thoughts about the moral permissibility to rescue them have "one thought too many."[22] The reasons is that, for him, true lovers do not really care about what is morally permissible or impermissible in situations such as this.[23]

There is certainly something strange about the idea of a lover who checks their moral rule book before jumping in to rescue their beloved. This lover would have to be sufficiently removed from the situation in order to reflect on it from the point of view of general moral principles, and being thus removed is at odds with how we imagine a lover to think, feel, and act in this kind of situation.

But being concerned about and emotionally affected by the plight of the stranger, and taking oneself to have reasons to also rescue them, is not the same as checking one's moral rule book. It is not a sign of being removed, but compatible with being entirely "in" the situation. If we tell Williams' story in that way, our intuitions change: if we imagine that instead of checking their inner moral rule book, the lover feels the weight of what it means that the stranger is drowning and recognizes that they also have reason to rescue them, we would not think that the lover has one thought too many. Intuitively, this kind of response towards the stranger is not at odds with loving the beloved.

In fact, given what I argued before (and in line with Velleman's point), if they did not have this response and were indifferent to the stranger's plight, then as a lover they would have one thought too few.

Love and our moral relations with others 213

Conclusion

I have argued that a certain type of "ruthless love" does not exist. Lovers think of their beloveds as objective ends in themselves on account of their humanity, and they also think of other human beings in this way. This means that they are not indifferent to the plight of others in the way the lover is in Pettit's cat case, and they would not be brutal in the way the father is in Korsgaard's organ case. Instead, loving someone comes along with recognizing that one has *prima facie* overriding reasons to at least not stand in the way of other people's existence and flourishing being protected and pursued, and sometimes also to actively protect and pursue it oneself (if no one else can do so, for instance). To that extent, there is an overlap of the reasons lovers and moral agents recognize as theirs.

This does not mean that lovers are not partial toward their beloveds: there is a difference between believing that something is an objective end in itself and it being one's own end. In conflict situations such as Williams' lake case, however, even though lovers *qua* lovers have overall reason to rescue their beloved, they still recognize that they also have reason to rescue the stranger.[24]

Notes

1. Pettit (2015, 14–15).
2. Pettit (2015, 19).
3. Korsgaard (2006, 73–76).
4. Another possibility might be that he is not acting on the basis of reasons at all, but on pure affect. I am not sure this distinction is very clear-cut, however. Acting on reasons does not have to mean acting on the basis of a conscious deliberation process. It can be very affect-laden, simply responding to what one consciously or unconsciously perceives as a normative pull in a particular situation.
5. Something that ought to be pursued in all conceptually possible situations must be something that ought to be pursued for its own sake. For things that ought to be pursued for the sake of some other end ought to be pursued in a limited range of conceptually possible situations only, namely only for as long as they continue to be related to this other end in the relevant way (e.g., for as long as they continue being a means to this end). At least, this is so if this relation between them (the means and the end, say) is contingent and not conceptually necessary. Arguably, if the relation is one of conceptual necessity, the two things in question are in fact part of one. But this would have to be investigated further.
6. If no one else is protecting and pursuing it, then believing that something is an objective end in itself does imply believing that one has reason to protect and pursue its existence and flourishing oneself (see also below).
7. Although, while I take this to be *prima facie* plausible, this would have to be defended some more: why accept a weighing of reasons where reasons correlated with public and universal values outweigh reasons that correlate with non-public and non-universal ones? See Korsgaard (1996), et al..

8. Frankfurt, Harry (2006, p. 27 ff). This means that, strictly speaking, Frankfurt is not a bestowal-theorist of love as he is sometimes called, at least not if "bestowal" means projecting valuable qualities onto the beloved or actually generating valuable qualities in the beloved by loving them. Lovers value their beloveds, according to Frankfurt, but valuing is not a cognitive attitude for him, it is purely volitional. So, for him, love is compatible with believing that the beloved is devoid of valuable qualities (independently of whether this belief is a projection or not), and love does not create any actual value in the beloved either. All it means for lovers to value their beloved is to treat their existence and flourishing as an end in itself.
9. If nobody studies art, then believing that studying art is an objective end in itself might commit one to also believing that one ought to either study art oneself or do something so that someone else suitable will study art. In other words, it might commit one to believing that one has a reason to do something so that studying art is instantiated in the world.
10. It does not necessarily mean that lovers will hope that someone else will love their beloved at t2, although I think this is common. We often want others to see what we saw in our beloveds and to care for them lovingly after we have died.
11. Someone might object that the fact that the lover would want their beloved's existence and flourishing to be pursued at t2 only shows that they consider it to be worthy of pursuit independently of their desires *at t2*, but not necessarily independently of their desires *at t1*. It would be a strange bias in favor of one's current desires, but perhaps the position could be made sense of. In response, we could think of a lover who at t1 imagines that at *t1* they did not have the relevant desire—say, they imagine a world in which they had never met and hence not fallen in love with their beloved. They would still want their beloved's existence and flourishing to be pursued for its own sake even if they never desired it as their own end. So it seems that they would want their beloved's existence and flourishing to be pursued independently of their current desires, too. In other words, they do not take their own desires to be the ground for the worthiness of this pursuit. If we extend the argument to other people's desires again, we arrive at the same conclusion: they locate the ground in the beloved, i.e., they take the beloved's existence and flourishing to be objectively worthy of being pursued for its own sake.
12. That lovers take their beloveds to be irreplaceable is also independently plausible. However, whether, as lovers, they take their beloveds to be irreplaceable not just *qua* beloved but *qua* objective end in themselves, as I am suggesting here, is a matter of controversy. Velleman (1999) argues that they do, but others offer different accounts of the beloved's irreplaceability. See Kolodny (2003), Frankfurt (2004), Grau (2010), Abramson and Leite (2011), Naar (2017), Kreft (2018), and others.
13. See the discussion in Setiya (2014, 262), about the potential differences between these terms.
14. Velleman (2013, 9).
15. Velleman (1999). Although see Velleman (2013), where he writes (in contrast to the 1999 paper): "I do not see much point in talking about what love is. Still, I think that there is one strand of emotion that almost always runs through love and for which we have no other term: it is the emotion that I have described as amazement at the personhood of another."
16. See also Kreft (2018), and Kreft (forthcoming).

17. What exactly this range includes might vary between cultures, but presumably there is a common core, see Pettit (2015, 18).
18. Strictly speaking, whether or not this is really partial depends on what justification there is for lovers taking their beloved's existence and flourishing to be their end in particular. If this is somewhat arbitrary, then lovers favoring their beloveds is indeed partial. But if there is a justification, this is not so clear.
19. Velleman (1999, 372–373). This also seems to be an impartial reason.
20. Pettit (2015, ch. 7).
21. Velleman (1999, 373).
22. Williams, Bernard (1981, ch. 1).
23. See Wolf, Susan (2012) for this interpretation of Williams' point.
24. I thank Michael Kühler and Andrew Stephenson for their very helpful comments on an earlier draft.

References

Abramson, Katy & Leite, Adam, 2011: 'Love as a reactive emotion', in *The Philosophical Quarterly*, Vol. 61/245.
Frankfurt, Harry, 2004: *The Reasons of Love*, Princeton University Press.
Frankfurt, Harry, 2006: *Taking Ourselves Seriously & Getting It Right*, Stanford University Press.
Grau, Christopher, 2010: 'Love and History', in *The Southern Journal of Philosophy*, Vol. 48/3.
Kolodny, Niko, 2003: 'Love as Valuing a Relationship', in *The Philosophical Review*, Vol. 112/2. Korsgaard, Christine, 1996: The Sources of Normativity, Cambridge University Press.
Korsgaard, Christine, 2006: 'Morality and the Logic of Caring' in Frankfurt, H., *Taking Ourselves Seriously & Getting It Right*, Stanford University Press.
Kreft, Nora, 2018: 'Love and Autonomy', in Grau, C., Smuts, A., *The Oxford Handbook of Philosophy of Love*, Oxford University Press.
Kreft, Nora, forthcoming: *Liebe*, de Gruyter.
Naar, Hitchem, 2017: 'Subject-Relative Reasons for Love', in *Ratio*, Vol. 30/2.
Pettit, Philip, 2015: *The Robust Demands of the Good*, Oxford University Press.
Setiya, Kieran, 2014: 'Love and the Value of a Life', in *The Philosophical Review*, Vol. 123/3.
Velleman, David, 1999: 'Love as a moral emotion', in *Ethics*, Vol. 109/2.
Velleman, David, 2013: 'Sociality and Solitude', in *Philosophical Explorations*, Vol. 16/3.
Williams, Bernard, 1981: 'Persons, Character, and Morality', in his *Moral Luck*, Cambridge University Press.
Wolf, Susan, 2010: 'One Thought Too Many: Love, Morality, and the Ordering of Commitment', in Heuer, U., Lang, G., *Luck, Value, and Commitment: Themes from the Ethics of Bernard Williams*, Oxford University Press.

12 Acting Out
How Personal Relationships Provide Basic Moral Practical Reasons

Shane Gronholz

- *Gretchen and Edgar are close personal friends, and Gretchen has applied for a job at Edgar's company. Edgar recommends Gretchen for this position to his boss, even though he has no reason to be confident that Gretchen would do a better job than any of the other applicants.*
- *Tony and Becky pay for their daughter to attend an expensive private college, despite the fact that there are much more pressing needs to which they could contribute those financial resources.*
- *Raquel's husband needs a pancreas transplant. She has access to the donor list and moves her husband up to ensure he will get a much needed pancreas.*

These are examples of people behaving partially toward their friends or loved ones. To behave partially is to show favoritism toward certain groups or individuals, to put their interests ahead of the interests of others, to treat them *better* than one treats everyone else. What are we to make of the above examples? Are those kinds of actions wrong? Are they permissible? Could they be morally required?

In this chapter, I will argue that we are morally permitted, and sometimes morally required, to give preferential treatment to those with whom we have certain kinds of personal relationships (hereafter, I refer to all such individuals simply as *friends*). This is because I believe such relationships provide *basic* moral practical reasons that apply to our treatment of our friends, but not to others.

I stress "basic" here because even the paradigmatic impartial moral theory, act utilitarianism, can allow some limited scope for treating one's friends differently than one treats strangers, for sometimes doing so leads to greater well-being. Of course, very often it does not, and when it does not, it is not permissible. For a view to be partial in a deep way, it must claim that it is permissible to prioritize my friends even when I would achieve less overall moral good than by doing some alternative. And my view is partial in an even deeper way, in the sense that it is the *relationship itself* that places special moral demands on me.

In the "Reasons and Relationships" section, I will explicate the concept of the reason these kinds of relationships provide, which I call a *relational reason*. In the "Partiality and Impartiality" section, I will explore the concepts of partiality and impartiality. Impartiality is not one thing—a view can be partial in one way but impartial in another way, and there are some senses of the term "impartiality" such that a moral view really must be impartial for it to be acceptable. In this section, I will make it clear in what sense my view is partial, and in what sense it is appropriately impartial.

In the "Why Partiality?" section, I will offer a novel argument for moral partiality by defending the existence of relational reasons. Like Troy Jollimore, who also defends partiality, I will begin with the feelings of love and affection that typically exist between friends. Jollimore argues that, conceptually, for an agent to have a friend the agent must love that friend—and love the friend in a way the agent does not love everyone. It also requires expression of that love, which requires action, but this action must be partial action, since the feelings themselves are feelings of favoring the friend over other individuals. My argument goes a step further. While Jollimore's argument rests on a conceptual claim about friendship, mine rests on a *normative* claim: we *ought* to love our friends.

I will then introduce a general principle, which I call Act Out.

> Act Out: If s has normative reasons to hold attitude a, then s has corresponding normative reasons to act out of a.

If this principle holds, and we do indeed have reason to have a special kind of affection for our friends, then it follows that we have reasons to *act out* of that attitude, which involves treating our loved ones in a special sort of way. I then offer two arguments for Act Out. One is that to deny Act Out would be to endorse a schizophrenic view of morality. It would be to say, for example, that while you are permitted (or even required) to have a certain kind of attitude, you must never act on that attitude.

My other argument begins with a metaphysical claim about the source of practical reasons: both our reasons to have certain attitudes as well as our reasons to perform certain actions are provided *by the very same facts*. Thus, when I have a reason to adopt a certain attitude, there will also be a reason to act in a corresponding way (at least provided that I'm in a position to act at all). I then show how Act Out has important implications for the epistemology of practical reasons: when we recognize the appropriateness of having a certain attitude (which can often start by simply *having* the attitude), we thereby recognize a reason to act out of that attitude.

I will close by pointing out that this account of partiality does an excellent job at satisfying what I call the Right Reasons Requirement. As Susan Wolf (1992, 2012) and Michael Stocker (1976) have noted, there is something unsettling about the idea that when our friends behave lovingly toward us, they do so merely because they believe it is their moral duty. Instead, we would hope that they treat us in these ways simply because they love us, because we are their friends. On the other hand, we don't think we should have to violate a moral duty by giving loving treatment to our friends. My account shows how one may be appropriately motivated by love and friendship while still living up to the demands of morality.

Reasons and Relationships

Consider a provocative scene from the television show *Game of Thrones*. The young Jon Snow has recently joined The Night's Watch, a special order of soldiers charged with protecting the kingdom from outside threats (Game of Thrones 2011). When they take their vows, they are required to renounce all property and personal commitments, and to promise to have no wives or children. But Jon is in a quandary: his father has been taken prisoner and his brother is leading a rebellion against the evil rulers of the realm, so Jon is considering breaking his vows and abandoning his post at The Night's Watch in order to help them. Jon has the following conversation with a wise elder of The Night's Watch, named Aemon:

AEMON: Tell me. Did you ever wonder why the men of The Night's Watch take no wives and father no children?
JON: No
AEMON: So they will not love. Love is the death of duty. If the day should ever come when your lord father was forced to choose between honor on the one hand and those he loves on the other, what would he do?
JON: He would do whatever was right, no matter what.
AEMON: Then Lord Stark is one man in ten thousand. Most of us are not so strong. What is honor compared to a woman's love? And what is duty against the feel of a newborn son in your arms? Or a brother's smile? [...] We're all human. Oh, we all do our duty when there is no cost to it. Honor comes easy then. Yet, sooner or later, in every man's life, there comes a day when it is *not* easy. A day when he must *choose*.

Is Aemon right when he claims that love is the death of duty? That we must choose between doing what is right and providing special care for our parents, or siblings, or friends?

Relational Reasons

I do not believe that love for our close relations is generally incompatible with moral duty. This is because I believe we have good reason to behave partially—to give special treatment to our friends and family.[1] My aim here is to defend the existence of such reasons, which I call relational reasons, and to explain the role they play in determining the moral status of this kind of special treatment.

Because I will be making regular reference to the broad category of those individuals with whom we enjoy personal relationships of many kinds (more on those relationships below), it is convenient to adopt a term to refer to all such individuals. I will refer to all such individuals simply as *friends*—this will include friends, in the normal sense of the word, but also other loved ones, (some) family members, and perhaps certain acquaintances as well.

I offer the following definition of a relational reason: a relational reason is a reason an agent has to treat individual s in certain ways, for s's own sake, in virtue of a personal relationship the agent has with s.

Relational reasons, if they exist, can justify, and perhaps require, certain kinds of partiality or favoritism that would be morally impermissible in the absence of such reasons. We have a general moral requirement to treat other individuals well. There is also a presumption in favor of equal treatment: we should treat people equally unless there is a good reason not to. If we have relational reasons, which apply only to the treatment of our friends, then we have more reason, or stronger reason, to treat our friends well. Such a reason can then overcome the presumption in favor of equal treatment, justifying treating our loved ones *better* than we treat everyone else (more on what better treatment entails below).

I in fact hold a stronger version of the view I just presented. I believe that agents are sometimes *obligated* to provide special treatment to those with whom they have a relationship. This is because I believe that one ought to do whatever one has most reason to do. If one is deciding to perform an action that will benefit a stranger or an action that will benefit a friend, then that the friend is a friend will provide additional reason for the agent to benefit the friend, and that means that, all else equal, the person ought to benefit the friend. Of course, the view that one should always do that which one has most reason to do and the view that there are relational reasons can come apart. They do not entail each other and one can endorse one without endorsing the other. For the most part, in this chapter, I will be defending the more modest version.[2]

I want to stress here that the relational reasons I will be defending are *basic* normative practical reasons. This is important to note, for even the paradigmatic impartial moral theory, act utilitarianism, can allow some limited scope for treating one's friends differently than one treats strangers, for *sometimes* doing so can lead to greater well-being.

Relational reasons are *basic,* by contrast: they do not arise from other values or goods but are instead provided by the very relationships we have with those to whom they apply.

Before saying more about what kinds of relationships I have in mind, let me explain the qualification "for *s*'s own sake" in the above definition. I may have reasons to see that my child receives an excellent education. One reason to do this may be for *my own* sake, for example, to gain the admiration and envy of my peers. But this would not be a relational reason in the present sense, since this is not a reason to do anything for my child's own sake. Rather, a reason to see to my child's education for his own sake would refer directly to *him*, to his well-being, or development, or whatever.

Personal Relationships

The kinds of relationships I have in mind are what we commonly refer to as *personal relationships*. These kinds of relationships are quite familiar: spouses, children, perhaps other family members, friends, and (at least some) acquaintances. I cannot give a complete and definite account of what constitutes a personal relationship since the concept by its nature is fuzzy and amorphous. But I take it that we all have an intuitive understanding of the concept. It is often obvious when we have such relationships and when we don't. I have a personal relationship with my spouse, my child, and my best friend. I do not have a personal relationship with Bob, a stranger in Minnesota whom I have never met. Of course, there are many cases around the margins where it is less clear. I may take an Uber ride and strike up a conversation with my driver. Do I now have a personal relationship with my driver? Do I have a personal relationship with a colleague whom I see around the office but hardly ever speak to? Sometimes it will simply be vague. But I think even in these cases, it is plausible that I have some minimal personal relationship with such people and therefore have minimal relational reasons to treat them well. For example, if I can benefit my colleague or a stranger, and I have equal agent-neutral reasons to benefit each, it is plausible that I have slightly more reason to benefit my colleague, and therefore ought to do so.

As these examples suggest, personal relationships come in degrees. On my view, the strength of our relational reasons correspondingly comes in degrees. For example, my relational reasons to care about and promote my spouse's well-being, all else equal, will generally be stronger than my relational reasons with respect to my treatment of my friend, which are in turn stronger than my relational reasons with respect to my treatment of a mere acquaintance.

Another issue these examples (the Uber case, the colleague case, etc.) raise is whether it is up to me whether I have the relevant kind of personal relationship with another person and the attendant relational reasons regarding my treatment of them. It seems to me that it must be up to me *in some sense*: I cannot simply be thrust into a personal relationship without any voluntary action on my part whatsoever. Thus, relational reasons based on personal relationships must be voluntaristic in some sense. But what sense?

To say that a relational reason is voluntaristic admits of at least three interpretations. One possible view of voluntaristic relational reasons is that one has such reasons only if one chooses to have them. I reject this view. One reason is that I do not believe that reasons in general are voluntaristic in this sense, at least not usually.[3] On my view, if we have a personal relationship with someone, we have relational reasons regarding our treatment of that person, regardless of whether we want to have such reasons. I have relational reasons to promote my friend's welfare even if I don't want to have those reasons. Of course, it may be that he moves away and we lose touch, and our relationship dissolves. In that case, I may no longer have relational reasons regarding my treatment of him. (Or not: maybe I will always have at least a minimal relational reason. I'm neutral on this point.)

A more plausible interpretation of the claim that relational reasons are voluntaristic is that I have them only if I voluntarily enter into a personal relationship. Or, slightly differently, I have them only if I take myself to be in a personal relationship. On this view, though I have relational reasons whether I want to or not, it is up to me whether I am in the kind of relationship that would generate relational reasons. But I reject this view as well. We can sometimes find ourselves in a personal relationship we did not intend to enter, and in those cases, we will still have relational reasons. Suppose I see the same stranger at my bus stop each morning. One morning, out of sheer boredom, I begin making idle chitchat with him. Over the course of months, our conversations naturally and gradually become more personal and we get to know each other in a somewhat intimate way. I now have a personal relationship with that person, and have relational reasons regarding my treatment of him, even though I at no time intended to enter into such a relationship. If there was an accident at the bus stop, and he and a stranger were pinned under a bus, and I could save only one, I should (all else equal) save him, because I have more reason to save him. So while I did not intentionally enter into a relationship with him, I voluntarily performed actions that led to that relationship.

So the voluntary condition I favor is the following:

> X has relational reasons with respect to Y only if X voluntary performs some (set of) action(s) that generate a personal relationship with Y.

This condition allows for the possibility that I have relational reasons regarding my friend at the bus stop, even if I never intended to become his friend. However, I also could have chosen never to perform any action, for example, engaging him in conversation, that would generate a personal relationship.

It bears mentioning that these choices are also available to him. He could have, for example, ignored my attempts at conversation and thereby avoided a personal relationship with me. Personal relationships, then, are reciprocal: they require voluntary actions on the part of each member. When a personal relationship is in place, both members have relational reasons with respect to the other.

What kinds of relationships does the voluntariness condition rule out? An important one would be that of mere biological relation. If I discover that I have a long-lost sister whom I have never met, I have no relational reasons regarding my treatment of her. It would also rule out relationships between a hostage and a captor. Though a hostage may get to know her captor quite intimately over the course of her imprisonment, she couldn't avoid those interactions without putting herself in danger. Thus, she has no relational reasons with respect to her treatment of her captor.[4]

The weak voluntaristic condition seems to capture the right morally relevant personal relationships. It entails we cannot be forced into them without our control. But it also entails that we often have morally relevant relationships we did not directly intend to have. In fact, many of our relationships are like this, in particular, relationships with our friends—"friends" in the ordinary sense, not in my technical sense. I have never had a friendship ceremony where I made a commitment to be a friend to someone. Friendships often form slowly, and sometimes even unintentionally. I might have a colleague whom I see regularly. We chat at parties and around the office and our relationship slowly grows more intimate. At some point, I may realize that this person has become a friend.

Now, it is plausible that making a commitment increases the moral significance of a relationship. A commitment is itself a voluntary action that can increase the reason-giving force of a relationship. This explains, in part, why marriages are among the most significant relationships we have.[5]

Relational reasons, in the current sense, are not to be confused with reasons one has in virtue of a *relation* one bears to other individuals, such as promiser-to-promisee, debtor-to-creditor, etc., nor those that arise from the role one occupies (though of course these relations often involve personal relationships). The President of the United States stands in a certain morally relevant relationship to all US citizens and has taken oaths to do certain things. These considerations may give him particular practical reasons, but they do not provide him with relational reasons, in the current sense, regarding his behavior as president. The same would go for a child I unknowingly fathered. Though I may have particular obligations toward such a child, such obligations would not be in virtue of any relational reasons I have.

Partiality and Impartiality

It should now be obvious that relational reasons rule out certain kinds of strict impartiality. This presents a challenge since it is natural to assume that morality should be impartial in some sense. Indeed, in some contexts, "impartial" and "morally right" are nearly synonymous. This challenge can be overcome by distinguishing, as Brad Hooker does, between different senses of the term "impartiality" (Hooker 2010). There is at least one sense in which my view is clearly *not* impartial. Hooker characterizes this form of impartiality as "impartial benevolence as *the* direct guide to decisions about what to do" (26). This type of impartiality is expressed in Singer's Principle of Equal Consideration (PEC), which

> "acts like a pair of scales, weighing interests impartially. True scales favour the side where the interest is stronger or where several interests combine to outweigh a smaller number of similar interests; but they take no account of whose interests they are weighing." (Singer 2011, 20–21)

Relational reasons are clearly incompatible with PEC, since they entail that agents have reasons, *inter alia*, to prioritize the interests of their friends over the interests of others. For the same reasons, relational reasons rule out Mill's famous injunction that we be "as strictly impartial as a disinterested and benevolent spectator" (Mill 1863, 19).

But my view *can* answer to the label of impartiality in a different sense. According to Hooker, another sense of "impartiality" is "impartial assessment of (first order) moral rules" (26). For a rule to be impartially assessable is, at a minimum, "to be defensible from an agent-neutral point of view" (35). Evaluating rules from an agent-neutral point of view, according to Hooker, involves "evaluating them apart from any special attachment of yours." He continues, "In your assessment of rules, you would not give extra weight to benefits that the rules produce for you, your friends, your family, etc." (35). For example, consider the rule, "the product of a collective enterprise should be divided in proportion to people's contributions to the enterprise" (29). Now suppose I am in charge of distributing the products and I reject this rule solely on the grounds that, were I to follow it, I would get the short end of the stick. This would amount to my failing to *assess* the rule impartially. As Hooker notes, assessing rules in an agent-neutral way has obvious appeal:

> In the assessment of rules, agent-neutrality does seem much more appealing than agent-relativity. The agent-relative assessment "Everyone's accepting these rules is good because this maximizes benefits for me" is utterly unconvincing. So is "everyone's accepting these rules is good because this maximizes benefits for my group". Agent-neutral assessment effectively eliminates explicit bias towards oneself, one's group, and indeed anyone with whom one has some special connection. (35)

Hooker is here referring to rules rather than reasons, but we can easily alter this account of "impartiality" to apply to reasons rather rules. We can then say that one can, upon assessment, endorse the view that one has basic reasons to prioritize one's friends in an agent-neutral way. In fact, nearly everyone does endorse it (at least implicitly), *including* those who could be made substantially better off if it were generally rejected. For example, I think a reasonable person could accept that I chose to invest in a college fund for my child, because he is my child, even though I could have used that money to provide a more fundamental need for her children. And she, in turn, might provide what she can for her children, even though she recognizes that she could produce more impartial good by doing something else. It need not be the case that she endorses relational reasons because she realizes that she and her child would be better off if relational reasons were generally acted upon. (This would constitute *partial* assessment.) Indeed, she might even be made worse off.

But the view that emerges if relational reasons are recognized is of course not impartial in other senses of the term. Relational reasons yield a partial view because agents often have more reason to treat their friends well than they do strangers. What counts as good treatment will depend on other substantive questions in normative ethics. But I take it that it involves, perhaps among other things, promoting their welfare. I should care about the interests of all individuals and I have reasons to make other individuals better off when I can. But if there are relational reasons, I often have more reason to care about and promote the interests of my friends. Practically, this means that it is often permissible to act so as to promote the welfare of my friend, even if I could promote more general welfare by choosing an alternative course of action. So, again, relational reasons are incompatible with Singer's PEC.

There may be other ways to treat people well besides by promoting their welfare. For example, there may be general, basic duties of fidelity, that is, duties to tell the truth and keep promises. If there is such a duty, it will be more pressing when it comes to the treatment of my friends. To see the intuitive appeal of this, we can contrast a case of my, say, lying to my spouse, with a case of lying to a stranger on the street. If someone approaches me and asks me if I have time to hear about the campaign to beautify the neighborhood, I might consider telling a lie by saying, "Sorry, I don't have any time right now," when this is not in fact the case. I may have some reason not to lie, but this reason does not seem especially strong, and it might be perfectly permissible to tell such a lie in light of other reasons to lie. But there seems to be something importantly different about telling a lie to my spouse. It seems like I have additional reasons not to lie to my spouse. Of course, some of these reasons are welfarist reasons. For example, she may be more likely to find out that I lied, and she may be hurt by my lying, and it may erode her trust in me. But it may be that I have extra reason not to lie to her even if I have good reason to believe there is very little chance of her finding out, and that reason seems to be *that she is my spouse*. This fact seems to be relevant to my practical reasons in a basic sort of way.

Another way of saying that agents often have reasons to treat friends better than strangers is that relational reasons are often stronger than agent-neutral reasons. What does this mean? I can think of two potential models, or ways of understanding this claim. Consider this case from Charles Fried (1970): an agent sees two people drowning. One is his wife. The other is a stranger. Assume he can save only one. We might say that the agent has equal agent-neutral reason to save each. If those were the only relevant reasons, he would have equal reason to save each. But the agent has an additional reason to save his wife, namely, that she is his wife. So he should save his wife. The problem with this model is that it might be, as Bernard Williams put it, "one thought too many" (1981, 18). It can seem odd or inappropriate for the agent to reason like this: "I realize they are both the kinds of individuals that I should save if I can. But since my wife is my wife, I have more reason to save her, so I will save her." Instead, we might think that the mere fact that she is his wife is all the reason he needs to save her. So we might prefer a model where the agent's reason to save his wife is simply that she is his wife. The problem with this model is that that isn't really the only reason he has, for he would have reasons to save her even if she were not his wife.

I propose that this dilemma can be avoided by noticing that in order for the agent's wife to be the sort of being with whom he can have a personal relationship in the first place, and thus have relational reasons regarding his treatment of her, she must already have the features that would make it the case that the agent would have agent-neutral reasons regarding his treatment of her if she were not his wife. When the agent saves his wife, he does so *because* she is his wife. But her being his wife entails that she has other features that would provide him with non-relational reasons to save her, even if she were not his wife. In short, relational reasons *entail* non-relational reasons. In this way, we might say that the non-relational reasons are subsumed by the relational reasons.

Why Partiality?

So far, I have been discussing the concepts of personal relationships, relational reasons, and partiality and impartiality. I now turn to defending partial treatment and the existence of relational reasons.

Begin by considering a case, to which I will give the name *Recommend*: The company I work for is hiring, and my friend, Gretchen, has submitted an application. I am considering whether to put in a good word to my boss on Gretchen's behalf. I know that doing so will give her a significant advantage. Suppose further that I have no evidence that Gretchen is more qualified for the job than any other candidate—I know she would do fine, but I have no idea whether she would be especially good. We can even suppose I know there is a candidate who would be slightly better. And suppose I'm not considering lying to my boss. I would only tell him that I think Gretchen is capable of doing the job. Still though, I know that even this modest endorsement will give Gretchen an advantage. To put in a good word for her, then, is to treat her partially, since I can assume most of the other candidates do not have an advocate on the inside. Should I recommend my friend?

To say that I should recommend my friend is to say that I should treat her partially. I now turn to defending this kind of partial treatment.

A variety of arguments have been made for defending this kind of view. It is common to begin with the premise that it is permissible to have friends (whatever that entails). The question then becomes, is it possible to have friends *and* behave in the ways impartial views—for example, consequentialism—prescribe? Susan Wolf and Michael Stocker both argue that even if this were possible, when a consequentialist acts in a way a friend is typically expected to act, she acts for the wrong reasons. To borrow Stocker's example, if I visit my friend in the hospital, I do not do so ultimately *because* he is my friend, but only because I realize that will maximize good consequences. It is not *his* good I care about, but just the good in general, and it just so happens that visiting my friend in the hospital is a way in which I can promote the good. I will briefly return to these arguments later.

Troy Jollimore takes a different approach. He argues that to be a friend requires that one act in a way that a consequentialist could not act (Jollimore 2000). He too begins with the premise that it is permissible to have friends. He then argues that to be a friend at all requires having certain kinds of feelings or sentiments toward one's friend, which we can describe as simply loving one's friend. The third premise is this: for friendship to exist, one must not only *feel* a certain way about one's friend, a way in which one does not feel about everyone, one must *express* that feeling through action. Interestingly, this premise is inspired by Kagan (1989), who accepts that for friendship to exist, love must be expressed in some way but denies that preferential treatment is necessary for that expression. Then comes the crux: "there can be no ... partiality-free expressions of love" (72).

To see whether this is true, we need an account of what it is for an action to express a feeling. Jollimore expresses this in terms of a counterfactual:

> CC: If an action A is an expression of feeling F, then it must be that if F had not obtained, A would not have occurred. (73)

He writes, "For an agent to express her feelings, her feelings must have significant influence over her actions: if she felt differently, she would act differently." He considers an example:

> I express my love for Joan by bringing about certain outcomes which I value: those in which Joan's desires are fulfilled (preferably by me); those in which Joan and I share enjoyable experiences; those in which I refrain from betraying Joan's trust, etc. If I felt differently toward Joan, I would not value those outcomes and would not act so as to bring them about. (73–74)

"But," he goes on, "this presents a problem for the consequentialist agent":

> According to consequentialism, we all ought to agree in ranking outcomes in order of value, and we all ought to bring about the best outcomes we can. Since such an agent's particular feelings play no significant role in determining which outcomes she is to bring about, she cannot express her feelings though her actions. (74)

One might think that the consequentialist can express love through speech, but as Jollimore notes, if my consequentialist friend tells me she loves me, I would have no reason to believe that she loves me—only that she believes that telling me she loves me promotes the good. Nor does it help to say that a consequentialist should adopt a policy of scrupulous honesty. Not only is such a policy unlikely to actually maximize the good, but the consequentialist who adopts such a policy "has no way to convince other people she has done so" (78) but, as before, her claim that she has done so only gives others evidence that she believes that claiming this is a way of promoting the good. If she hides the fact that she is a consequentialist, then she cannot explain why, although I am her friend, she is forbidden from showing me any favoritism. Jollimore writes,

> Such an agent is caught in a dilemma: she can only justify her conduct to people she cares for by revealing her moral commitments; but once her moral commitments are known, those around her will have no reason to believe her when she tells them she cares for them. (78)

So for Jollimore, for an agent to have a friend requires the agent loving that friend—loving the friend in a way the agent does not love everyone. It also requires expression of that love, which requires action, but this action has to be partial action, since the feelings themselves are feelings of favoring the friend over other individuals.

Acting Out

I now want to offer an additional argument in favor of partial treatment toward friends that shares some similarities with Jollimore's argument. Like Jollimore, I assume it is permissible to have friends. Hardly anyone denies that. And, like Jollimore, I think there is something important about the attitudes one has regarding one's friends. For Jollimore, it is simply analytic that friendship requires love. He says, "A friendship cannot exist where feelings of love and affection are not present. If Bill does not like Susan, if he does not feel any warmth toward or attachment to her, then they are not friends" (72).

I agree with Jollimore that friendship requires love in this way. But I now want to make a normative claim about the attitudes one takes toward one's friends: Not only is it analytically true that one loves one's friends, one also has reasons to love ones friends, such that one is *prima facie* required to love one's friends.[6] Now, this might seem odd: if love is required for friendship to exist in the first place—I simply will love my friend if she is in fact my friend—what is the point in saying that I *ought* to love my friend? Is the normative claim not otiose?

It is not otiose. It is one thing to say that if I stop loving my friend, we are no longer friends.[7] It is another thing to also say that I have reasons to continue loving my friend, which entails that I have reasons to maintain the friendship. But this is intuitive—most people don't think I should abandon my friendships for no reason. Of course, reasons do not always give rise to obligations. I may sometimes have reasons to stop loving my friend and thereby end the friendship, for example, my friend might betray me, or I may discover my friend has a deep moral flaw.

To say one ought to love one's friends is to say that one should be partial in one's attitudes toward one's friends. Indeed, if I say I am partial to something, I am expressing that I like it or love it. To be partial toward someone is to care about that person more than you care about others. As C.S. Lewis says, "To say 'These are my friends' implies 'those are not'" (1993, 40–41).

Ought one to love one's friend? Should one be partial in one's attitudes toward one's friends? For most, the answer is obviously "yes." But to say something in support of this, think back to Recommend. Suppose I fail to recommend Gretchen. She might ask, "Why did you not recommend me? Didn't you want me to get the job?" It would be one thing to say, "Listen Gretchen, *of course* I wanted you to get the job. But I believe morality requires impartiality, and I'm therefore not permitted to give you special treatment." That response would be problematic for the reasons Jollimore has already noted. But an even *worse* response would be, "Gretchen, frankly, I don't really care whether you get the job or not. The only thing I care about is that the best person gets the job." We could expect Gretchen to respond, "Some friend you are!" Interestingly, this response admits of two possible interpretations that parallel the analytic and normative claims, respectively, that I mentioned earlier. Gretchen might be implying that although I am in fact her friend, I'm being a bad friend, and have (relational) reason to be a better friend, in this case, to care about her success and well-being. Or, she might be implying, and it is perhaps true that we have ceased to be friends. Whether it is true may depend on, for example, how deep my lack of regard for her goes, or how persistent it is. If it is in fact true that we are no longer friends, it would then be true that I no longer have relational reasons toward her (analytic), but this would be so because I wrongly failed to properly regard her as a friend when we *were* friends (normative).

I now introduce a general principle. The principle I have in mind is motivated by the simple thought that there seems to be some kind of important connection between the appropriateness of our attitudes and the appropriateness of our actions. The principle is this:

ACT OUT: If *s* has normative reasons to hold attitude *a*, then *s* has corresponding normative reasons to act out of *a*.

If we have normative reasons to love our friends, and if Act Out is true, then we also have normative reasons to act out of this love. The normative practical reasons to act out of the love we have for our friends can at a minimum justify, but may also require, partial treatment toward our friends. In Recommend specifically, it is permissible for me to have Gretchen as a friend. If Gretchen is in fact my friend, it is permissible for me to have partial attitudes toward Gretchen. In this case, it is appropriate that I hope that Gretchen gets the job. What kind of friend would I be if I were indifferent? And if Act Out is true, then it is appropriate, at least *prima facie*, for me to act out of this hope, that is, to recommend Gretchen for the job.

Here, I am making the fairly safe assumption that there is a relationship between normative practical reasons and the moral status of actions. Precisely how relational reasons help to determine the moral status of an action will depend on whatever other reasons are at play in a particular situation and on what the correct view is about the relationship between reasons and the moral status of actions.

There can be reasonable disagreement about the precise nature of this relationship. I hold the view that one should always do whatever one has most reason to do. On this view, it may well indeed be the case that, once my relational reasons get added to the totality of genuine normative reasons at play, I have most reason to recommend, and so that is what I ought to do. But there are other views about the relationship between reasons and the moral status of actions. The relationship may be more attenuated. For example, one might hold a kind of satisficing view about practical rationality, on which an action is rationally justified as long as one has sufficient reason to perform it, even if there is *even more* reason to perform an alternative action.[8]

Either way, whether it is right to recommend will also depend on the totality of relevant practical reasons in the particular scenario. And indeed, there are reasons, even strong ones, *not* to recommend. The practice of recommending and providing other kinds of professional favors to those we like or prefer can perpetuate and entrench various kinds of unfair advantage. Our relationship in the first place might be due to our belonging to privileged and influential professional and social networks, as a result of our socio-economic class, having both attended the same prestigious university, etc. As a result of knowing me, Gretchen has an unfair advantage over other candidates. And Gretchen's getting the job will then put her in a position to help out other members of our network, leaving behind those who are less well connected, and so the cycle continues. So recommending isn't just some benign act of friendliness and it should not be taken lightly.

Of course, it may also be that Gretchen is in a *less* privileged social position. If this were the case, then, on the assumption that we have reasons to promote values like fairness or equity (whether these reasons are basic or derivative), I would have quite strong reasons indeed to recommend.

But, cases like Recommend are exactly what makes Act Out, and partiality in general, interesting. It wouldn't be all that interesting to posit very weak relational reasons that can seldom justify or require actions, except perhaps in cases where, in the absence of such reasons, there would be near parity between reasons for various alternatives, or that can merely "break ties," so to speak. To put it starkly, I believe there is *something* positively wrong with Recommending. And yet, I believe it can be the right thing to do, given that our relational reasons can be quite strong, depending on, among other things, the strength or importance of the relationship in question.

But is Act Out true? One reason for thinking that it is is that it is very *prima facie* plausible. What Act Out does, in essence, is connect the morality of our attitudes and affections to the morality of our actions. There is simply something attractive about this kind of connection, or moral harmony, between the moral status of attitudes and that of actions.

If nothing else, we should very much want Act Out to be true. It would be agonizing to hold that morality tells us to have certain attitudes, but also that we must never act out of those attitudes. One might liken morality to a cruel master, holding out a tempting treat to a dog but never letting him have it. Or one might think of morality as being like Lucy from Peanuts, holding out the football for Charlie Brown, only to remove it the moment he tries to kick it. As Stanley Kowalski screams in anguish to Stella in *A Streetcar Named Desire*, we might scream at morality (so to speak), "You're tearing me apart!"

Relatedly, borrowing a term from Bernard Williams, a view that denied the truth of Act Out would be *alienating* (1973), especially in the context of intimate relationships. In a real sense, morality would require that we ignore some of our most deeply held attitudes—attitudes that are intertwined with, and even constitute, our very identity. As Ross noted, I am not simply an agent who stands to promote the good: I am a father, a son, a husband, a friend (Ross 1930).

Consider just how strange it would be if morality turned out to be this way. How could it be that certain attitudes are good, desirable, or appropriate, but no action motivated by that attitude is ever good, desirable, or appropriate? It is one thing to say that *some* actions motivated by good attitudes are impermissible. For example, it would be wrong for me to kill all of Gretchen's competitors in hopes that she gets the job. But to say that there are some attitudes that, though themselves good, can *never* be acted on, would represent a schizophrenic view of morality.

Apart from its intuitive appeal, I think there are deeper reasons for thinking Act Out is true. One reason is metaphysical, the other epistemic, though the two are related.

I begin with the metaphysical reason. The kinds of considerations that constitute reasons for having certain attitudes are the same kinds of considerations that constitute reasons for action. That is to say, when I have reasons for having a certain attitude, I will also have reasons for acting in some way that corresponds with that attitude, because the reasons for having the attitude and the reasons for acting are provided *by the very same fact*.

Suppose I see a blind woman about to step out into oncoming traffic. I have reasons to hope she does not do this, and I have reasons to prevent her from doing this. And the reason for having the attitude and the reason to perform the action of stopping her from doing this are provided by the same facts, that is, that she will get hit by a car and be seriously injured if she steps out into oncoming traffic.

Or suppose there are reasons related to desert. Here, I would have reasons to hope that a deserving person is rewarded, and I would have reasons to do certain things to bring it about that a deserving person gets rewarded. And these reasons are provided by the same facts: that the person deserves the reward. Or consider justice. That an injustice has occurred is a reason to feel angry. It is also a reason to act out of that anger by trying to correct the injustice that has occurred.[9]

In saying that the reasons for attitudes and the reasons for actions are provided by the same kinds of facts, I do not mean to suggest that there is necessarily only one right or appropriate way to respond to a given set reasons (themselves based on a given set of facts). There may be cases where there are several equally appropriate, perhaps mutually exclusive, ways to respond. The same may also go for attitudes. What I am saying is that facts that provide reason(s) to hold some attitude (or set of possible attitudes) are also facts that provide reasons for performing some action (or set of possible actions).[10]

This metaphysical observation leads to an epistemic one: If we grant the metaphysical claim that the reasons that justify certain attitudes and the reasons that justify actions are provided by the same facts, then recognizing a reason to hold a certain attitude can be a way of recognizing a reason to act in a certain way. In Recommend, that Gretchen is my friend is a reason to hope she gets the job. If reasons for attitudes and reasons for actions are provided by the same facts, then I have some practical reason to act in a way toward Gretchen that I do not have with respect to her competitors. Provided I have no special reason to help anyone else get the job, and since I *do* have a special reason regarding my treatment of Gretchen, this reason can become a decisive reason in favor of recommending Gretchen.

There may be a variety of ways of recognizing a reason to have an attitude. One might simply be via intuition. It may simply seem appropriate for me to hope that Gretchen gets the job. Of course, we often do not adopt attitudes by rationally reflecting on what attitudes we have reasons to have. Rather, attitudes often arise spontaneously, without any intention to adopt them. This is particularly true of a certain subset of attitudes, that is, emotions. There is a robust feminist literature on emotions, and particularly, the relationship between emotion and knowledge. For instance, Alison Jaggar argues that "[E]motions may be helpful and even necessary rather than inimical to the construction of knowledge" (Jaggar 1989, 146). I think this is especially true when it comes to moral knowledge. As Jaggar herself points out, "emotions and values are closely related.... If we had no emotional responses to the world, it is inconceivable that we should ever come to value one state of affairs more highly than another" (153).

There are many ways in which emotions and values may be related, but one way may be that having an emotion can be evidence of a reason to have a certain attitude, that is, that very emotion. This is because emotions are often reasons-responsive, even when they arise spontaneously. Anger, even spontaneous anger, is very often a response to something that is actually worth being angry about. As Jaggar writes, "Only when we reflect on our initially puzzling irritability, revulsion, anger, or fear may we bring to consciousness our 'gut-level' awareness that we are in a situation of coercion, cruelty, injustice, or danger" (161). I may find that I am angry about a situation, and this can be evidence that I actually ought to be angry.

That an emotion arose spontaneously, as opposed to being the result of rational reflection about what one ought to feel, does not entail that it is not reasons-responsive. Beliefs also often arise spontaneously—I see a tree, and I form the belief that a tree is there. But we should not conclude from the fact that the belief arose spontaneously that I am not responding to my reasons to believe that a tree is there or that this belief has no rational basis.

Because emotions can be reasons-responsive, having an emotion can be evidence that one has a reason to have that emotion. If, as I argued above, reasons for attitudes and reasons for actions are provided by the same facts, then having an emotion can be evidence of a practical reason. So my anger about an injustice can be evidence that I actually ought to do something about the injustice. In cases such as these, emotions can be indispensable in leading me to recognize the moral facts and the duties they entail, for I may never have discovered those facts in the absence of having the emotion in the first place. And because our emotions are often more apparent to us than our practical reasons—they "leap out" at us—our emotions can lead to the recognition of practical reasons we might otherwise have missed. Far from being quirky cases on the margins, it seems to me that this phenomenon is extremely common. If so, then emotions occupy a very important role in the epistemology of practical reasons.

Of course, as Jaggar herself eloquently states, "Although our emotions are epistemologically indispensable, they are not epistemologically indisputable. Like all our faculties, they may be misleading, and their data, like all data, are always subject to reinterpretation and revision" (163). I can easily grant this. We may sometimes feel angry and then discover that this anger is unjustified, just as we can form beliefs based on our perceptions, but then discover that our perceptive faculties in question are unreliable under the circumstances.

I note that one need not accept the view that emotions can be evidence of a practical reason in order to accept Act Out. One could insist that emotions are not reasons-responsive, and whether an emotion, or any attitude for that matter, is justified must be evaluated on other grounds, and still accept the argument. Act Out says only that *if* an attitude is justified, then some way of acting out of that attitude is also justified.

A Counterexample

Are there counter-examples to Act Out? That is, are there cases where a certain attitude would be justified by certain reasons, but no way of acting out of that attitude would be even *prima facie* justified? One might argue that one is often justified in feeling anger with one's small child—especially if one has been the parent of a small child. But perhaps one is never justified in acting out of that anger. There are two ways to respond to this concern without rejecting Act Out. First, we could say that being angry with a small child is not justified. Or we could say that it is justified, and that acting out of that anger is also sometimes justified. In order to see whether this second response is plausible, we need to ask what acting out of anger toward one's child entails. Maybe it need not entail hurting the child, or yelling at the child, or in any other way taking one's anger out on that child. It could simply entail leaving the room and punching a pillow. I want to resist this response, for it seems to me that to act on one's anger toward another individual entails some sort of behavior toward that individual. As my earlier comments suggested, anger toward an unjust political regime is not merely evidence that one has a reason to punch one's pillow. Instead, it is evidence that one has a reason to, say, oppose that political regime. Therefore, it seems to me that to act out of anger toward one's child entails some sort of behavior directed at the child—perhaps striking her, or yelling at her. However, while losing one's temper and yelling at one's child is certainly *understandable*, I do not think it is justified in the sense that it is best supported by one's practical reasons.

Thus, I prefer to say that one is in fact not justified in feeling anger at one's small child. Jaggar writes, "Simply describing ourselves as angry... presupposes that we view ourselves as having been wronged" (159). If by "presupposes" she means "entails," then I disagree. I think I can be angry at the bench on which I just stubbed my toe without thinking the bench has wronged me. However, I do think that to say that we are *justifiably* or *rationally* angry entails that we view ourselves (or others) as having been wronged. Assuming that young children are not yet moral agents, I then cannot be justifiably angry at my child. If this sounds odd, I think it is because, as I have mentioned, it is certainly *understandable* for a parent to be angry at one's child, and perhaps even to yell at one's child. It may also be *excusable*, in certain cases. And we sometimes use "justifiable" in these ways, to imply "understandable" or "excusable." But it is not justifiable in the sense that it is supported by normative reasons. There is a big difference between saying that something is understandable, or excusable, as in the case of someone on a diet being tempted by some tasty morsel, and saying that something is justified in the sense that it is well supported by reasons. Of course, there are explanatory reasons why one is angry at one's child. But it is difficult to see why one would have most normative reason to by angry at one's small child, or at a bench, for that matter. After all, wouldn't it be *better* if I could always avoid being angry at my child if my child is not a morally responsible agent?

Right Reasons

A view that one has a reason to be partial to one's friends, and that that reason *is* the fact that they are your friends, is appealing because it meets what I will call the "right reasons" requirement. I noted above that Wolf argues that even if a consequentialist could behave toward a friend the way in which we ordinarily expect friends to behave, such a consequentialist agent would be behaving for the wrong reasons. This agent does not favor her friend *because* the friend is her friend; rather, she does it simply because she recognizes she can produce more value by doing so. Consider Stocker's famous example:

> [S]uppose you are in a hospital, recovering from a long illness. You are very bored and restless and at loose ends when Smith comes in once again. You are now convinced more than ever that he is a fine fellow and a real friend-taking so much time to cheer you up, traveling all the way across town, and so on. You are so effusive with your praise and thanks that he protests that he always tries to do what he thinks is his duty, what he thinks will be best. You at first think he is engaging in a polite form of self-deprecation, relieving the moral burden. But the more you two speak, the more clear it becomes that he was telling the literal truth: that it is not essentially because of you that he came to see you, not because you are friends, but because he thought it his duty, perhaps as a fellow Christian or Communist or whatever, or simply because he knows of no one more in need of cheering up and no one easier to cheer up.
>
> Surely there is something lacking here—and lacking in moral merit or value. (Stocker 1976, 462)

Interestingly, Stocker uses this example to critique both consequentialism as well as certain kinds of deontology. If Smith's friend asks him why he came to visit, "because the categorical imperative demands that I come to visit you" is as unacceptable an answer as "because it promotes the good." As Stocker suggests, the right answer, or at least the answer that would satisfy his friend, seems to be simply "because you are my friend." That he is Smith's friend just *is* the reason—both the explanatory reason and the normative reason. And as Stocker notes, we should seek harmony between our motives and reasons, values, and justifications (453).

My view satisfies the "right reasons" requirement in the most direct and straightforward way that any view can. If my friend asks me why I came to visit him in the hospital, my answer, "because you are my friend" is literally and basically true. Of course, if a consequentialist answered this way, her answer would be true in some sense, but it would be incomplete. For a complete answer, she would have to say something like, "Because you are my friend, I am especially well placed to promote your well-being by coming to visit you."[11]

Conclusion

I have argued for the existence of relational reasons, which can justify special treatment of our friends and loved ones. In some ways, this conclusion is totally unsurprising, at least in the sense that nearly everyone does treat their loved ones differently than they treat everyone else. But that this kind of behavior is nearly universal does not make it justifiable. It still needs to be defended. In fact, for all I have said here, I believe most people are *too* partial toward their friends (and too selfish, for that matter). A simple but profound thought that impresses itself upon me is this: the world could be so, *so* much better than it currently is. What I share with my consequentialist friends is a deep longing for the world to be as good as it can possibly be for everyone. I believe we all have very strong reasons to work toward that goal, *in addition to* the relational reasons I have argued for. In many cases, such reasons happily coincide. The world would be a dreary place without loving relationships. It is often good for the world when parents act on their relational reasons to love and nurture their children, since this produces better children, and eventually, better adults.

But I have also claimed that relational reasons are basic—that is, not derived from any more basic or fundamental reason, for example, the reason to promote the overall Good. If these relationships are valuable *because* they serve the overall Good of everyone, then they are merely instrumentally valuable. That is of course a position some take, though it's one I obviously reject. If it is true, as I believe it is, that both relational reasons and reasons to promote the Good are both genuine basic reasons, then we should expect that they will at times be at odds. (Should I pay for my child to attend a good college or donate that money to a Givewell-approved charity?)

The same, I would think, could be said for the other themes in this volume as well. Love, justice, and autonomy, in addition to the overall Good of everyone, are all important values. It is possible that some of these values can be cashed out in terms of others, though I suspect that they cannot (at least not all of them). I am a pluralist, rather than a monist, about values and reasons. If pluralism is true, if more than one thing is of value and reasons can have a variety of sources, then it seems natural to expect that there will be occasions where certain intrinsic values and reasons are at odds. And yet, in such cases, we still must decide. This decision often is not simple or easy and we run the risk of getting it wrong.[12] As a pluralist, I like to think that a significant part of the elusive virtue of wisdom is being sensitive to the normative pull from all of our competing reasons, and judging, with increasing expertise, where the strongest pull is coming from.

Notes

1. Of course, I do not deny that there are impermissible acts of favoritism. For example, it would be wrong for me to poison a child to make room for my own child at an elite private school. This would be an impermissible way of behaving partially toward my child. Alternatively, consider Susan Wolf's case of a woman whose son has committed a crime and she must decide whether to hide him from the police (253). Though I suspect some may consider hiding him a form of impermissible partiality, Wolf thinks this is a hard case, and I agree. So sometimes it is unclear whether an action is impermissibly partial. See also Stephen T. Asma's *Against Fairness* for many more examples and a provocative treatment of favoritism for our loved ones (Asma, 2013).
2. I will return to the topic of how reasons help to determine the rightness of actions again briefly in the "Why Partiality?" section.
3. See Chang (2010) for potential exceptions to this. Relatedly, Tim Oakley (2017) has argued there may be some moral duties from which one may choose to release oneself.
4. Of course, Stockholm Syndrome may occur, but this is merely a descriptive psychological phenomenon. On my view, no one has any reason to acquire Stockholm Syndrome, and that is as it should be.
5. See Chang (2013) for an illuminating discussion of the normative significance of commitments.
6. I stated earlier that I was going to use the term "friend" in a technical sense to refer to all individuals with whom an agent has a personal relationship. I should note here that while Jollimore's analytic claim seems to hold for all friends, in the everyday sense of 'friend', it does not hold for all personal relationships. I may stop loving my child, but that does not by itself entail that that personal relationship has dissolved. And, crucially, even if I stop loving my child, I may still have reasons to love my child, and to behave partially toward my child.
7. I should note that it is probably more accurate to say that we are not friends if I'm not *disposed* to have special feelings for her. If in a moment those feelings vanish, it is not as though our friendship has vanished, too.
8. See McElwee (2007) for such an account. And there are still further options regarding the role of practical reasons. Joshua Gert has recently introduced the intriguing possibility of *purely justifying reasons*: reasons that can justify certain actions, but never require them (Gert 2018). Gert argues that reasons to seek revenge may be such reasons: there are reasons to seek revenge that can justify doing so, even though no one is ever required to seek revenge. Relational reasons *could* be of the purely justifying sort. One might find this alternative attractive if it seems strange to say that the scrupulously impartial agent behaves impermissibly. Being scrupulously impartial is at least permitted, one might think, though being partial may also be permitted in some instances. Even if there are purely justifying reasons, I am inclined to think that relational reasons are not of this kind. But I won't explore this here. I offer it here as yet another possibility as to how relational reasons might figure in to the overall moral status of an action.
9. See Elizabeth V. Spelman (1989).
10. Whether two (or more) different actions can be supported by the same set of facts and reasons is something people can disagree about. It will depend on what one thinks the precise nature of the relationship between reasons and the moral status of actions is. My point isn't to come down on any position here. It is enough that reasons support actions *in some way*.

11. It may be that sophisticated consequentialism could satisfy this requirement. According to sophisticated consequentialism, one should not always, perhaps not even often, apply the utility calculus to each and every decision (Railton 1984). Instead, one should try to develop character traits and patterns of behavior that will in general promote the good. It may be that if one cultivates love and affection for one's friends, such that providing care for one's friends (like visiting them in the hospital) becomes almost second nature, at least in general, conduces to the good. Thus, if you asked your sophisticated consequentialist friend why she came to visit, she could truly, and more completely, answer, "Because you are my friend." On the one hand, this answer would indeed be more satisfying than "because it promotes the good" because the former has something to do with *you*, in particular. Of course, it is also true that the reason your sophisticated consequentialist friend developed this particular affection for you was because she thought it would promote the good. I'm unsure whether it makes sense to be bothered by this fact, but perhaps sophisticated consequentialism does a fairly good job satisfying this requirement as well.
12. As noted pluralist W.D. Ross rather famously stated, "it is more important that our theory fit the facts than that it be simple" (Ross 1930, 19). I am aware that in making these final remarks, I reveal some Rossian, or pluralist, or intuitionist commitments. Nothing I've said so far depends on any of these substantive views. I have merely argued for the existence of relational reasons. How these reasons get factored into making final deontic assessments will just depend on what substantive views one takes about such matters.

References

Asma, Stephen T. *Against Fairness*. Chicago: University of Chicago Press, 2013.
Chang, Ruth. "Commitment, Reasons, and the Will." In *Oxford Studies in Metaethics, Vol. 8*, edited by Russ Shafer-Landau, 74–113. Oxford: Oxford University Press, 2013.
Chang, Ruth. "Do We Have Normative Powers?" Unpublished manuscript, 2010. http://fas-philosophy.rutgers.edu/chang/10normpowersdist11-30-10.pdf.
Fried, Charles. *An Anatomy of Values: Problems of Personal and Social Choice*. Cambridge: Harvard University Press, 1970.
Gert, Joshua. "Revenge Is Sweet." *Philosophical Studies* 177, no. 4 (2018): 971–186.
Game of Thrones. "*Baelor*." Season 1, episode 9. Directed by Alan Taylor. Written by David Benioff, D.B. Weiss, and George R.R. Martin. HBO, June 12, 2011.
Hooker, Brad. "When Is Impartiality Morally Appropriate?" In *Partiality and Impartiality: Morality, Special Relationships, and The Wider World*, edited by Brian Feltham and John Cottingham, 26–41. Oxford: Oxford University Press, 2010.
Jaggar, Alison M. "Love and Knowledge: Emotion in Feminist Epistemology." *Inquiry* 32, no. 2 (1989): 151–176.
Jollimore, Troy. "Friendship Without Partiality?" *Ratio* 13, no. 1 (2000): 69–82.
Kagan, Shelly. *The Limits of Morality*. Oxford: Oxford University Press, 1989.

Lewis, C.S. "Friendship – The Least Necessary Love." In *Friendship: A Philosophical Reader*, edited by Neera Kapur Badhwar, 39–47. Ithaca: Cornell University Press, 1993.
Mcelwee, Brian. "Consequentialism, Demandingness and the Monism of Practical Reason." *Proceedings of the Aristotelian Society* 107, no. part 3 (2007): 359–374.
Mill, John Stuart. *Utilitarianism*. Kitchener: Batoche Books Limited, (1863) 2001.
Oakley, Tim. "How to Release Oneself from an Obligation: Good News for Duties to Oneself." *Australasian Journal of Philosophy* 95, no. 1 (2017): 70–80.
Railton, Peter. "Alienation, Consequentialism, and the Demands of Morality." *Philosophy and Public Affairs* 13, no. 2 (Spring, 1984): 134–171.
Ross, W.D. *The Right and the Good*. Oxford: Oxford University Press, 1930.
Singer, Peter. *Practical Ethics*. New York: Cambridge University Press, 2011.
Spelman, Elizabeth V. "Anger and Insubordination." In *Women, Knowledge, and Reality: Explorations in Feminist Philosophy*, edited by Ann Garry and Marilyn Pearsall, 263–274. New York: Routledge, 1989.
Stocker, Michael. "The Schizophrenia of Modern Ethical Theories." *Journal of Philosophy* 73, no. 14 (1976): 453–466.
Williams, Bernard. "A Critique of Utilitarianism." In *Utilitarianism: For Against*, by J.J.C. Smart and Bernard Williams, 75-150. Cambridge: Cambridge University Press, 1973.
———. "Persons, Character, and Morality." In *Moral Luck: Philosophical Papers*, 1–19. Cambridge: Cambridge University Press, 1981.
Wolf, Susan. "Morality and Partiality." *Philosophical Perspectives* 6 (1992): 243–259.
———. "'One Thought Too many': Love, Morality, and the Ordering of Commitment." In *Luck, Value, and Commitment: Themes from the Ethics of Bernard Williams*, edited by Ulrike Heuer and Gerald Lang, 71–92. Oxford: Oxford University Press, 2012.

13 Love for One's Own or Justice for All?

Marilyn Friedman

Loyalty to One's Own

Many people identify themselves, and are identified by others, in terms of one or more social groups to which they belong and to which they may feel a strong attachment. Social identity groups fall into a variety of types, including but not limited to those of race, religion, nationality, and gender. When a human group provides an identity for some persons in this way, let us call it a "social identity group" (or simply "identity group") for each person who identifies in those terms.

It is possible for one person to regard more than one human group as her social identity group. Most people have a complex identity that merges at least two identities together. A sexual or gender identity is usually integrated with a racial, ethnic, religious, or national identity. Sometimes this sort of merger is referred to as an "intersectional identity." However, for the sake of simplicity in this discussion, I shall regard each person as having only one (non-intersectional) identity. I shall consider someone's identity to be the classification in terms of which she would identify herself first and foremost.

People often form deep attachments to some persons whom they regard as members of their own identity group. Someone who identifies as white probably forms attachments to at least some other white persons; someone who identifies as Muslim probably forms attachments to at least some other Muslims, and so on. These attachments can include feelings of liking and love, attitudes of loyalty, readiness to defend and support one's own group members, and tendencies to associate with at least some other members of one's own group. Members of the same group often have shared histories and may face common problems.

Some identity groups such as racial groups have been widely regarded over the years as having a biological or genetic basis. More recently, however, many theorists have denied that there is a biological or genetic basis for differentiating among people in racial terms. Yet the racial categories, which most people use to identify themselves and others, seem to persist stubbornly in popular culture despite scientific discredit. My discussion avoids entering that dispute and simply takes for granted the racial and other identity categories used in everyday life. Thus, this discussion will pertain to any social identity category that is widely accepted and that ordinary people use to differentiate among each other.

For the rest of this discussion, the term "identity group" should be thought of as shorthand for a "group which is the basis of identity for at least some of its members." Whether or not a group is some particular person's identity group is relative to the attitudes of the person being considered and to whether or not she considers herself to have the requisite identity traits. Identity groups usually differ from each other in regard to norms, values, typical attitudes, or typical behaviors that characterize their members. These identity traits might be "social constructions" rather than biologically based traits yet may still sufficiently differentiate someone's identity and self-conception from outsiders who belong to other groups instead.

Social identity groups are the bases of activities and relationships that ground much human happiness and fulfillment. Someone who is strongly attached to the members of her own identity group probably feels a variety of positive attitudes toward them such as enjoyment, affection, empathy, and pride. These and similar attitudes can all be thought of as forms or manifestations of love. Under ordinary circumstances, group members who are strongly attached to their respective groups tend to support or defend their beloved identity group members against threats and attacks by other groups and individuals.

However, social identity groups can also be the bases of intergroup aggression and violence. Here is where the problem of this essay begins. One group may initiate serious moral wrongdoing or injustice toward another group. The group that is doing wrong might well be the identity group for some of its members. A group member, call her X, may come to believe with good reason that her identity group is treating outsiders wrongfully, in the form, for example, of sexism, racism, violence, oppression, and so on. Some white persons, for example, recognize injustices that many whites commit against persons of color.

The group members who recognize such wrongdoing in their own identity groups often do so in terms of moral norms that call for treating all other persons, not just one's own group members, as morally equal to oneself. The assumption of this moral approach is that *all* persons are equally deserving of moral consideration, respect for rights, and the promotion of their well-being. On this view, in regard to certain matters such as granting loans, registering voters, and trying people accused of crimes, moral agents are supposed to be impartial among all persons and to harm none. Let us use the expression "general impartial moral norms" for the norms that call for this treatment. General impartial moral norms (to repeat) pertain to how one should treat all others in certain domains, regardless of one's specific relationship to them. These norms contrast with particular partial norms, which pertain to how one should treat those with whom one has a special relationship.

A moral agent who reasons impartially will judge all persons who do wrong with equal severity. She will react in the same critical way to both the wrongdoing by her own group members toward insiders and outsiders and the wrongdoing by members of other groups toward anyone. If a moral agent is openly critical of her own identity group or active in her opposition to their wrongful actions toward outsiders, her relationships with members of her own group might suffer. She might feel pressure from her own group members to stand loyally by them in their opposition to outsiders. After all, she is one of them. This pressure may well influence her behavior, given the love and loyalty she probably feels toward at least some of her own identity group members. She is likely to feel a normative pull toward being loyal toward members of her own group, with whom her life is likely to be intertwined, regardless of how they treat outsiders.

Thus, a person who believes with good reason that her identity group members are doing wrong toward another group seems to face a painful dilemma. If she criticizes or opposes the wrongdoing by her group, she may alienate herself from her group and disrupt her relationships with its members, even though the group defines her identity and is probably linked to her in otherwise loving relationships. On the other hand, if she remains attached to her group despite its wrongdoing, she thereby fails to uphold the general moral norms that ground her general recognition of certain kinds of wrongdoing. Her general moral convictions would seem to be weakening if she overlooks the way her identity group members wrongfully treat outsiders.

A person facing this sort of dilemma, let us call her X, may be forced or pressured to choose between supporting her identity group under the circumstances or withholding support from them. Suppose X sides with and supports her identity group and does nothing in regard to what its members do wrong. In this case, what can be called the morality of *love* predominates. This partial particular response manifests love for X's own kind, but it also involves a weakening of her general impartial moral convictions against harming others. The extreme form of this attitude is exemplified in the patriotic fervor of "My country, right or wrong." On the other hand, if she upholds her general moral convictions and criticizes or opposes the injustices committed by her identity group against outsiders, the morality of *justice* predominates. In that case, X risks alienating beloved members of her own identity group and disrupting her relationships with them.

One's own group probably exerts a strong *psychological* pull on one's moral allegiance. It is likely that most human identity groups exert pressure on their respective members to remain loyal toward their own group. Loyalty generally includes supporting one's own group in their various struggles, verbally or physically, against other groups. Obviously, just because a group is one's own does not guarantee that it always acts rightly toward all other groups. The morality of loving commitment and group attachment seems to conflict directly with the general impartial morality of equal concern for all persons.

Is there any way a person should typically respond to dilemmas of this sort? In general, what should someone do when she recognizes that her identity group is acting wrongly toward others? Which side should a person choose? Ultimately, this dilemma cannot be fully resolved in particular cases until we know what the groups in question stand for. However, it may be possible to make some headway at the general level by considering this dilemma in abstraction. That is the aim of this essay.

The Dilemma

> E.M. Forster wrote that "...if I had to choose between betraying my country and betraying my friend I hope I should have the guts to betray my country."
>
> (Forster, 1938, 66)

Forster was weighing in on the dilemma that might arise when attachments to two different sorts of particulars (one's country and one's friend) compete with each other.

What if Forster had posed a hypothetical choice between a particular other and general *impartial moral norms*? Would Forster have wanted to choose loyalty to, say, a friend who had *murdered* someone? Would attachment to a friend who was a murderer have been more important to Forster than the option of reporting the friend's crime to the state? Just as a state or its officials can be corrupt and oppressive, and thereby diminish their entitlement to one's loyalty, cannot a particular person to whom one has an interpersonal attachment also be seriously immoral in ways that diminish her claims to one's support for her? (I might help my friend out with her legal fees, but should I regard my murderer friend as above the law?)

Plato has an answer for dilemmas of this sort. In the *Euthyphro*, Socrates expresses surprise and disappointment that Euthyphro has chosen to report to the authorities that his (Euthyphro's) father had murdered a slave (Plato, 2002, 1–20). Socrates' moral commitments fall on the side of showing loyalty to the particular person who is one's father, even when he is a murderer, rather than seeking the justice that is owed to the father's murder victim as it would be owed to any murder victim.

If one's very identity is defined by a particular group, then, granted, one might have as much psychological difficulty in accusing any of the members of that group of wrongdoing as Socrates would have had in accusing his own father of homicide. One way to frame this dilemma is to regard it as a conflict between the moral pull of norms that cover one's relationships to particular others who ground one's very identity and who are owed a measure of personal loyalty, on the one hand, and, on the other hand, the moral pull of general impartial norms of justice and the right. The general impartial norms of justice and right tell us how to treat all persons regardless of the existence or nature of one's personal connections with them.

Are the two sorts of moral pull equally morally weighty? I venture to suggest that many if not most people would support their identity group or persons in it against threats and dangers. However, in the type of situation under consideration here, one or more members of one's identity group are *harming or wronging* members of another group. This is an essential part of the hypothetical dilemma described here.

General impartial moral norms do not differentiate among human beings on the basis of their specific identities. General impartial moral norms apply equally to all other persons, ranging from persons with whom a moral agent is intimate and deeply involved to persons who are complete strangers to her. According to general impartial norms, when a moral agent considers persons who have done wrong and judges what they have done, she is not to show favoritism to those wrongdoers who happen to be close or special to her. If she finds, for example, that some members of her family engaged in racist treatment toward the members of a different racial group, she should judge that wrongdoing in the same way she would judge strangers who were equally racist.

Of course, sometimes there are forms of moral privilege that are appropriate and even called for in the treatment one owes to those who are specially related to oneself. Parents, for example, should favor their own children to a substantial degree when it comes to taking care of the vulnerable people within each society. That a particular child is my child is the moral reason that I have for favoring her with positive benefits—and anyone else may, indeed should, do the same each for her own children. Special relationships thus tend to call for some forms of favoritism that may not be called for in regard to strangers. They do so equally, of course, for any persons who have similar types of special relationships.

Yet such permissible favoritism has its limits. Some contexts call for impartiality even toward one's close relations. If I am a judge in a court of law, I should not give my sister a lighter sentence when she is tried for a crime than I would give to anyone else who commits exactly the same type of crime under exactly the same sorts of circumstances. Actually, a judge who is related closely to a defendant should recuse herself altogether from hearing that case. This requirement is imposed because we grasp the difficulty for most people of remaining impartial and being fair when judging their "own." A judgeship is a public office which is supposed to serve the needs of all members of the community equally, guided by the requirement of fairness on the judge's part toward all those persons.

Thus, there are at least the two divergent modes of moral understanding in practice that guide how we act toward others. One mode of moral understanding calls for the moral agent to take account of how other persons are specifically related to her. The relationships and circumstances may call for favoring close others with positive benefits even if one is not required to treat anyone else similarly.

At the same time, a second mode of moral understanding calls for the moral agent to apply moral concepts impartially and universally to all involved persons. Thou shalt not kill—unless thou hast a justification or excuse that would be acceptable for *any* moral agent to use under the same sorts of conditions. Whereas special relationships often call for special positive benefits to be conferred on those to whom one is specially related, non-special relationships typically do not do so.

Let us return to the dilemma that arises when a moral agent belongs to an identity group some of whose members are acting wrongfully toward another group. Let us call X's identity group "Group A" and the victim group "Group B." We are assuming that Group B consists of persons with whom X does not identify and to whom she feels no special connection. She may not even know them by acquaintance. Suppose that X is not herself acting wrongly toward Group B; she herself is not violating general impartial requirements to do no harm to others. However, the members of her identity group, Group A, may very well expect her to support *them* in *their* wrongful treatment of Group B and to avoid criticizing or obstructing those Group A members.

How should a moral agent treat her identity group members regarding their wrongful treatment of others? And does the moral agent owe the group of victim strangers any attempts to end or compensate for the harm to them that is perpetrated by her identity group?

There are at least two sorts of responsibilities in this situation that conflict with each other. On one side are X's responsibilities to show *loyalty and support* toward her identity group and to refrain from obstructing them unreasonably. Her identity group might well include her family and other persons who have taken care of her over the years and promoted her well-being. She would owe them gratitude for their lifelong love and support.

On the other side, X and all the other members of X's identity group A share with all persons the general impartial obligation to avoid harming any persons, including members of Group B. We are further assuming that X comes to recognize that her identity group's treatment of Group B is seriously unjust and unwarranted under the circumstances. The members of Group A are responsible for attempting to stop the harm they are inflicting on Group B. They may also owe to Group B compensation for the harm they have already done to Group B. Does X share in these responsibilities with her Group A?

Also, is a moral agent responsible for trying to *prevent the other members* of her identity group from doing wrong to still others? Are we each obligated to try to change the behavior of members of our respective identity groups so as to lessen, if not to eliminate, the wrongs they do to others, even if we do not participate in those wrongdoings? Should we go so far as to *defend* the groups that are being mistreated by our own identity group?

Let us suppose that the moral agent has reflected on her moral dilemma conscientiously. After communicating with members of both groups and taking careful account of what she has learned, she continues to regard her own identity group members overall as wrongfully mistreating members of group B. What are some of the responses that X might consider, abstractly speaking, under those fictional circumstances? Here are five of the possible responses that a moral agent might consider:

1. Stay out of the conflict as completely as one can.
2. Support one's own identity group loyally and uncritically in its treatment of group B.
3. Defend Group B against one's own group A.
4. Support in some ways but also criticize one's own group's treatment of Group B; try to make that treatment more just.
5. Be alert to possible misunderstandings by either group of the interaction between them; try to eliminate misunderstandings on either side if one can.

Are there any moral guidelines that can help someone to decide which of those options she should select in general, that is, in the absence of further considerations? Is one of those options always or generally the best choice for moral dilemmas of the sort described above? Let us consider each of the above options in more detail.

Beginning to Resolve the Dilemma

Option (1): Stay out of the conflict as far as one can

This option involves doing nothing to help or hurt either side. In actual practice, it seems to be the *de facto* stance which many people take when dealing with conflicts they witness in their daily lives. Many people try simply to avoid trouble.

I have been assuming that it *matters* if the group that is doing wrong in a two-group conflict is the *identity* group of a moral agent who encounters the conflict. At the outset, we should ask why it matters if a moral agent becomes aware that others of her nationality, race, religion, or gender are acting wrongly toward yet another group. Wouldn't a moral agent face a moral dilemma of deciding what to do even if she encountered a group with which she did not identify, that was acting wrongly toward yet another group with which she also did not identify?

Love for one's own or justice for all? 247

Intervening in a conflict to stop wrongdoing by members of her identity group seems to differ psychologically and pragmatically for the moral agent from intervening to stop wrongdoing by members of a group not connected to her identity. For one thing, the moral agent's own well-being is likely to depend more on the fortunes of her identity group than it does on the fortunes of other groups. She is more likely to do well in general if her group (A) does well than if some non-identity group does well instead. The moral agent X might be inclined to support the group on whose fate her own well-being is more likely to depend, even if she regards their behavior as wrong.

Also, it is not implausible to think that when people take sides in a conflict between groups, they are more likely to side with a group that is implicated in their own identities (if one is involved in the conflict), regardless of whether that group is the victim or the wrongdoer in the conflict. If the moral agent's own identity group is the victim group, it is obvious why she would intervene on their behalf. Yet, even if a moral agent's group is the aggressor in the situation, a psychological tendency for a moral agent to side with her own group would not be surprising.

Someone's identity group is connected to who she is. Each person may see the worth of her own identity as somehow at stake in how well her identity group fares—or is perceived to fare—when engaged in conflicts with other groups. It may matter to a person's sense of self as the particular *sort* of person she is that persons of that sort behave respectably and are regarded as doing so. Many persons would not want to admit that their own identity groups do wrong to others. In the event of a struggle between one's own identity group and a non-identity group, many people, I believe, would prefer to think that the brunt of the wrongdoing fell on the side of the non-identity group. If the facts of a given case do not support this interpretation, a moral agent might try to reconceptualize the situation so as to obscure the wrongful nature of what her own group members were doing (e.g., portraying violent actions by her own group members as mere self-defense).

Furthermore, a person is likely to have important relationships with other members of her own identity group and to spend significant amounts of time interacting with them. Acting in opposition to people with whom one has been personally close can be a wrenching experience. Reasons to criticize or oppose one's identity group have to be strong enough to overcome the psychological weight of an identity connection. Even if a person breaks off contact with her identity group, she may, depending on the nature of the identity in question, still remain someone who is socially identified as a person of that kind, both in the way others conceive of her and in how she conceives of herself. She may not be able socially to escape her identity.

This suggests that, in the sort of conflict situation we are considering (Group A does wrong to Group B), many, if not most, people would take the side of their own identity group rather than substantially avoid the conflict. If this is accurate as a general tendency, then Option #1 is not psychologically realistic for many moral agents regarding conflicts in which their respective identity groups are one of the opponents.

Thus far, I have made only psychological and pragmatic suggestions about how people might react when their respective identity groups are involved in conflicts with non-identity groups. Those suggestions pertain only to the ways in which I believe persons are *likely* to act when an identity group to which they belong behaves wrongfully toward another group. Those suggestions are not as such *moral* claims. They do not settle the normative question posed here, namely (to repeat): What is it *right* for a person to do when an identity group of hers is harming or treating wrongfully the members of another group? How *should* a person react to such conflicts?

Suppose that belonging to a particular identity group, on the face of it, imposed a *moral responsibility* on each capable adult member of that group to support the group in times of trouble, including times of conflict with other persons or groups? According to that sort of outlook, one would be acting wrongly if one failed to support or defend one's identity group in its conflicts with other groups. If the only moral outlook that existed were one of particular partial morality, then the dilemma would dissolve: one should simply and always favor one's own group overall. There would be no other available morally right choice.

However, as suggested earlier, many human beings also subscribe to general moral norms that articulate obligations owed to all persons, not just those of one's own group. This morality of general impartial moral respect changes the moral arithmetic. In contrast to partial particular morality, this contrasting moral outlook calls for each person to avoid harming, and to treat impartially and with equal respect, *all* human beings with whom she interacts. The moral agent is to "do no harm" to any persons.

However, our hypothetical situation also involves the wrongful treatment by the moral agent's identity group toward certain other human beings. Might this sort of situation create new responsibilities for a moral agent, even if she has done nothing to contribute to the moral wrong done by her identity group? Might the moral agent have the responsibility to try to *stop* the mistreatment of outsiders by others in her identity group (assuming that she could do something effective toward that end)?

This thought might begin with a claim about the responsibilities falling on any *group* that has done wrong to another group, thus: If Group C has on balance harmed or treated wrongfully another group, Group D, and has done so without adequate reason or excuse, then Group C is obligated to cease its mistreatment of Group D and, if possible, to rectify the situation or compensate Group D members adequately for the harm done.

Love for one's own or justice for all? 249

Those who exercise the agency of a group are the ones who bear, in the name of the group, the responsibilities and obligations that befall the group. A group based on a shared identity can lead its members to stick together and support each other in case the group as a whole determines that they have common opponents or enemies in virtue of being members of that group. Shared traits that are publicly noticeable allow group members to recognize each other and band together easily from different paths in life.

Roughly speaking and allowing for exceptions, it seems that interrelationships and bonding are enhanced among persons of the same identity group, more so than among persons of divergent identity groups. These connections make it easier for moral agents to support the respective identity groups that protect each from harm than it would be for moral agents to support non-identity groups to which they were not connected. This practical ease lends plausibility to the following claim for *individual* members of identity groups that harm other groups: If a person has played any sort of role in the wrongful treatment that her identity group A has inflicted on others, then she shares with the other agents of her group the responsibility to try to cease the harmful and wrongful behavior and to rectify, or compensate the victims, for the harm done.

Members of a shared identity group may not need to think twice about how to behave when they encounter recognizable others of their group, even others who have never met before. A gathering crowd whose members recognize that they share a common identity may impel its members to act violently together with little or no reflection when they gather, say, to protest their victimization by outsiders. However, personal features that facilitate bonding in the search for justice can also facilitate the perpetuation of wrongdoing. Group members can engage in harming third parties without warrant, and their shared similarities can make it easier for newcomers to join the group, feel loyalty to it, and act in concert.

Does a member of an identity group have the above responsibilities even if she did not play any sort of role in her group's wrongful treatment of Group B? If so, then we may extract a further claim: Any group member with at least an adult level of moral agency shares in the responsibility to try to stop her own group from wronging outsiders without warrant. Even though X did/does not actively contribute to the harm done by Group A to Group B, nevertheless X shares some of the responsibility for those wrongs. X shares some of Group A's responsibility to cease, prevent, or compensate for the harm or wrongdoing it has done to members of Group B.

Finally, the implication for Option #1 is this: A person X who shares in the responsibility of her identity group, A, for wrongdoing done to Group B should not completely ignore the conflict between Groups A and B.

What if a wrong is done by a random, motley group of persons who happen to act together but do not share a uniform identity? Suppose that a crowd gathers spontaneously and is whipped up into a frenzy by hateful speakers and goes on to lynch innocent victims who happen to be at the wrong place at the wrong time. In this case, even though the crowd members do not share a common identity, they all still share in the responsibility for the wrong they did together or enabled together. Thus, a shared identity is *not a necessary* condition for a number of people to share responsibility for wrongdoing. However, it may be a sufficient condition.

Suppose a group with which one does *not* identify is treating others wrongfully. Does one have a responsibility to intervene in that sort of situation to protect or defend the victim group? There may indeed be responsibilities that befall non-identity bystanders, but I suggest that these are typically less demanding than responsibilities that befall agents who *belong* to the membership group that is wronging others. If I am, say, an American living in the US, and I witness a group of Americans who together mistreat certain others, I have an obligation to try to do something to stop this wrongful treatment. This responsibility would be weaker (although not absent) if I were, say, an Algerian living in the US and not an American citizen. In situations in which one's own identity group in particular is harming others, one has obligations to combat that harm that are stronger than those that pertain when the group that is harming others is not one's identity group.

At this point, we have reached this tentative intermediate thought: *a person who is aware of a two-group conflict in which one of the groups is her identity group should not simply ignore the conflict, especially if her group is the aggressor.*

Uncritical Loyalty to One's Own

Option (2): support one's own identity group A loyally and uncritically against Group B

This alternative sounds like what many people actually do when caught up in a struggle between their own identity group and some other group. People in general seem to favor their "own kind" when those persons are engaged in a struggle with people of "different" kinds. Option #2 construes this behavior as normatively right. On this approach, one *should* defend one's identity group, both verbally and/or physically if possible, against threatening outsider groups and individuals. One would thereby be giving priority to partial, particular moral norms (favor one's own) over general impartial moral norms (treat all persons equally). On this approach, defending one's identity group would override any general impartial principles that called for one to criticize or oppose one's identity group.

We are assuming that one's identity Group A is indeed treating Group B wrongfully. In both Option #1 as it was first formulated (ignore the conflict) and Option #2 (support one's identity group uncritically), one would be doing nothing to try to stop one's identity group from treating the other group wrongfully. Option #1 involves merely *ignoring* the wrongdoing by one's own group. Option #2 involves actively *supporting* one's own group while it carries out its wrongdoing against other persons.

Unfortunately, there is no guarantee that any particular group will make correct moral choices all the time. The best moral choice in any situation is likely to be relative to the particular circumstances in question. When circumstances change, what it is right to do may also change. Without critically evaluating the circumstances at hand, one would not know whether uncritical loyalty to one's own identity group was warranted *under the circumstances at hand*. The problematic attitude here is not mere loyalty to one's identity group but rather *uncritical* loyalty to them.

Could it sometimes be right to support one's identity group loyally and uncritically? What about the preference in caretaking that most people show for their own families over other families? When widespread in a society, family preference can be defended as part of an efficient system for distributing familial caretaking widely throughout the society. If all parents direct their caretaking resources toward their own children first and foremost, the well-being of many, if not most, of the children in the society could be thereby secured. However, as shown by Plato's example in the *Euthyphro*, a preference for family members might not be justified in case one's family member has done serious wrong. Young children, when preferred by their parents, have typically not done serious wrong. More mature family members toward whom people show preference have also often not done serious wrong. Loyal preference and support for one's family members seems warranted in those cases in which the family members in question can be presumed innocent under the given circumstances and to deserve that loyalty and support. Because of this presumption, the loyalty and support are not genuinely uncritical. In the two-group conflict problem we are considering, one's family members are known to be wronging some other party. In that situation, it seems that uncritical loyalty is not warranted.

Examining Other Options

Option 3: Defend Group B against one's own group

On this alternative, one may publicly criticize one's own group A for harming group B or even forcefully try to prevent one's own group members from harming group B.

Suppose that the loyalty owed to one's own group is not absolute but is a matter of degree. If so, then in some situations, it might be overridden by weightier responsibilities. One of those weightier responsibilities might be the responsibility to try to defend a group of outsiders, Group B, from aggression started by one's own group members, Group A. In some cases, the responsibility to try to protect others *from* "one's own" kind might be weightier than one's responsibility to protect and support "one's own" from threatening others. Suppose one's own state invades another state that did nothing to warrant the invasion. The responsibility to try to defend the *invaded* state may fall, at least partly, on all or most members of the invading state, even those members that have not participated in carrying out the invasion.

In actual practice, someone who acts in this manner is likely to be attacked by members of her own identity group as if she were a traitor to them. Many groups retaliate strongly against criticism and opposition from within by their own members—sometimes more strongly than they react against outside enemies. Even mild reprimands to other members of one's identity group can evolve into difficult and bitter arguments that strain emotional ties. The possible cost of Option #3 to the moral agent includes that of disrupting interpersonal, in-group relationships that are deeply intertwined with her very identity. Yet the moral agent might be required to bear this cost in those cases in which, as we have been supposing, the agent's responsibility to defend outsiders against aggression by her own group overrides her responsibility to support her own group.

If the two sorts of responsibility are roughly equivalent, then the moral agent could seek a response that would not risk estranging her from her "own kind" yet was still minimally good enough to count as *trying* to prevent her "own" group from harming others. There may be many ways in which one can both defend an opposition group against one's own group and at the same time blend this resistance to one's own group with forms of loyalty toward one's own group.

Option (4) Support but also criticize one's own group; try to make it more just

This option is one of *critical* loyalty. Initial attempts to pursue this option could involve trying to use loving criticism toward one's own group members to get them to stop treating others wrongly (e.g., "I know you mean well and want to do what's best, but..."). However, Group A members might persist in their wrongful treatment of Group B and merely become annoyed or antagonized by one's loving criticisms. Or Group A members might agree that they have already harmed Group B but argue that this harm was small by comparison to what they have previously suffered at the hands of Group B.

Of course, it is possible that the members of Group A have some reason for mistakenly thinking that Group B members have harmed Group A more than Group A members have harmed them in return. To see whether Group A members think this way, one must try to understand the various Group A points of view. Group A members might overestimate the harms they have suffered from group B, and this mistake might be inadvertent. Yet if they honestly think Group B harmed them first and the hardest, it would seem that in *some* respects the harms done

Love for one's own or justice for all? 253

by group A and group B should now be reconceptualized as an attempt at self-defense. (More on this in Option #5.) At the same time, a claim of self-defense that is grounded on a mistaken moral evaluation might *excuse* the harmful treatment of others but still does not *justify* it.

Thus option #4 permits the moral agent to show loyalty toward her own group but requires that this loyalty be grounded in her critical thinking about what her group has done to Group B and the circumstances in which they did it. Assuming that one's own group is not in danger of imminent or substantial attack, there is no reason on the face of it to let its mistreatment of others go unrecognized. One does not treat one's "own kind" well by *failing* to criticize or intervene when they mistreat others.

Euthyphro might have gone too far when going to the authorities to accuse his father of murder, a charge that might have opened his father up to execution. However, at least from a twenty-first century perspective, Euthyphro would not have been amiss if, instead, he pleaded with his father to *recognize* the wrong done to the slave and to turn *himself* in to the authorities with the hope that a full confession would elicit a lesser sentence. At the very least, Euthyphro could have pleaded in general with his father to stop killing slaves. Thus, being defined by a particular group or its members does not entail being required to have *uncritical* loyalty to that group. Indeed, intervening in the behavior of one's identity group members to try to stop them from mistreating others could be regarded as a way of trying to promote the moral *improvement* of one's group members. Although a demanding response, it is also a caring response.

There is another end served by the critically reflective dimension of critical loyalty. A moral agent's critical reflection on the viewpoints of members of her identifying group opens up the possibility of a kind of content-neutral autonomy in her loyalty to her group. If one's identity group is truly mistreating a second group B without adequate justification or excuse, then supporting one's identity group uncritically makes one an enabler, an abettor of that treatment. One is not acting as an autonomous agent. One's actions follow someone else's lead. One exhibits greater autonomy by basing one's loyalty to one's identity group on one's own conviction that one's group members are doing what is right and (better yet) have reason to do it (more on this in section VI).

Option (5) Be alert to possible misunderstandings by either group of the interactions between the groups; try to eliminate misunderstandings on either side if one can

One's own group may regard Group B not simply as a group of outsiders but also as their enemy. They may consider their own harsh treatment of Group B to be justified self-defense. As a result, moral agent X's own Group A might regard X's attempts to get Group A's members to stop mistreating Group B as an expression of X's sheer ignorance about the situation or as a betrayal of X's own group A. If the persons to whom a moral agent directs loving criticism regard the criticism as ignorant or as a betrayal, then, despite X's best intentions, she may not be able to change their wrongful behavior while still preserving undamaged a loving relationship with them. As long as Group A members seem to understand correctly their relationship to Group B, the moral agent who is a member of Group A has no overriding reason to try to prevent them from defending themselves against Group B. This option combines the two apparently divergent types of moral thinking we discussed earlier: first, special concern for the members of one's identity group to which one is attached, and, second, abstract commitment to the well-being of persons in general.

The Role of Autonomy

So how should the moral agent choose from among these five options?

Can the consideration of moral autonomy help to make the final choice? Can it help to decide how someone should respond under the complex circumstances in which the people one loves and identifies with are treating others unjustly?

Autonomy can be defined in various ways. The conception that I endorse is a formal, or *content-neutral*, sense of autonomy (Friedman, 2003, Chapter 1). It involves choosing or acting according to norms or values that one has already affirmed as one's own, and subsequently reaffirmed. One reflects on the available options in light of one's basic norms and values, which constitute a second-order reflective standpoint that defines one's deepest commitments. The autonomous choice would not be flippant or capricious but instead would reflect these deepest normative commitments about what really or ultimately matters to oneself.

A content-neutral sense of autonomy, as the name suggests, does not dictate a particular content that one must choose in order to be autonomous. Rather, it tells us *how* to choose. I should reflect on the situation at hand, to repeat, in light of my basic norms and values and follow their implications. I should also take the time to reconsider those basic norms and values in light of my still deeper (if any) norms and values. In that way, the norms and values that provide the touchstone for someone's autonomy are *her* norms and values, to the extent that this is possible. They could be either particular and partial or general and impartial—or both as combined in a ranking or merger. Nothing about autonomy precludes either of these kinds of principles. Any of the five options listed above, for dealing with one's identity group when it is harming others, could be autonomous for a particular person depending on which alternative best accords with her deepest norms and values.

As one considers the nature and demands of the situation, if one's overriding moral norms and values that govern the situation at hand are partial and particular, then one's autonomous choice would probably involve supporting one's identity group (either Option #2 or #4).

My attachment to the particular persons who comprise my identity group might be profoundly meaningful to me in all its social significance. Assuming I was raised by persons of the same religion, race, nationality, etc., I doubtless developed a strong lifelong commitment to those persons. Profound loving concern is likely to be my reaction to those persons who have been an important part of my life. I want to care for and support them. I am probably like them in important ways. I might locate myself in the larger human community from a standpoint that reflects my particular identity group. My emotional reactions might often be anchored by the history and current needs of my group. I probably know some of these people in rich familiarity; I have shared their joys and sorrows. My own well-being likely incorporates aspects of their well-being. It is rare to find a human being whose life lacks a web of connections with at least a few others who share an identity with her that gives some meaning and direction to her life.

By contrast, if one's overriding norms and values that survive reflection are general and impartial, then, in the hypothetical situation we have been considering, one is likely to lean toward defending Group B against one's own Group A (either Option #3 or #4). Choosing this way would be more autonomous for that sort of moral agent.

My general and impartial commitments can connect me to humanity at large, something my partial and particular attachments are likely unable to do. Instead of a parochial attachment simply to one group of human beings, my general impartial commitments might lead me to think of myself as a citizen of the world. Thinking this way, I might venture more openly and enthusiastically out into that greater world and assimilate more readily what is to be seen and understood of the lives of diverse people out there. It might give me great satisfaction to rise above parochial attachments and treat all persons with respect and due consideration, especially those persons whom I barely know or have never met.

If a person's reflection according to her deepest norms and values does not dictate one specific choice but results in a tie between two or more of them, then it would seem that for her, those choices are morally equivalent.

According to the content-neutral conception, diverse people with differing basic norms and values may each realize autonomy even when they act very differently under the same circumstances. They might end up as opponents in conflicts between their different identity groups. A content-neutral conception of autonomy allows us to say that people on opposite sides of a conflict with each other may all be morally autonomous.

One may reaffirm or transform oneself over time through struggling to cope with moral challenges or threats. One might never have previously encountered a situation like the one that one now faces, so the outcome of one's reflections might be a surprise. One might come to recognize that a previous, particular identity-defining attachment is unworthy of one's commitment. One may find, upon reflection, that the partial, particular community one has trusted, venerated, and followed over the course of one's life (a particular attachment) has betrayed that trust by acting in ways that one finally realizes one must condemn. Alternatively, one might fail to find a foundation for one's long-standing universal moral commitments. Resolving a moral dilemma might change one's basic values so that one ceases to be exactly the same person one was before.

However, a formal or content-neutral conception of autonomy does not help us to decide *substantively* between universal morality and particular morality. Each sort of normative connection—to particular, known others and to humanity in general and in the abstract—has its distinctive sort of appeal and its particular way of fitting into the emotional and intellectual currents of a life.

The fifth option listed above for resolving the moral dilemma (try to eliminate misunderstandings on either side) merges general impartial moral norms with particular partial moral norms. According to this option, I am required, at one and the same time, to show loyalty and caring in word and in deed to those to whom I am specially related, *and* to show respect to all persons including those whom my own identity group treats unjustly. As well, I bear a share of the responsibility for putting an end to the excessive moral mistreatment by my identity group toward the opposing group.

I have surveyed five solutions to the dilemma of how to act when one's identity group is wronging another group: (1) stay out of the conflict, (2) support one's own aggressor group uncritically, (3) defend the victim group uncritically, (4) support one's own group critically, and (5) eliminate misunderstandings. Briefly I outlined a content-neutral conception of autonomy according to which a person's own normative fundamentals govern her substantive moral convictions. Any of the five options presented here for dealing with wrongdoing to outsiders by one's beloved identity group could be autonomously chosen by a moral agent provided it accords with her own deepest norms and values.[1]

Note

1. I am grateful to all the editors for very helpful suggestions toward the final version of this chapter.

References

Forster, E. M. 1938. "Two Cheers for Democracy." *Nation* 147 (3), 65–68.
Friedman, Marilyn. 2003. *Autonomy, Gender, Politics*, 3–29. Oxford: Oxford University Press, 2003.
Plato. 2002. "Euthyphro." In *Five Dialogues*, 1–20, translated by G. M. A. Grube, revised by John M. Cooper. Indianapolis: Hackett, 2002.

Section III
The Political Dimension of Love and Justice

14 Love's Extension

Confucian Familial Love and the Challenge of Impartiality

Andrew Lambert

Introduction

The question of possible moral conflict between commitment to family and to impartiality is particularly relevant to traditional Confucian thought, given the importance of familial bonds in that tradition. While Confucian thought does recognize commitments beyond familial attachments, and does give expression to forms of justice and fairness, it consistently prioritizes family. Classical Confucian ethics also appears to lack any developed principled commitment to impartiality as a regulative ideal and a standpoint for ethical judgment, or to universal equality (all people matter equally). The Confucian prioritizing of family has prompted criticism of Confucian ethics, and doubts about its continuing relevance in China and beyond.[1]

This chapter assesses how those sympathetic to the Confucian vision of the good life might respond. It first explores Confucian conceptions of love and highlights the importance of familial love. Next, problems arising from this commitment to partiality are discussed, and how a modern Confucian ethics might respond. One possible defense is that classical Confucian thought does, in fact, contain robust notions of impartiality and justice-as-fairness. Another response is to advocate the introduction of norms and institutions from outside the tradition, in order to strengthen conceptions of the public interest, ethical impartiality, and moral equality. On this view, such values, though largely absent from the tradition, can function alongside traditional Confucian concerns about family without conflict. Another argument prioritizes indigenous Confucian normative ideals, such as harmony; these take priority over impartiality, which emerges from a different historical and cultural milieu. In what follows, I review these responses and discuss their shortcomings.

I then explore a different response, which begins by accepting the primacy of familial attachments to the Confucian ethical life. I explore what notions of impartiality—understood largely pragmatically, as a value that functions in everyday social life rather than as an explicit moral principle that guides deliberation or judgment—can be derived from an ethics that focuses on family commitments. Stated another way: how can particularistic motivations, rooted in personal attachments, give rise to greater benefit or concern for those outside the family, but who share civic or public space? While this reconstruction of traditional Confucian ethical ideas might not entirely assuage the concern over impartiality, it will nevertheless raise interesting questions for the ethics of liberal individualism and suggest areas in which Confucian ethics and contemporary ethical theorizing might develop a dialogue.

Love in Classical Confucian Thought

How has love been understood in the Confucian tradition? What relevant love-like states or ideas appear in the classical texts such as the *Analects* and the *Mencius*? Answers to these questions are not straightforward, as no single term entirely equates to "love." The most obvious match is *ai* (愛)—which is also the modern term for romantic love. In the *Analects*, Confucius is asked to explain the key Confucian virtue, *ren* (仁, variously translated as humaneness, goodness, or exemplary conduct), which is central to the aim of personal cultivation:[2] "Fan Chi asked about *ren*. The Master said: It is to love (*ai*) all men" (12.22, James Legge, trans.).[3] In so far as love involves personal familiarity and strong feelings of attachment, however, such translations can be misleading. *Ai* does sometimes indicate some form of intimate personal regard and affection in the early Confucian literature.[4] However, *ai* is often an attitude directed toward non-intimates, or those of limited or no personal acquaintance.[5] In the Analects, it often refers to a ruler's attitude toward his subjects or people in general, and here a better translation is arguably "care," albeit with some degree of affection or feeling.[6] We return to the theme of love-as-care below, but here note that *ai* as a single attitude or affection is not, by itself, central to classical Confucian ethics.[7]

Another obstacle to understanding the nature of love in the Confucian texts is the muted interest in some familiar forms of love, particularly romantic or sexual love. *Ai* does occasionally refer to something like romantic love,[8] and the erotic occasionally features in the *Book of Odes* (*Shijing*).[9] Desire (*yu* 欲) is also recognized as a powerful force in human conduct, to be harnessed rather than suppressed.[10] The desire for food and sex is recognized as the most prevalent and generic of human desires.[11] However, discussions of desire, including those of a sexual nature, often arise in the context of urging appropriate levels and the avoidance of excess, issued as advice to rulers.[12] Furthermore, the relationship between husband and wife (marriage in general), although one of the key relationships mentioned in the Analects, receives less attention in the texts than other relationships[13] and is often described in vague and dutiful terms.[14] In general, romantic love does not feature strongly in classical Confucian social thought.

Another form of love mentioned sparingly is friendship. Confucian texts lack the detailed analysis found in Aristotle's *Nicomachean Ethics* or Plato's *Lysis*. Friendship is often presented in moralized terms, as a means through which people can learn from others as a means of self-cultivation (*Analects* 1.9), or a relationship of mutual exhortation and moral improvement (*Mencius* 3B30). While friends (and virtue) are valued in the text, they are not a locus for discussions of love.

Evidently, many forms of love found in the Western canonical tradition are treated cursorily in the classical Confucian tradition. There is little interest in strong feelings or passions, physical attraction, attraction to mind or soul, the sense that another can make up for some deficiency in oneself, or the importance of finding another self. One form of love is found throughout the Confucian texts, however: feelings and attachments centered on the family.

The Chinese term that most closely approximates to family is *jia* (家). As Ambrose King notes (1985, 61), however, *jia* has a range of meanings. This includes the nuclear family, clan or kinship relations, and even feudal estates. To retain the broad scope of the Chinese notion, the term *familial* will sometimes be used.

The importance of the familial to classical Confucians can be articulated in several ways. First, the topic of family pervades the early texts. Discussions of family affairs and the use of familial language or motifs to describe social life are commonplace. In the *Analects*, for example, these include the importance of the father-son relationship (*Analects* 1.11, 4.20), instructions for children regarding treatment of parents (4.18–4.21), and normative guidance for relations between older and younger (9.16, 13.20, 14.43). Teacher-student relations are also conceived in familial terms (11.11), as are ruler and the ruled (*Mencius* 1A4), and even the relation between states (13.7). The family is thus the focus for much "moral discourse." The *Mencius* declares: "What is the most important duty? It is one's duty towards one's parents" (4A19).

Second, the texts feature a wide range of inter-personal attitudes found in familial relationships, with each—including *ai*—comprising an aspect of a Confucian notion of familial love. These attitudes often appear to be normative—desirable forms of family-like relations to be fostered or cultivated. For example:

"A humane man (*ren* 仁) does not lay up anger, nor cherish resentment against his brother, but only regards him with affection and love (*ai*)" (*Mencius* 5A3).

Wan Zhang said, "When his parents love (*ai*) him, a son rejoices and forgets them not" (5A1).

Besides *ai* (love/care), many other psychological states and forms of conduct are implicated in loving familial relations. These include: filial piety or family reverence (*xiao* 孝), fraternal responsibility (*ti* 悌), nurturing or nourishing (*yang* 養), concern or anxiety (*you* 憂), reverence or respect (*jing* 敬), affection (*qin* 親), loyalty or commitment (*zhong* 忠), deference (*rang* 讓), giving honor or esteeming (*gong* 恭), bringing comfort or respite (*an* 安), cherishing (*huai* 懷),[15] and shame (*chi* 恥). The *Mencius* illustrates both the range and the significance of familial feelings:

> Children carried in the arms all know to love (*ai*) those giving affection (*qin*), and when they are grown a little, they all know to respect (*jing*) their elder brothers. To be affectionate (*qin*) towards parents – this is humaneness (*ren*). To have respect for elders – this is appropriateness (*yi*). All that remains is to extend these to the entire world.' (7A15, original translation, Legge, translation modified for clarity.)

Here, the cardinal Confucian values of humaneness (*ren*) and appropriateness (*yi*) are equated with care, affection, and respect for family and kin.[16] A full account of the various affective states involved in Confucian family life is beyond the scope of this paper, but this brief survey illustrates some key points. While familial love is the most important form of love for the Confucians, it is not characterized by a single property or feeling. Also, the psychological states and experiences involved in loving relations are not symmetrical or generic, common to both or all parties; this differs from unitary characterizations of love such as longing for the other, lovingly gazing upon another, and so on. Instead, distinctive affective experiences or psychological states attach to particular relationships or social roles, and their distinctive perspectives within the web of familial relations. For example, the older should be kind to the young, while the young should feel respect for elders (*Mencius* 6B6). The "Liyun" chapter of the *Book of Rites* (*Liji*) illustrates this point:[17]

> What are "the things which men consider right?" Kindness on the part of the father, and filial reverence on that of the son; gentleness on the part of the elder brother, and obedience on that of the younger; righteousness on the part of the husband, and submission on that of the wife; kindness on the part of elders, and deference on that of juniors; with benevolence on the part of the ruler, and loyalty on that of the minister – these ten are the things which men consider to be right. (Legge, trans. modified)

Each of the above attitudes or stances—kindness, filial reverence, gentleness, obedience, deference, etc.—entails a range of habits, actions, and feelings, which are cultivated through ritual and social practice; these attitudes, along with ritual, direct inter-personal interactions and maintain larger social networks. The deference expected of juniors, for example, is not a simple psychological state but also entails certain thoughts and feelings that direct behavior. Filial reverence (*xiao*) includes warm affective experiences—such as gratitude for parents' care and reverence for the more experienced or accomplished—and also patterns of behavior action. *Xiao* involves gratitude, which leads to trust, and so to obedience, which itself is a method of learning (*xue*). Obedient children learn through thoughtful attentiveness to how the more experienced construct their lives (*Analects* 1.11). Conversely, the attitudes of elder brothers (gentleness) or elders (kindness) suggest support, patience, and even forgiveness for junior parties striving for competence in the social world.

This web of related attitudes collectively constitutes familial love and explains another feature of Confucian familial love: it is instrumental in realizing the Confucian notion of the good life. This well-functioning "eco-system" of interpersonal attitudes and roles produce both virtuous individuals and social harmony and stability. Such wide-reaching effects of well-ordered family life are expressed in *Analects* 1.2:

> Master You said, "A young person who is filial and respectful of his elders rarely becomes the kind of person who is inclined to defy his superiors, and there has never been a case of one who is disinclined to defy his superiors stirring up rebellion.
> "The gentleman applies himself to the roots. 'Once the roots are firmly established, the Way will grow.' Might we not say that filial reverence and respect for elders constitute the root of humanness (*ren*)?"[18]

The long process of personal cultivation (*ren*) begins with familial love and includes the development of the right kinds of interpersonal attitudes and affective responses.[19] The emergence of patterns of deference (and remonstrance—*jian*諫—which prevents deference becoming mere submission) serves to integrate the subject into a social web of relations and shared traditions, which enables people to find "meaning in life" (Rosemont 2015, 90). Ultimately, the result of such cultivation through the family was the capacity for political authority—which was guided by the same attitudes of reverence, deference and sympathetic response.[20]

A final feature of classical Confucian thinking about love is "graded love" or "love with distinctions." Love toward one's family should be stronger than love toward other families or strangers. This contrast informs the disputes between Mencius and another early philosophical school, the Mohists. The latter promoted a kind of general care or concern (*jianai*), in which one's own family did not receive special consideration.[21] All fathers were to be treated as fathers, all sons as sons, etc. Other families were treated in the manner of one's own family. Mencius believed this was psychologically implausible and perhaps against human nature (*xing*性).[22] Basic motivations to care about others originate in the family and have one's family as their immediate object;

ideally, conditions permitting, such motivations are to be extended (*tui*推) toward more distant others, ultimately covering all under heaven (Mencius 1A7, 4A1, 7A15). How such extension might proceed is discussed below.²³

Problems of Familial Love: A Failure of Fairness and Impartiality?

The priority of familial love in the Confucian tradition has engendered an ethical dilemma among contemporary Confucian scholars. The motivations and commitments associated with the family seem frequently in tension with the moral requirements of impartiality or justice. The locus classicus for this tension is *Analects* 13.18:

> The Duke of She said to Confucius, "Among my people there is one we call 'Upright Gong.' When his father stole a sheep, he reported him to the authorities."
>
> Confucius replied, "Among my people, those who we consider 'upright' are different from this: fathers cover up for their sons, and sons cover up for their fathers. 'Uprightness' is to be found in this."

Confucius advocates "covering up" for the thieving father, which constitutes being "upright" or a "true person" (*zhi*直). However, justice demands that wrongdoing be addressed and due consideration given to the broader community. The commitment to family members appears to conflict with duties to a more impersonal public realm; and which side Confucius is on seems clear.

This passage has been widely discussed.²⁴ Some interpretations attempt to ameliorate the tension and portray Confucius sympathetically. Interpretations include: the passage cautions against the failure to understand filial reverence, comparable to Plato's *Euthyphro*, rather than disregards public interest; it describes a profound ethical conflict and, while respecting and not dismissing justice, prioritizes familial values; it indicates that surrendering a loved one for a minor crime is unnecessary or counterproductive, with the wrong-doing better dealt with via familial structures (e.g., the son remonstrates with the father to make amends to those harmed).²⁵ This passage is not an isolated example, however. The second Confucian classic, the *Mencius*, contains a similar problem:

> Tao Ying asked, "When Shun was Son of Heaven, and Gao Yao was his Minister of Crime, if 'the Blind Man' [Shun's father] had murdered someone, what would they have done?"
>
> Mengzi said, "[Justice Minister] Gao Yao would simply have arrested him!"

Tao Ying asked, "So Shun would not have forbidden it?"

Mengzi said, "How could Shun have forbidden it? Gao Yao had a sanction for his actions."

Tao Ying asked, "So what would Shun have done?"

Mengzi said, "Shun looked at casting aside the whole world like casting aside a worn sandal. He would have secretly carried him [his father] on his back and fled, to live in the coastland, happy to the end of his days, joyfully forgetting the world." (7A35)

The conflict between public interest or justice and the actions of an exemplary Confucian is clear. The emperor Shun would flee with his father, helping him to evade justice. Such are the demands of familial love. Here, the crime and normative roles involved (emperor, minister, father, son) leave less room for interpretation than the sheep-stealing passage. Shun is aware of due process, and what the minister for justice ought to do. While Shun did not abuse his power by granting immunity to his father, he nevertheless prioritized his father's well-being, and at the cost of governing the empire.[26]

Many have found this prioritizing of the family over the interests of the wider community morally troubling, due to the apparent neglect of moral impartiality. This might be explained as the failure to adequately recognize the interests of those with whom no ties of affection exist. Stated in modern terms, Confucian ethics has been accused of failing to recognize moral equality between persons and impartiality as foundational moral principles: differential treatment of people is justified only if meaningful differences in cases exist, and family ties or particularistic affections are insufficient reason in many cases. Furthermore, in Western liberal democratic traditions, such moral ideals have informed the construction of social and political institutions that govern public life, fairly and impartially administering goods and burdens (as well as punishments). In contrast, traditional Confucian ethics has been accused of fostering nepotism and corruption (Liu 2003, 7). This raises doubts about the viability of Confucian ethics, and whether it can serve as a resource for modernizing China, as well as global and comparative ethical theorizing (Tu Wei-Ming 1985; Robert Neville 2010).

The difficulty facing Confucian ethics might be summed up in two points. The first is the lack of a strong distinction between the familial and the public or political realm. Contemporary sociologist Ambrose King locates the problem in a Confucian classification of the human community into three categories: the individual, the family, and the group (or non-familial group, *qun*); in Confucian theory, however, "there is no formal treatment of the concept of *qun*" (King 1985, 61). King writes, "The root of the Confucian problematik lies in the fact that the boundary between the self and the group has not been conceptually articulated" (King 1985, 62). It is difficult to conceive of society as a community of separate and equal persons, upon which impartial institutions are constructed, because the self has not been considered independently of the relationships that constitute it. As Ci Jiwei notes, "those who have absorbed the Confucian concept of human relations would be socially and ethically at sea if they were to enter into relations with strangers, where the conjunction of hierarchical-reciprocal relations and kinship ties simply does not exist" (Ci 1999, 334).

This failure to distinguish the two realms leads to a second issue in traditional Confucian thought: treating the familial as a model for the political realm. This is seen in the reoccurring motif of the ruler as the father (or parent) of the people (*minzhi fumu* 民之父母).[27] This equating can be understood in various ways, but all invite objections. One gloss is the claim that good sons make good rulers: excellence in one realm ensures excellence in another. But someone can be a good son without being an effective leader, since the requirements of political leadership differ from those of family life. Good sons do not obviously develop good administrative skills by being sons. A second gloss is that how one acts as a father just is how one should act as a ruler. However, this seems insufficient for effective political leadership, since the two are very different social or professional roles. Furthermore, Chinese critics frequently regard the familial model of political organization as the basis for authoritarianism, hierarchical social structures, and political subservience.

This apparent failure to distinguish the partiality of familial life from a public or political realm characterized by impartiality has led to damning assessments of the Confucian tradition in modern China. The late Qing dynasty (1644–1911) saw intense debate about how to modernize China and respond to the hegemony of the Western powers, and prominent intellectuals such as Kang Youwei (1858–1927) and Tan Sitong (1865–1898) argued that the bonds of family were holding China back.[28] Complex modern political and economic realities required bureaucratic forms of regulation and impartiality in public administration; traditional Confucian family-based ethics, however, struggled to meet this demand. This led many to question the worth of traditional Confucian social ethics in post-imperial China.[29] New Confucian thinker Xiong Shili (1885–1968) claimed "Family is the source of all evil and the root of decline [...] It is because of family that the Chinese people lack ideas of country, of nation, and of public life" (Xiong 1996, 336–337).

What then might be said in defense of the Confucian ethical tradition? Can it move beyond the commitment to familial life and its tendency to favor partiality over more impartial or impersonal perspectives? In what follows I explore four possible ways to rehabilitate Confucian ethics and establish its relevance to modernity and to meta-ethical theorizing. The four responses are: Confucian ethics does value impartiality; Confucian social thought can import (and is consistent with) modern ideals such as impartiality and political equality; Confucian thought offers alternative moral ideals, which can trump impartiality; and Confucian partiality can bring about states of affairs roughly approximate with the demands of impartiality (in its local and bounded forms) without treating the latter as a foundational moral ideal—by harnessing the motivational force of familial love and attachments.

Confucian Responses to the Challenge of Impartiality

Confucian Impartiality?

Some have argued that traditional Confucian thought does value non-familial relationships and also limits the family-as-state analogy (Joseph Chan 2004, Erin Cline 2007). Chan (2004) points out that while avoiding harm to the father-son bond is a prominent demand in the texts (Mencius 4A17), the ruler-minister (ruler-subject) relationship lacks such privileged status. Ministers can refuse to serve and, in extremis, rulers can be disposed (Mencius 1B8). The ruler's fatherly concern for the people's welfare is better understood as an expression of paternalism and perfectionism; while political liberals might reject such values, they do not equate the state with the family. Furthermore, the texts distinguish between civil virtues and relationship virtues (Chan 2004). Civic virtues are found throughout the early texts—such as tolerance, trustworthiness and generosity—and apply to all relationships, not merely familial ones. The rudiments of a public realm and the means to limit the influence of familial ties are present in the tradition.

Others (e.g., Cline 2007) argue that the *Analects* is concerned with questions of fairness beyond special relationships. Confucius did not discriminate when accepting students, for example, and the virtue of rightness or appropriateness (yi義) limits the pursuit of profit or self-interest. Cline draws on John Rawls' account of a personal *sense of justice* that underpins his formal principles and argues that the exemplary person or *junzi* in the *Analects* can be similarly understood.[30] This sense of justice has three aspects (Cline 2007, 367–369): a sense of fairness (the *junzi* is neither for nor against anything, 4.10, 16.1), sympathy toward people's suffering (6.30), and a sense of responsibility to the wider community (benevolent rulers respond to people's needs, Mencius 1A7). Both accounts are developmental, with a sense of justice cultivated over time: Rawls follows Jean Piaget, while the Confucian-Mencian tradition recognizes four incipient moral responses (*siduan*; 2A2, 6A6) to be nurtured. A sense of justice is thus part of a Confucian ethical naturalism—a guiding "moral" sense that naturally develops, conditions permitting.

These arguments claim, in effect, that Confucian familial love coexists alongside impartiality or fairness in the public realm. They are inconclusive, however. First, the textual evidence is unclear. There is some awareness of the need for fairness and extended concern for others (rulers for their subjects, etc.); but whether these constitute a robust commitment to impartiality is unclear. For example, the so-called civic virtues identified by Chan are still relational virtues, guiding everyday social interaction. Such virtues might induce a widening sphere of moral concern, but this extension arguably proceeds within networks of personal attachments and affect (see the discussion below). Also, Chan (2004, 69–70) translates *gong* (公) in the *Xunzi* as impartiality, suggesting explicit recognition of this ideal. But this seems forced and possibly anachronistic. The text defends a profoundly hierarchical social structure, in which common people must defer to sagely rulers and the norms of ritualized order.[31] *Gong* can mean "public mindedness," and a ruler might be mindful of public need; however, it is ritual propriety and the ruler, advised by ministers, who ultimately determines what is just and fair (*ping*).[32]

The issue here is whether judgments of fairness or rightness (*yi*) in early Confucian thought are sufficiently detached from historical context and personal prejudices. A ruler's or minister's "impartial" judgments, although made in good faith, could nevertheless be shaped by ritualized norms and traditional precedents that are not impartial in a more expansive sense—e.g., reflecting the moral equality of persons. After all, the tradition regards as appropriate the prioritizing of family. There is no meta-level reflection on the dominant social institutions and their role in propagating hierarchical Confucian social roles.

Furthermore, justice appears in the text mainly as a personal virtue of the ruler (though a version of the Golden rule in the *Analects* suggests some role for abstract principle). But a personal sense of justice does not itself ensure critical perspective on institutions and historical precedent. In Rawls' account, the development of a sense of justice or fairness starts with the family, strengthens through the community, and arrives at recognition of an impersonal public realm where personal ties are unimportant; but the Confucian texts lack this final step. One example of this historically conditioned sense of rightness or justice is the texts' critical view of the "barbarians" in the hinterlands surrounding the early Chinese states (Mencius 3A4). This shows little regard for difference or otherness, and also confidence in the superiority of Confucian culture. Thus, the Confucian ethical code appears more important than abstract notions of moral community and equality.

In sum, there is reason to believe that the early Confucian understandings of fairness and impartiality are shaped by traditional norms and established social practices, and while some forms of justice and impartiality are recognized, these do not trump familial priority. The texts lack higher level commitments to institutional forms or regulative ideals of justice or impartiality that might curb personal vagaries or cultural norms.[33]

Importing Impartiality from the Western Liberal Tradition

Given that the strength of the commitment to impartiality in traditional Confucian social ethics' is unclear, a possible response is to introduce to the tradition novel institutions and mechanisms that cultivate awareness of impartiality as a personal value and ensure impartiality in the public realm. On this view, the tradition of authoritative virtuous rulership, grounded in familial attachment, is inadequate for the needs of modern East Asian societies. Economic, technological, and social changes have led to value pluralism and disagreement about the good life (as well as concerns about gender equality, and the rejection of caste systems and legal restrictions on self-determination). This situation pragmatically justifies the adoption of ideals and political institutions from outside the tradition, such as political equality (the right to participate in decisions affecting oneself) and democracy (one person one vote), and institutions that ensure the impartiality of legal and political processes (Sungmoon Kim 2018, 6). In turn, these regulate the influence of particularistic ties and ensure substantive impartiality.

Ideally, a Confucian heritage is not rejected but enriched, and a distinctively Confucian modernity can emerge. Robust notions of impartiality and impartial public institutions are to exist alongside the Confucian commitment to familial attachments. For example, in some East Asian countries, public debate and political institutions have produced laws promoting filial piety, making children legally responsible for the care of aging parents.[34] Confucian particularistic attachments are thus reimagined within institutions guided by explicit regulative ideals of impartiality, equality, and fairness. This is perhaps the most convincing response to the sheep-stealing dilemma above, since here impartiality is enshrined in institutions and is not merely a personal virtue.

However, the problem with this approach is that the extent to which such a society remains Confucian is debatable. If diversity and disagreement are such that an impersonal and impartial system of decision making is required, with Confucian values merely one competing vision of the good life, is this a meaningful continuation of the Confucian tradition?[35] Confucian culture becomes a sub-set of a multi-cultural society, and its influence might wane over time. Furthermore, in the face of social disagreement and conflict, people might be increasingly compelled to appeal to self-conceptions based on individual autonomy and self-determination; but this elides the Confucian emphasis on a relational and role-constituted self.

Rejecting the Priority of Impartiality

As a path to a Confucian modernity, another defense of Confucian familial love and partiality involves rejecting the *priority* of ideals such as justice and impartiality, without rejecting them per se. Instead, an ideal internal to the Confucian tradition is deemed more fundamental, and constitutive of human flourishing within that tradition. Harmony (*he* 和) is such an ideal. Contemporary thinker Li Zehou has argued that "emotional harmony is higher than rational justice" (Li 2016, 1098–1100). On this view, the priority of justice and impartiality assumes a particular kind of human subject, which can be questioned. This is one characterized by desires. Desires explain action and lead to an influential conception of rationality (means-end reasoning). People have different desires and pursue different ends; rather than judge which desires are most worthwhile, the moral task is to enable all to pursue personal projects within ethical constraints (fairness, not harming others, etc.). Justice entails impartially adjudicating between competing ends or projects. On Li's view, however, this focus on personal desires bound up in individuated conceptions of a single life is misguided. He draws on Liang Shuming (1893–1988) and Chinese interpretations of Yogacaran Buddhism, which understand desires as originating in the body. Being bodily in nature, desires are experienced as private and individual. This in turn generates the impression of the self as a discrete independent entity, with its own life plans. This is the self that informs liberal political theory and drives concern with impartiality.[36]

Emotions, and their origins, however, are understood differently. The classical Chinese term for emotion, *qing* (情), also means situation or state of affairs, or even reality or essence.[37] This suggests that the origin of emotion lies partly outside the body. That is, emotions inhere in the social situations in which people find themselves (they have a quasi-objective quality and are not simply inner feeling). In Li's account, a species of historical materialism, material conditions, and social structures partly determine consciousness, including emotions. In the Confucian tradition, personal relationships are highly structured and ritualized. Such relationships are not understood as freely chosen or voluntary, a response to a liking a person's character, and so on. Rather, they arise within existing social and historical contexts; the emotions experienced in these relationships—including those of familial love—partly reflect the social practices and roles that constitute those relationships. Being partly derivative of the social practices in which the subject exists, and orientated toward those situations, emotions thus have a veridical or action-guiding quality.[38] Also, since these practices have been refined over time within the tradition they exhibit stability and coherence, and so the emotions experienced through them have a measure of order—i.e., they harmonize with each other.

In Li's account, emotions motivate action. Being inseparable from the concrete situations, however, they cannot be subsumed under abstract moral principles; the two are incongruent. The latter aim to make diverse considerations commensurable and facilitate judgments of fairness across an extended community (such as all humans or all rational beings).[39] For Li, committing to such principles means detachment from the motivating and guiding emotions embedded in the lived social world; but the meaning found in such everyday life contexts is a fundamental good (Li 2019, 317–322). Such meaning can be characterized in terms of the Confucian ideal of harmony. This broad notion might be summarized as the integration of various elements into a collaborative whole. Exemplified in various ways, it includes the harmonizing of emotional experiences through the practices and interactions that constitute relationships.[40] The partiality found in the Confucian tradition is thus justified since attention to particulars and the contexts of social interaction (i.e., familial love) create harmony. While the emotions experienced might differ, each participant in a relationship derives emotional satisfaction from the interactions. These emotional rewards are central to the Confucian good life, with the pleasure of such coordination compared to the effects of musical coordination and harmony.[41] This is why "emotional harmony is higher than rational justice."

This defense of partiality, by placing harmony above impartiality, is speculative and awaits fuller articulation.[42] Its account of emotion (and the difference with desire) is questionable; and even if accepted, the account arguably better suits traditional societies with less social mobility and more settled forms of life. The more complex and numerous the social forms, the more elusive is "emotional harmony." Still, even if social diversity complicates how harmony might be generated, the latter could still serve as an alternative regulative ideal, with conceptions of flourishing that ignore such affective satisfactions poorer for that omission. Furthermore, this approach raises valid questions of approaches to morality that begins from a strongly individuated conception of self—to which attach highly individual life plans. The separate but equal nature of such innumerable life plans requires a moral idea such as impartiality to ensure fair treatment. But the metaphysical assumptions behind such a self can be questioned; and if the self is not understood in such terms, then perhaps impartiality (as impersonal adjudication) matters less. Similarly, perhaps the emphasis on pluralism and separateness undervalue emotional solidarity built on some degree of shared social life.

How Familial Attachments Contribute to Impartiality

Rather than pursuing alternative foundational moral ideals, however, Confucian familial love can be developed in another way. This does not directly contest the value of impartiality but shows how familial attachments yield limited and localized forms of impartiality for the shared spaces of everyday social life. Here, impartiality means expanding one's sphere of concern: giving greater consideration to, or making available more goods or resources to, those with whom no particularistic ties exist (initially). In so far as the bulk of most people's lives and concerns focus on the local and concrete, rather than the distant and abstract, then this form of impartiality may be significant.

The route to such impartiality starts from Confucian convictions about the moral worth of particularistic motivations, and the emotions deriving from family life. Instead of reigning in these motivations and sensibilities, they are cultivated and harnessed. When directed toward social life beyond the family, these motivations can bring about forms of impartiality, without necessarily aiming at it—in a manner somewhat analogous to Adam Smith's "invisible hand." Examining the psychological and practical effects of Confucian familial attachments can thus partially address the objections about Confucian values from the standpoint of impartiality. The ways of directing conduct that emerge might not satisfy the loftiest or most abstract notions of impartiality, since these effects will generally be limited and local. But this approach suggests reasons for continued interest in Confucian ethics beyond the Chinese tradition, and possibilities for a Chinese modernity informed by its own traditions.

Confucian Care: Care-as-modeling

The first illustration of how partiality can generate forms of impartiality derives from the conception of care inherent in Confucian familial love. An important form of such loving care is *care-as-modeling*.[43] Such care originates in the family, but its benefits can extend beyond kith and kin. Confucian care-as-modeling can be explained as follows.

Confucian thought recognizes the natural unevenness of most close relationships; at any given moment, one party is typically stronger, wiser, more capable, etc., in some aspect of the relationship or interaction. Equality in such relationships is an abstraction. Confucian familial relations are typically hierarchical and role-bound and include father-son, older-younger (sibling), mentor and mentee, and teacher and pupil. These relationships feature disparities in age, experience, and even ability or competence, and classical Confucians emphasize the differing experiences, duties, and emotional experiences that characterize each type of relationship. The *Mencius* notes:

> He [the sage-ruler Shun] appointed Xie minister of education in order to teach people about human relations (*lun*): that between parents and child there is affection (*qin*); between ruler and minister rightness (*yi*); between husband and wife, separate functions (*bie*); between older and younger, proper order (*xu*); and between friends, trustworthiness (*xin*). (3A4 trans. Irene Bloom and Ivanhoe)

Differing forms of loving care arise within these relationships, such as affection (*qin*) and kindness (*ci*) from parents toward children, and filial reverence (*xiao*, which encompasses obedience, loyalty, respect, and gratitude) of (adult) children toward parents. In the context of such differentiation, one aspect of loving care becomes important. Namely, the more senior party is responsible for educating those more junior. This is done partly by modeling or setting an example. Rooted in a motivation that the other succeeds in the world, care consists in showing the cared-for or mentee "how it's done."

The *Analects* offers a detailed study in how Confucius sets an example for his students. Book 10, for example, is a study in the care with which Confucius conducts himself—the reverence he displays toward others, his caution about speaking, his attention to demeanor as a guide for conduct, and so on. The exemplary figure of Confucius is a reference point for human conduct, around which others can find their moral bearings. Confucius cares about his disciples' development, modeling excellence to ready them for positions of responsibility in government. As Mencius notes, "The compass and square produce perfect circles and squares. By the sages, the human relations are perfectly exhibited" (4A2).[44]

Beyond the classical texts, a more recent, albeit gendered, image that embodies this care is the traditional Chinese *shifu* 師父: someone "teacher-like" (*shi*) and "father-like" (*fu*) invested in training junior cohorts in a skill or vocation. This form of care involves imparting knowledge and skills, but from a position of relative authority and motivated by personal attachment. "Care" is a concern that the cared-for succeed in the complex social world that they find themselves in, and a readiness to help. Such caring enables the cared-for to do something they were previously incapable of, did not want to do, or had not considered. Such caring applies to children preparing to enter a more structured and responsibility-laden environment; but—drawing on the extended sense of familial love—it includes junior acquaintances unfamiliar with the requisite standards and skills inherent in practical tasks or social situations, such as in the workplace. Concerned and experienced mentors often prepare the cared-for to fulfill social roles and navigate situations in which conduct is largely prescribed or customary (everyday greetings, weddings, professional roles, etc.). However, models are also beneficial in less structured situations, including dealings with neighbors or friends, which bring more room for interpretation and error. In all of these contexts, the ideal is to attain competency, fluency, or even mastery.

How does care as modeling work? An obvious mechanism is imitation—observing and copying successful behaviors and strategies. But care-as-modeling is also characterized by its suggestiveness. It is prospective and pre-emptive. It invites the cared-for to thoughtfully study those around her and imaginatively adapt what is found there. Confucius notes,

> "In strolling in the company of just two other persons, I am bound to find a teacher. Identifying their strengths, I follow them, and identifying their weaknesses, I reform myself accordingly." (7.22)

As this passage illustrates, learning via modeling often proceeds by interpersonal comparison (*pi*譬). This is expressed explicitly in 6.30, and the possibilities of learning from what is close at hand:

> ... Authoritative persons [*ren* 仁] establish others in seeking to establish themselves and promote others in seeking to get there themselves. Correlating (*pi*) one's conduct with those near at hand can be said to be the method of becoming an authoritative person. (Ames and Rosemont 2010, trans.)

One seeking to "establish others" and "promote others" provides a personal example that invites interpersonal comparison, analogy, and appropriation. Friendship promoted in the *Analects*—exemplified by Confucius' students—has a similar structure: people of similar virtue learn from and inspire each other (13.1, 16.4).

Care-by-modeling can be extrapolated beyond the original Confucian context. For example, older brothers offer a model to younger family members or friends in how they cope with bullying at school, which helps the cared-for to prepare for similar situations. Similarly, in the choice of career, children and pupils observe how teachers and parents make a success (or not) of their professions, compare the observees' characters with their career demands, and gain insight into the suitability of such careers.

Care-as-modeling contrasts with prominent Anglophone accounts of care. The latter prioritize attentiveness, empathy, and motivational displacement—allowing one's own motivations and actions to be directed by the cared-for (Noddings 2002; Held 2006). In the Confucian account, however, these are secondary to ensuring the cared-for attains the applicable competencies.[45] "Care" is not primarily psychological access to the cared-for's emotions and mental states, or responding to the individual's immediate or stated needs. Rather, attention focuses on the interface of the individual and the surrounding environment, with its social practices that the cared-for must master. Furthermore, this conception of care does not rely on a comprehensive understanding of the cared-for's interests or good—i.e., a concern for how their desires and goals form a unified life plan that the caregiver helps to realize. Instead, the caregiver is motivated by success in specific social practices and contexts, each with their own internal standards of excellence.

How Modeling-as-care Mitigates the Problems of Partiality

Modeling as care addresses some objections to Confucian ethics deriving from concerns about partiality. This is because the example set or the model offered can be a public resource. Acts of care intended to benefit a select group (broadly, those in the web of familial relations) also benefit a broader range of people—including those for whom the agent lacked caring motivations.

The benefits to the wider group of such caring motivations can be expressed in various ways. The first is the public model provided by the caregiver. For example, a father coaches a football team primarily because of his desire to introduce his son to the joys and challenges of football, but all who join the team benefit from his teaching and example. Initially, the model, i.e., the coach, is not strongly motivated to benefit the other children, but his particularistic motives generate a quasi-public benefit.

The psychological or motivational implications of such care can be explored further. In the Confucian tradition, models or exemplars are not simply resources, from which others might learn if motivated to improve. Modeling is also implicated in a complex social psychology, which emphasizes the non-consensual effects of models on those around them. For example, people do not emulate models only because of a desire to learn or profit. The Confucians suggest that they are also moved by a sense of shame, by wanting to measure up more favorably to the example set: *Analects* 2.3 reads, "Lead them with excellence... and they will develop a sense of shame and, moreover, will order themselves."[46] The classical texts also assume that, as a matter of basic human dispositions, people emulate exemplars without consciously choosing to do so.[47] Modeling motivated by familial love can thus stimulate interpersonal reactions and comparisons that have broader social effects. Other parents see the coach's example and are shamed, inspired or simply disposed to make a contribution, sharing the burden of running the team, etc. In this way, caring enriches the goods or resources available to a community, benefiting a range of people beyond the original familial attachments.

Another relevant Confucian insight concerns the extension of caring, to include people connected to the original cared-for person. The practically relevant motivations are not limited to the cared-for, but rather "spill over" or, to use the classical Confucian term, *extend* (*tui* 推; Mencius 1A7[48]): sympathy and affection for one's own family can be extended to more distant others. In the football coach example, the other children are not merely foreseen but unintended beneficiaries; the claim is that the powerful affective attitude of care for the son often stimulates a degree of personal interest in the other children on the team. Caring about the project, as a result of caring for the son, induces caring for others involved in it.[49] This motivation to care might be less strong, but nevertheless, these other relationships acquire some of the qualities of particularistic ties. As a result the children's interests matter more to the coach. Through this extension of concern, partiality is redirected and again drives broader concern for others.[50] Familial love should thus not be understood in terms of clearly delimited commitments, with distinctions between inner and outer, but is somewhat malleable and "extendable."

It might be objected that, so far, the ways in which familial love generates wider concern or public benefit is limited; impartiality requires more extensive consideration for others than examples such as the football coach suggest. What about, for example, conditions of scarcity, when families chose between prioritizing their own and strangers? When waiting lists for medical treatment are long, should families "pull strings" to have family members treated early (Marcia Baron 1991, 855)? Similarly, it might be asked whether such extensions of motivation and concern are psychologically plausible.

I address the motivational question in the next section, but the following can be said about the extent to which impartiality can be indirectly achieved through familial love. First, it is unlikely that that familial love can generate an idealized standpoint for moral judgments; as noted above, impartiality in public life and policy is perhaps best addressed through institution reform. Of greater interest here is how familial love can generate more local and socially specific forms of fairness or impartiality—e.g., greater willingness to share goods with those in the same community. That said, perhaps particularistic care and the exemplary conduct it motivates can sometimes realize more abstract and global forms of impartiality.

One possible route involves the subject's own commitment to serving as a model. Caring about the son makes the father desire to be a good model for him. Fathers, for example, often want their sons to acquire general character virtues, such as kindness or fairness. This can elicit motivations in the father to treat others in ways that models tolerance, fairness, etc. Furthermore, such motivations, if sustained, become part of the father's character and habitual conduct. As a result, conduct guided by values such as fairness or tolerance becomes routine, even in situations where such conduct is neither observed by the son nor affects him.[51] Indeed, it is common for parents to hold themselves to higher standards because of their child; anecdotally, people can experience a change of mindset in response to the birth of a child, becoming more socially responsible in general. While further study of such anecdotal evidence is needed, the key point is that this expanded sense of moral responsibility and fairness are motivated by particularistic ties.

A second example of how familial love might motivate more global notions of impartial fairness concerns the environment. Some parents become concerned about the world's ecosystems when considering the future from their children's perspective (and their children's children). Desire that the world still be habitable for children can motivate parents to take on their share of the burden to ensure sustainable resource use. Here, too, parents are prompted to value fairness, to do their fair share, by particularistic concern for their children; previously, they might have been unmotivated to act or motivated by narrower self-interested calculations.

Familial Love as an Obligation to Develop a Basis for Familiarity

On the question of a moral psychology that connects familial love with wider concern, we return to classical Confucianism's *extension* (*tui*) of family-like concern and attachments.[52] The dominant paradigm of Confucian social ethics, articulated in canonical texts such at the *Great Learning* (*Daxue*), is expanding circles of concern, influence, and harmonious interaction, with exemplary people at the center. In the original formulation, extension is explained in terms of potency or an ordering force (*de*), rooted in the effects of exemplary conduct on ever larger communities: exemplars transform households, households transform communities, and so on. The importance of personal attachment in the texts suggests that these expanding ripples of order and connection also proceed via the extension of family-like attachments.[53] Exploring this guiding metaphor and Confucian prescriptions for family-like attachments suggests a moral psychology that connects particularistic affections with a wider realm and the common good.

In the liberal social contract tradition, the expansion of personal attachments is often understood as voluntaristic, with rational individuals choosing or consenting to closer ties with others. Here, friendship is idealized: an alternative to the bonds of family or traditional ties, where relationships are chosen on judgments of character, common interest, a sense of attraction or amusement, etc. Outside these consensual networks—strangers or those with whom no personal attachment exists—different modes of relatedness apply, such as recognizing a shared human dignity; here, the formal demand for impartiality or fairness seems most apt.

Confucian thought challenges this picture, offering a different account of the expansion of networks of personal attachment. Here, expansion is not primarily voluntary or consensual; for the Confucian subject it is the result of a cultivated sense of obligation that is rooted in familial life. This sense of obligation can be described as *an obligation to identify a basis of familiarity* with each person who enters the subject's local social world.[54] This means a disposition to identify features of those encountered, such that a more particularistic tie can be established, and which can then guide action toward that person and facilitate affection. Such moments of familiarity can be varied—an obvious commonality, a prominent trait, a particular piece of knowledge, etc. An example is seeing a new acquaintance as being similar in some way to a sibling or parent, which then suggests how to act toward that person and even affective responses.

This sense of obligation to "familiarize" others is the cumulative effect on the subject of exposure to family life, which consistently sensitizes the subject to the roles and relationships that constitute her social world. This heightened awareness and conditioning is prominent in the

Analects. The text is a study in internalizing the demands of the many roles and relationships that constitute so much of the subject's everyday experiences. This conditioning begins with filial reverence (*xiao*): the junior person's adjustment to multiple social roles and relations—son, father, mother, teaching, minister, ruler, and so on. Most fundamentally, junior parties should be concerned about their parents. Children are to avoid giving parents cause for concern (*Analects* 2.5), care for them with a genuine feeling (2.6), control their speech toward parents (4.18), know their parents' age, and refrain from changing the affairs of a deceased father (4.20). Junior members of the community—younger brothers and sons—are also instructed on behaving at home and in the community (1.6). The effect of the practices and habits of filial reverence and fraternal deference, I suggest, is to cultivate a subject consistently concerned about relationships, who experiences a sense of obligation to establish familiarity with others. It is evoked whenever new acquaintances are encountered, with attempts made to "familiarize" the other and develop particularistic connections.[55] Such a sensibility explains why deliberation or reflection in the *Analects* is construed as a meditation on one's performance in various relationships (4.1).

This felt compulsion to identify personal qualities or features instrumental to the expansion of the web of affective connections is, for the Confucians, a form of ethical obligation. This contrasts with rationalist ethics in which impartiality is central. In the latter, ethical obligation is grounded in rational deliberation, and the identification of agent-neutral reasons for action. The Confucians, however, seem to suppose that the most fundamental obligations are social—demands to adopt certain practices or attitudes—and their force is created through the effects of practice and conditioning on the subject through ritual, habit, and custom. Such obligation is confirmed as ethical obligation on account of the shared social goods generated through familial attachments, and the broader social harmony realized in this approach to the good life. This point is significant because rational obligation, which underlies an abstracted impartial moral viewpoint, typically encounters the problem of how to motivate the subject to meet such obligation. Some insist that if we are fully or properly rational, then we will be sensitive to appropriate reasons (Christine Korsgaard 1996). But the Confucian approach to ethical obligation avoids such problems about practical motivation by locating ethical obligation in the conditioning effects of sustained practice, ritual, and habit as these pertain to other people who share a social space.

The same forms of obligation and sensitivity can be identified in contemporary Confucian cultures. One example is the power of fictive kinship relations—establishing relationships with strangers or non-kin by "extending" the features and emotions of kinship-relations.[56] Consider the younger brother-older brother relationship. The unique collection of actions, habits, and emotional experiences that constitute two people's experience of that familial relationship forms the basis for relating to other people judged to be similar to "younger brother" or "older brother." Contemporary examples of the extension of familial relations and affections include: appeal to native places or "hometowns" to generate solidarity, or parents instructing children and playmates to call one another by a fictive kinship term (William Jankowiak 2009, 77). In factories, young female factory workers address more experienced female workers or managers as "older sister" (*jiejie*) (Yang 1994, 114). This creates mutual affection and establishes modes of interaction and expectations—of assistance on the one hand, and cooperation on the other. Fictive kinship relations are not limited to China, but they illustrate this cultivated disposition to incorporate new connections into an existing web of family-like relations and ties. In contemporary China, this urge to generate a basis for familiarity is also seen in the importance of social networks or *guanxi*.[57] Importantly, *guanxi* relations are more particularistic and emotionally involved than mere lists of social contacts, favor exchange, or fee-for-service bribery. We return to the practical significance of *guanxi* below.

How then does this obligation to identify a basis for familiarity, and so to "familiarize" relationships with new acquaintances, accord with or further the demands of impartiality? Clearly, the expansion of family-like relationships to an ever-wider community does not constitute conduct or judgments that are impartial per se. But the drive to expand the web of relations does involve an attitude that is impartial. This sense of obligation is blind and impersonal. Any person entering the subject's social world becomes the object of this attempt to find familiarity. The attitude transcends particularistic ties, since it is not limited to particular favored others. It is an open-ended disposition; it is agent-neutral. This attitude is defeasible, given sufficient cause; nevertheless, one subject at a time, the web of particularistic ties expands. According to the Confucian ideal, this process has no endpoint; ultimately, for exemplary persons, "all within the fours seas are my brother" (12.5). This impartial attitude can thus generate wider concern for a greater number of people, within the context of localized social life.

Another consequence of the extension of the thoughts, feelings, and practices of familial ties is that subjects' conceptions of their self-interests are made malleable and convergence of interests more likely. Enhanced deference and openness to suggestion are features of friendship and even love (Amelie Rorty 1986); and the coordinating and consensus building effects of such attitudes can bring about states of affairs that are equitable without direct appeal to impartial judgments of fairness.

The limits of familial attachments to generate objectively fair outcomes must be acknowledged, however. This approach is most plausible when analysis of human conduct starts from recognition of a shared everyday social world constituted by numerous social interactions. Consequently, its relevance to justice within extended or global communities (all human beings, all sentient beings, and so forth) is limited. There are distant others who cannot be brought within networks of personal familiarity but who remain morally considerable. Furthermore, it is possible to yield, defer, and find consensus in ways that, from an impartial viewpoint, might involve unequal or unfair arrangements. False consciousness and insufficient appreciation for social structures and power dynamics are genuine challenges for this approach.

Guanxi Networks as Civil Society

Here too, however, something might be said for the Confucian approach presented here. Some (Lo and Otis 2003; Lambert 2012, ch. 7) have explored how networks of familiarity and particularistic ties can constitute a form of civil society. They can generate social stability and create sensitivity to others and a culture of respect. In this respect, extending networks of familiarity might contribute to fairness or justice in the wider public realm, albeit through a distinctive mechanism. This involves the effects of large-scale social networks on public policy.

Consider again the social phenomenon of *guanxi*, or affect-laden networks of personal attachment. Arguably, *guanxi* networks can function as an ethical corrective for "unethical" laws produced by a putatively impartial centralized authority. Lawmakers, striving for impartiality, can nevertheless be insufficiently sensitive to local conditions and the needs of local populations. Laws that appear impartial and fair to lawmakers—on account of their social identities, particular vantage points on society, or even constraints on their ability to understand local conditions—might be reasonably rejected by those distant from legislative centers. Under such circumstances, *guanxi* networks can induce reform by resisting or undermining unjust laws—perhaps by making enforcement infeasible.

Such effects are somewhat analogous to civil disobedience although the latter involves other forms of organization. Use of the black market during the Chinese communist government's restrictions on free-market exchanges is another example.[58] Given the scarcity of goods that citizens might reasonably expect access to, the use of *guanxi* networks to secure such goods "illegally" might, from an impartial standpoint, be justified, while also undermining nominally impartial but unreasonable economic policies. Indeed, historically, such informal personal networks help the under-privileged to resist or survive objectionable laws.[59]

Particularistic ties achieve their effect by providing alternative channels for resources and information, and by connecting affected individuals. The effect on policy might be achieved through a single social network, or several networks with the same concern emerging independently. In all such networks, no single person need be personally familiar with all others, with each network partly maintained by a loose rhizomatic collection of personal ties.[60]

In this way, the obligation to establish a basis of familiarity can sometimes lead to outcomes that accord with an impartial moral standpoint—but without aiming at the latter. The experiences and goods of particularistic attachments can thus have ethical significance that extends beyond the confines of their obvious biases and partial concerns.

Conclusion

Attempting to show how Confucians can satisfy the demands of impartiality, within a tradition that has not recognized it as a foundational ethical ideal, might seem misguided. One either directly embraces impartiality as a regulative ideal or one does not. But there are at least two reasons for exploring Confucian responses to the ideal of impartiality. The first is theoretical, and concerns ethical theorizing. The Confucian ethical tradition is rooted in familial love and partiality. However, showing that the Confucian tradition can respond to concerns about impartiality shows the viability of the tradition moving forward, and its value to ethical theorizing in general. The novel ideas found in the tradition are worthy of inclusion in global dialogue about the nature of the good life and right action. There is much scope for ongoing comparative dialogue.

The second reason is political. Faced with the question of what a Chinese modernity might be like, it is important to consider China's native resources for answering this question, rather than assuming the inevitability of liberal or neo-liberal frameworks for understanding persons and the relation between them. Returning to Li Zehou's Marxist-informed critique of Western thought, perhaps the Confucian tradition can raise helpful questions about whether the market-based view of society, comprised of self-interested and fair-minded rational contractors, has exerted disproportionate influence on ethical theorizing. If this view—and the role of impartiality within it—is challenged, different ethical ideals and norms might emerge. Traditional Confucian thought—about the human subject, human flourishing, and what social or political structures best realize such flourishing—can inform discussions of Chinese modernities.

Notes

1. For a contemporary critique of the Confucian commitment to family, and to filial piety (孝 *xiao*) in particular, see Liu Qingping (2003, 2007). See also notes 24, 28, and 29.
2. Confucian personal cultivation can be helpfully glossed via agricultural metaphors of nurturing and growth. See Don Munro (1971).

3. A similar definition is found in *Mencius* 4B28: "That whereby the superior man is distinguished from other men is what he preserves in his heart – namely, benevolence and [ritual] propriety. The benevolent man loves others" (Legge trans.). Translations from ctext database [ctext.org] unless otherwise indicated; I hope that using an accessible database will help interested readers to explore texts cited in the paper.
4. See *Mencius* 5A3, quoted below. Another example of ai-as-love is found in the "Tan Gong I" chapter of the *Book of Rites* (*Liji*), where *ai* is one source of mourning, alongside fear: "there are two grounds for the wailing; one from love, and one from fear." In the same chapter, the Confucian Zengzi uses the term *ai* when lecturing his followers about authentic "love": "Your love of me is not equal to his. A superior man loves another on grounds of virtue; a little man's love of another is seen in his indulgence of him" (Legge trans.; ctext.org).
5. In fact, the term for person (*ren* 人) that appeared in the passage 12.22 above, and translated as "loving others," often refers to the people in general rather than people understood personally (Lau 1979, *Introduction*).
6. See *Analects* 1.5 and 17.4. *Analects* 1.6 makes the ruler's commitment to subjects more explicit with the injunction to "broadly care for the masses" (汎愛眾).
7. *Mencius* 7A37, for example, compares *ai* to caring for domestic animals and also places it below respect/reverence (*jing* 敬) in a hierarchy of values.
8. In *Mencius* 1B5, a ruler argues that he is incapable of true rulership because he is fond of beauty or sex (*haose* 好色). Mencius reassures the ruler by pointing out that an ancient sage-king was also found of beauty and "loved his concubines," yet became a great ruler.
9. See Ulrike Middendorf (2007).
10. *Analects* 2.4; *Mencius* 4B30; *Xunzi* 19:1.
11. *Mencius* 5A1, 6A4; *Book of Rites* 9:19.
12. *Analects* 4.5.
13. In *Analects'* 5.1, Confucius approves of his daughter's marriage to a man unjustly accused of an unspecified crime; Cf. 11.6; but such references are largely tangential.
14. For example, *Mencius* 4B30.
15. *Analects* 5.26.
16. The same ideas are often repeated across early Confucian texts, reinforcing their importance. In the *Doctrine of the Mean*, another influential Confucian text, we find: "Humaneness (*ren*) is the characteristic element of humanity, and its most important aspect is to affection for kin" (Sec. 20.5).
17. A similar set of prescriptions for the ordering of relationships appears in the *Mencius* 3A4, cited below.
18. Slingerland, trans; translation modified for clarity. See also, e.g., the Han Dynasty text the *Classic of Filial Piety*: "It is familial reverence (*xiao*) … that is the root of excellence (*de*), and whence education (*jiao*) itself is born" (Ch. 1, Rosemont and Ames, trans., 2009, 105).
19. "Confucian moral epistemology … begins at home, in the role of son or daughter with which every human being begins their life. We learn loyalty and obedience by deferring to our mother and father, but … do not see deference (positive) as subservience (negative)" (Rosemont 2015, 98).
20. See *Mencius* 1A7; or the familial devotion of the legendary sage-ruler Shun in the *Mencius*, 5A2–3.
21. For the Mohist critique, see Burton Watson (1964, 39–41); the Mohists have been described as "the first consequentialists" (Chris Fraser 2016).

22. In 3A5, Mencius asks the Mohist Yi Zhi "Does Master Yi believe that a man's affection for his brother's child is just like his affection for the child of a neighbor?" On this passage, and the disagreements between the Mencian notion of a single root of feeling (the family) and the "two roots" of the Mohists (family and generalized concern for all), see David Nivison (1996).
23. On the extension (*tui*) of care and concern, see Mencius Book 1A and 1B. In several dialogues, rulers are encouraged to share their wealth and resources with their subjects, thereby sharing and enhancing the pleasures of all involved. For example, a ruler is encouraged to open up his private enclosures and ponds to the public. Such extension remains limited, however, and does not go beyond a ruler's state. The question remains about how far motivation can be extended, and whether it can include the interests of those who are distant strangers. The Mencius has little to say about the details here in terms of mechanism, psychological or otherwise, which raises doubts about whether a highly generalized concern for humanity as such can be generated from a concern for family and kin.
24. For an overview of the debate, see Hagop Sarkissian (2010, forthcoming 2020).
25. See Chan's account of this passage below. Another possibility is to focus on historical and sociological context. For example, brutal collective punishments in pre-Qin China (including the execution of entire families for the crimes of one member) could suggest a utilitarian defense for not reporting.
26. Another example of prioritizing family is Mencius 5A3. Here, Shun, a paragon of family devotion, became emperor and enfeoffed his inhumane and murderous brother, while also punishing other offenders. His justification for such unequal treatment includes, "A humane man does not store up anger against his brother, nor harbor grievances against him. He simply loves him; that is all. Loving him, he desires him to be honored; loving him, he desires him to be wealthy" (Bloom and Ivanhoe, Trans 2011, 101). Liu Qingping (2003, 234) argues that *Analects* 1.11, 17.21 provide further examples. The Mencius also shows concern to avoid situations that would harm the affection between fathers and sons (4A18, 4B30).
27. See, for example, the *Nan Shan You Tai* (南山有臺) and the *Jiong Zhuo* (泂酌) odes in the *Book of Poetry* (*Shijing*). The phrase also appears in the *Book of Rites*, the *Great Learning*, the *Xunzi* (王制, 正論, 禮論 chapters) and chapter 1 the *Classic of Filial Piety* (*Xiaojing*). In modern times, Liang Qichao (1873–1929) (2017 [1930]) was an influential proponent of the view that the state was the family writ large; for English language interpreters of this view, see Frederick Mote (1989 [1971]).
28. Kang Youwei (2010), Tan Sitong (1984). In contrast, Hsu Dau-Lin (1970) argued that the exaggerated importance of the filial piety and the bonds between father and son or ruler and minister was a product of Song Dynasty Neo-Confucian thought, rather than a philosophical commitment of the classical Confucians. According to Hsu, Song metaphysics and moral philosophy became the orthodoxy for later generations, up to the end of the imperial dynastic period in 1911.
29. See Liu Qingping (2003, 2007), Yong Li (2011), Hu Pingsheng (1999). Rosemont and Ames (2009) and Rosemont (2015) offer a defense of traditional familial values.

30. Rawls (1958, 61). Cline cites various passages that suggest a sense of justice was important to the early Confucians: *Analects* 1.6, 4.5, 4.10, 6.30, and 16.1.
31. Chan translates *li* 理 as "reason" (70), but perhaps "order" is a better translation. See Eric Hutton's translation of the Xunzi (2016, ch. 27, lines 171–178). In this passage, Xunzi clearly subordinates rightness (*yi*) to ritual propriety or precedent: "The gentleman dwells in *ren* by means of *yi*, and only then is it *ren*. He carries out *yi* by means of ritual, and only then is it *yi*."
32. Similarly, Cline claims *Analects* 13.18 as evidence that Confucius is concerned with justice. Confucius might be concerned here with rightness, in accord with his own ethics, but it is unclear whether a robust notion of impartiality is central to this vision.
33. Alasdair MacIntyre (2004, 217) sums up this view: "But my view does involve a denial that any modern state, Asian or Western, could embody the values of a Mencius or Xunzi. The political dimensions of a Confucianism that took either or both of them as its teachers would be those of local community, not of the state."
34. Singapore's 1996 *Maintenance of Parents Act* is one example of legislating for filial piety. Similar laws exist in China, Taiwan, and India (Serrano, Saltman, & Yeh 2017), and, though rarely enforced, in some US states.
35. For an alternative account of a modern Confucian polity, one less sympathetic to value pluralism and democracy, see Jiang Qing (2013); Lee Ming-Huei (2017, ch. 7) opposes Jiang's approach.
36. See Rosemont (2015) for an argument against this "autonomous" self from a Confucian perspective.
37. On *qing*, see A.C. Graham (1986, 59–65), Chad Hansen (1995), and Brian Bruya (2001). Hansen explains *qing* as "inputs from reality" (196) that are relevant to following a guide (a *dao*). As motors of action, such inputs are distinct from desire.
38. This is why, as discussed above, fathers are not to teach sons (Mencius 4A18)—to preserve emotional harmony between them and avoid interactions that cause resentment, anger, etc. Moral duties (children's education) matter but are partly constrained by the contours of emotional life.
39. One might insist there is nevertheless a moral obligation to do this—a question discussed below.
40. Confucian harmony is expressed in multiple realms, only some of which are emotional: internal harmony within the body, upholding social roles, absence of social discord, consensual generation of policy, accord between humans and broader cosmos forces, etc. See Chenyang Li (2008, 2014).
41. On musical harmony, see Erica Brindley (2012).
42. Li sees harmony as a regulative ideal realized slowly, as a historical process; this ideal state transcends liberalism but, for now, the right (of the individual) takes priority over the good (Li 2014, 1136).
43. For a detailed discussion of the relation between Confucian thought and the ethics of care, see Chenyang Li (1994), Daniel Star (2002), and Andrew Lambert (2016).
44. Mencius 4A2 outlines the importance of role models in achieving sagely rulership, and the example set by the exemplary sage rulers of antiquity, Yao and Shun.
45 This explains why the Mencius (4A18) advises against parents teaching their own children—since there will be arguments, feelings will be hurt and intimacy threatened.

46. See also 4.22, 13.20, and 14.1. On the psychology of Confucian shame, see Bongrae Seok (2016) and Nathaniel Barrett (2015).
47. See, for example, the Mencius' discussion in Book 1 of how exemplary rulers influence their subjects. See also the related discussion in P.J. Ivanhoe (1993).
48. Mencius 1A7 describes how the ideal ruler is able to take his sympathetic response to what is near at hand and extend it to others.
49. Propinquity might also play a role in this psychological extension: exposure to others who share common cause with one's son. This accords with social psychology research that suggests the key variable in developing friendship is not a particular characteristic of a person but proximity and prolonged exposure. See Newcomb (1956).
50. Nationalism provides another example. Upon discovering that a stranger belongs to the same nation, a particularistic connection, a commonality, is established and one's attitude towards that person can change—*if* one is disposed to identify and be moved by such ties (see the discussion below).
51. Here fairness or impartiality is valued directly, as morally desirable traits; however, the motivation to so value them—to "wake up" to these values—resides in particularistic ties.
52. For an alternative use of Mencius' notion of extension to generate concern for non-intimates, comparing it to the Golden Rule, see Eric Schwitzgebel (2019).
53. The Zhou Dynasty (c. 1046–221BCE), for example, expanded and sustained power through the use of strategic marriages and the creation of vassal states. See Melvin Thatcher (1991).
54. The disposition to establish a basis of familiarity, which can guide conduct, is derived from anthropologist Mayfair Yang's work on Chinese social relations (Yang 1994, 111–123 and passim).
55. This explains why some Chinese intellectuals, such as 20th-century scholar Xu Fuguan, have characterized the Confucian tradition as a culture of "concern" (*you* 憂, sometimes translated as anxiety; Xu 2005). See also Tea Sernelj (2013).
56. Arguably, fictive kinship relations are important in early Confucian thought. Clan lineages (*zong*宗), which unified clans by tracing a common lineage, also involve imaginary affect-laden relationships analogous to fictive kinship. I thank Thomas Barlett for this point.
57. On *guanxi*, see Mayfair Yang (1994), Andrew Kipnis (1997), and Gold, Guthrie, and Wank (2002).
58. See Ren Xin (1990).
59. See, e.g., Carol Stack (1975). Another example is migrant workers in China who use "native place ties" to find employment and a foothold in large cities, in defiance of residency laws that often exclude migrant workers from local services (Li Zhang 2001). If those laws are exclusionary or unfair, then networks of particularistic ties are a justified form of resistance.
60. There might be cases where opposing networks emerge, pursuing contradictory aims with regard to a policy. In such cases, in so far as the eventual outcome was fair from an impartial viewpoint, then particularistic ties would still be instrumental in bringing about fairness, without directly aiming at fairness. More importantly, the original point still stands: particularistic ties can sometimes mitigate for the epistemic deficiencies or other failings of centralized lawmakers.

References

Ames, Roger T., and Henry Rosemont, Jr. 2010. *The Analects of Confucius: A Philosophical Translation*. Ballantine Books.
Baron, Marcia. 1991. "Impartiality and Friendship." *Ethics* 101 (4): 836–857.
Barrett, Nathaniel F. 2015. "A Confucian Theory of Shame." *Sophia* 54 (2): 143–163.
Bloom, Irene, and Philip J. Ivanhoe. 2011. *Mencius*. Columbia University Press.
Brindley, Erica Fox. 2012. *Music, Cosmology, and the Politics of Harmony in Early China*. SUNY Press.
Bruya, Brian. 2001. "Qing (情) and Emotion in Early Chinese Thought." *Ming Qing Yanjiu* 2001: 151–176.
Chan, J. C. W. 2004. "Exploring the Non-Familial in Confucian Political Philosophy." In *The Politics of Affective Relations: East Asia and Beyond*. Edited by Bell, Daniel, Hahm Chiahark. Lexington Books.
Ci, Jiwei. 1999. "The Confucian Relational Concept of the Person and Its Modern Predicament." *Kennedy Institute of Ethics Journal* 9 (4): 325–346.
Cline, Erin M. 2007. "Two Senses of Justice: Confucianism, Rawls, and Comparative Political Philosophy." *Dao* 6 (4): 361–381.
Dau-Lin, Hsü. 1970. "The Myth of the "five Human Relations" of Confucius." *Monumenta Serica* 29 (1): 27–37.
Fraser, Chris. 2016. *The Philosophy of the Mòzǐ: The First Consequentialists*. Columbia University Press.
Gold, Thomas B., Doug Guthrie, and David Wank. 2002. *Social Connections in China: Institutions, Culture, and the Changing Nature of Guanxi*. Cambridge University Press.
Graham, Angus C. 1986. *Studies in Chinese Philosophy and Philosophical Literature: Logic and Reality*. SUNY Press.
Hansen, Chad. 1995. "*Qing* (Emotions) in Pre-Buddhist Chinese Thought." *Emotions in Asian Thought*. Edited by Marks, Joel & Ames, Roger, 181–211: SUNY Press.
Held, Virginia. 2006. *The Ethics of Care: Personal, Political and Global*. OUP.
Hu, Pingsheng. 1999. *An Annotated Translation of the Xiaojing (Xiaojing Yizhu 孝經譯註)*. Beijing Zhonghua Publishing.
Hutton, Eric L. 2014. *Xunzi: The Complete Text*. Princeton University Press.
Ivanhoe, Philip J. 1993. *Confucian Moral Self Cultivation*. Hackett Publishing.
Jankowiak, William. 2009. "Well-being, Cultural Pathology, and Personal Rejuvenation in a Chinese City, 1981–2005." *Pursuits of Happiness: Well-being in Anthropological Perspective*. Edited by Mathews, Gordon & Izquierdo, Carolina, 147–166: Berghann Books.
Jiang, Qing. 2013. *A Confucian Constitutional Order: How China's Ancient Past can Shape its Political Future*. Princeton University Press.
Kang, Youwei. 2010. *Datong Shu* [The Book of the Great Community]. Beijing Renmin Publishing.
Kim, Sungmoon. 2018. *Democracy after Virtue: Toward Pragmatic Confucian Democracy*. Oxford University Press.
King, Ambrose Y. C. 1985. "The Individual and Group in Confucianism: A Relational Perspective." *Individualism and Holism: Studies in Confucian and Taoist Values. Center for Chinese Studies*. Edited by Donald J. Munro. University of Michigan Press.

Kipnis, Andrew B. 1997. *Producing Guanxi: Sentiment, Self, and Subculture in a North China Village*. Duke University Press.
Korsgaard, Christine M. 1996. "The Sources of Normativity." Cambridge University Press.
Lambert, Andrew. 2012. "What Friendship Tells Us about Morality: A Confucian Ethics of Personal Relationships." PhD Dissertation, University of Hawaii.
Lambert, Andrew. 2016. "Confucian Ethics and Care: An Amicable Split?" In *Feminist Encounters with Confucius*. Edited by Foust, Mat & Tan, Sor-hoon, 171–197: Brill.
Lau, Dim Cheuk (DC). 1979. *The Analects*. Penguin.
Lee, Ming-Huei. 2017. *Confucianism: Its Roots and Global Significance*. University of Hawai'i Press.
Legge, James, trans. 2013. *The Book of Rites (Li Ji): English-Chinese Version*. Createspace Publishing.
Li, Chenyang. 1994. "The Confucian Concept of Jen and the Feminist Ethics of Care: A Comparative Study." *Hypatia* 9 (1): 70–89.
Li, Chenyang. 2008. "The Philosophy of Harmony in Classical Confucianism." *Philosophy Compass* 3 (3): 423–435.
Li, Chenyang. 2014. *The Confucian philosophy of harmony*. Routledge.
Li, Yong. 2011. "Evolution, Care and Partiality." *Asian Philosophy* 21 (3): 241–249.
Li, Zehou. 2016. "*A Response to Michael Sandel and Other Matters*." *Philosophy East and West*, 66 (4): 1068–1147.
Li, Zehou. 2019. *A History of Classical Chinese Thought*. Translated by Andrew Lambert. Routledge.
Liang, Qichao. 2017 [1930]. *History of Chinese Political Thought During the Early Tsin Period*. Routledge.
Liu, Qingping劉清平. 2003. "Filiality Versus Sociality and Individuality: On Confucianism as" Consanguinitism"." *Philosophy East and West* 53(2): 234–250.
Liu, Qingping. 2007. "Confucianism and Corruption: An Analysis of Shun's Two Actions Described by Mencius." *Dao: A Journal of Comparative Philosophy* 6 (1): 1–19.
Lo, Ming-Cheng M. and Eileen M. Otis. 2003. "Guanxi Civility: Processes, Potentials, and Contingencies." *Politics & Society* 31 (1): 131–162.
MacIntyre, Alasdair. 2004. "Questions for Confucians." *Confucian Ethics*: 203–218.
Middendorf, Ulrike. 2007. "*Resexualizing the Desexualized: The Language of Desire and Erotic Love in the Classic of Odes*." Accademia Editoriale.
Mote, Frederick. 1989 [1971]. *Intellectual Foundations of China*. Knopf.
Munro, Donald J. 1971. "The Concept of Man in Early China." *Philosophy East and West* 21 (2): 203–217.
Neville, Robert C. 2000. *Boston Confucianism: Portable Tradition in the Late-Modern World*. SUNY Press.
Newcomb, T. 1956. The prediction of interpersonal attraction. *American Psychologist,* 11 (11): 575–586.
Nivison, David S., and Bryan W. Van Norden. 1996. *The Ways of Confucianism Investigations in Chinese Philosophy*. Open Court.

Noddings, Nel. 2002. *Starting at Home: Caring and Social Policy*. University of California Press.

Rawls, John. 1958[1999]. "Justice as Fairness." From *John Rawls: Collected Papers*. Edited by Freeman, Samuel, 1999. Harvard University Press.

Ren, Xin. 1990. "The Second Economy in Socialist China." In *The Second Economy in Marxist States*. Edited by Maria Los, 140–156: Springer.

Rorty, Amelie Oksenberg. 1986. "The Historicity of Psychological Attitudes: Love Is Not Love Which Alters Not When It Alteration Finds." *Midwest Studies in Philosophy* 10: 399–412.

Rosemont, Henry. 2015. *Against Individualism: A Confucian Rethinking of the Foundations of Morality, Politics, Family, and Religion*. Lexington Books.

Rosemont, Henry, and Roger T. Ames. 2009. *The Chinese Classic of Family Reverence: A Philosophical Translation of the Xiaojing*. University of Hawaii Press.

Sarkissian, Hagop. 2010. "Recent Approaches to Confucian Filial Morality." *Philosophy Compass* 5 (9): 725–734. doi:10.1111/j.1747-9991.2010.00319.x.

Sarkissian, Hagop. Forthcoming 2020. "Do Filial Values Corrupt? How Can We Know? Clarifying and Assessing the Recent Confucian Debate." *Dao: A Journal of Comparative Philosophy*.

Schwitzgebel, Eric. 2019. "How Mengzi Came Up with Something Better than the Golden Rule." *Aeon*, November 2019. Accessed December 12, 2019.

Seok, Bongrae. 2016. *Moral Psychology of Confucian Shame: Shame of Shamelessness*. Rowman & Littlefield International.

Serrano, Roy, Richard Saltman, & Ming-Jui Yesh. 2017. "Laws on filial support in four Asian countries." *Bulletin of the World Health Organization*, 95(11): 788–790. doi:10.2471/BLT.17.200428.

Sernelj, Tea. 2013. "Xu Fuguan's Concept of Anxiety and Its Connection to Religious Studies." *Asian Studies* 1 (2): 71–87.

Stack, Carol B. 1975. *All our Kin: Strategies for Survival in a Black Community*. Basic Books.

Star, Daniel. 2002. "Do Confucians really Care? A Defense of the Distinctiveness of Care Ethics: A Reply to Chenyang Li." *Hypatia* 17 (1): 77–106.

Tan, Sitong. 1984. *An Exposition of Benevolence: The Jen-hsüeh [Renxue] of T'an Ssu-t'ung*. Translated by Chan Sin-wai. The Chinese University Press.

Thatcher, Melvin P. 1991. "Marriages of the Ruling Elite in the Spring and Autumn Period." In *Marriage and Inequality in Chinese Society*. Edited by Watson, Rubie & Ebrey, Patricia. 25–57: University of California Press.

Wei-Ming, Tu. 1985. *Confucian Thought: Selfhood as Creative Transformation*. SUNY Press.

Xiong, Shili. 1996. "Letters on Chinese Culture [論中國文化書簡]." In *The Foundation of Modern New- Confucianism: An Anthology of Xiong Shili* [現代新儒學的根基: 熊十力新儒學論著輯要]. Edited by Qiyong Guo, 331–351. Zhongguo Guangbo Dianshi Publishing.

Yang, Mayfair Mei-hui. 1994. *Gifts, Favors, and Banquets: The Art of Social Relationships in China*. Cornell University Press.

Zhang, Li. 2001. "Migration and Privatization of Space and Power in Late Socialist China." *American Ethnologist* 28 (1): 179–205.

15 Love as Union and Political Liberalism

Michael Kühler

Introduction

One of the hallmarks of political liberalism is its individualism. Each person is treated as an individual, i.e., as a separate subject independent of any group affiliations. Moreover, everyone is treated as an equal whose individual autonomy and freedom needs to be respected, as long as no one else's (equal amount of) freedom is compromised. As John Rawls has famously put it in his first principle of justice (in the restated version): "Each person has the same indefeasible claim to a fully adequate scheme of equal basic liberties, which scheme is compatible with the same scheme of liberties for all" (Rawls 2001, 42). The role of individual autonomy is succinctly highlighted by John Christman: "Autonomy is the chief characteristic of the model citizen whose perspective and interests locate the source of legitimacy for just political institutions and who frames the basic goals which provide content to the principles governing such institutions" (Christman 2009, 135). Union accounts of romantic love, on the other hand, claim that lovers abandon their individual identities and form a shared *we*-identity. The crucial idea is that each lover no longer sees him- or herself as a separate (autonomous) individual but lovers see themselves as fundamentally belonging together, even including a "pooling" of their autonomy (cp. Nozick 1990, 71). Taken together, this raises the question of whether or to what degree liberalism is compatible with union accounts of love. Does liberalism leave (sufficient) room for this age-old and still influential understanding of romantic love? If not, should this be taken as a reason to reconsider liberalism or rather our corresponding idea of romantic love—given that there is no shortage of alternative positions in both respects?

At first glance, one might easily think that there should be no problem to begin with. After all, is marriage not the prime traditional example of treating different individuals as fundamentally belonging together—assuming, of course, that marriage may be considered an institutional manifestation of love as union (for a critical overview, see Brake 2016)? For instance, married couples may undertake officially recognized joint decision-making, may share bank accounts, are generally taken to share certain responsibilities, may enjoy differential treatment as a couple, e.g., in case of visiting rights if one of them is in the hospital, and each lover is seen and treated with the authority to speak for the married couple's *we* as a whole.

However, liberalism's treatment of married couples as a *we* obviously has its limits. For instance, lovers will not be treated as jointly responsible and punishable if only one of them has committed a crime. Lovers still get one vote each in public elections and, in turn, get not elected as a couple if one of them is elected for public office. The same holds for liberal society, e.g., in a company's hiring procedures or a variety of other civil contracts. Even if there is the possibility, for example, to have shared property as a married couple, this is always seen against the individualist background of individual property (rights). In general, marriage is taken to consist of (traditionally) two individuals who remain being seen and treated as individuals when it comes down to it. The latter is most importantly evidenced by continuously granting each individual person an *individual right to exit*, just like in case of other community memberships. As Susan Moller Okin has put it succinctly: "Any consistent defense of group rights or exemptions that is based on liberal premises has to ensure that at least one individual right—the right to exit one's group of origin—trumps any group right" (Okin 2002, 205; cp. also Christman 2009, 201). Obviously, this also holds for marriages, as is shown by the individual right and possibility to get divorced and end the loving relationship, which would, thus, also include ending the shared we-identity. If so, doubts about the compatibility between liberalism and love as union do not seem that far-fetched.

Accordingly, in the following, I argue that, while stronger versions of union accounts are, indeed, incompatible with liberalism's individualism, liberalism still leaves sufficient room for a weaker version of love as union. Hence, liberals do not need to give up this age-old idea of romantic love completely. First, I sketch liberalism's individualism and its emphasis on individual autonomy. Second, I elaborate on love as union and distinguish between a variety of versions the idea may spin. Third, based on this mapping of the theoretical landscape, I discuss the compatibility between different versions of union accounts and liberalism's individualism and argue for liberalism's limited capability of including love as union. Finally, I draw a brief conclusion, summarizing the results of the discussion.

Liberalism's Individualism and Its Emphasis on Individual Autonomy

Liberalism's individualism can roughly be summarized as follows: individual human beings are the centerpiece of political liberal theory. It is

Love as union and political liberalism 291

individual human beings to whom and based on whose perspective political norms and institutions need to be justified and are supposed to be justifiable. It is individual human beings whose interests and preferences primarily have to be taken into account. It is primarily individual human beings who are thought to have rights and liberties. Finally, when it comes to analyzing a liberal society, groups or smaller and more personal communities are considered to be created and maintained by individual human beings who autonomously want to be and stay a part of them.

Obviously, this very general description of liberalism's individualism is far from being uncontroversial, both in terms of how liberalism and its individualism should be spelled out as a political theory in more detail (for an overview of the variety of liberal positions, see Gaus, Courtland, and Schmidtz 2018) and, as especially the extensive debate over the communitarian critique of liberalism has shown (for an overview, see Bell 2020), whether the individualism involved is a plausible position to analyze our self-understanding as (political) persons to begin with. Still, concerning both how to spell out liberalism's individualism in more detail and how this may invite (communitarian) criticism, the debate has undoubtedly been shaped by John Rawls's *A Theory of Justice* and his later works (Rawls 1971, 1993, 2001).

Rawls's *Theory* prominently includes an individualistic point of view in the "original position," in which the principles of justice for society's basic structure are to be determined. Rational deliberation on how to pursue one's interests best in the resulting society takes place behind a "veil of ignorance," which strips the individuals of any knowledge about their personal characteristics and future position in society. This is supposed to ensure a fair deliberation (cp. Rawls 1971, 17–9). This characterization of the original position and the supposedly anthropological basis upon which individuals make their rational choice has sparked the communitarian critique of the liberal self (see most notably Sandel 1998, ch. 1). While Sandel grants that Rawls's position does not imply an overly egoistic individual person who is necessarily devoid of any social ties (cp. Sandel 1998, 60f.; see also Kymlicka 1989), he argues that "there is a deeper sense in which Rawls' conception is individualistic" (Sandel 1998, 62). He goes on to describe this as follows: "We can locate this individualism and identify the conceptions of the good it excludes by recalling that the Rawlsian self is not only a subject of possession, but an antecedently individuated subject, standing always at a certain distance from the interests it has. One consequence of this distance is to put the self beyond the reach of experience, to make it invulnerable, to fix its identity once and for all. No commitment could grip me so deeply that I could not understand myself without it. No transformation of life purposes and plans could be so unsettling as to disrupt the contours of my identity. No project could be so essential that turning away from it would call into question the person I am. Given my independence from the values I have, I can always stand apart from them" (Sandel 1998, 62). In this passage, Sandel refers to Rawls's further elaboration on how citizens consider themselves as moral persons: "[A]s free persons, citizens recognize one another as having the moral power to have a conception of the good. This means that they do not view themselves as inevitably tied to the pursuit of the particular conception of the good and its final ends which they espouse at any given time. Instead, as citizens, they are regarded as, in general, capable of revising and changing this conception on reasonable and rational grounds" (Rawls 1980, 544).

Assuming that what or who a person loves may be considered a part of the person's conception of the good, Rawls's individualistic view of the person would, thus, include the idea that we are capable of reconsidering our love. This may arguably cast doubt on the view's compatibility with the idea of love as union, which apparently seems to leave behind such an individualistic stance on the lovers' union. Moreover, Sandel then concludes that this kind of individualism "rules out any conception of the good (or of the bad) bound up with possession in the constitutive sense" (Sandel 1998, 62), i.e., any understanding of the self, according to which it is constituted by personal attachments, from which, for this very reason, we cannot distance ourselves. This strengthens the abovementioned doubt even more, for it arguably excludes the idea that the lovers' shared we-identity may be constitutive in this sense, i.e., beyond the lovers' joint capability of reconsidering and possibly abandoning it—let alone the lovers' respective individual capabilities.

However, in his later works Rawls effectively sidestepped this metaphysical debate on the constitution of the self. Instead, he developed a decidedly *political* conception of the person, according to which persons are *regarded* and *regard themselves* as free and equal individuals (cp. Rawls 2001, 18–24; 2005, 29–35). This still includes the abovementioned idea of persons being capable of revising and changing their conception of the good but reformulates it in terms of persons only being *seen* and *treated* as such in political theory and practice. That is, regardless of how a person's identity is constituted and whether the person is actually capable of distancing herself from her conception of the good or other personal ties, as a citizen, the person will be regarded and treated *as if* she could. Essentially, this means that persons are regarded as free, i.e., as having a right, to do so, even though Rawls readily admits that, in addition to this political identity as an individual citizen, a person's moral identity may very well include constitutive attachments in the sense Sandel describes. "It can happen that in their personal affairs, or in the internal life of associations, citizens may regard their final ends and attachments very differently from the way the political conception supposes. They may have, and often do have at any given time, affections, devotions, and loyalties that they believe they would not, indeed could and should not, stand apart from and evaluate objectively. They may regard it as simply unthinkable to view themselves apart from certain religious, philosophical, and moral convictions, or from certain enduring attachments and loyalties" (Rawls 2005, 31). The political conception of the person, therefore, certainly looks like it can easily leave sufficient theoretical and practical room for "union" lovers' self-understanding as sharing a constitutive we-identity that may even be immune to active reconsideration and revision.

Still, Rawls mentions two further aspects of the political conception of persons. "A second respect in which citizens view themselves as free is that they regard themselves as self-authenticating sources of valid claims" (Rawls 2005, 32). This second aspect, thus, highlights once again that it is individual persons who are considered central to liberalism. Ultimately, valid claims are traced back to individuals, arguably including claims of communities or more intimate personal affiliations as consisting of parallel or shared claims of the individuals who are part of and constitute the community, group, or couple, in question. If so, this might very well again raise the question of how the lovers' we-identity must be constituted in order to be compatible with even the political conception of the person.

This worry is strengthened even more when considering Rawls's third aspect. "The third respect in which citizens are viewed as free is that they are viewed as capable of taking responsibility for their ends" (Rawls 2005, 33). While Rawls explains this in terms of a capability of taking responsibility for one's aims against the political background of matters of justice, this aspect again highlights liberalism's individualism, as it is ultimately individual citizens who are considered to be capable of taking responsibility. Arguably, this would seem to include also taking responsibility for one's ends in terms of one's love, i.e., taking individual responsibility for pursuing and sharing a we-identity. If so, liberalism's individualism appears to imply a picture of love as union, according to which the lovers' shared we-identity is necessarily constituted and maintained by separate individuals. At the very least, following the political conception of regarding and treating persons as if they were free and equal, "union" lovers would be regarded and treated *as if* this were (still) the case. Consequently, it does not seem far-fetched to question whether this practical regard of how to see and treat lovers is actually sufficient in acknowledging the implications of union accounts of love.

To sum up, two levels of liberalism's individualism may be distinguished:

1. a *constitutive level*, marking the metaphysical debate on how persons and their identities are constituted, whereas liberalism initially included the claim that persons are actually individually capable of reconsidering and revising their conception of the good and personal ties, and

2. a *political level*, following Rawls's political conception of the person, according to which persons are merely regarded and treated *as if* they were capable of reconsidering and revising their conception of the good and personal ties.

While Rawls seems to have successfully sidestepped the first level by introducing the second, the latter's implications might actually prove to be more complex and possibly raise issues belonging to the constitution of the self, more particularly the lovers' we-identity, after all. Yet, in order to elaborate more on this worry and render it plausible, liberalism's individualism needs to be explained in some more detail concerning its connection to individual autonomy.

Notably, John Christman has discussed this in helpful detail in connection to a comprehensive overview of different accounts of the constitution of the self and autonomy, while following up on Rawls's political conception of the person (Christman 2009; for further discussions on autonomy in relation to liberalism, see Christman 1989; Christman and Anderson 2005; Sneddon 2013; Oshana 2014; Christman 2015). Christman's position is especially helpful for the purpose at hand because he explicitly wants to allow liberalism's political conception of the person to include social constituents of the self. "In our rejection of the classic liberal individualist conception of the self, we said that the various ways in which identities can be specified with essential reference to social connections must be part of a replacement, non- or less-individualist conception of the person. This means that room must be made for the various (and varying) ways in which social relations constitute selves and their self-conceptions in the models utilized in political principles" (Christman 2009, 111). While this may easily be read as including a lovers' we-identity, Christman actually rejects such particular social ties. For, he continues: "What we found, though, is that such connections can be seen either at a very general and abstract level, such as the constitution of the self by way of the social practices of language, or at a specific one, such as the relation to particular significant others in one's life. We found, or so I claimed, that the latter kinds of relations are not plausible elements for any general conception of the self, for such relations are subject to change in structure and significance. No matter how much one identifies oneself, say, as this person's mother or that person's spouse, the centrality of that relation to one's sense of self may well shift as one's life circumstances change, through death, estrangement, or renegotiation of the relationship" (Christman 2009, 111). Given that Christman aims at a general political conception of the person that can be utilized in liberal political theory and practice, this rejection is perfectly plausible. Yet, it gives rise to the question discussed here of whether his conception actually allows liberalism taking the idea of love as union seriously enough and acknowledging the lovers' we-identity sufficiently.

In this respect, the notion of individual autonomy Christman deems necessary needs to be spelled out in more detail. Christman explicitly defends a relatively weak version of autonomy to be included in the political conception of the person in order to allow for the variety of social constituents, which for some time now have been highlighted by relational accounts of the self and personal autonomy (see Meyers 1996; Mackenzie and Stoljar 2000; Oshana 2006; Helm 2010; Christman 2015). Accordingly, the notion of personal autonomy Christman defends merely requires that "the person does not feel deeply *alienated* from [one of the person's characteristics or traits] upon critical reflection. [...] To be alienated is to experience negative affect, to feel repudiation and resistance. It is, moreover, to feel a need to repudiate that desire or trait, to reject it and alter it as much as possible, and to resist its effects" (Christman 2009, 143f.). Furthermore, the critical reflection Christman has in mind must be authentic in the sense that it is not the result of manipulation or otherwise autonomy-endangering social conditions (cp. Christman 2009, 146, 185). Yet, it does not need to be the traditional and overly individualistic liberal "foundational" self-reflection, which includes the claim that we are always able to step back from our convictions and values and reflect on "whether, for any commitment or relation X, there are good and sufficient reasons to maintain one's connection to X" (Christman 2009, 130). This is essentially the version of critical self-reflection that Sandel criticized in Rawls. Instead, Christman argues that a less demanding idea of "embedded self-reflection" suffices, which essentially describes only a critical self-*understanding* in terms of a person's acknowledgment of her deeply held convictions and values in light of how these came about and the person's social embeddedness (cp. Christman 2009, 131, 185). If so, and Christman's rejection of concrete social ties for *general* representative purposes in liberal theory notwithstanding, this seems to leave conceptual room for acknowledging also a lovers' we-identity as constitutive of an authentic self and fitting basis for personal autonomy in *concrete* cases. Put in another way, while it makes perfect sense to reject concrete social ties, i.e., a specific social content, as a necessary condition of being considered autonomous in liberal theory *in general*, liberalism may very well allow for the *possibility* of specific social ties serving as constituents of personal autonomy in concrete cases. Hence, if "union" lovers are not deeply alienated from their shared we-identity, it seems to be plausible from a liberal point of view like Christman's to consider them as (sufficiently) autonomous, at least for the time being. Thus, it seems that liberalism is able to acknowledge the lovers' shared we-identity, after all.

However, first, it should be noted that Christman's focus, and indeed that of relational accounts as well, is still on *individual* autonomy, regardless of whether it is analyzed in terms of solely individualistic criteria or in allowing for social, relational aspects of the constitution of the *individual* self. As he states explicitly, "there is nothing about a social conception of 'self' that is incompatible with an individual conception of autonomy" (Christman 2009, 166). Focusing on individual autonomy is, of course, perfectly plausible for a liberal approach, which has individual human beings as its centerpiece. Yet, it still raises the question of which implications this has for the compatibility between liberalism and love as union.

Second, one might question if Christman's idea of "embedded self-reflection" can really be employed independently of the traditional liberal "foundational" self-reflection. For, if "embedded self-reflection" successfully leads a person to understand herself and her deeply held convictions and values better, such reflection arguably does not just end with this kind of self-knowledge, especially if, as Christman claims, this knowledge is gained through considering questions such as "What is the *importance* of X? What are the *implications* for myself and others of pursuing, respecting, enjoying (etc.) X? How central is X to my self-concept?" (Christman 2009, 131). Even if it is granted that the person may not be able to change the constitutive impact of X on her identity at will, it seems fair to assume that Christman's questions naturally lead to, or at the very least allow for, further *practical* questions about whether one's self, being (at least partially) defined by X, should be welcomed or rather seen critically, whereas this does not imply that one actually needs to succeed in changing it. In any case, such questions are precisely the type of questions Christman (rightly) associates with the traditional liberal "foundational" self-reflection. If so, in addition to the general focus on *individual* autonomy, liberalism's political conception of the person would still include at the very least a person's capacity for *posing* and *facing* practical questions associated with "foundational" self-reflection. If it then turned out that the person could in fact do nothing to change her deepest convictions and values, although she considers them and thus her accordingly constituted *self* critically, this would admittedly be tragic. Yet, assuming that such cases are not completely uncommon, this raises serious doubt on Christman's "embedded self-reflection" as an independent option. If so, this would imply that the liberal political conception of the person and her autonomy still includes the idea that persons are seen and treated as if they were individually autonomous in this stronger sense, i.e., capable of reflecting on and at least taking an evaluative stance toward the constituents of their selves. Obviously, this would also have to hold for "union" lovers and their shared we-identity. In fact, Christman seems to acknowledge this result in general terms himself: "The lesson of relational theories, then, is that socially constituted and interpersonally embedded selves, in all their varieties and complex perspectives on value and justice, are autonomous only when that variable and multiplex position in those social relations reflects the authentic and self-imposed standards of the free person. [...]

Therefore, in any such cases, socio-relational conditions will have to obtain for any such person to maintain the ability to engage in the kind of reflection required of autonomy" (Christman 2009, 185f.). Now, if my above criticism is plausible, mere "embedded self-reflection" would appear to be insufficient as the kind of reflection required of autonomy.

The upshot of this discussion is that even for liberalism's political conception of the person, according to which persons are only seen and treated *as if* they were individuals and capable of individual autonomy, regardless of how socially embedded the constitution of their selves and personal autonomy in fact is, this individualistic representation of persons in liberal political theory and practice raises the question of whether, or to what degree, it is actually compatible with the idea of love as union, i.e., seeing and treating "union" lovers as a *we*. However, union accounts of love come in different flavors and include different claims, which have different implications for the question at hand. The following section will provide an overview of the variety of union accounts relevant for the topic.

The Variety of Union Accounts of Love

The idea that love consists in a *union* or *merging* of the lovers can be traced back at least to Plato (the following depiction of union accounts is partially based on earlier work of mine; cp. Kühler 2011, 2014, 2020). In the *Symposium*, Aristophanes tells the myth that we were all once "double-creatures" with four legs, four arms, and two heads. Because of our strength and hubris, we even posed a threat to the gods themselves, which is why Zeus split us in two halves, i.e., in our current appearance. Each individual half then desperately looked for their other half and yearned to be reunited again. Love is, thus, nothing but the desire for unity and, if fulfilled, the union itself (cp. Sheffield and Howatson 2008, 189c–93).

The main idea that romantic love is about the lovers' desire for or accomplishment of being united or merged into one is, unsurprisingly, still prevalent in current union accounts (for recent defenses of union accounts, see Fisher 1990, 26–35; Nozick 1990; Solomon 1994, 194–99; for a partially critical assessment, see Delaney 1996; Soble 1997; Friedman 1998; Merino 2004; Kühler 2009, 2011). However, no one, of course, takes the union metaphor literally, i.e., as a physical merging of two separate human beings into one. Accordingly, union accounts typically do not include a—rather implausible—ontological claim about the creation of a new entity (yet, see Fisher 1990, 27; Nozick 1990, 70–3, whose positions could be interpreted this way). Instead, it is merely claimed that lovers no longer see themselves as independent individual persons but as fundamentally belonging together, which, in turn, manifests itself in a shared *we*-identity. For example, any plausible answer to the question who Romeo is would have to consist primarily in a depiction of his loving relationship with Juliet, and vice versa. Both Romeo and Juliet would be considered belonging together in a way that makes it virtually impossible to define their identities independently. Moreover, neither of them would likely be inclined to do so anyway. It is always Romeo *and* Juliet, as Robert Solomon remarks (Solomon 1994, 192f.).

Still, given that lovers obviously remain separate and individual physical beings, it is far from clear how the idea of a shared we-identity relates to this fact and how it may be spelled out in more detail (for concise discussions of possible options, see Friedman 1998; Merino 2004). For the purpose at hand, a distinction between *weak* and *strong* union accounts will suffice. Mark Fisher, for instance, defends a decidedly strong version of love as union (Fisher 1990, 26–35). He argues that lovers develop a "fused self." "As a lover [...] I will tend to absorb not only your desires but your concepts, beliefs, attitudes, conceptions, emotions and sentiments. [...] In coming to love you I will undergo a process of coming to see everything through your eyes, as it were" (Fisher 1990, 26f.). Since this absorption is reciprocated, the lovers will form "a single fused individual," even if this "personal fusion can never be complete" (Fisher 1990, 27). Likewise, Robert Nozick states that "[i]n a *we*, the people *share* an identity and do not simply each have identities that are enlarged" (Nozick 1990, 82). It is, thus, a *redefinition* of the lovers' individual identities that leads to the formation of a shared we-identity. "That is what shared identity means—not a loss of individual identity but a redefinition of personal identity in terms of the other person" (Solomon 1994, 193). Both Fisher and Nozick then readily admit that this poses a threat to individual autonomy but claim that the lovers gain a shared *we*-autonomy. According to Fisher, the "fused couple retains its own autonomy" (Fisher 1990, 28). Likewise, Nozick emphasizes that "[p]eople who form a *we* pool not only their well-being but also their autonomy. They limit or curtail their own decision-making power and rights; some decisions can no longer be made alone" (Nozick 1990, 71). So understood, strong union accounts include the claim that the lovers' new we-identity completely redefines, or replaces, their prior individual identities and serves as authentic shared basis for the lovers' we-autonomy.

However, especially Nozick leaves room in his analysis of love as union for a weaker interpretation. "The individual self can be related to the *we* it identifies with in two different ways. It can see the *we* as a very important *aspect* of itself, or it can see itself as part of the *we*, as contained within it" (Nozick 1990, 72). While even the latter option arguably allows the lovers still to have an individual identity, especially the former option makes this explicit and also includes the claim that this individual identity still takes precedence. In both cases, the crucial underlying question is how important the new shared we-identity is for each individual lover and for their remaining respective individual identity. In general, weak union accounts, thus, claim that the lovers' new we-identity merely supplements or only partially modifies the lovers' individual identities.

The difference between strong and weak union accounts might be illustrated by way of a trivial example. Imagine the lovers moving in together and having to decide on their apartment's decoration. Weak union accounts would still allow each lover to have an individual perspective on the matter and to have individual preferences, say about the style and color of the couch. Yet, assuming that each lover takes their love to be of prime importance, these individual preferences would always be considered to be less important than the shared we-perspective. Put simply, a lover might reason thusly: "I know what I would prefer if it were (only) up to me. But I value our *we* more, so I take up our shared we-perspective to decide on the matter."

For strong union accounts, such reasoning would no longer make sense. Due to the complete redefinition of the lovers' identities in terms of their shared we-identity, the lovers would no longer have individual perspectives or preferences to begin with. Accordingly, the lovers' reasoning based on their shared we-identity would always and solely be a *joint* reasoning in light of the question: "How would *we* like to design *our* apartment?"[1] Consequently, it is no wonder that strong union accounts appear to be incompatible with individual autonomy (for a detailed discussion in this respect, see Soble 1997; for an attempt at reconciling strong union accounts with individual autonomy, see Kühler 2011).

However, addressing the challenge that love as union poses for individual autonomy ultimately rests on an analysis of how authentic and autonomous the constitution and maintenance of the shared we-identity may be for each lover. In this respect, both constitution and maintenance of the lovers' *we* and we-identity may be passive or active. Put briefly, it may either be something that just happens to the lovers and which the lovers may only discover, or it may be the result of the lovers actively bringing it about (for a more encompassing discussion of activity and passivity in romantic love, see Kühler 2014). Accordingly, passive union accounts closely resemble the prominent idea in everyday life that love is something that just happens to us, as highlighted, for instance, in the phrase "*falling* in love." Similarly, Harry Frankfurt's influential essentialist account of the self rests on the idea that we can merely discover who we are in terms of discovering what we love (see Frankfurt 1994, 1999, 2004). As discussed in the previous section, this is also exactly what Sandel has in mind when he emphasizes an understanding of the self in the "constitutive sense" (cp. Sandel 1998, 62). The idea can easily be applied to passive union accounts, which then include the claim that when we discover that we love a specific person, we discover this in the sense of a (complete or partial) redefinition of our identity in terms of a shared we-identity.[2]

In contrast, active union accounts deny that there is nothing we can do about love and the formation of the shared we-identity. For instance, Erich Fromm has famously claimed that "[t]o love somebody is not just a strong feeling—it is a decision, it is a judgment, it is a promise. If love were only a feeling, there would be no basis for the promise to love each other forever. A feeling comes and it may go" (Fromm 1956, 52). If so, active union accounts include the claim that the lovers face both an *individual* and a *shared* practical task. Lovers first need to decide individually on bringing about their shared we-identity, including its content in terms of shared values, preferences, etc. Afterward, the shared we-identity needs to be maintained, including the possibility of changing its content, as the lovers may very well make adjustments over time.[3] This may be seen as a shared practical task for the lovers' *we* or additionally as an individual task for each lover, in which they need to decide on whether they still want to be a part of the current *we* or a revised version of it.

Finally, Fromm's position may even allude to an existentialist account of the self and autonomy, according to which we can—and in fact must—radically choose who we want to be and how we want to act (see Sartre 1943, part 4, ch. 1; Crowell 2017). Following this existentialist take, each lover *necessarily* needs to decide individually, if they (still) want to identify themselves with the we-identity or make changes or even ending the love.[4] However, if so, the question might be raised how much "union" there still is in such an existentialist active union account. In any case, the existentialist active union account can, thus, only come in a weak flavor, for it would require a constant distinct individual perspective on the shared we-identity, which strong union accounts explicitly exclude—while existentialism would deny the very idea that this individual perspective could ever be excluded to begin with.

The crucial upshot for the purpose at hand is that the distinction between passive and active union accounts essentially mirrors the discussion between liberalism and communitarianism about the constitution of the self. Passive union accounts would, thus, be an exemplar of what Sandel labels constitutive features of the self, while active union accounts would fit liberalism's idea of bringing one's identity about by, what Christman calls, "foundational" critical self-reflection and possible revision. However, it should be noted that the focus of the debate is significantly different. The debate between liberalism and communitarianism has been a debate about the constitution of the *individual* self, more precisely about whether certain social conditions need to be acknowledged for this—which Christman has answered affirmatively, at least to a certain degree. In contrast, love as union starts from the assumption of individual selves and asks how the formation or constitution of the *shared we-identity* should be analyzed and how or to what degree the lovers' individual selves might still be featured in it.

To sum up, the variety of union accounts of romantic love can be mapped as follows:

1. *Strong* union accounts claim that the lovers' identities are completely redefined or replaced by the shared we-identity.
2. *Weak* union accounts claim that the shared we-identity is only a partial redefinition of or a supplement to each lover's individual identity, whereas the shared we-identity is typically more important to each lover than their individual perspective.
3. *Passive* union accounts claim that love and the shared we-identity is something that we merely experience and discover. Passive union accounts may come in a strong or weak flavor and imply a corresponding passive or essentialist theory of the self and personal autonomy.
    a. Strong passive union accounts are, then, only compatible with the lover's individual autonomy if the shared we-identity is taken to be an appropriate authentic basis for it, like in Christman's notion of "embedded self-reflection."
    b. Weak passive union accounts do not pose a threat to individual autonomy but rather require it, albeit in an essentialist or, to use Sandel's characterization, "constitutive" version.
4. *Active* union accounts claim that love and the shared we-identity is something that the lovers actively need to bring about and maintain. Active union accounts may then also come in a strong or weak flavor.
    a. Strong active union accounts assume that the shared we-identity is brought about by the lovers' initial, individually autonomous contributions. However, once the we-identity has been formed, it can only be maintained by the lovers together in terms of a shared practical task. The corresponding practical question for the lovers is always: do *we* still want to remain who we are now or do *we* want to change our we-identity? This makes strong active union accounts ultimately incompatible with individual autonomy.
    b. Weak active union accounts likewise assume that the shared we-identity is brought about by the lovers' initial, individually autonomous contributions. Yet, the latter remains necessary for maintaining the we-identity as well, as each lover is still able to reason individually on the we-identity's standing in relation to their own individual identity. The corresponding practical question for each lover is thus: do *I* still want to be part of the *we* so far or do *I* want our we-identity to change? Weak active union accounts, therefore, do not pose a threat to individual autonomy but, again, rather require it—arguably even in existentialist or, to use Christman's characterization, "foundational" terms, whereas it should be noted that this would imply that strong active union accounts are inconsistent to being with.

Liberalism's Limited Compatibility with Love as Union

The above mapping of the theoretical landscape finally allows addressing the main question more precisely. Whether or to what degree is liberalism compatible with union accounts of love?

As noted above, liberalism's point of reference is the political conception of the person, which serves as theoretical representation of individual citizens in liberal political theory and practice. Following this conception, people are seen and treated *as if* they were individuals and capable of individual autonomy, regardless of how socially embedded the constitution of their selves and personal autonomy may be. Yet, the question for the topic at hand is whether this individualist political conception, including its sidestepping of the debate on the constitution of the *individual* self, can do justice to love as union's emphasis on the lovers' *shared we-identity*, i.e., to the idea that persons with previously individual identities and autonomy now would need to be seen and treated as fundamentally belonging together. Accordingly, while the central question is indeed to be located on the *political level* mentioned above, as it is about the *social and political recognition and treatment* of the lovers as a *we*, there might be more to it when it comes to acknowledging the formation or constitution of the lovers' shared we-identity and its relation to individual autonomy.

Following the discussion of Christman's account of individual autonomy in the political conception of the person, liberalism's underlying assumption necessarily must still be that each lover is at least taken as being able, i.e., as being individually autonomous, to reflect on whether he or she does not feel deeply alienated from the shared we-identity ("embedded self-reflection") and arguably whether he or she still has sufficient reasons to continue being a part of it ("foundational self-reflection"). If so, liberalism's sidestepping of the constitutive level in favor of the political level simply does not work for the challenge that love as union and the formation of a shared we-identity poses. For, even if persons are only regarded and treated as if they were individuals and individually autonomous, this clashes with some versions of union accounts, according to which such a regard and treatment would run precisely against the idea of the lovers forming a *we*, as this idea would no longer allow for a fitting political representation of the lovers as separate individuals. Put differently, "union" lovers would then consider themselves *misrepresented* in political theory and practice. Consequently, liberalism's individualism at least implicitly implies a claim about which kind of constitution or formation of the lovers' *we* is acceptable against a liberal background.

The conclusions to be drawn regarding which of the previously distinguished versions of love as union is acceptable on liberal grounds should be fairly straightforward. In general, any acceptable union account obviously needs to allow for the lovers to be and remain individually autonomous. This excludes strong union accounts which take the "pooling" of autonomy in terms of a we-autonomy seriously, i.e., strong active union accounts. Strong passive union accounts, on the other hand, may still be considered compatible with liberalism's individualism if the shared we-identity is accepted as an authentic basis for individual autonomy, as in Christman's notion of personal autonomy and a mere "embedded self-reflection." However, as I have argued above, liberal individual autonomy may very well still require a more demanding "foundational" critical self-reflection, including the capability of reconsidering and possibly revising one's identity—which may even allude to an existentialist take on the self and personal autonomy. If so, union accounts need to allow for this as well. This would then exclude both strong and weak passive union accounts, which both take a constitutive approach to the lovers' we-identity in the sense that it is only to be discovered but not subject to such active "foundational" reconsideration or even revision.

This leaves one with weak active union accounts. This version of love as union is not only compatible with the lovers' respective individual autonomy but in fact requires it for both bringing about the shared we-identity and maintaining it. Moreover, weak active union accounts include the possibility of an individual "exit," one of liberalism's central aspects of treating persons as individuals with individual rights when it comes to community memberships. Finally, weak active union accounts also allow for the lovers' individual autonomy to be analyzed in existentialist or "foundational" terms. Hence, weak active union accounts are the only version of love as union that proves to be compatible with liberalism's individualism.

While this might be an unwelcome result for everyone preferring a strong version of love as union and a more inclusive liberalism—after all, there seems to be little "real" union left in love as union[5]—liberalism's emphasis on seeing and treating persons as individuals whose individual autonomy needs to be respected may in fact be welcomed. For, it not only allows for but even requires a critical perspective on how the lovers' we-identity is formed in detail and whether its content may be deemed a fair representation of each lover, so that the lovers "union" may be regarded as a love between equals (cp. Wilson 1995), not the least from each lover's individual perspective. Such an undoubtedly important critical perspective clearly should not be given up lightly, especially when considering the pervasive experience of social relations, including relationships of love, being unfair or even oppressing (see, e.g., Oshana 2014).

Conclusion

Whether or to what degree is liberalism compatible with union accounts of love? I have argued that liberalism's individualism and emphasis on individual autonomy severely limits its compatibility with love as union. The political conception of the person, which only includes seeing and treating persons *as if* they were individuals and individually autonomous, does not succeed in sidestepping the debate on the constitution or formation of the lovers' *we* and we-identity. "Union" lovers are still unavoidably—and for good liberal reasons—represented in liberal theory and treated in liberal political practice as if they were individually autonomous persons and separately capable of reflecting, possibly revising, and even abandoning their shared we-identity. This has proven to be incompatible with all versions of union accounts with the exception of weak active accounts, which require the lovers to be individually autonomous for both bringing about the shared we-identity and maintaining it, including being continuously able to reconsider their shared we-identity, initiate changes, or even abandon it altogether from their own individual point of view. In doing so, weak active union accounts not only prove to be compatible with political liberalism and fit the initially mentioned practice of regarding and treating lovers as a *we* only in some respects, like in the case of marriage, but also leave sufficient theoretical and normative room to incorporate and address questions of justice *within* love as union.

Notes

1. It should be noted that both strong and weak union accounts raise questions about the degree to which each lover's prior identity, including each lover's values and preferences, is represented in the shared we-identity. For, such representation could very well be substantially unequal and unfair, which is why the details of the lovers' *we* can and need to be discussed against a moral background. Hence, love as union is also subject to a moral discussion about justice *within* loving relationships as depicted in section I of this volume.
2. If so, it should be noted that this would pose a special challenge to the moral discussion of justice *within* love as union, as we would apparently have no control over whether the formation of the we-identity is, in fact, fair.
3. Following an active union account, it should, thus, be easy to see how fairness and justice *within* love as union can be addressed, for the lovers are now explicitly conceived of as being able to decide on how they want to define and continuously refine their shared we-identity, not the least in light of moral considerations of fairness. Yet, so far, this does not necessarily include an individual perspective, which, it might be argued, is an additional condition for addressing justice within love as union comprehensively and convincingly.
4. Following an existentialist account, therefore, would satisfy the aforementioned additional condition for justice within love as union.
5. A possible line of criticism at this point could be that weak active union accounts are in fact nothing but interpersonal accounts of romantic love, which explicitly abandon the idea of a union (for an exemplary such account, see Krebs 2014, 2015, and her contribution to this volume). In any case, the line between those two types of theories of romantic love would be significantly blurred.

References

Bell, Daniel. 2020. "Communitarianism." In *The Stanford Encyclopedia of Philosophy*, edited by Edward N. Zalta, Summer 2020. Stanford, CA: Metaphysics Research Lab, Stanford University. https://plato.stanford.edu/archives/sum2020/entries/communitarianism/.

Brake, Elizabeth. 2016. "Marriage and Domestic Partnership." In *The Stanford Encyclopedia of Philosophy*, edited by Edward N. Zalta, Winter 2016. Stanford, CA: Metaphysics Research Lab, Stanford University. https://plato.stanford.edu/archives/win2016/entries/marriage/.
Christman, John, ed. 1989. *The Inner Citadel: Essays on Individual Autonomy*. New York: Oxford University Press.
Christman, John, ed. 2009. *The Politics of Persons. Individual Autonomy and Socio-Historical Selves*. Cambridge: Cambridge University Press.
Christman, John, ed. 2015. "Autonomy in Moral and Political Philosophy." In *The Stanford Encyclopedia of Philosophy*, edited by Edward N. Zalta, Spring 2015. Stanford, CA: Metaphysics Research Lab, Stanford University. http://plato.stanford.edu/archives/spr2015/entries/autonomy-moral/.
Christman, John, and Joel Anderson, eds. 2005. *Autonomy and the Challenges to Liberalism*. Cambridge: Cambridge University Press.
Crowell, Steven. 2017. "Existentialism." In *The Stanford Encyclopedia of Philosophy*, edited by Edward N. Zalta, Winter 2017. Stanford, CA: Metaphysics Research Lab, Stanford University. https://plato.stanford.edu/archives/win2017/entries/existentialism/.
Delaney, Neil. 1996. "Romantic Love and Loving Commitment: Articulating a Modern Ideal." *American Philosophical Quarterly* 33: 339–56.
Fisher, Mark. 1990. *Personal Love*. London: Duckworth.
Frankfurt, Harry G. 1994. "Autonomy, Necessity, and Love." In *Necessity, Volition, and Love*, by Harry G. Frankfurt, 129–41. Cambridge: Cambridge University Press, 1999.
Frankfurt, Harry G. 1999. "On Caring." In *Necessity, Volition, and Love*, by Harry G. Frankfurt, 155–80. Cambridge: Cambridge University Press, 1999.
Frankfurt, Harry G. 2004. *The Reasons of Love*. Princeton: Princeton University Press.
Friedman, Marilyn. 1998. "Romantic Love and Personal Autonomy." *Midwest Studies in Philosophy* 22: 162–81. https://doi.org/10.1111/j.1475-4975.1998.tb00336.x.
Fromm, Erich. 1956. *The Art of Loving*. New York: Harper Perennial, 2006.
Gaus, Shane D., Gerald Courtland, and David Schmidtz. 2018. "Liberalism." In *The Stanford Encyclopedia of Philosophy*, edited by Edward N. Zalta, Spring 2018. Metaphysics Research Lab, Stanford University. https://plato.stanford.edu/archives/spr2018/entries/liberalism/.
Helm, Bennett W. 2010. *Love, Friendship, & the Self-Intimacy, Identification, & the Social Nature of Persons*. Oxford: Oxford University Press.
Krebs, Angelika. 2014. "Between I and Thou – On the Dialogical Nature of Love." In *Love and Its Objects. What Can We Care For?*, edited by Christian Maurer, Tony Milligan, and Kamila Pacovská, 7–24. Basingstoke: Palgrave Macmillan.
Krebs, Angelika. 2015. *Zwischen Ich und Du: Eine dialogische Philosophie der Liebe*. Berlin: Suhrkamp.
Kühler, Michael. 2009. "Liebe Als Vereinigung Im Anschluss an Adam Smith." *Allgemeine Zeitschrift Für Philosophie* 34: 197–220.
Kühler, Michael. 2011. "Love as Union vs. Personal Autonomy?" In *Love on Trial: Adjusting and Assigning Relationships*, edited by Nadine Farghaly and Corazón T. Toralba, 93–104. Oxford: Inter-Disciplinary Press. http://www.inter-disciplinary.net/wp-content/uploads/2009/10/kuehlerpaper.pdf.

Kühler, Michael. 2014. "Loving Persons. Activity and Passivity in Romantic Love." In *Love and Its Objects. What Can We Care For?*, edited by Christian Maurer, Tony Milligan, and Kamila Pacovská, 41–55. Basingstoke: Palgrave Macmillan.

Kühler, Michael. 2020. "Love and Conflicts Between Identity-Forming Values." In *International Handbook of Love: Transcultural and Transdisciplinary Perspectives*, edited by Claude-Hélène Mayer and Elisabeth Vanderheiden. Dordrecht: Springer. https://doi.org/10.1007/978-3-030-45996-3.

Kymlicka, Will. 1989. "Liberal Individualism and Liberal Neutrality." *Ethics* 99 (4): 883–905.

Mackenzie, Catriona, and Natalie Stoljar, eds. 2000. *Relational Autonomy: Feminist Perspectives on Autonomy, Agency, and the Social Self*. Oxford: Oxford University Press.

Merino, Noël. 2004. "The Problem with 'We': Rethinking Joint Identity in Romantic Love." *Journal of Social Philosophy* 35: 123–32.

Meyers, Diana Tietjens. 1996. *Feminists Rethink the Self*. Boulder: Westview Press.

Nozick, Robert. 1990. "Love's Bond." In *The Examined Life. Philosophical Meditations*, by Robert Nozick, 68–86. New York: Simon & Schuster.

Okin, Susan Moller. 2002. "'Mistresses of Their Own Destiny': Group Rights, Gender, and Realistic Rights of Exit." *Ethics* 112 (2): 205–230. https://doi.org/10.1086/324645.

Oshana, Marina. 2006. *Personal Autonomy in Society*. Aldershot: Ashgate.

Oshana, Marina, ed. 2014. *Personal Autonomy and Social Oppression*. New York: Routledge.

Rawls, John. 1971. *A Theory of Justice*. Cambridge: Belknap Press.

Rawls, John. 1980. "Kantian Constructivism in Moral Theory." *Journal of Philosophy* 77 (9): 515–72.

Rawls, John. 1993. *Political Liberalism*. New York: Columbia University Press.

Rawls, John. 2001. *Justice as Fairness. A Restatement*. Cambridge: Belknap Press.

Rawls, John. 2005. Political Liberalism. *Expanded Edition*. New York: Columbia University Press.

Sandel, Michael. 1998. *Liberalism and the Limits of Justice. 2nd edition*. Cambridge: Cambridge University Press.

Sartre, Jean-Paul. 1943. Being and Nothingness. *A Phenomenological Essay on Ontology*, translated and with an introduction by Hazel E. Barnes, New York: Washington Square Press, 1992.

Sheffield, Frisbee C. C., and M. C. Howatson, eds. 2008. *Plato: The Symposium*. Cambridge: Cambridge University Press.

Sneddon, Andrew. 2013. *Autonomy*. London: Bloomsbury Academic.

Soble, Alan. 1997. "Union, Autonomy, and Concern." In *Love Analyzed*, edited by Roger E. Lamb, 65–92. Boulder: Westview Press.

Solomon, Robert C. 1994. *About Love. Reinventing Romance for Our Times*. Indianapolis: Hackett Pub. Co., Reprint 2006.

Wilson, John. 1995. *Love between Equals. A Philosophical Study of Love and Sexual Relationships*. Houndmills: Palgrave Macmillan.

16 The Freedom that Comes with Love

Niklas Forsberg

Introduction

When we think of freedom, we often think of "freedom to act." From this perspective, the question of freedom is intimately intertwined with actions, one's abilities to act as one wants to, and with the presence or absence of obstacles that hinders one to "act freely." The political undertow to the question of freedom is the number of issues that we can come up with that concern what kinds of limitations a government may induce upon its citizens to act and choose freely as well as on the kinds of efforts that can be done to make sure that various power structures enhance the citizens' capabilities to be free responsible agents. It is within this idiom that a Sartrean distinction between an existential-ontological notion of freedom as the (necessary) ability to transcend one's situation (as expressed and discussed in *Being and Nothingness*) and a political-material notion (as expressed and discussed in *Critique of Dialectical Reason*), is applicable (Sartre 2015; 2004). It is also within this idiom that discussions like that about the Rawlsean "veil of ignorance" come into play (Rawls 1999). The rational activity that we engage in when we think about freedom along these lines—i.e., when we think philosophically about freedom understood as "freedom to act"—will naturally revolve around how to contemplate alternative courses of action (given the restriction of one's political and cultural set-up).

Of course, this focus on actions and judgments is well motivated. Intentional action is, and will remain, central to all reflections about the notion of freedom, and it's equally central to the grammar of responsibility. It is hard to imagine that one could make sense of morality without having something to say about how and on what grounds we can hold each other responsible; and without a notion of freedom to act, it's hard to see how we could judge each other fairly. Praise and blame are measured by reference to if what I did was intentional or unintentional, a stroke of luck, or a deed of painful heroism, done clumsily or carefully, by accident or by mistake. Intentional action, moral judgment, and the question of justice all seem to be connected and central to any and all attempts to explicate morality.

It is well known that Iris Murdoch is highly critical of the focus on actions and judgments in moral and political philosophy (Murdoch 1999, 80), so one may assume that *she* has little to teach us about freedom and even less to say about justice—especially on a communal level.[1] That's true, however, only under the assumption that "freedom" needs to be understood in immediate relation to "voluntary actions." It is also well know that Murdoch thought that love was her main subject, which comes into view clearly in this passage from an interview, where Murdoch distances herself from the idea that "freedom" is central to her philosophy:

> No. I think love is my main subject. I have very mixed feelings about the concept of freedom now. This is partly a philosophical development. I once was a kind of existentialist and now I am a kind of Platonist. What I am concerned about really is love, but this sounds very grandiose.
>
> (Dooley 2003, 25)

What is clear from the two points just mentioned—that she is critical of the idea of a one-sided focus on actions in moral and political thinking, and that she sees love and not freedom as her primary interest—is that Murdoch's eventual contribution to ethico-political discussions about freedom will not consist of additional theorizing about freedom understood in accordance with the most standardized manner of thinking about it just described. However, having "mixed feelings" about the concept of freedom does not mean that one is not interested in it. Indeed, where there are mixed feelings involved, there is something to be sorted out. In what follows, I will show how Murdoch's mixed feelings about the concept of freedom invite us to broaden our horizon and to seek to attain a more complex understanding of freedom that reaches beyond, but does not cancel, the link between voluntary action and freedom.

The Critique of the One-sided Focus on Will

In a deliberately scornful passage, Murdoch characterizes the idea of the free and rational agent, which she thinks of as the predominant picture of man that guides contemporary (her contemporary at least) moral and political philosophy, like this:

> We ought to know what we are doing. We should aim at a total knowledge of our situation and a clear conceptualization of all our possibilities. (...) My responsibility is a function of my knowledge (which tries to be wholly impersonal) and my will (which is wholly personal). Morality is a matter of thinking clearly and then proceeding to outward dealings with other men.

> On this view one might say that morality is assimilated to a visit to a shop. I enter the shop on a condition of totally responsible freedom, I objectively estimate the features of the goods, and I choose. The greater my objectivity and discrimination the larger the number of products from which I can select. Both as act and reason, shopping is public.
>
> (Murdoch 1999e, 304)

Murdoch does not want to deny that there are quite sensible ways of talking about morality in these terms, where we strive to objectively and neutrally estimate the alternative outcomes of alternative courses of action. Of course, we are forced to do so. It is quite easy to come up with examples of scenarios where we are forced to choose between different routes and where we do need to "calculate" the outcomes. Should I go to this or that university? Should I have another drink with my friend that needs my support and company, or should I go home and complete tomorrow's lecture? Should I have an abortion or not? But that fact does not mean that those moments capture the core of, and exhaustively describe, what morality is and freedom amounts to. Murdoch suggests that these moments are not the core of morality. In fact, one may even say that what she suggests, is that these kinds of decisions we have made on the basis of estimating, or calculating, various outcomes, where we choose between different routes on the basis of estimated outcomes, is precisely what we do when we do *not* know the moral truth. We reason hypothetically like this, when we do *not* know what is right, good, true. Moral truth, for Murdoch, comes into view when there are *no* choices (Murdoch 1999b, 159; 1999e, 331).

This claim may seem perplexing, given the emphasis on action and choice that is prevalent in contemporary moral philosophy. Murdoch's view on this matter is grounded in two central thoughts of hers. One is her concept of attention (that I will return to shortly). The other, which ought to be discussed first, is her view that vision precedes choice. In an oft-quoted passage, Murdoch claims that "I can only choose within the world I can *see*" (Murdoch 1999e, 329). In its simplest explication, this means that what one can choose between depends on what's in one's field of vision. But vision, as Murdoch conceives it, is not an ocular question. It is not a matter of *what* you see, but of what you *can* see and *how* you see it. You can have a thing right under your nose and still not *see* it, and if a person accuses another of not seeing her, she is not accusing the other for not including her in her ocular field. Thus, we need to broaden, or open up, the connotative logic of "vision" in order to see what Murdoch is after.

The most immediate way of doing that is to think about the fact that we all *have* various forms of visions. We have visions of our future, of who we are, of who *I am*, of what I ought and could become. These forms of visions are very far from crystal ball like premonitions. These are ways of conceptualizing oneself and one's future, ways of giving direction. And one does not do that without attending to one's world and one's surrounding. So it's a way of looking at the world and one's place in it. Similarly, how we perceive the world also partakes in forming the connotative logic of Murdoch's talk about vision. We may say that we have a worldview, a way of seeing, a vision of the world. These are most likely not private (though one can imagine a person having his or her own private worldview—which is, I take it, the same as imagining insanity when taken to its extreme).

When Murdoch suggests that vision precedes choice, she is to be seen as bringing the full connotative logic of the concept of vision into play. How we choose depends on who we are, how we picture ourselves, how we perceive our world. As such, vision forms the backdrop to, or ground beneath, all choices. Thus, Murdoch can be said to try to push us to ask the deeper questions: we should not only ask about what do to in a given situation, but also about how that particular situation came about, what gave it its importance, and how the particular choices that we seem to stand before got singled out as "the options," and so on and so forth. Here, the philosophical questions about "what to do" and "what a good person is" transpose themselves into questions about who "we" are (about history, society, politics), who I am (questions of roots, of belonging, of desires and dreams, of identity, the loss of identity), and of where ideas and values come from (a question about concepts, importance, and our most fundamental beliefs, i.e., the kinds of beliefs and desires that we are more likely to *not* know that we have, than we are to be in command of them, since they guide each of our commands).

> We do continually have to make choices – but why should we blot out as irrelevant the different background of these choices, whether they are made confidently on the basis of a clear specification of the situation, or tentatively, with no confidence of having sufficiently explored the details? Why should attention to detail, or belief in its inexhaustibility, necessarily bring paralysis, rather than, say, inducing humility and being an expression of love?
> (Murdoch 1999g, 88)

Importantly, Murdoch's claim that vision precedes choice is not meant to be a philosophical hypothesis that needs philosophical arguments to make it credible. That each choice has a background is a simple fact. It's one of those thoughts that are meant to sound familiar and true just by being highlighted. You can only choose between A and B in a world where there are As and Bs, and the choice can only become real if you can see A *as* A, and B *as* B, for what they are. The choice between having an abortion and not having an abortion is not possible without a culture in which abortion is a practice, and if it isn't a practice, the termination of a pregnancy would be something else—it would, as it were, fall under a different concept. One can only be a vegetarian in a world where people eat animals and have eaten animals for some time. You can't divorce someone in a world where there are no marriages. You may think about this as bringing the present unseen into something present seen. Notice that the world "seen," as used on this scale, is not a question of "obscured from view" versus "clearly in sight," but of "not attended to" versus "attended to" (and one can here begin to see why the question of attention took on the central role it has in Murdoch's philosophy). Uncovering the background, trying to shift our focus from the explicit choices to the world that brought these choices forth *as* choices, is a quest for truth, and of truthfulness, since this is a matter of finding out what something *is*.

> [I]f we attend to more complex regions which lie outside "actions" and "choices" we see moral differences as differences of understanding (…), more or less extensive and important, which may show openly or privately as differences of story or metaphor or as differences of moral vocabulary betokening different ranges and ramifications of moral concept. Here communication of a new moral concept cannot necessarily be achieved by specification of factual criteria open to any observer ('Approve of *this* area!') but may involve the communication of a completely new, possibly far-reaching and coherent vision; and it is certainly true that we cannot always *understand* other people's moral concepts.
>
> (Murdoch 1999g, 82)

The part of this passage that is hard to swallow is her claim that the communication of a new moral concept may involve the communication of a new "far-reaching and coherent vision," and that we won't always "understand other people's moral concepts." This may make it seem as if we are doomed to fall short of truth at times, since we are not even in agreement about what our moral concepts mean.

Murdoch's response to that challenge is twofold. On the one hand, any moral and political philosophy that abstains from attending to (or fails to see the importance of) issues pertaining to how vision and conceptual change come together and make up the field in which deliberation later on may take place, will be even worse off, since such forms of philosophizing will take a faulty picture as its departure in the quest for truth. On the other hand, the one-sided focus on actions and choices will give us little to say in, or about, cases where understanding is blocked. When *a* and *b* disagree about what *x is*, arguments about whether *x* is *y* or not won't work. One of the main problems with much contemporary moral philosophy, Murdoch shows, is that it is a mistake to think that our (moral) concepts have a singular defined meaning, that we can establish once and for all. The concepts we live by are not names. They grow and change, and we grow and change with them.

Murdoch here talks about the introduction of a new moral concept. This introduces history as a fundamental notion. Our vision of the world has a history, and our concepts have been formed throughout that history. This means, as Murdoch conceives it, that because "moral differences are conceptual differences," morality must be studied historically. And this may be disappointing to some since it makes "the reduction of ethics to logic" impossible (Murdoch 1999e, 84; cf. Forsberg 2018). Moral truth about a moral choice (should I do *a* or *b*?) is never, or hardly ever, merely a matter of determining which alternative has the best, and the highest number of, arguments speaking in its favor. These kinds of deliberations may help us choose when we are bewildered, but we are bewildered, Murdoch would say, precisely because we do *not* know what the good thing to do here is. Murdoch's alternative—studying ethics historically—does not involve the claim that the task of the moral philosopher is to write the history of the concept, or to trace the etymology of a word back to its supposed "origin," as if that would teach us what to do or even how to think. The unearthing of the historical dimension serves to make clear "where we are" and how we have come to be what we are, that is, how our worldview was formed—but it also points forward, as it were, marking out future's possibilities and impossibilities. If you want to speak "Wittgensteinian," you may say that the historical study serves to bring our "form of life" into view. If you speak "Foucauldian" you may say that Murdoch's perspective shows how we are structured, conditioned, and that questions of power (and hence freedom) cannot be reduced to questions about distribution, choices and actions (with the caveat that, on a superficial level, Murdoch emphasizes the importance of the subject's inner life whereas Foucault is critical of the traditional humanistic notion of the human). What the Murdochian effort of deepening our concepts and of unearthing the background to our choices, achieves, is not more support for one of the hypothetical paths forward, but a deepened understanding of what the concept you are deliberating about means, or indeed *is*.

Words and Concepts

At this juncture, it is absolutely crucial to realize that Murdoch's talk about the introduction of a new moral concept is not to be understood as the introduction of a new *word*.

> Words may mislead us here since words are often stable while concepts alter; we have a different image of courage at forty from that which we had at twenty. A deepening process, at any rate an

altering and complicating process, takes place. There are two senses of "knowing what a word means", one connected with ordinary language and the other very much less so. Knowledge of a value concept is something to be understood, as it were, in depth, and not in terms of switching on to some given impersonal network. Moreover, if morality is essentially connected with change and progress, we cannot be as democratic about it as some philosophers would like to think. We do not simply, through being rational and knowing ordinary language, "know" the meaning of all necessary moral words. We may have to learn the meaning; and since we are human historical individuals the movement of understanding is onward into increasing privacy, in the direction of the ideal limit, and not back towards a genesis in the rulings of an impersonal public language.

(Murdoch 1999e, 322)

Murdoch's view of how we are "mislead by words" is worth underlining here, not only because she has an original take on the distinction between words and concepts but also because it gives us a handrail into an understanding of the nature of the problem Murdoch is wrestling with. When we are confronted with a choice, we have two (or more) alternatives in front of us. Now, these choices—the sense of the conceptual paths forward—are often clear to us. But sometimes, that clarity is deceptive or even illusory. Being "mislead by words" is being under the assumption that we are in command of our concepts and that the sense of our words is not really what is at stake. At the very core of Murdoch's philosophy lies a very complex and profound sense of the nature of our philosophical questions that often become veiled by the suggested responses to this problem (love, attention, and an emphasis on the development of a person's inner life). One of her most fundamental philosophical discoveries lies in how she understands the very nature of our philosophical difficulties. Because we are familiar with our words, we tend to be blind to the slow and (often) unintentional changes of our conceptual habitat, our world. What is in the background remains in the background, and we thereby fail to pay attention to the most fundamental and important issues. Murdoch's more positive sounding "responses" to this kind of difficulties will sound shallow, too subjective (even ego-centered), and, well, "cute" —it would be better if we all had an attentive and loving gaze instead!—if one have not attained a good sense of the very nature of the questions that they are meant to be answering.

There are a number of points that need to be explicated as one unpacks Murdoch's view about the relation between words and concepts, as it is expressed in the passage just quoted. First: Murdoch makes the striking observation that the relation between words and concepts is, in reality, quite the opposite of what philosophers often are prone to think. The idea of a concept is regularly understood as the idea of a (desired) consistency hidden under the fluctuating uses of words. Murdoch shows how this thought turns reality inside out. Murdoch's example here is that "we have a different image of courage at forty from that which we had at twenty." It's a simplified example, of course. The youngster's idea of courage (say, "I dare to climb the highest tree") is quite different from a middle-aged man's (say, "I am ready to face my demons in therapy"). But if we think about what's involved in this kind of change, it should become clear that the answer must be quite a lot. I am inclined to say that what has changed is not one man's opinion about the sense of a concept, but that the 20-year old and the 40-year old inhabit different worlds. This is, of course, a metaphor, but it's a pregnant one, and one Murdoch herself uses (Murdoch 1999e, 82). As one's concept of courage changes, it is clear that a lot of other concepts, practices, and ways of seeing and valuing have changed too. Moving from one concept of courage to another one is not a matter of being proved wrong or of changing one's definition, but of a changed, and indeed deepened, understanding of *life*. So when a concept changes, it is not merely a word that has been redefined. What is solid and remains unchanged over time is the word, not its sense—and this, clearly, will make philosophical clarity hard to achieve since concepts change slowly, and often unbeknown to us, while they remain the same on their surface. The illusion of sense is a constant threat.

At this point, it seems natural to raise the question about the dynamics between social or communal changes on the one hand, and personal or existential changes, on the other. Indeed, it may seem as if we have two very different tales about conceptual change in play here. One is strictly communal or historical. The other strictly personal. The worry lurking behind this question about dynamics is of course a fear that Murdoch's view makes all philosophical positions "subjective"—a matter of personal development and existential particularities (and perhaps even preferences and peculiarities).[2] Just because one person's idea about what "courage" means changes, it doesn't seem to follow that the person in question knows *more*, that is, that the concept really is deepened. Neither does it seem to follow that there's progress. Different, yes. But better? How do we tell which direction is "better"? And even if it's better for me, why think of it as more true? The second remark about progress depends, of course, on the view that progress always is a relevant thing to discuss and strive for in relation to morality. As long as one talks about morality in the abstract like this, it seems inevitable that one ought to endorse such a view of the centrality of progress.

As an example, think about a concept like equality and what it really means to us. For us, it seems clear that the woman's right movements and the abolishment of slavery are to be understood as forms of progress. We had less equality before; more after. This is due, I would say, to a deepened concepts of equality. It didn't use to extend to women and slaves,

The freedom that comes with love 315

now it does. One cannot talk about all humans being equal, while at the same time excluding half of the world's population from all democratic discussions, or claiming to own and systematically and violently mistreating fellow human beings. In the case of courage, and my example of climbing the highest tree as a paradigmatic instance of courage for my imagined 20-year-old self, and being brave enough to pursue therapy in my imagined 40-year-old self, we may certainly see a form of deepening that is intertwined with maturation. The difference between the two cases seems to be that the first (about equality) concerns an obviously social phenomenon, and that the deepening and progressive development has very little to do with a *person's* development. There's no reason to speak of this as a particularly subjective form of advancement. But it is easier to think that the example of courage at 20 versus courage at 40 pertains more, if not only, to subjective changes. The concept as employed by the imagined 40-year-old self is richer, broader, more nuanced, its web spun over a larger area of human life. It covers more and reaches deeper into the human mind and life. But if the deepened concept of courage covers a larger area of human life, it seems strange to say that that personal development is cut off from the communal. So even though we need to be able to distinguish between personal and existential changes of one's concepts, there is also a sense in which the personal struggle to earn sense is not cut off from the changes of the communal sphere. And this should lead us to see that the rather common way to understand Murdoch as someone who only cares about personal development does not only go wrong because it focus almost exclusively on passages of her texts that talks about, or at least alludes to, personal development, but because it hears them in the wrong key.

The key here is to recognize that the ability to draw distinctions does not necessarily cancel out the ability to discern similarities and make connections. Thus, there are ways of seeing questions about personal change as distinct from matters of social change, and there are ways of seeing how the personal and the communal changes interact. Conceptual changes (which, as we have seen, for Murdoch are intertwined with changes of moral vision and moral development) are complex things and need to be handled with care—attentively. Think, for example, about the concept of marriage. One may easily see that the concept has changed because of changes in social, legal, religious, economic, and sexual ways of thinking and being. So, as an example, it is obvious today (to most liberal-minded persons) that gay marriage makes perfect sense and that the effort to deny people in love to marry is nothing but a form of violation of their rights as citizens of one's community. The situation was very different in a not-too-distant past—when religious convictions had a different orientation, the economic system was different, and ideas of homosexuality as a form sin, and later on as a form of illness, were prevalent. A gay couple could not marry then, whereas they can (or can at least rightfully claim their right to) now. This seems to be a change on the communal level only. And it can and should be studied as such. Now, compare that with a couple struggling to attain a clear sense of what their marriage means to them—a question I guess all married couples need to work with, quite regardless of "objective" criteria (what the law says, if the marriage was done properly, if they have a marriage certificate, etc.). Here, there is a sense in which each married person has to struggle to inherit the concept. For some, it's achieved easily; for others with great difficulty; for some, it's not achieved at all. So there is a sense in which social change can be distinguished from the personal, existential struggles we are called to go through. But then again, what would those personal struggles be (like), if they were not only performed in relation to a given social order? And how could those social forms of structuring a concept even come about, if people were not challenging them? I want to say that the difference between these two sides is real and of great importance, but also that it would be a mistake to think that they don't intermingle.

A clear case of why this is so can be found in Murdoch's well-known example of M and D, where M (a mother in law) attends to her daughter in law (D), and transform her view of her by means of attending to her lovingly (Murdoch 1999e). She first found her undignified and juvenile and then, after attending to her lovingly, she found her to be refreshingly simple and delightfully youthful. Now, this may seem as if a very personal change of perspective has taken place. By choosing to attend to D lovingly, M has become more kind and open-minded. This is often how the example is perceived. However, pace the predominant reading, the kinds of changes that M goes through, are achieved by a form of self-criticism, and what she discovers through the process is that she is out of tune with society. What she discovers is that she has perceived D from the point of a privileged bourgeois lady, and that she has sifted her view thought that. Attending lovingly to D means discovering that she, as an ethico-political being, has lost touch with reality that her concepts distort reality. That's the conceptual level at which her vision transforms. She doesn't just *choose* to look at D "lovingly" (See Forsberg 2017a, 2020). So the existential development is never disconnected from the social; and the social transformations are never cut off from personal struggles with the relevant concepts (Forsberg 2017b; Antonaccio 2012, 256; Hämäläinen 2015, 757n9). The deepening of a concept is never wholly a personal matter.[3]

A second point about Murdoch's view of the relation between words and concept that needs to be discussed is this: Since our concepts are not names of things that remain the same, and since their senses are in constant renegotiation in relation to other concepts and, indeed, to life as a whole, clarity about complex areas of life (such as one's moral and political being) can only be achieved, Murdoch contends, by a process of "deepening" of our concepts, and by *complicating* things, rather than seeking manageable definitions. This is, Murdoch argues, particularly true about our moral concepts. Even though I personally find it too restrictive to say that there is such a thing as a moral language made up by a limited set of concepts (we do, after all, use language in its entirety as moral and political beings, and praise and blame, and perform responsible and evasive maneuvers, and so on and so forth, without the use of overtly "moral concepts"), Murdoch is most certainly right to suggest that concepts that are central to most moral discourse—like, say, good, bad, evil, freedom, justice, virtue, generosity, love, harm, and so on—are very different from concepts like bicycle, pencil, treehouse or apple pie. When it comes to "moral concepts" we need to understand them "in depth" and that is not a matter of on and off. Either you have a bicycle or you don't. Our moral concepts are much more complex than that. You may, for example, be politically and morally free to do what you want (though, of course, legally restricted), yet feel completely paralyzed, not knowing where to go next and why and how.

Murdoch (provokingly to some, I assume) claims that since morality is "essentially connected with change and progress," it is not a "democratic" issue. Now, what this means, I take it, is not that morality is anti-democratic but that democratic decision making tends to be called for precisely because our moralities are different. We deliberate, count pluses and minuses, try to be fair, try to give everyone his or her share, in a lot of situations, many of which are clearly moral. But when we do, it's because there's no single road forward. When we "ride with the best hypothesis," we know that we are not morally at peace.

Thus, the take home message from Murdoch's comment about how words stay the same, whereas concepts change, and that morality is essentially connected to change and progress, is that moral understanding, and a truthful relation to one's moral reality, is not about choosing as rationally as possible between different alternatives, assuming that one is in command of the central concepts that the question is about, but about seeking clarity about the relevant concepts and the entire changing fabric of language in which they take their present form(s). The movement of thought here is not toward simplified precision—say, a more precise, more strictly delimited definition—but one toward complexity, and truthfulness toward that complexity. What the most difficult part of this is might very well be the admittance required, that we do not *know* all the relevant concepts (that we naturally assume we already are in command of).

> For political purposes we have been encouraged to think of ourselves as totally free and responsible, knowing everything we need to know for the important purposes of life. But this is one of the things of which Hume said that it may be true in politics but false in fact; and is it really true in politics? We need a post-Kantian unromantic

> Liberalism with a different image of freedom. The technique of becoming free is more difficult than John Stuart Mill imagined. We need more concepts than our philosophies have furnished us with. We need to be enabled to think in terms of degrees of freedom, and to picture, in a non-metaphysical, non-totalitarian and non-religious sense, the transcendence of reality.
>
> (Murdoch 1999a, 293)

Murdoch is here working with an opposition between what she calls "The Natural Law View" and the "Liberal View" of the human being. The "Liberal notion of the human is the notion of the human as a free and responsible agent that moves around in a neutral world of facts and chooses. It's the image of the non-conditioned man, the non-historical monarch" (Murdoch 1999a, 288–289; 1999c, 70). In the opposing "Natural Law" view, the "individual is seen as held in a framework which transcends him, where what is important and valuable is the framework, and the individual only has importance, or even reality, in so far as he belongs to the framework" (Murdoch 1999c, 70; See also Forsberg 2011). But even though we may rightfully describe ourselves as "free to choose" in this "liberal" sense, it narrows down the concept of freedom to such a point where the idea of "becoming free" eventually disintegrates on us. What is needed is a notion of freedom that comes in degrees, and which is deepened by means of "the transcendence of reality."

Now, the idea of transcending reality may indeed seem too metaphysical (even paraphysical) to today's philosophical sensibilities. That Murdoch is a self-confessed Platonist doesn't help here either, since it leads people to think that she thinks there's a Platonic "elsewhere"—contrary to Murdoch's explicit rejections of such views. For Murdoch, "metaphysics" basically means the background against which all our actions and words and thoughts are formed. So in that sense, we are *always* guided by metaphysics, no matter how critical one is of "metaphysics" (Murdoch 2003, 399; Robjant 2012; Forsberg 2019; Hämäläinen 2013). Thus:

> Of course virtue is good habit and dutiful action. But the background condition of such habit and such action, in human beings, is a just mode of vision and a good quality of consciousness. It is a *task* to come to see the world as it is. A philosophy which leaves duty without context and exalts the idea of freedom and power as a separate top level value ignores this task and obscures the relation between virtue and reality. We act rightly "when the time comes" not out of strength of will but out of the quality of our usual attachments and the kind of energy and discernment which we have available. And to this the whole activity of our consciousness is relevant.
>
> (Murdoch 1999f, 375)

Freedom is not a "separate top level value," and it is a notion we won't understand is we fail to get "the background condition" of our virtues into view; and to achieve *that* we have to engage in the *task* of seeing the world (not a singular action, or person, or deed) *as it is*. And this (perpetual) task of coming to see the word as it is, is achieved by the work of attention.

In *Metaphysics as a Guide to Morals*, Murdoch argues that the "Liberal" view of freedom inserts a rift between "the person as a citizen and the person as a moral-spiritual individual" and goes on to say that this is a "fictitious" citizen since we are not divided in that way as "real, whole persons" (Murdoch 2003, 357; Cf. Browning 2019, 182). This does not mean, however, that Murdoch thereby would argue that the public and the private are the same thing. Public politics requires a different form of reflection and is darting toward different aims than one is as a person (Browning 2019). This may appear somewhat contradictory: On the one hand, Murdoch claims that the distinction between "person as a citizen and the person as a moral-spiritual individual" is fictitious. On the other hand, she claims that personal morality and politics work differently and have different aims. But this contradiction is only apparent. *As a person* we are never disconnected from the social and political world of which we are a part and that partakes in forming who and what we are. But that does not mean that the aims of the political and the methods of reflection and deliberation that there take place and have their home are easily transposed and adequate for us as individuals (moral *and* political). In fact, one may say that the rather recent idea of freedom and deliberation and justice that come together with the notion of the "liberal man" is rooted in a misguided adoption of political and economic ways of thinking in moral registers—registers that are far more complex and diverse (and also private) than the politicized and economized notions of freedom and deliberation and responsibility allow for.

> A simple-minded faith in science, together with the assumption that we are all rational and totally free, engenders a dangerous lack of curiosity about the real world, a failure to appreciate the difficulties of knowing it. We need to return from the self-centred concept of sincerity to the other-centred concept of truth. We are not isolated free choosers, monarchs of all we survey, but benighted creatures sunk in a reality whose nature we are constantly and overwhelmingly tempted to deform by fantasy. Our current picture of freedom encourages a dream-like facility; whereas what we require is a renewed sense of the difficulty and complexity of the moral life and the opacity of persons. We need more concepts in terms of which to picture the substance of our being; it is through an enriching and deepening of concepts that moral progress takes place. Simone Weil said that morality was a matter of attention, not of will. We need a new vocabulary of attention.
> (Murdoch 1999a, 293)

Love, Attention, and Degrees of Freedom

This is where our exploration has taken us so far: Murdoch argues that the idea of the human being as neutral and free, where "free" is reduced to "free to choose," is a misguided image that we naively are letting ourselves be guided by. (We tend to think about ourselves in this reductive way, and we tend to think about freedom in this reductive way—hence we are letting these images guide us as we reflect upon ourselves and our concepts and as we project ourselves and our concepts into a future.) The major philosophical mistake in play here is a faulty view of the human and of our conceptual world. The complexity of reality has been purged away—thereby allowing ourselves to believe that we are rational and in command, leaving us with a diminished view of human nature and freedom. Freedom, for Murdoch, is not an on or off thing, and we need to make conceptual room for an understanding of freedom as something that comes in degrees. As long as we think of freedom in terms of will alone—of ourselves as neutral agents that acts in a world of fact—we won't be able to discern reality for what it is, and we need to make room for, and find ways to comprehend, the deepening of our concepts, and the changing (historical) nature of our moral reality. A richer, more nuanced, more true, concept of freedom (as one that comes in degrees and is not locked to "will") can only be attained if we find ways to see and explore this "deepening process" and the "transcendence of reality." In order to do *that*, attention (and love) will be the most central concepts.

Murdoch's use of the concept of attention is a difficult one. I think it would be a mistake to think that she has established a well-defined technical concept. But it's a rich concept, and she is allowing for that connotative richness to be in play, so if one understands that concept too narrowly, one will misunderstand Murdoch. First of all, it is clear that she does not just mean "look really closely" at something. In fact, she introduces the concept of attention as a contrast to "looking" (Murdoch 1999e, 329). Seeing "attentively" is not just perceiving, or having something in one's ocular field. Following Weil, Murdoch emphasizes *waiting* as a central aspect of attention (Weil 1970, 335). Attention, as Murdoch and Weil understand it, is very hard to cash out as a method of sorts, as something we can choose to do. But neither is it well explicated as a form of passivity. The French word, *attendre*, literally means" to wait," but the Latin root, *at tendere*, means" to reach out," and both these features are in play in Weil's and Murdoch's use of the term (Larson 2009, 66–67; Forsberg 2017c). The movement of attention is, characteristically, *away from the self*, and to the reality. Love comes in here, as *the ability to do so* (Murdoch 1999d, 354). This is also the Murdochian route to realism in philosophy: not hypothesizing, but waiting and acknowledging what is there, seeing what is there apart from my desires and fantasies and wishes.

> The place of choice is certainly a different one if we think in terms of a world which is compulsively present to the will, and the discernment and exploration of which is a slow business. Moral change and moral achievement are slow; we are not free in the sense of being able suddenly to alter ourselves since we cannot suddenly alter what we can see and ergo what we desire and are compelled by. In a way, explicit choice seems now less important: less decisive (since much of the "decision" lies elsewhere) and less obviously something to be "cultivated". If I attend properly I will have no choices and this is the ultimate condition to be aimed at.
>
> (Murdoch 1999e, 331)

For Murdoch, coming to see the world rightly, through the "work" of attention, means struggling to take oneself to a point where there are *no* choices. However, for Murdoch, that does not mean that freedom is cancelled. It means that it is realized. Now, this is not as strange as it may seem. For what is cancelled out here, if anything, is certainly not man's freedom, if "free" is understood as that which is negatively defined as the opposite of "determined." So waiting, paying attention "to such a point that we no longer have a choice" (Murdoch 1999b, 159) means, above all, seeing the world rightly so we are released from hypothetical doubt; *not* that one's ability to choose is cancelled out. Being released from hypothetical doubt is also becoming more free, liberated. This kind of freedom, however, is not an on or off thing. "More free" suggests a notion of freedom that comes in degrees. And that is no wonder, since the kind of freedom that we now are unearthing is intimately intertwined with seeing the world aright. Attaining a truthful understanding of our world is not a choice between two alternative courses of actions, but a continuous process. Obviously, in the course of this process, one will have to make choices of this kind and there will never be a moment at which one will run out of choices along life's way.

This thought about degrees of freedom as attainable through the work of attention is complex and layered. The most accessible layer is probably this: Most moral philosophical theories approach the field of ethics as a set of questions and problems best addressed through the image of a human being as a rational agent forced to make a difficult choice. Murdoch's response to this "pay attention to such a point that you no longer have a choice" means, at its simplest and most explicit level, that you know what is right when all paths forward but one are closed, have fallen out of the picture as alternatives altogether. The demand that moral truth places on us is that we find a way to move out of the realm of hypothetical calculation and "theories." The basic thought here can be brought into view by this simplified example in which moral and political issues have been reduced to a minimum: Suppose you are a scientist working to solve a particular problem that you have discovered in your lab. You want x to happen, so you develop a variety of theories about how to best achieve that. And then you test these theories by way of hypothetical and deductive reasoning. As long as you have more than one theory in competition—does solution a or solution b lead to x?—you have not reached the true solution to your problem. Not until there is only one way forward, not until you don't have any alternative theories to choose from, have you reached the truth.

If one transposes this example to an overtly moral case—as is typical of contemporary moral philosophy—things quickly become more difficult of course. A very common form of examples in contemporary moral philosophy is to present the reader with a scenario where one has to choose between two or three courses of action. And then one is supposed to calculate the goods of each, and choose. The trolley example is one of the most famous ones (Foot 2003). Now, "trolley examples" are not meant to be direct instructions for how to act in a given situation but serve primarily to test our intuitions. And they tend to highlight differences between various ethical standpoints (such as varieties of consequentialism and deontological theories). But they also serve as a model for how to reason theoretically while doing moral philosophy attempting to solve difficult problems that we supposedly may face, and to some extent, they may even serve to form how we reason in everyday life. And it's true, one cannot go through life without finding oneself caught in dilemmatic situations. A young woman asking herself whether or not to have an abortion will be forced to think about the pros and cons of two very concrete alternatives. Since a woman is under temporal pressure in such a situation, she may be forced to make a decision based on weighing pros against cons. Personal differences and differences in moral universe come to the fore here. But it's a drastic mistake to think that such choice merely is a matter of choosing between two alternatives courses of action. What is at stake is so much more, and the question itself cannot even be approached without thinking about who one is, how one perceives one's future and one's future self, where one comes from, how one's beliefs and convictions have been formed and why, and so on and so forth.[4]

Coming to see clearly, attaining a clear vision of one's world and one's language is thus something that is hard to achieve. But it is here that true freedom is to be found. And it can only be attained in degrees. The work of attention—enabled by love—is the way to do that. For that is precisely the effort to see what is there, in *its* reality, rather than as guided by my own fantasies and pre-conceptions. (For a more detailed discussion of other aspects of Murdoch's concept of love, see Forsberg 2017c.) Our moral world is constantly formed and always (though slowly and unbeknownst to ourselves) renegotiated. And that is what we need to learn to see: "if we consider what the work of attention is like, how continuously it goes on, and how imperceptibly it builds up structures of value around us, we shall not be surprised that at crucial moments of choice most of the business of choosing is already over" (Murdoch 1999e, 329). Given that "structures of value" are all the time built up around us, without us noticing, it follows that it is indeed quite easy to rely on, and be misled by, faulty images. "The act of attention is the effort to counteract such states of illusion" (Murdoch 1999e, 329).

Responsibility: We Are Guilty for What We Are

The "traditional" notion of freedom—which should I choose?—becomes relevant once the table has been set, and there's food to distribute or dishes to choose from. Murdoch suggests that when we get to *that* point, most truly relevant and fundamental issues have already been settled. This is the core idea of her claim that vision precedes choice, later explored under the image of us always being guided by metaphysics. When we come to the moments of choice, the fundamental issues have already been staged, if not addressed or settled. This does not mean that vision is important because it is a prerequisite for action (Cf. Jollimore 2011, 152). This would mean that if I see clearer, attentively, it's easier to choose. Murdoch's point is rather that the notion of freedom that permeates this model of freedom is illusory, at least as long as we don't see that freedom also is a concept that changes and that we need to deepen our understanding of that concept too.

Thus, Murdoch's "mixed feelings" about the notion of freedom can be said to come down to this: yes, we do have to make choices, continuously. But there is a sense in which these choices are illusory. Not in the sense of "oh, so determinism is true!", but in the sense that freedom itself is layered. Genuine freedom does not consist of the ability to make a choice, but of the seeing the world rightly. But knowledge about oneself and one's world is not a "have or have not" affair. It comes in degrees. Freedom—political and moral—is achieved through a deepening of one's concepts. Real freedom comes in degrees. It is hard earned, and there's no end-point. The route to freedom here suggested is a work of deepening one's concepts, with the aim of reaching understanding of one's situatedness, one's heritage if you like, and of seeing the world for what it really is. This is, admittedly, a rather austere idea of moral truth, as perfection of a form of truth that is "glimpsed but never reached" (Murdoch 2003, 304). So we survive by blocking it out, trying to convince ourselves that the state of not knowing (and riding along with the best hypothesis) is the best we can do.

The deepening of one's concepts is a task without end, which means that morality is inherently concerned with change and progress. And changes come about because we become clear about how we have failed to see the world rightly and projected our fantasies and wishes upon it. This is the also the central reason why love becomes a central concept for Murdoch. When Murdoch claims that love, and not freedom, is her central concept, she is not saying that she does not care about public and social and political issues and concerns. She is saying that public and social and political issues are today approached and dealt with through a diminished view of what a human being is, and a naïve faith in her powers to choose. Hence, rather than turning away from those kinds of concerns, she is trying to turn our attention to them.

Given that freedom is not to be locked to actions only, moral responsibility is not something that is restricted to our overt moral actions. With a friendly nod to Schopenhauer,[5] Murdoch claims that "we are guilty not of what we do but of what we are" (Murdoch 2003, 69). Murdoch is here pushing us to see that our responsibilities stretch far beyond the most obvious: the effects of our actions. Whether you are white or black, happen to be rich or poor, a man or a woman (or neither), and so on and so forth, will affect how you are judged. Whether we like it or not (most of the time, I guess we don't), people will measure our words and deeds in relation to who we are and where we come from. We may want to think of ourselves as equal (in front of Lady Justice, in front of each other). The reality, however, is different. Murdoch's call for realism in moral philosophy is a call to take this into account (and not rely on idealizations, fantasies). Attention, love for a reality beyond our fantasies of a just world, of a reality other than the one I would like to be real, is the way to do that. But the question of responsibility, and hence of freedom, reaches deeper than that. Since we are creatures who partake in forming the very horizon against which actions and deeds make sense and can be measured, we are to be held responsible for how we relate to that fact too. Freedom comes in degrees. We attain it, we become responsible citizens, by acknowledging that, and by taking responsibility for how we relate to our words, to how we partake in forming our world by doing so. "We cannot over-estimate the importance of the concept-forming words we utter to ourselves and to others. This background of our thinking and feeling is always vulnerable" (Murdoch 2003, 260).[6]

Notes

1. Martha Nussbaum has, for example, suggested that Murdoch avoids questions about "social justice and human well-being" and focuses instead on "each person's struggle for self-perfection" (Nussbaum 2001). This is a view that has been rightly criticized by Maria Antonaccio (Antonaccio 2003, 2012) and is further and fruitfully discussed in White (2018).
2. This is, for example, Nussbaum's understanding, as we saw in note 1.
3. For a good illustration of how this thought may function when put to work (particularly in relation to the concept of autonomy), see Mackenzie and Stoljar (2000).
4. My example of the young adult reflecting on the question of whether or not he ought to be circumcised is meant to illustrate how much is involved in what looks like "simple decisions" (Forsberg 2013, 136–137).
5. I thank Maria Gila Moreno for pointing out Murdoch's connection to Schopenhauer on this point (Moreno 2019, 57n.55; Forsberg 2015).

6. I thank Nora Hämäläinen for valuable comments to an earlier draft of this chapter. This publication was supported within the project of Operational Programme Research, Development and Education (OP VVV/OP RDE), "Centre for Ethics as Study in Human Value," registration No. CZ.02.1.01/0.0/0.0/15_003/0000425, cofinanced by the European Regional Development Fund and the state budget of the Czech Republic.

References

Antonaccio, Maria. 2003. *Picturing the Human: The Moral Thought of Iris Murdoch*, 1st edition. New York: Oxford University Press USA.

Antonaccio, Maria. 2012. *A Philosophy to Live By: Engaging Iris Murdoch*. Oxford, New York: Oxford University Press.

Browning, Gary. 2019. "The Metaphysics of Morals and Politics (MGM Chapter 12)" in *Reading Iris Murdoch's Metaphysics as a Guide to Morals*, eds. Nora Hämäläinen and Gillian Dooley (Palgrave MacMillan, 2019), 179–194.

Dooley, Gillian, ed. 2003. *From a Tiny Corner in the House of Fiction: Conversations with Iris Murdoch*. Columbia, SC: University of South Carolina Press.

Foot, Philippa. 2003. "The Problem of Abortion and the Doctrine of Double Effect." In *Virtues and Vices: And Other Essays in Moral Philosophy*, Reprint edition, 19–32. New York: Oxford University Press USA.

Forsberg, Niklas. 2011. "Knowing and Not Knowing What a Human Being Is." *SATS* 12 (1): 1–17. https://doi.org/10.1515/sats.2011.002.

Forsberg, Niklas. 2013. *Language Lost and Found: On Iris Murdoch and the Limits of Philosophical Discourse*. London: Bloomsbury Academic.

Forsberg, Niklas. 2015. "A New Conception of Original Sin?" *The Heythrop Journal* 56 (2): 272–284. https://doi.org/10.1111/heyj.12244.

Forsberg, Niklas. 2017a. "M and D and Me: Iris Murdoch and Stanley Cavell on Perfectionism and Self-Transformation." *Iride* 30: 361–372. https://doi.org/10.1414/87773.

Forsberg, Niklas. 2017b. "Iris Murdoch on Love." In *The Oxford Handbook of Philosophy of Love*. https://www.oxfordhandbooks.com/view/10.1093/oxfordhb/9780199395729.001.0001/oxfordhb-9780199395729-e-26.

Forsberg, Niklas. 2018. "Taking the Linguistic Method Seriously: On Iris Murdoch on Language and Linguistic Philosophy." In *Murdoch on Truth and Love*, 109–132. New York, Secaucus: Palgrave Macmillan.

Forsberg, Niklas. 2019. "Unity and Art in a Mood of Scepticism (MGM Chapter 1)." In *Reading Iris Murdoch's Metaphysics as a Guide to Morals*, edited by Nora Hämäläinen and Gillian Dooley, 33–49. New York, Secaucus: Palgrave Macmillan.

Forsberg, Niklas. 2020. "Perception and Prejudice: Attention and Moral Progress in Iris Murdochs Philosophy and C. S. Lewis 'A Grief Observed.'" *Partial Answers* 18 (2) 259–279.

Hämäläinen, Nora. 2013. "What Is Metaphysics in Murdoch's *Metaphysics as a Guide to Morals*?" *SATS* 14 (November): 1–20. https://doi.org/10.1515/sats-2013-0001.

Hämäläinen, Nora. 2015. "Reduce Ourselves to Zero?: Sabina Lovibond, Iris Murdoch, and Feminism." *Hypatia* 30 (4): 743–759. https://doi.org/10.1111/hypa.12172.

Jollimore, Troy. 2011. *Love's Vision*, 1st edition. Princeton, NJ: Princeton University Press.

Larson, Kate. 2009. *"Everything Important Is to Do with Passion": Iris Murdoch's Concept of Love and Its Platonic Origin*. Uppsala: Department of Philosophy, Uppsala University. http://urn.kb.se/resolve?urn=urn:nbn:se:uu:diva-9532.

Mackenzie, Catriona, and Natalie Stoljar. 2000. "Introduction: Autonomy Refigured." In *Relational Autonomy: Feminist Perspectives on Autonomy, Agency, and the Social Self*, 1st edition, 3–31. New York: Oxford University Press.

Moreno, María Gila. 2019. "Análisis de los Conceptos de Responsabilidad y Deber en Iris Murdoch." Madrid: Universidad Complutense de Madrid.

Murdoch, Iris. 1999a. "Against Dryness." In *Existentialists and Mystics: Writings on Philosophy and Literature*, 287–295. New York: Penguin.

Murdoch, Iris. 1999b. "Knowing the Void." In *Existentialists and Mystics: Writings on Philosophy and Literature*, 157–160. New York: Penguin.

Murdoch, Iris. 1999c. "Metaphysics and Ethics." In *Existentialists and Mystics: Writings on Philosophy and Literature*, edited by Peter Conradi, 59–75. New York: Penguin.

Murdoch, Iris. 1999d. "On 'God' and 'Good.'" In *Existentialists and Mystics: Writings on Philosophy and Literature*, 337–362. New York: Penguin.

Murdoch, Iris. 1999e. "The Idea of Perfection." In *Existentialists and Mystics: Writings on Philosophy and Literature*, 299–336. New York: Penguin.

Murdoch, Iris. 1999f. "The Sovereignty of Good Over Other Concepts." In *Existentialists and Mystics: Writings on Philosophy and Literature*, 363–385. New York: Penguin.

Murdoch, Iris. 1999g. "Vision and Choice in Morality." In *Existentialists and Mystics: Writings on Philosophy and Literature*, 76–98. New York: Penguin.

Murdoch, Iris. 2003. *Metaphysics as a Guide to Morals*. New edition. London: Vintage Classics.

Nussbaum, Martha C. 2001. "When She Was Good." *The New Republic*, December 31, 2001. https://newrepublic.com/article/122264/iris-murdoch-novelist-and-philospher.

Rawls, John. 1999. *A Theory of Justice*, 2nd edition. Cambridge, MA: Belknap Press: An Imprint of Harvard University Press.

Robjant, David. 2012. "The Earthy Realism of Plato's Metaphysics, or: What Shall We Do with Iris Murdoch?: Philosophical Investigations." *Philosophical Investigations* 35 (1): 43–67. https://doi.org/10.1111/j.1467-9205.2011.01455.x.

Sartre, Jean-Paul. 2004. *Critique of Dialectical Reason: V. 1 by Sartre, Jean-Paul (2004) Paperback*. New edition edition. London & New York: Verso Books.

Sartre, Jean-Paul. 2015. *Being and Nothingness: An Essay on Phenomenological Ontology*, 2nd edition. London: Routledge.

Weil, Simone. 1970. *First and Last Notebooks: Supernatural Knowledge*, translated by Richard Rhees. Oxford: Oxford University Press.

White, Frances. 2018. "'It's Brown, It's Not in the Spectrum': The Problem of Justice in Iris Murdoch's Thought." In *Murdoch on Truth and Love*. New York; Secaucus: Palgrave Macmillan Springer.

17 Love, Activism, and Social Justice

Barrett Emerick

> I am more and more convinced that true revolutionaries must perceive the revolution, because of its creative and liberating nature, as an act of love.
>
> —*Pedagogy of the Oppressed*—Paulo Freire

It's common for those who are concerned with countering injustice to appeal to love as a remedy.[1] My project here is to think about the relationship between love and social justice activism, focusing in particular on ways in which activists rely on popular versions of traditional theoretical accounts of love or on claims that can be illuminated by those theoretical accounts. I will focus on three in particular—what I call the union, sentimentalist, and fate accounts of love, respectively.

I'll argue that all three, while appealing, can be seriously problematic when interpreted through too shallow a lens, as they tend either to obscure important differences in the ways that various groups are socially situated or to overlook the ways in which injustice can be structural. They also encourage inaction by suggesting that individuals' responsibility is adequately discharged simply by being differently oriented to oppressed others or by letting things unfold naturally.

None of this is to suggest that love has no place in social justice or in activists' efforts. Indeed, I follow Martin Luther King Jr. in claiming that we ought to be "extremists for love."[2] But that means rejecting empty platitudes that obscure structural social difference and going well beyond Pollyanna-style optimism that love is inevitably fated to secure justice in the long run. In short, though love is indeed valuable in working to achieve social justice, it is crucial that we be clear about to what that value amounts. It is my aim here to try to achieve some of that clarity.

In focusing on injustice, I'll not focus on the demands of interpersonal morality. I'll adopt Iris Marion Young's account of oppression—understanding it to be synonymous with injustice—specifically with regard to two important features of her view. The first is that oppression is a structural phenomenon that applies primarily to groups and only derivatively to individuals in virtue of their group membership.[3] Indeed, as Young argues much of our identities are "thrown" onto us and we find ourselves members of social groups, often involuntarily. Moreover, structural oppression is part of what causes that thrownness; you might well come to understand that part of what it means to be gendered or raced, to be able-bodied or disabled, to be of a particular nationality or cultural group, is determined by your social positioning relative to others. In short, part of what it means to say that oppression is structural is to say that it non-voluntarily helps to determine who we are. Second, part of what it means to say that oppression is structural is that it does not require particular perpetrators who overtly aim to oppress others. Indeed, few people in contemporary society likely have the power to affect whole social groups. (Heads of state, religious organizations, large corporations, etc., might all be exceptions to this claim.) Young's point is that, in general, we err if we think that eliminating oppression is as simple as eliminating individual bad actors or their actions. Instead, oppression is a part of the very fabric of contemporary social arrangements and is the kind of thing that can exist in an otherwise well-meaning and liberal society.[4]

By way of terminological definitions: I'm going to use the term "activist" very broadly to refer to those who aim to change social arrangements for the better. (Think, for instance, of those who after the 2016 U.S. election adopted the term "resistance"—either claiming to be a member of "the resistance" or using the hashtag "#resist" on bumper stickers or social media.) Obviously, this definition refers to a huge collection of people, many of whom might not think of themselves as activists, and some of whom might think of themselves as activists but whom we might want to exclude. My main reason for casting the net so wide is for ease of language and to be able to talk about both those who create hashtags or bumper sticker slogans and those who protest and engage in direct action. But I should say that this is primarily aimed at the former: at well-meaning, usually privileged folks who are concerned about social justice but who stay pretty superficial, both in act and analysis. My aim is not to attack those folks. Indeed, for reasons I'll unpack below the motivation to "resist" the global rise of fascism—literal Nazis marching in the streets—and the horror of such a display is totally understandable. But simply labeling one's self a part of "the resistance" is of course not enough to actually oppose or counter such horrors. My aim here is not to tell people that they *ought* to engage in such efforts but is instead to help unpack what doing so amounts to for those who sincerely claim to bear such commitments. I'll argue that some uses of "love" obscures just what making good on such commitments entails.

Finally, I want to be clear that I do not intend this accounting of love and its relationship to the achievement of social justice to be exhaustive. Indeed, love is a concept both broad and deep, with multiple meanings across cultures with deeply important personal implications, if not religious or cosmological implications, for most people. So, I want to stress that my goal here (despite its curmudgeonly undertones) really is to be constructive. Following Marilyn Friedman, philosophers rarely seem so silly as when they try to write analytically about something as central to human welfare and meaning-making as love.[5] It's easy for such work to appear bloodless and reductionist in a way that utterly ignores the significance of love itself. I have no interest in engaging in such reductionism, or of writing about love in a way that is utterly devoid of poetry. Nevertheless, I think there is value in turning an analytical lens toward the concept precisely because there is something of real significance to the relationship between love and social justice. Indeed, as someone who strives to be an "extremist for love," it's my aim to try to achieve some clarity about that relationship—to clear away some distracting underbrush—in order to enable it to flourish.

Part 1—Love as Union

The first account of love I'll consider is sometimes called the union, merger, or "federation" view. Developed notably by Robert Nozick and Marilyn Friedman, the union account says that to love someone involves extending the boundaries of the self, thereby creating a new entity—a "we"—in addition to the two already existing individuals.[6] You share in the fate of the one you love; when things go well or badly for the other, there is a meaningful sense in which they also go well or badly for you.[7] And, since love changes who you are, it affects what you perceive and how you experience the world.[8]

Both Nozick and Friedman talk about such merger primarily in terms of romantic love, but there is nothing in principle that prevents us from understanding the same expansion of the self to include those with whom we have non-romantic relationships. In her article, "You Mixed? Racial Identity Without Biology," Sally Haslanger describes her experience (as a white woman) of adopting and parenting two black children. Over time, her perceptions and experiences of the world changed. She says, "Racism is no longer just something I find offensive and morally objectionable; I experience it as a personal harm. There is an important sense in which a harm to my kids is a harm to me; by being open to the harm, I am more fully aware of the cost of racial injustice for all of us."[9] Since the boundaries of her identity are now broadened to include her children, when they are harmed, she is harmed as well.

If someone only loves people who occupy social locations similar to their own, it is no surprise when they fail to recognize oppressive social structures or ideologies. In this way, love can be transformative; though it is not guaranteed, truly loving someone who is differently socially located can help motivate profound shifts of one's perceptual abilities.

So far I've been talking about the union view of love in terms of interpersonal relationships. Can it be applied more broadly to refer to social groups rather than individuals? Does it make sense to say that you love (are part of a "we" with) a whole group of people, many of whom you have never met and will never meet? Even if we think those challenging ontological questions can be answered adequately, there are other equally serious worries we might have.

Consider that some activists (at least those who create hashtags and bumper stickers) rely on the concept of merger or union by making use of slogans like, "We're all in this together." Others claim something like: "When one person is oppressed everyone is oppressed." Perhaps here they riff off of King who said in his famous "Letter from Birmingham City Jail" that "Injustice anywhere is a threat to justice everywhere."[10] Environmental activists create the bumper sticker slogan that says, "We're all downstream," recognizing that pollution and climate change are global phenomena that affect everyone, and so everyone has a stake in combatting them. They might here be following Deep Ecologists like Warwick Fox who claimed that "The reason we should care about another's fate is not merely because it affects us, but because they are us."[11] This claim is an extension of the position's ontological holism, which breaks down boundaries between objects altogether.[12]

These are attractive sentiments; it's compelling to find solidarity and unity in thinking about oppressive social structures, since it's often the case that oppression operates by way of isolation and division. I have two concerns about such sentiments. The first is that each of these claims obscures real and significant differences in social position. We might all "be downstream" from corporate pollution, in that everyone faces some toxic elements in at least some food they eat or air they breathe, but some people are more downstream than others. Climate change is indeed a global phenomenon that will affect every living person, but of course some people will be (and already have been) vastly more affected by it than others. If you can afford to access food that is more (rather than less) free of toxic pollutants, if you can afford to live in an area that has cleaner air, then even though there might not be any food or any air that's perfectly clean, there is a world of difference between what you consume and what others who don't have that economic freedom can afford to consume.[13]

Furthermore, as I write this, the COVID-19 pandemic is ravaging the planet. As a great many people struggle with the economic, psychological, and physical costs of "social distancing" and having to "shelter in place," it's common to hear that "we're all in this together." As with climate change, of course the nature of a pandemic is that we *are* all affected by the virus in one way or another. However, when you contrast news reports of celebrities receiving excellent treatment for the virus with the staggering lack of adequate treatment (and even of tests) for the virus that will result in hundreds of thousands of avoidable deaths, it makes crystal clear that in reality we are *not* all in this together in the same way.

In short, my first worry with the focus on union or merger, when taken up by well-meaning activists who aim to stress solidarity, is that in doing so they embrace sameness of social position (or at least a framework that makes it harder to recognize difference of social position) and that doing so not only fails to achieve the goals activists set for themselves (the promotion of justice) but can positively hinder it.[14]

One common, underlying truth to each of the slogans above is that they recognize that humans are deeply vulnerable and profoundly social beings. Consider the appeal to "ubuntu"—following largely from Archbishop Desmond Tutu. One common definition says that "ubuntu" means "I am because we are" or "the belief in a universal bond of sharing that connects all humanity."[15] Ubuntu is a rich and complicated concept that has much to recommend it. Nothing I'll say here is intended to imply that it should be rejected. However, as it stands that definition is easy to misuse.

Consider as an alternative definition of ubuntu Antjie Krog's view which she analyzes as "interconnectedness-towards-wholeness," which understands persons to be importantly interconnected so that "one can only become who one is, or could be, through the fullness of that which is around one."[16] Both definitions reverse the order of the traditional Western account of the relationship between individuals and communities. Instead of focusing first on individuals and then recognizing the way that they make up communities, we instead start with the community and think about ways that they constitute individuals.

Finally, though not specifically about ubuntu, consider King's famous claim that "In a real sense, all life is interrelated. All men are caught in an inescapable network of mutuality, tied in a single garment of destiny. Whatever affects one directly affects all indirectly. I can never be what I ought to be until you are what you ought to be, and you can never be what you ought to be until I am what I ought to be. This is the interrelated structure of reality."[17]

Each of these claims is consistent with Young's analysis of social groups which recognizes that part of who we are is thrown on to us; that the social groups of which we are members help to determine our identities, often without our consent. I am very sympathetic to the claim that people are mostly socially constructed beings and that we all become who we are always via social connection with others. However, despite our profoundly social nature we should resist a conclusion that blurs the lines between individuals altogether, not only because (as I've been arguing) some people are more "downstream" than others) but also because the focus on being bound up in the same circumstances precludes from the beginning the possibility of exit from those circumstances, which is often what oppressed people want or need. Some people don't *want* to be "in this together"; indeed, very often the aim of liberatory efforts is to help oppressed people to no longer be in oppressive relation to others and to escape social positions of domination or subordination. Sometimes such escape is impossible. But sometimes escape *is* possible; sometimes oppressed groups *can* leave those who contribute to or benefit from their oppression behind and not continue to be interconnected with them. We can agree that we are all interconnected with others, and that through that interconnectedness we might be able to become more full and complete people, and deny that any particular relationship (in this case that of the oppressed and the privileged) ought to be maintained.

This point is seen more clearly through an interpersonal lens. Though I won't argue for it here, I believe that we all have duties not only to promote the welfare of others but also to promote our own welfare.[18] One way to satisfy that duty might be to avoid interconnectedness with those who are harmful. In short, socially constructed though we may be, we are capable of choosing (at least some of the time) who to be interconnected with and we satisfy our self-regarding duties by exiting those relationships of interconnectedness that do not promote our welfare. The same is true when viewing things structurally: sometimes what justice requires is for groups *not* to continue to interact or be bound up with each other, for colonizing countries to leave, for companies to stop polluting, for capitalism to stop disrupting local economies, etc. In short: we should be reluctant to embrace too deeply the claim that "we're all in this together" because sometimes the best way forward is for someone to be able to jettison harmful others from their lives.

One might object that I am being overly optimistic in thinking that exit is possible, given how thoroughly interwoven are the various systems of oppression in our profoundly unjust world. Though one might be able (some of the time) to exit harmful interpersonal relationships (and to *not* be "in this together" with particular agents of oppression), in the world as it is there might not be a place to which one could escape from white supremacy, sexism, and capitalism (and the myriad ways in which they relate, build off of, and exacerbate each other). I don't deny this. Nevertheless, it's important that we remain critical of the slogan that we're all in this together, since our goal should be not to coexist within oppressive systems but to overthrow those systems. The goal should not be to find a way for rich people and poor people to get along; instead, we should aim for the abolition of poverty and wealth and the economic systems that make such disparity possible. Return to the COVID-19 pandemic. If we are to take away from the fact that the wealthy and powerful are "in this together" with everyone else, we lose some of the conceptual space that we need to overthrow a system that privileges the wealthy in such circumstances. Thinking that we are all in this together reentrenches the existence of that system by encouraging us to focus on how to operate within it, rather than to challenge it.

So, the superficial account of merger is problematic because it obscures important features of the social world that need to be clear. And, the deep account of merger (relying on the ontological claim about our socially constructed nature) is problematic because it seems to obscure the possibility of severing oppressive relationships between groups or of challenging the oppressive systems themselves. Is there another way forward?

Consider U.S. presidential candidate Bernie Sanders' conclusion to a speech when he asked the crowd: "Are you willing to fight for that person who you don't even know as much as you're willing to fight for yourself?" he asked. "Are you willing to fight for young people drowning in student debt even if you are not? Are you willing to fight to ensure that every American has health care as a human right even if you have good health care? Are you willing to fight for frightened immigrant neighbors even if you are native born?"[19] Sanders is here calling people to be willing to fight on behalf of strangers—those they do not know and will never know. He therefore cannot be endorsing the type of union account of love that relies on intimacy and close connection. He also doesn't suggest that people ought to fight on behalf of others who are similarly socially situated; indeed, in each example he asks if the crowd would fight for others who are oppressed even if they themselves are privileged. This, it seems to me, is calling for real and meaningful political solidarity that does not erase difference but recognizes that social structures position some people hierarchically relative to others.[20]

To be clear, I am not suggesting (nor, I take it, was Sanders suggesting) that privileged folks ought to jump in to organizing work without understanding the implications of their efforts, nor should they do so in a way that centers attention on them or refocuses the larger narrative around their efforts or agency. Following Linda Alcoff, I'm arguing that privileged folks ought to "wherever possible aim to speak with rather than for"[21] others—to not make the conversation about them, but to ensure that those who might otherwise be easy to ignore, and with whom they are in deep solidarity, are able to speak and be heard.[22]

Few write so beautifully about love and its relationship to activism as Paulo Freire in his classic *Pedagogy of the Oppressed*. In it he argues that what he calls dialogue or revolutionary and liberatory remaking of the world "Cannot exist in the absence of a profound love for the world and for people. The naming of the world, which is an act of creation and re-creation, is not possible if it is not infused with love. Love is at the same time the foundation of dialogue and dialogue itself.... Because love is an act of courage, not of fear, love is commitment to others. No matter where the oppressed are found, the act of love is commitment to their cause—the cause of liberation."[23] Later, he argues that "Solidarity requires that one enter into the situation of those with whom one is solidary; it is a radical posture.... [T]rue solidarity with the oppressed means fighting at their side to transform the oppressive reality which has made them these 'beings for another'."[24] But being in true solidarity is not mere endorsement of a political position or concern for/caring about the situation of others. Instead, what Freire calls for, and what true solidarity involves, is that privileged people should be "Accomplices, not allies."[25] I take this at least to mean that privileged people ought not be a bystander or superficial support from the sidelines for those who are doing the actual liberatory work but should instead be deeply invested in that work in a way that both implicates them and leaves them exposed to penalty or sanction. It does not imply hierarchy or separateness, where one person fights for (and is the hero of) another, but instead means working side by side in a horizontal relationship that avoids maintaining a relationship where one party is subordinate (because one party needs saving).[26]

In short: the deep rather than shallow union account of love enables genuine collaboration between parties rather than mere support from the sidelines. But even then it should always do so self-critically in a way that aims to avoid reinscribing power relations that center already privileged voices and perspectives while continuing to marginalize others. One way to do this is for privileged activists to make their aim to promote the autonomy of those who have less power. Marilyn Friedman defines autonomy as "reflecting on one's deeper wants, values, and commitments, reaffirming them, and behaving and living in accordance with them even in the face of at least minimal resistance from others."[27] This conclusion goes beyond simply asking how to achieve the goals that oppressed others would autonomously pursue, but to help create the conditions where oppressed others are able to act autonomously in the first place.[28] Indeed, when we recognize (following Young) that oppression is structural, our aim should be to transform social circumstances to enable autonomous action.[29]

Part 2—Love and Sentiment

The second type of love that is sometimes employed by activists regards the attitudes we take up toward others—most notably toward our adversaries. I call this account the "sentimental" account of love, and I take it to have at least two features.

The first is that love is fundamentally affective or attitudinal; it's about how we feel or are oriented toward one another, and the fundamental problem with politics or social arrangements more generally is that we aren't oriented toward each other in the rights ways. The second feature, born from the first, is that it calls us to harken back to an earlier time when people were simply kinder, more patient, more willing to work with and understand those who hold different perspectives, and more concerned with decency, civility, and respectful citizenship than they were within the divisive tribalism we now face.

As an example of the sentimental account of love, consider Gandhi's famous claim that one should "be the change you want to see in the world." There are at least two ways to interpret what that means, one shallow, and one deep. I'll turn to the deep meaning shortly, but for now I take it that, when adopted superficially, what this claim amounts to is simply that everyone needs to be nicer to each other, that small acts of kindness when added together can be revolutionary, and that we all ought to find something to like or value about those with whom we disagree.

Sometimes those who employ the sentimentalist account of love and who make this kind of argument do so by appealing to King's repeated calls for us to love our enemy. And, of course he did—but the kind of love he called for was not reducible to mere sentiment.[30] King drew the traditional distinction between three types of love and then argued repeatedly and across many sermons and speeches for the last: agape, which he defined as creative, redemptive goodwill toward everyone. Agape requires that we recognize the spark of divinity in all people, believe in their capacity in every moment to go in a new direction, and always to hope that they will do so.

This forward-looking pursuit of positive change in your enemy is not the same thing as finding something to like about the other, nor does recognizing the spark of divinity require that you feel positively about them. Indeed, King notes in multiple texts that it's possible to love without liking the other person at all. Instead, it is precisely because agape is forward-looking that it sets demands for the other, not to take them as they are and find something to appreciate or value about them, despite their terrible politics or past actions, but to expect them to transcend their old ways and become better.

Note also that this does not imply that the loving activist ought to be willing to work together with their adversary to find common ground. Indeed, when dealing with fascists or Nazis there may be no common ground to find, nothing with which to be patient. This is perhaps in tension with the Gandhian tradition of nonviolence which starts from the fallibilist assumption that no knowledge is perfect and that everyone has something to say so we ought to be open to engaging in dialogue or argumentation with those whom we oppose.[31] Indeed, I think we've all heard quite enough from the Nazis and members of the Klan and there's nothing more to learn from them (at least regarding things like race).

Much ink has been spilled in the last few years debating not only whether it's ok to "punch Nazis" but whether we ought to engage in dialogue with "the other side," and whether we ought to "reach across the aisle" to find common ground with interlocutors with whom we disagree. I won't explore the first question (when physical violence is justified) and I won't settle any debate about the limits and requirements of civil discourse here (though I have written about it elsewhere[32]). However, I do want to spend some time exploring the claim that activists ought to be motivated by love, or that love ought to guide their actions, and that both suggest that we ought to be nice or kind to our enemies. In other words, even if you agree that we don't need to "hear out" the other side, you might still think we need to "work with" the other side, or to be willing to compromise. And, in particular, you might take the sentimental account of love to mean that, at the end of the day, we simply need to be loving toward each other, and that means being civil or nice to each other.

It is obviously true that there are times, strategically, where compromise is called for, in which you make concessions on some points or in negotiating certain outcomes but judge those concessions to be worthwhile, since making them serves some larger end. I cannot here specify when such compromise is called for, since doing so would require real-world knowledge of particular political gains that activists anticipate they would secure by making such concessions. Instead, my point here is to note that when people invoke King (or Christianity, or vaguely Christian norms more broadly) when calling for us all simply to be nicer to and more civil toward one's adversary, they fail to remember what I noted at the outset, which is that King calls not for moderation, but for extremism, not for compromise, but for the defeat of injustice wherever it lives. There is no reason whatsoever for thinking that the kind of love King was after—agape—means being either merely nice or civil.

Consider two recent cases of this kind of niceness and civility, both of which might (when pressed) get bound up with a more foundational commitment to being loving. In 2019, comedian and talk show host Ellen DeGeneres was roundly criticized for being friends with former U.S. President George W. Bush. The next day DeGeneres addressed the controversy on her show saying, "I'm friends with George Bush. In fact, I'm friends with a lot of people who don't share the same beliefs that I have. Just because I don't agree with someone on everything doesn't mean that I'm not going to be friends with them," Ellen concluded. "When I say, 'Be kind to one another,' I don't mean only the people that think the same way that you do. I mean, 'Be kind to everyone, it doesn't matter.'"[33] What could be wrong with universal kindness? And don't we, after all, "Defeat our enemies when we make them our friends"[34]? Isn't the way to bring about a world devoid of violence and conflict to regard everyone else *not* as an adversary to be opposed but as someone with whom you can watch a football game?

Poor George W. Bush; just a few weeks later his friendship with former First Lady Michelle Obama also caused public scrutiny. In an interview on The Today Show Obama said of Bush: "Our values are the same. We disagree on policy but we don't disagree on humanity. We don't disagree about love and compassion. I think that's true for all of us."[35] What Obama meant is unclear, and to be fair, she made that statement in an interview (and not as a prepared statement) so it might not have been as carefully worded as it otherwise would have been. But to try to achieve some of that clarity now, and with an eye toward charity, it seems like the best interpretation we can offer is that both Bush and Obama are committed to being loving in two capacities: the first is to do so within interpersonal relationships; the second is to do so more broadly and impersonally. We can grant that the first is true of Bush, that he loves his family, friends, and the members of his church, for instance. But Bush is a former two-term president of the United States of America whose actions in that office caused innumerable, hugely significant, and enormously horrific global effects. To think of Bush as manifesting the shared value of love only in an interpersonal sense is at best to fail to say anything interesting about love itself and at worst to dramatically distort our understanding of the issue at hand.

Consider an analogue: it is common in the United States for politicians to claim that we ought to apply the same principles to the U.S. economy that families do to their own budgets; in short, they claim that we ought to have "kitchen table" conversations about how to not overspend as a country. This is, on but a moment's reflection, an utterly ridiculous comparison to make, since the two budgets are many orders of magnitude different both in size and complexity (not to mention that the economy is what sets the terms for personal financial decisions to be possible in the first place). Obama makes the same error when thinking about the ways in which she and Bush share the same values: his commitment to the value of love clearly did not extend to the brown bodies that he bombed in Iraq and Afghanistan, nor to the LGBTQ bodies whose rights he undermined and violated, nor to those bodies who have been and will be destroyed by climate change, and on, and on. Those are not just disagreements about "policy"; if someone can do the things that Bush did and still be someone who should be viewed as committed to the value of love, then we should abandon that commitment.

What about DeGeneres' claim that what we all ought to do is be kind to one another (and in this case, to be kind to Bush and to be his friend, despite their policy disagreements)? DeGeneres does "kindness" a disservice here, for she interprets it to be far more vapid and empty than she should. I'm not saying that DeGeneres should have made a scene on national TV and I recognize that moments like that often sail by before we realize we have an opportunity to act. But in DeGeneres' case she went on to defend not just sitting next to Bush and having a pleasant time at the game with him, but to claim friendship with him, along with a fundamental commitment to being kind to everyone. Kindness is not niceness, nor is it civility. Real kindness that moves beyond exchanging simple pleasantries or maintaining a pleasant disposition involves caring about others as complete people, including as moral agents. That means holding them to account for what they have done and expecting them to be better than their past selves.[36] If DeGeneres really cares about Bush and really wants to be kind to him as his friend, she should hold him to account for his past and press him to do all that he can for the rest of his life to try to make up for it.[37]

One might object that all this holds DeGeneres and Obama (and all of us) to too high a standard; we can only control our own actions (and cannot control what others do) and so we ought to set for ourselves the commitment to being kind and loving and leave it at that. Not only does this account of responsibility encourage inaction (a point to which I'll return in the next section), it also encourages an account of friendship, love, and indeed of what it means to be a person (as deeply social beings) that are unworthy of those terms. What a lonely world it would be if everyone truly only was concerned for their own actions and didn't participate in the identity formation and moral development of others. To the contrary, we should adopt a deep understanding of Gandhi's claim that we should be the change we want to see in the world. Instead of letting ourselves off the hook for bringing about real structural change by focusing exclusively on our own emotional dispositions—on not having hatred in our hearts or on being nice to others—we should aim to prefigure the future we want to bring about by focusing hard on the redemptive aspect of agape. Love, for King, is an *expectation*, a *demand*, that all of us exercise agency responsibly, that we dedicate ourselves to promoting justice, and that in truly loving our neighbors we see them as whole people who are flawed but could be better. And, it means doing the same thing for ourselves; it means that we all must strive to recognize the ways in which everyone who operates within oppressive social structures can be complicit in their maintenance or caught up in their enforcing ideologies and then doing the hard work of expressing through our actions a claim to the dignity and equality of everyone. In short, we can't achieve the redemptive aspect of agape without an honest accounting of the wrongs for which agents must be redeemed, and niceness and civility do not achieve such an accounting.

Part 3—Love and Fate

The final type of love is what I'll call "love as fate." Activists have at times relied on the idea that a loving orientation to or regard for oppressed others (or for those privileged groups who maintain oppressive relations) inevitably achieves social justice. For instance, consider popular slogans like "In This House, Love Wins," or "Love Trumps Hate" along with hopeful sentiments like the claim that it is in love's nature to triumph over hatred and injustice or the claim that "love is all you need."

One reason to be concerned about using such slogans is that they send the message that love is a force that exists independent of human agency. All we have to do is open our hearts and let love take over. Just as gravity causes a book to fall to the ground when bumped off a table, love causes things to get better, causes the "moral arc of the universe to bend towards justice," causes the inevitable downfall of those wicked people who are in power, and the inevitable victory of those who oppose them.[38]

But of course love is not a force like gravity and acting like it is enables inaction. As the recent global resurgence of fascism has made enormously clear, to believe that states of affairs in the social world inevitably move toward any outcome—including progress—is folly. Instead, *social movement happens because there are social movers*—those who work to change social arrangements, either for the better or worse.

Indeed, Kathryn Norlock argues convincingly that it's a mistake not only to think that our moral trajectory is toward something better, but that it's a mistake to think that there is a moral trajectory at all. She says, countering the claim that social justice advocacy is a Sisyphean task, "There is no hill. There is no upwards and no backwards. Our attraction to directional metaphors betrays a wishful thinking that moral progress and ambitious policies are achievements with endpoints that we can reach if we just get closer to them."[39] Instead, there is only the diligent work of imperfect human agents who have chosen to strive toward particular outcomes. Though it is tempting to take the long view of history and draw some common thread from a series of events, ideological developments, or changes in the social imaginary, we should be careful not to attribute any causal origin to those things other than that diligent work.

One reason why this point is worth making is that to view love as a force that brings about goodness in the world—to believe not only in fate but in fate that spirals progressively upwards toward justice—is that it encourages inaction or quietism. If love really does win, if it is the destiny of love to vanquish hate, then I don't have to work to bring that about. This concern becomes more pronounced when coupled with the sentimental account of love developed in the previous section: if love really is *all* that others need, if it is the most powerful tool or weapon at our disposal, and if love is an emotion or an attitude internal to me, then by simply having love in my heart or being lovingly oriented toward the world, I have done what morality requires of me and am in that way a conduit for that force to do its work, a place for fate to unfold. In short, understanding love as fate helps to justify my inaction.

Such inaction is totally understandable: there is so much injustice in the world that having to take on the task of working to make it better is terribly overwhelming. It is therefore very tempting to adopt a worldview that relieves you of that responsibility. Moreover, it's not just tempting but often positively needed. Research in social psychology supports the claim that we need to believe in the just world hypothesis: that the world is basically just, that social arrangements are fundamentally stable and dependable, and that I as an individual actor am essentially good, even if I sometimes do bad things.[40] To fail to take up this perspective is to open oneself to the threat of being crushed not just by the weight of how much work there is to be done, and not only to my own near constant moral failure, by the utter horror that pervades the world and of which people are capable.

Indeed, this is perhaps part of why King wrote things like, "Love is the most durable power in the world. It is the most potent instrument available in mankind's quest for peace and security,"[41] and "Evil is doomed; good is inexorably the victor."[42] Those kinds of claims can be read to imply the kind of fated, guaranteed outcome that could enable quietism. And, when reduced to a slogan or put on a bumper sticker they might have that effect. However, to reiterate, King's view was considerably more complex than it is often taken to be and he called many ways of talking about love "sentimental bosh."[43] My point here is that we can acknowledge, on one hand, the need to believe that the fight not only can but will be won while remaining committed to the fight itself and remembering, on the other hand, that there being a fight implies there are fighters who actively work to bring about that victory.

In other words, the shallow version of love as fate enables inaction while the deep version recognizes both the magnitude of the fight and the frailty of human motivation. I have much more patience for this latter implication than the former—much more patience for needing to believe that "love wins" because the alternative is too horrible rather than wanting to believe that love wins because doing so let's you off the hook. But it is worth noting that despite the need to believe in the inevitable and fated progress love ensures we will achieve as a society, that belief is not true and if we want to take seriously the psychological need to believe it, we tell ourselves a noble lie in order to continue going about our days and getting out of bed in the morning. All that said, the second sense of this thesis—that we need to believe that love wins— serves to avoid the pitfalls of the first—that love's fated victory lets us off the hook. If we don't believe and bet on the outcome that love wins, it would indeed be very difficult—perhaps impossible—to go about trying to achieve that outcome. So, instead of a noble lie perhaps we should understand it as a version of Pascal's wager: it's better to bet on love winning than not, because even though we might lose, if we don't make that bet we are sure to do so.

Part 4—Conclusion

It's attractive for activists to employ love (or related concepts) in their work for a variety of reasons—motivational, epistemic, perceptual, prefigurative, and to break down oppressive group boundaries by merging groups altogether. But it's also perilous to do so, since it can reentrench oppressive relations between privileged and subordinated groups, inspire quietism, justify a retreat to the interpersonal and away from the structural, and cause a failure to recognize the ways in which social location leaves some groups more exposed to oppressive harm than others. It's vital, then, for activists to retain a clear understanding not only of what they mean when employing the language of love, but what outcomes such theoretical commitments imply.

At the same time, I am persuaded by King and Freire's repeated claims that we must remain hopeful about both the achievement of justice and about the lives and potential of those privileged people who benefit from or maintain oppressive social structures. What King called agape we might tie with Freire's account of hope. He says, "Hope is rooted in men's incompletion, from which they move out in constant search—a search which can be carried out only in communion with others."[44] We should start from the open-endedness of human agency that Norlock describes; though there is no guarantee that people will act rightly or be better in the future than they have in the past, we can work actively to encourage each other to do so.

Though I said at the outset that I join King in thinking that we all should be extremists for love I admit that at times I struggle to understand what that entails. Such struggle is both necessary and always ongoing; being an extremist for love is the kind of identity it takes a lifetime to explore and cultivate. That said, I also feel certain that part of what being an extremist for love means is that we can use love not only to inspire our efforts but to help set our agendas in the first place, to help determine the aims of the political struggles we take up. At the end of the introduction to *Pedagogy of the Oppressed* Freire says, "From these pages I hope at least the following will endure: my trust in the people, and my faith in men and women, and in the creation of a world in which it will be easier to love."[45] What if we set that as our goal: *to create a world in which it will be easier to love?* Surely such a world would be worth fighting to achieve.

Notes

1. Many thanks to Rachel Fedock, Jennifer Kling, Michael Kühler, Mark Lance, and Audrey Yap, for their invaluable insight and critique.
2. King (1986, 297).
3. Young (1998, 273–276).
4. Young (1998, 271).
5. Friedman (2003, 116).
6. Nozick (1989, 71).
7. Friedman (2003, 122).
8. Friedman (2003, 122).
9. Haslanger (2005, 282).
10. King (1986, 290).
11. Fox (1984, 200).
12. Fox (1984, 199).
13. See Tessman (2005, 98–106) for a helpful discussion of this point.

14. I recognize that many activists might call for solidarity or union without appealing (or intending to appeal) to love. I'm not suggesting that whenever one does the former one necessarily does the latter. But I think it's not unusual to hear well-meaning folks refer to how we should "love the world" or "love humanity" while also talking about being in solidarity with them in a way that suggests the two sometimes go together in people's minds. In short, these kinds of claims, though not explicitly invoking love (the word doesn't appear in the slogan that "We're All Downstream"), are at least love-adjacent appeals.
15. As with many of the slogans I'll consider, these definitions are commonly said and it's hard to pinpoint an originating source. As evidence that these rich concepts can be watered down (and commodified), consider that you can learn about "the essence of ubuntu" by staying at a resort named Ubuntu Luxury Villa that employs both of these quotes: https://www.ubuntuvilla.com/the-essence-of-ubuntu/
16. Krog (2008, 355). Krog is here relying on and further unpacking the moral concept of "ubuntu." For very helpful additional analysis of the concept, see Metz (2007).
17. King (2010, 69).
18. The claim that we have self-regarding duties is controversial in contemporary Western normative ethics; many think that we have merely prudential (but not moral) reasons to commit self-regarding actions. I cannot argue for the stronger position here but just note that traditional normative theories (like Kantian and Rossian deontology) both make clear that it is not only rational to act in ways that demonstrate self-respect or promote our own welfare but are morally obligatory as well. For instance, according to the Kantian it would be wrong (and not merely imprudent) to treat myself as a mere means to an end. For the Rossian it would be wrong (and not merely imprudent) for me to fail to cultivate my own wisdom and virtue.
19. Ember (2019).
20. See Krishnamurthy (2013) for a very helpful analysis of political solidarity and survey of views in the literature.
21. Alcoff (1992, 23).
22. Also very helpful is Mark Lance's discussion in his manuscript, "Speaking For, Speaking With, and Shutting Up: Models of Solidarity and the Pragmatics of Truth Telling."
23. Freire (2012, 89).
24. Freire (2012, 49).
25. Indigenous Action (2014).
26. Freire says, "No pedagogy which is truly liberating can remain distant from the oppressed by treating them as unfortunates and by presenting for their emulation models from among the oppressors. The oppressed must be their own example in the struggle for their redemption." Freire (2012, 54).
27. Friedman (2003, 99).
28. One might worry that union views threaten to erase distinctions between individuals which would render such autonomy promotion impossible (see Soble 1997). One reason why I adopt Friedman's account is that she aims to preserve the separateness of individuals who make up a particular union and thereby enable such autonomy promotion, while reframing autonomy (and autonomy competence) as being grounded in our relational nature. In short, because we are profoundly social beings we are able to develop (or are prevented from developing) the capacity to act autonomously always

via social interaction with others. So, on Friedman's account the following three things are true: (1) We are relational beings; (2) Loving relationships entail union among their members; and (3) We are discrete beings who can (in principle if not always in practice) disrupt or leave those relationships.
29. Serene Khader raises important concerns about the ways in which Westerners might try to promote the autonomy of non-Westerners but end up reinforcing oppressive structures, especially capitalism. Truly promoting the autonomy of others is tricky, to say the least. See Khader (2019, 76–98).
30. King (2010, 46).
31. May (2015, 75).
32. Emerick (Forthcoming).
33. Grady (2019).
34. This quote has been attributed to a variety of people including Abraham Lincoln. King says something similar when he tells us that "Love transforms enemies into friends." King (2010, 48).
35. Henderson (2019).
36. Emerick (2016).
37. One might object that challenging Bush publicly would humiliate him and not only undermine the obligation to be kind but would undermine the goal of pressing him to be better (since he might then become more defensive and less willing to take responsibility for his past wrongs). I am not calling for DeGeneres to humiliate Bush. However, in portraying him as someone with whom she merely disagrees politically, she surely swings much too far in the other direction and lets him off the hook entirely.
38. King (1986, 252). With this famous quote, King was paraphrasing 19th century Unitarian minister Theodore Parker.
39. Norlock (2019, 16).
40. Jost (2002).
41. King (2010, 51).
42. King (2010, 76).
43. King (2010, 46).
44. Freire (2012, 91–92).
45. Freire (2012, 40).

References

Alcoff, Linda. 1992. "The Problem of Speaking for Others." *Cultural Critique* 20 (Winter): 5–32.

Ember, Sydney. October 19, 2019. "Proclaiming 'I Am Back,' Bernie Sanders Accepts Ocasio-Cortez Endorsement." *The New York Times*. https://www.nytimes.com/2019/10/19/us/politics/bernie-sanders-aoc-queensbridge-park.html.

Emerick, Barrett. 2016. "Love and Resistance: Moral Solidarity in the Face of Perceptual Failure," *Feminist Philosophy Quarterly*, 2 (2): 1–21. http://ir.lib.uwo.ca/fpq/vol2/iss2/1 DOI: 10.5206/fpq/2016.2.1.

Emerick, Barrett. Forthcoming, "The Limits of the Rights to Free Thought and Expression," *Kennedy Institute of Ethics Journal*, Johns Hopkins University Press.

Fox, Warwick. 1984. "Deep Ecology: A New Philosophy of Our Time?" *The Ecologist* 14 (5, 6): 194–200.

Freire, Paulo. 2012. *Pedagogy of the Oppressed*. New York, NY: Bloomsbury Academic.

Friedman, Marilyn. 2003. *Autonomy, Gender, Politics*. Oxford: Oxford University Press.

Grady, Constance. Oct. 9, 2019. "Ellen Built Her Brand on Being Nice to Anyone, Even George W. Bush. That Brand Might Not Be Viable Now." Vox.com: https://www.vox.com/culture/2019/10/9/20906371/ellen-degeneres-george-w-bush-controversy.

Haslanger, Sally. 2005. "You Mixed? Racial Identity without Racial Biology." In *Adoption Matters: Philosophical And Feminist Essays*, edited by Sally Haslanger and Charlotte Witt. Ithaca, NY: Cornell University Press: 265–289.

Henderson, Cydney. Dec. 11, 2019. "Michelle Obama Defends Friendship with George W. Bush." *USA Today*: https://www.usatoday.com/story/entertainment/celebrities/2019/12/11/michelle-obama-defends-friendship-george-w-bush/4402339002/.

Indigenous Action. 2014. "Accomplices Not Allies: Abolishing the Ally Industrial Complex.": http://www.indigenousaction.org/accomplices-not-allies-abolishing-the-ally-industrial-complex/.

Jost, John, and Orsolya Hunyady. 2002. "The Psychology of System Justification and the Palliative Function of Ideology." *European Review of Social Psychology* 13: 111–153.

Khader, Serene. 2019. *Decolonizing Universalism: A Transnational Feminist Ethic*. New York: Oxford University Press.

King Jr., Martin Luther. 2010. *Strength to Love*. Minneapolis, MD: Augsburg Fortress Press.

King, Jr., Martin Luther. 1986. "Letter from Birmingham City Jail," in A Testament of Hope: The Essential Writings and Speeches of Martin Luther King, Jr., edited by James M. Washington, New York, NY: HarperCollins Publishers: 289–302.

Krishnamurthy, Meena. 2013. "Political Solidarity, Justice and Public Health," *Public Health Ethics*, 6 (2): 129–141.

Krog, Antjie. 2008. "'This Thing Called Reconciliation…' Forgiveness as Part of an Interconnectedness—Towards-Wholeness." *South African Journal of Philosophy* 27: 353–366.

Lance, Mark. Manuscript. "Speaking For, Speaking With, and Shutting Up: Models of Solidarity and the Pragmatics of Truth Telling."

May, Todd. 2015. *Nonviolent Resistance: A Philosophical Introduction*. Cambridge: Polity Press.

Metz, Thaddeus. 2007. "Toward an African Moral Theory." *The Journal of Political Philosophy* 15: 321–341.

Norlock, Kathryn J. 2019. "Perpetual Struggle," *Hypatia*, 34 (1): 6–19.

Nozick, Robert. 1989. "Love." In *The Examined Life*. New York, NY: Simon & Schuster: 68–86.

Soble, Alan. 1997. "Union, Autonomy, and Concern." In *Love Analyzed*, edited by Roger E. Lamb, Boulder: Westview Press: 65–92.

Tessman, Lisa. 2005. *Burdened Virtues: Virtue Ethics for Liberatory Struggles*. Oxford: Oxford University Press.

Young, Iris Marion. 1988. "Five Faces of Oppression." *The Philosophical Forum* 16 (4): 270–290.

Contributors

Barrett Emerick is an Associate Professor of Philosophy at St. Mary's College of Maryland. He works in social philosophy, moral psychology, and normative ethics, focusing in particular on gender, racial, and restorative justice. Related publications include "The Limits of the Rights to Free Thought and Expression," *Kennedy Institute of Ethics Journal*, Johns Hopkins University Press, forthcoming; "The Violence of Silencing," *Pacifism, Politics, and Feminism: Intersections and Innovations*, edited by Jennifer Kling. Leiden, The Netherlands: Brill Rodopi, 2019; "Love and Resistance: Moral Solidarity in the Face of Perceptual Failure," *Feminist Philosophy Quarterly*, 2 (2), 2016: 1–21, URL: http://ir.lib.uwo.ca/fpq/vol2/iss2/1. DOI: 10.5206/fpq/2016.2.1.

Rachel Fedock is a Senior Lecturer and Honors Faculty Fellow at Barrett, the Honors College at Arizona State University. She is also an affiliate faculty member of the Center for the Study of Race and Democracy at Arizona State University. Her research interests include ethics, feminist ethics, Black feminism, gender, race, moral psychology, the philosophy of love, and care. Currently, she is revising her paper, "The Moral Phenomenon of Care," while also exploring the intersections between love, care, and respect from a feminist perspective.

Niklas Forsberg is the Head of Research at the *Centre for Ethics as Study in Human Value*, Department of Philosophy, University of Pardubice, Czech Republic; and Docent (associate professor) in Theoretical Philosophy at Uppsala University, Sweden, and in Philosophy at University of Helsinki, Finland. A large portion of Forsberg's research deals with problems found at the intersection between theoretical philosophy, ethics, and aesthetics. He has written papers about thinkers such as Austin, Cavell, Coetzee, Collingwood, Emerson, Murdoch, Kierkegaard, and Wittgenstein, discussing various topics such as pain, sin, love, language, and literature's relation to philosophy and philosophical argumentation. He is the author of *Language Lost and Found: On Iris Murdoch and the Limits of Philosophical Discourse* (New York: Bloomsbury, 2013 [pbk. 2015]).

Contributors

Marilyn Friedman is a retired professor of philosophy whose final appointment was as W. Alton Jones Professor of Philosophy at Vanderbilt University in Nashville, Tennessee. Her research interests fall in the areas of ethics, social philosophy, and feminist thought, and they include works on the topics of autonomy, friendship, justice, and women's social and political standing. In these areas and among other works, Friedman has authored: *What Are Friends For?: Feminist Perspectives on Personal Relationships and Moral Theory*, Cornell University Press, Ithaca, New York, 1993; and *Autonomy, Gender, Politics*, Oxford University Press, New York, 2003. Friedman has also edited *Women and Citizenship*, Oxford University Press, New York, 2005.

Shane Gronholz is a lecturer in the philosophy department at Gonzaga University. He works on metaethics, practical rationality, special obligations, and well-being. His recent publications include "Welfare: Does Thinking Make It So?" in: *Social Theory and Practice* 46/2, 2020, 299–316; and "Moral Reasons as Other-Regarding Reasons," in: *Ethical Perspectives* 25/2, 2018, 285–319.

Carter Johnson is a doctoral candidate in philosophy and instructor at the School of Historical, Philosophical, and Religious Studies at Arizona State University. His research interests include philosophy of sex, philosophy of love, and ethics. Currently, he is working on his dissertation entitled *Universal Love as a Moral Ideal*.

Troy Jollimore is a Professor in the Philosophy Department at California State University, Chico. His research interests include normative ethics (especially personal relationships), esthetics (especially philosophy of poetry), practical reasoning, and applied ethics. He is also a poet and has published three books of poetry, the first of which (Tom Thomson in Purgatory, 2006) won the National Book Critics Circle Award. He was a Guggenheim Fellow (poetry) in 2013. His academic publications include *Love's Vision* (Princeton, 2013); "'This Endless Space Between the Words': The Limits of Love in Spike Jonzes's *Her*." *Midwest Studies in Philosophy*, vol. 39, 2015; "Miserably Ever After: Forgetting, Denying and Affirming Love in *Eternal Sunshine of the Spotless Mind*," in Christopher Grau, ed., *Eternal Sunshine of the Spotless Mind (Philosophers on Film)*, Routledge, 2009.

Angelika Krebs holds the chair for practical philosophy at the University of Bâle in Switzerland. Her research focuses on applied and general ethics, the philosophy of emotion, aesthetics, and political philosophy. She edited together with Aaron Ben-Ze'ev the four-volume collection *Philosophy of Emotion* with Routledge in 2017. Her two major books on love are *Arbeit und Liebe* with Suhrkamp in 2002 and *Zwischen Ich und Du. Eine dialogische Philosophie der Liebe* again with Suhrkamp in 2015.

Nora Kreft is an Assistant Professor at the Institute of Philosophy at Humboldt University, Berlin. She works on the philosophy of love, moral psychology, and philosophy of antiquity. Her recent publications include "Love and Autonomy," in: *The Oxford Handbook of Philosophy of Love*, edited by Chris Grau & Aaron Smuts, Oxford University Press, 2018; "Aristotle on Friendship and Being Human," in: *Aristotle's Anthropology*, edited by Geert Keil & Nora Kreft, Cambridge University Press, 2019; and a monograph on the philosophy of love titled *Liebe*, forthcoming with de Gruyter Press.

Michael Kühler is a Research and Teaching Fellow at the Academy for Responsible Research, Teaching, and Innovation (ARRTI) at Karlsruhe Institute of Technology (KIT) and "Privatdozent" (roughly equaling Associate Professor) at Münster University, Germany. His research interests include ethics, metaethics, political philosophy, and the philosophy of love. His publications include "Love and Conflicts Between Identity-Forming Values," in: *Handbook of Love in Cultural and Transcultural Contexts*, edited by Mayer, Claude-Hélène/Vanderheiden, Elisabeth, Dordrecht: Springer, 2020, forthcoming; "Romantische Liebe und die Freiheit zu gehen," in: *Die Freiheit zu gehen. Ausstiegsoptionen in politischen, sozialen und existenziellen Kontexten*, edited by Dietz, Simone/Foth, Hannes/Wiertz, Svenja, Wiesbaden: Springer, 2019, 195–222; and "Loving Persons. Activity and Passivity in Romantic Love," in: *Love and Its Objects. What Can We Care For?*, edited by Maurer, Christian/Milligan, Tony/Pacovská, Kamila, Houndmills: Palgrave Macmillan, 2014, 41–55.

Andrew Lambert is an Assistant Professor of Philosophy at City University of New York, College of Staten Island. His research focuses primarily on ethics and Chinese thought, particularly the relationship between conceptions of moral conduct and personal attachment. His recent publications include *"Impartiality, Close Friendships and the Confucian Tradition,"* in: *Conceptualizing Friendship in Time and Place*, edited by Marlein van Raalte and Carla Risseeuw, Leiden: Brill, 2017, 205–228, and *"Confucian Ethics and Care: An Amicable Split?"* in: *Feminist Encounters with Confucius*, edited by In Mat Foust and Sor-Hoon Tan, Leiden, Netherlands, 2016, 173–197. He has translated several works in Chinese philosophy, including contemporary Chinese thinker Li Zehou's book, *A History of Classical Chinese Thought*, published by Routledge in 2019.

Getty L. Lustila is a Visiting Lecturer in the Department of Philosophy and Religion at Northeastern University, in Boston, Massachusetts. His research lies at the intersection of early modern philosophy and ethics. Lustila's research has appeared in the *Canadian Journal of Philosophy*, the *European Journal of Philosophy*, *Utilitas*, and *Hume Studies*. He is currently at work on the topic of self-love and the writings of Sophie de Grouchy and Damaris Cudworth Masham.

348   Contributors

Christian Maurer is a SNSF Professor at the Philosophy Department of the University of Lausanne, Switzerland. He works on various themes in moral and political philosophy, both from historical and systematic perspectives. He is the author of *Self-love, Egoism and the Selfish Hypothesis* (Edinburgh University Press: 2019), the co-editor with Tony Milligan and Kamila Pacovská of *Love and Its Objects: What Can We Care For?* (Palgrave Macmillan: 2014), and the co-editor with Giovanni Gellera of the special issue *Contexts of Religious Tolerance: New Perspectives From Early Modern Britain and Beyond* in Global Intellectual History (2/2020).

Tony Milligan is the Senior Researcher with the Cosmological Visionaries Project, Department of Theology and Religious Studies, King's College London. His specialism is applied ethics, with particular interest in otherness: other people, places and creatures, and how the concept of love can shed light upon these matters. Previous publications include *Love* (2011); and the co-edited volume *Love and its Objects* (2014). His next book, including an examination of the politics of love, will be *The Ethics of Political Dissent*, due for release with Routledge in 2021.

Arina Pismenny is a Lecturer at the University of Florida. Her research interests cover moral psychology, ethics, philosophy of emotion, and philosophy of sex and gender. Her recent projects include elucidating the relationship between romantic love and morality, analyzing the rational structures of affective states and complexes such as emotions, sentiments, and syndromes, and exploring the bearing of implicit biases on theoretical and practical rationality. Her publications include "The erotic as a value" (in French "L'Érotisme") with Ronald de Sousa. In J. Deonna, & E. Tieffenbach (Eds.), *A Small Treatise on Values* (Petit Traité des Valeurs) (pp. 132–139). Paris: Editions d'Ithaque, 2018; and "Is love an emotion?" with Jesse Prinz. In C. Grau & A. Smuts (Eds) The Oxford Handbook Of Philosophy Of Love. New York & Oxford: Oxford University Press, 2017.

Raja Rosenhagen is an Assistant Professor of Philosophy and Associate Dean of Academic Affairs at Ashoka University in Sonipat, Haryana (India). His interests span philosophy of science, philosophy of mind, epistemology, logic, Indian philosophy, and, of course, philosophy of love and friendship. He has a philosopher's crush on Iris Murdoch and among his current projects is a book project in which he seeks to combine his interest in Murdochian just attention and his interest in the notion and role of experience. Past publications have appeared in *Synthese* and in various edited collections, among them, the following essay is pertinent to the present volume: "Toward Virtue: Moral Progress through Love, Just Attention, and Friendship" (2019), in: *Love and Justice. Consonance or Dissonance*, edited by I. Dalferth and T. Kimball (Religion in Philosophy and Theology, Book 101), Tübingen: Mohr Siebeck, 217–240.

Index

Page numbers in *italics* refer to figures

abandonment 168, 174, 178–179
Abelson, R. P. 51
abortion 158, 160, 309–311, 322
About Love (Solomon) 131–132
Abramson, Kate 28, 29–31
acquaintance 107
acting out (Act Out) 228–234; *see also* partiality
active union 300, 301; existentialist 300; strong 301; weak 301
activism/activists 17–18, 327–341; fate 338–340; sentiment 334–338; union 329–334
adultery 160
affect-laden networks of personal attachment *see guanxi* networks
agape 6, 7, 132, 172, 177, 335, 336, 338, 341
Alcoff, Linda 333
American Psychological Association 52
Analects 260, 261, 263, 264, 267, 268, 273, 274, 275, 278
anger 26, 32, 170, 231, 232–234
anxiety 12, 79–100
appearances 108
aptness 25–26
Aquinas 153, 154, 164n7
Archard, David 45
Aristophanes 8, 89, 131, 297
Aristotle 2, 7, 18n1, 68, 123n5, 132, 261
Armstrong, John 89
Arneson, Richard J. 45
art works 138
Astell, Mary 63
attachment style 23, 24, 36

attention 309, 320–323; *see also* just attention
Austen, Jane 174, 180–181
authenticity 5, 9, 10
autonomy: as an internal matter 87; content-neutral conception 254–256; Frankfurt's approach to 5; individualist accounts 4–5; Kantian definition 4; receptivity and 53–56; relational accounts 5–6; respect for 3–4, 11, 62, 66–69, 161–163; risk of giving up/surrendering 44–45; threats to 43–48; *see also* personal autonomy; individual autonomy
awareness 48–49

Being and Nothingness (Sartre) 307
being with 50
bell hooks 43
benevolence 46–47
Bennett, Christopher 47
Bentham, Jeremy 2
Ben-Ze'ev, Aaron 36, 145, 148n1
bias/biases 51; *see also* careless expectations
Black, John B. 51
Bollnow, Otto Friedrich 146
Book of Odes (Shijing) 260
Book of Rites (Liji) 262
Bowen, Murray 54
Bower, Gordon H. 51
Bowlin, John 13, 153–155
Bratman, Michael 147
Buber, Martin 50, 148
Bush, George W. 336–337

Camus, Albert 94
Capra, Frank 82
care-as-modeling (Confucian) 272–276
care/caring 32–34; Confucian familial love 272–276; helping strangers 201–212; love as a paradigm of 33; moral action 33; receptivity 49
careless expectations 50–52; biases 51; paternalism and 53–54; receptivity and 54–55; social scripts 51–52
Care View of reasons of love 32–34
categorical imperative 3
Chan, Joseph 267
charity 7, 63, 153–155, 236, 337
Chaturvedi, Aditi 122
choice: vision preceding 309, 310–311
Christianity 14, 167–181; egalitarian constancy 169–172; saintly intimate love 173–181
Christman, John 289
Ci Jiwei 266
civic virtues 267
Civilization and its Discontents (Freud) 89
civil society, *guanxi* networks as 280–281
climate change 330
Cocking, Dean 89
commitment 14, 16, 24, 33–34, 36, 45, 61, 66, 71–72, 105, 117–118, 120, 121, 122, 169, 171, 176, 218, 222, 227, 243, 254–256, 259–260, 268–269, 275–276, 295
communitarianism 291, 300
community feeling/mourning 143, 144
companionate love 24–25; *see also* romantic love
compassion 112
complex identity 240
compulsion 52
compulsive expectations 52–53; paternalism and 53–54; receptivity and 54–55
concepts and words 312–319
conceptual changes 315–316
Confucian conception of love 260–264; *see also* familial love/ attachments (Confucian tradition)
Confucius 260, 264, 267, 273–274, 284n32

consciousness 108–109, 118, 207, 270, 280, 318
consequentialism 226–227, 235, 238n11, 322
content-neutral conception of autonomy 254–256
cooperative joint practice 147
Corrigan, John 167, 179–180
COVID-19 pandemic 330–331, 332
critical self-reflection 295
Critique of Dialectical Reason (Sartre) 307
Cudworth, Ralph 62
Culver, Charles M. 45
curative model 132
Current Opinion in Behavioral Sciences 53

D'Arms, Justin 26
deeply objectionable differences 150–155; in robust-yet-fragile love 156–158
defense mechanisms 52
DeGeneres, Ellen 336, 337–338
Delaney, Neil 102–103
desires 63–64, 260, 270; sexual 260
dialogical love 10, 13, 132–133; internal rules 147–148; mature 147–148; young 148
differences in values 150–153; *see also* deeply objectionable differences
dilemma 242, 243–246; resolving 246–254; *see also* identity group
Dillon, Robin 192
Discourse (Masham) 63, 68
A Discourse Concerning the Love of God (Masham) 62
dispositions 48; rules characterizing 117; *see also* receptivity
Doctrine of the Mean 282n16
duties: moral 34–35; of reciprocity and gratitude 34; of trust 34; of vulnerability 34
"Duties of Love" (Wallace) 34
Duties of Trust View of reasons of love 34–35, 37
Dworkin, Gerald 45

Earp, Brian 73–74
Ebels-Duggan, Kyla 12, 61, 66, 76n12–13
egalitarian constancy 169–172
embedded self-reflection 295, 296

emotional identification 134, *136*, 138
emotional infection 134, *136*, 138
emotional keenness 134, 137
emotional rationality 11, 23, 25–27
emotional sharing 145–146
emotions: fittingness 25–28, 30; intentional states 25; motivations 32; objects of 25; rationality and 25–27; standard of correctness 25–26
empathy 134
Epistles to the Romans (Paul) 153
equality 1–2; concepts 314–315; moral action 2
eros 6, 7, 123n5, 131
essentialism (essentialist) 1, 3, 5, 11, 13, 25, 31, 33, 46, 116, 120, 131–133, 142–143, 169, 188–189, 244, 291, 292, 295, 299, 301, 313, 317
ethical non-monogamy 35–36
ethical obligations, Confucian approach to 278
ethical polyamory 73–74
Euthyphro (Plato) 243, 251, 264
exclusivity 69, 71–72
expectations: compulsive 52–53
experience: presentationalism 108–110; relationalism 107–108; representationalism 106–107

fairness 1, 28, 148, 230, 259, 264, 267–270, 277, 279, 280, 285n51
familial love/attachments (Confucian tradition) 16–17, 259–281; care-as-modeling 272–276; fictive kinship relations 278–279; *guanxi* networks 279, 280–281; importance of 261–264; inter-personal attitudes 261–262; obligation to develop a basis for familiarity 277–280; overview 259–260; problems of 264–267
fate, social justice activism and 338–340
favoritism 15, 216, 219, 227, 237n1, 244
fear 25, 27, 32, 83, 86–87, 90, 92, 96, 99, 107, 116, 118, 174, 178, 232, 314, 333
Fedock, Rachel 102
"fictitious" citizen 319
fictive kinship relations 278–279

filial reverence 262, 263, 264, 272–273, 278
Fisher, Mark 298
fittingness 25–28, 30
flourishing 6, 132, 134, 155, 162, 192–195, 198n17, 203–206, 208–212
Foot, Philippa 322
forbearance 13; in robust-yet-fragile love 160–162; tolerance *vs.* 152–155
forgiveness 159–160
Formalism in Ethics and Non-Formal Ethics of Values (Scheler) 137, 138
Forster, E. M. 243
Foucault, M. 312
foundationalism 106, 107; *see also* representationalism
"foundational" self-reflection 295, 296
Fox, Warwick 330
fragility 71; *see also* vulnerability
Frankfurt, Harry G. 5, 7–8, 32–33, 38n10, 38n11, 98, 132, 196n1, 205, 214n8, 299
Frederick, Shane 51
freedom 323–324; actions and 307–308; degrees 320, 321; liberal view of 319; Murdochian presentationalist 115–116
Freire, Paulo 333–334, 341, 342n26
Freud, Sigmund 89
Fried, Charles 225
Friedlander, Myrna 54
Friedman, Marilyn 329, 334
friendship 4, 24, 88–89, 122, 154, 156, 217, 222, 226–227, 261, 277, 279
friend zone 30
Fromm, Erich 300
fusion model 131–132

Gaita, Raimond 170–173, 176, 177, 178
Game of Thrones 218
Gandhi, Mahatma 169, 335, 338
gaslighting 6, 194
gay marriage 315–316
gender 6, 14, 47, 51, 53–54, 158, 169, 175, 177–178, 240, 269
general impartial moral norms 241–242
Gert, Bernard 45

Gert, Joshua 237n8
Gilbert, Margaret 87–88, 146–147
Gilligan, Carol 49, 186–187
God 63
good of love 202
Great Learning (Daxue) 277
Groundwork (Kant) 66
guanxi networks 279; as civil society 280–281
Gupta, Anil 108, 109

harmony 122, 230, 259, 263, 270–271, 278, 284n40
Haslanger, Sally 329
Hegel, G. F. W. 50, 142
Held, Virginia 186
Helm, Bennett 122
helping strangers 201–212
history 312
Hitchcock, Alfred 12
Hooker, Brad 223–224
hope 341
humaneness (*ren*) 260–263, 282n16
humanity 61, 66–67, 171–172, 203, 204, 205–210
humility 112

ideal lovers 104–105
ideal lovers' pledge 105, 121, 122
identity 9; constitutive sense of 295–296, 303; group 16, 240–256; redefinition 10, 298–299, 301; we-identity 7–10, 17, 102, 289, 290, 292–304
identity group 240–256; attachments 240, 241; critical loyalty 252–253; defending the victim group uncritically 251–252; dilemma 242, 243–246; eliminating misunderstandings 253–254; resolving dilemma 246–254; shared histories 240; staying out of the conflict 246–250; uncritical loyalty 250–251
immorality 23, 27, 34, 37, 155, 209, 243
impartiality 1, 2, 9, 10; Confucian familial love 264–281; rejecting the priority of 269–271; relational reasons and 223–224
inappropriate adaptive preferences (IAP) 193, 194
Individual and Community (Stein) 143

individual autonomy 102, 289, 295–297; interpersonal accounts 9–10; preserving or fostering 102–103, 119–121
inequality 2
injustice 327–328, 330
intentional action 307
intersectional identity 240
intimacy 69, 70–71
intimate sexualized love 168–169; *see also* saintly intimate love
It's a Wonderful Life 82

Jacobson, Daniel 26
Jaggar, Alison 232–233, 234
Jenkins, Carrie 73, 74
joint practice 146–147
Jollimore, Troy 217, 226–229
Jung, Carl 52
just attention 12–13, 103, 104; clear and realistic vision 114; as theoretical task 104
justice 1–2; Aristotle on 2; Rawls' principles of 2–3; *see also* autonomy; love and justice dichotomy (LJD)
Justinian 2

Kagan, Shelly 226–227
Kahneman, Daniel 51
Kang Youwei 266
Kant, Immanuel 2, 4; conception of persons 3; formulations of categorical imperative 3
Kantian ethics 3
Kennett, Jeanette 89
Khader, Serene 192–193, 194, 343n29
Kierkegaard, Soren 87, 169, 171
King, Ambrose 261
King, Martin Luther, Jr. 327, 338, 340, 341, 343n34
Kittay, Eva Feder 44
Kompridis, Nikolas 49
Korsgaard, Christine 202–205
Krebs, Angelika 47
Krog, Antjie 331, 342n16
Kühler's contention 102, 103, 104

Leite, Adam 28, 29–31
"Letter from Birmingham City Jail" (King) 330
Letters Concerning the Love of God (Norris and Astell) 63

Levinas, Emmanuel 50
Lewis, C. S. 228
Liang Shuming 270
liberalism 17; communitarianism and 300; compatibility with union 302–303; individualism 17, 290–297
life-community 138, *139*, 141
Li Zehou 270–271
Locke, John 62
lovability 28–31
love: *agape* 6, 7, 132, 172, 177, 335, 336, 338, 341; as apt 29; as complaisance 64; Confucian conceptions 260–264; curative model 47, 132; egalitarian constancy 169–172; *eros* 6, 7, 123n5, 131; helping strangers 201–212; as inapt 29–30; individualist accounts 7–8, 9; interpersonal accounts 7, 8, 9–10; as a moral achievement 64–66; moral duties 34–35; notions of 6–7; *philia* 6–7, 132, 158–159; theoretical approaches 7–10; threatening aspect of 98; union accounts 8–9, 10, 17; *see also specific entries*
love and justice dichotomy (LJD) 14, 185–196; challenges to 189–191; history of 186–189
"Loving Villains: Virtue in Response to Wrongdoing" (Pacovská) 172–173
loyalty 15–16, 240–256; critical 252–253; uncritical 250–251; *see also* identity group
Lysis (Plato) 261

M and D 316
Machery, Edouard 51
Malebranche, Nicolas 63
marriage 289, 290; concept of 315–316; Gilbert on 87–88; threat to 79–100
married couples 289–290
Masham, Damaris Cudworth 12, 62–68, 72; *see also* minimalist account of love
mass 137, 138, *139*
membership feeling/mourning 143
Mencius 260, 261–262, 264–265, 272
metaphysics 318
Metaphysics as a Guide to Morals (Murdoch) 319

Mill, John Stuart 2, 4
minimalist account of love 12, 61–74; lessons to be taken from 72–73; loving relationships 72–74; moral achievement 64–66; objections to 69–72; respect/value of others 66–69; transformation 64–65
mistaken acts of beneficence 36
monogamous relationships 26, 73–74
monogamy 36, 97
moral achievement 64–66
moral agent: Schaubroeck on 33
moral concepts 317
Moral Deliberation View of reasons of love 35–36
moral emotions 28, 29, 31, 38n4
moralistic fallacy 11, 23, 24, 26, 27–28, 29, 31
morality: modern, core element of 2; romantic love and 11, 27–37
moral progress 112, 113
moral reasons: reasons for love as 28–31; reasons of love as 31–37
moral saints 33
More, Henry 62
Murdoch, Iris 12, 17, 65, 103–105, 108, 110–115, 119, 174, 181, 185, 189–190, 192, 308–321; on metaphysics 318; on vision 310–312; on words and concepts 312–319
Murdochian presentationalism 110–122

The Nature of Sympathy (Scheler) 133, 137–138
Nedelsky, Jennifer 49, 80, 100n5
Nehamas, Alexander 89, 90, 91
Nicomachean Ethics (Aristotle) 132, 261
Noddings, Nel 49, 186
non-cooperative joint practice 147
Norlock, Kathryn 339, 341
Norris, John 62, 63
Nozick, Robert 329
Nussbaum, Martha 49, 177, 324n1

Obama, Michelle 336–337
objects of emotions 25
Occasional Thoughts in Reference to a Vertuous or Christian Life (Masham) 62–63
Okin, Susan Moller 290
one thought too many 212, 225
"on pain of consistency" 204

354 Index

oppression 327–328; structural 328
Orwell, George 83

Pacovská, Kamila 172–173, 174
parents 43
partiality 4, 9, 10, 15; acting out (Act Out) 228–234; modeling-as-care mitigating 274–276; relational reasons and 224–236; right reasons requirement 235–236
passionate love 24, 25; *see also* romantic love
passive union 299–300, 301; strong 301; weak 301
paternalism 45–47; benevolence and 46–47; careless or compulsive expectations 53–54; definitions 45–46; patterns of behavior and 47–48; as risk for relationships 47; *see also* receptivity
patient endurance *see* forbearance; tolerance
patterns of behavior 47–48
Pedagogy of the Oppressed (Freire) 333–334, 341
person(s): as a citizen *vs.* as a moral-spiritual individual 319; indifferent/malicious 46; Kant's conception of 3; as moral equals 2; political conception 292–293; Rawls' principles of justice 2–3; unconditional moral worth 28–29
personal autonomy 4–5, 295
personal community 137, 140, 141
personal feeling 143
personal relationships 220–223
personhood 28–29, 31, 37, 192; accounts of love 61–62, 65–66; universal abstract property 29
personhood accounts of love 61
Pettit, Philip 14–15, 201–202, 205, 209–210, 211, 213
philia 6–7, 132, 158–159
Plato 2, 6, 8, 64, 89, 131, 243, 251, 261, 264, 297
political liberalism 289–304
Pollyanna-style optimism 327
polyamory 73–74
presentationalism 105; motivating 105–110; Murdochian 110–122
Pride and Prejudice (Austen) 174, 180–181
Principle of Equal Consideration (PEC) 223

Protasi, Sara 84
prudence 26, 30, 36–37, 72, 151
public politics 319
public value 203

Qing dynasty (1644–1911) 266

racial groups 240
rationality and emotions 25–27
Rawls, John 4, 289, 291–294, 295
really looking 190–191
Rear Window 12, 79, 80–91
reasons for love 7, 11, 23, 24, 27, 28–31
reasons of love 11, 31–37, 202; Care View 32–34; Duties of Trust View 34–35, 37; Frankfurt on 32; Moral Deliberation View 35–36
receptivity 11–12, 48–56; autonomy and 53–56; as being with 50; components 48–49; concept of 11–12, 44, 48–49; cultivation of 56; expectations and 54–55; feminist work on 49; psychological account of 50; reflective 49; shortcomings of philosophical understandings 44; *see also* autonomy; paternalism
reflective receptivity 49
relationalism 107–108
relational reasons 219–223; as basic practical reasons 219–220; defined 219; impartiality 223–224; non-relational reasons 225; partiality 224–236; personal relationships 220–223; voluntaristic 221–222
religious emotion/experience 167–181
remonstrance (*jian*) 263
representationalism 106–107
resistance 328
respect for autonomy 3–4, 11, 62, 66–69, 161–163
right reasons requirement 235–236
The Robust Demands of the Good (Pettit) 201
robust-yet-fragile love 155–164; concept 155–156; deeply objectionable differences in 156–158; forbearance in 160–162; forgiveness in 159–160; tolerance in 162–164
romantic heros 30
romantic love 11, 23–38; defining 24–25; in Eastern cultures 26; emotional rationality 25–27; models of 131–133; morality and 11, 27–37; as moral phenomenon 23;

motivational component 31–32; psychological profile 24–25; reasons of love 11, 31–37; social narratives 35; in the West 26
ruthless love 202

Sadler, Brook 33, 35–36
saintly intimate love 173–181; concern about 175–179; Elizabeth Bennett case 174–175, 179–181
Sandel, Michael J. 291–292, 295, 299–300
Sanders, Bernie 333
Sartre, Jean-Paul 307
Savulescu, Julian 73–74
Schank, R. C. 51
Schaubroeck, Katrien 33
Scheler, Max 13, 131, 133–144, 145
scripts 51–52
self: authentic self 295; constitutive sense 299; essentialist accounts of 5, 299, 301; existentialist account of 300; individualist conception of 294; relational conception of 295; sacrifice of 36
selfishness 71, 111, 116, 118–119
self-knowledge 99
self-reflection: embedded self-reflection 295–297, 301–303; foundational self-reflection 295–296, 302
sensible values 138
sentiment, social justice activism and 334–338
Setiya, Kieran 12, 61
sexual desires 260
sexual love 260
shared feeling/sharing 13, 132–148; emotional 145–146; joint practice 146–147; normative fabric 146–148; sympathy/fellow-feeling 134–137, *135–136*; unity of feeling 141–143
shared *we*-identity 9–10, 289–304; *see also* union
Shiffrin, Seana Valentine 45
Skowron, Elizabeth 54
social contract theory 3
social identity group *see* identity group
social justice activism 327–341; fate 338–340; sentiment 334–338; union 329–334
social norms 35–36
social relationship 84, 86

Index 355

social scripts 51–52
society 137, 138, *140*
Socrates 76n10, 243
solidarity 271, 279, 330–331, 333–334
Solomon, Robert 32, 298
spiritual values 138
Stein, Edith 13, 131, 143–144, 145
Stocker, Michael 218, 226, 235
strong active union 301
strong passive union 301
strong union 10, 298–299, 301
survival circuits 53
suum cuique 2
sympathy 133–137; four forms of 134–137, *135–136*
Symposium (Plato) 8, 76n10, 89, 131, 297

Tan Sitong 266
target of emotion 25, 26
Tennov, Dorothy 24
A Theory of Justice (Rawls) 291
tolerance 13–14, 150–155; attitude of 151; core of 151; forbearance *vs.* 152–155; misplaced 151; as a practice of non-intervention 151; reasons for 151–152; robust-yet-fragile love 162–164; as a virtue 151, 153
Tolerance Among the Virtues (Bowlin) 153
trading-up 174
transformative love 12, 87–91
trolley example 322
Tronto, Joan 49
trust 24, 31, 34, 88, 120, 256, 263
truth 32, 92, 99, 113, 132, 224, 231, 235, 309, 311–312
Turner, Terrence J. 51
Tutu, Desmond 331
Tversky, Amos 51

ubuntu 331
Ulpian 2
unconditional love 14, 167–169
union 8–9, 10, 17; active 300, 301; Kühler's contention 102, 103; liberalism 302–303; passive 299–300, 301; social justice activism 329–334; strong 10, 298–299, 301; weak 10, 298–299, 301
union theorists 102–103

unity of feeling in shared feeling 141–143
universality 147, 187–189
universal value 203
unrequited love 26
utilitarianism 2

value(s): differences in 150–164; of human beings 66–69
value-content 134
veil of ignorance 3, 291, 307
Velleman, David 12, 28–29, 38n4, 61, 70, 75n2, 185, 186, 187, 189–191, 192, 193, 194, 196, 207, 208, 210–211
Vertigo 12, 79, 80, 83, 85, 86, 89, 92–99
virtue 7, 13, 26–27, 30–32, 61, 66, 85, 103, 106, 131, 151, 153–154, 158, 160, 162–163, 168, 172, 180, 195, 219, 222–223, 267–268, 276
vision(s) 73, 95, 114–121, 165n14; connotative logic of 309–312; preceding choice 309, 310–311; of the world 312
voluntary actions 222, 307
vulnerability 34, 45, 70, 92, 160, 168; *see also* fragility

Waiting for God (Weil) 169
Wallace, R. Jay 34–35, 38n14

weak active union 301
weak passive union 301
weak union 10, 298–299, 301
we-identity 7, 8, 9–10, 17, 102, 289–304; *see also* union
Weil, Simone 74, 103, 122, 168, 169, 171, 320
well-being 1, 3–4, 7, 12, 14, 30–34, 63, 98, 155, 163, 186, 220, 247, 251, 254, 298
Wettstein, Howard 167
wholeheartedness 14, 161, 163, 180, 181
Williams, Bernard 202, 212, 225, 231
Winterson, Jeanette 97
Wolf, Susan 33, 175, 218, 226, 235, 237n1
words and concepts 312–319
Works of Love (Kierkegaard) 169
worldview 310, 312, 339
Written on the Body (Winterson) 97
wrongdoing 16, 156, 159–160, 241–247, 249–251, 256, 264; *see also* identity group

Xiong Shili 266
Xunzi 268, 284n31

Yogacaran Buddhism 270
Young, Iris Marion 327–328